THE LIFE OF
JOHN WESLEY

Also by Roy Hattersley

The Life of

JOHN WESLEY

A Brand from the Burning

ROY HATTERSLEY

DOUBLEDAY

New York   London   Toronto   Sydney   Auckland

PUBLISHED BY DOUBLEDAY
a division of Random House, Inc.

DOUBLEDAY and the portrayal of an anchor with a dolphin are registered
trademarks of Doubleday, a division of Random House, Inc.

Library of Congress Cataloging-in-Publication Data
Hattersley, Roy.
The life of John Wesley: a brand from the burning /
Roy Hattersley.—1st U.S. ed.
p.   cm.
Includes bibliographical references (p.) and index.
1. Wesley, John, 1703–1791. I. Title.
BX8495.W5 H36 2003
287'.092—dc21
[B]   2002040917

ISBN 0-385-50334-2

PRINTED IN THE UNITED STATES OF AMERICA

June 2003

First U.S. Edition

First published in Great Britain by Little, Brown in 2002

1   3   5   7   9   10   8   6   4   2

CONTENTS

ACKNOWLEDGMENTS

John Wesley's place in history—for his leadership of the Second Reformation, the creation of a new church and the effect of those achievements on the character of the industrial working class—was secured through the triumph of his belief that thought should be followed by action. The scholar-evangelist was not an original thinker. But he was a lifelong student of other men's ideas. My understanding of the often arcane Wesleyan theology, which was the product of that study, was helped immensely by Canon John Shepherd, rural dean of Battersea, and the Reverend Howard Mellor, principal of Cliff College. Both read the third draft of my text and suggested invaluable improvements.

Anthony Howard, whose erudition and eye for detail have saved me from making embarrassing errors in earlier books, was again generous with both time and advice. His effective sub-editing of the whole manuscript went far beyond the demands of friendship. Cynthia Shepherd produced six versions of the text, either typing them herself or supervising others. She invariably made corrections along the way.

I am deeply grateful to all of them. Of course, the shortcomings which remain are entirely my responsibility.

1

Faith Alone

The Victorians, emboldened by the confidence that comes with success, convinced posterity that modern England began in the nineteenth century. After Trafalgar, a nation secure from Continental invasion could concentrate its interest and energy on industry and empire. A country unified by railways used its coal and iron to become the workshop of the world. Between 1832 and 1867 manhood (as distinct from universal) suffrage made Britain think of itself as a democracy. After 1870 compulsory elementary education ensured that the sons and daughters of the poor were taught to read and write. London became the undisputed financial and maritime capital of the world, providing insurance for the new iron ships which had been pioneered in British dockyards. And in the middle of the century the Great Exhibition of 1851 confirmed that Britain could make anything and everything and had become the crossroads of international trade. It is easy enough to believe that the historical (as distinct from the numerical) nineteenth century—from the Battle of Waterloo in 1815 to the outbreak of the First World War in 1914—was the time when old ideas were replaced by new. It is easy, but it is wrong.

The genius of the nineteenth century was the single-minded determination with which it exploited the ideas which it had inherited from the early Hanoverian age. The Industrial Revolution was the eighteenth century's bequest. After the Darbys of Coalbrookdale smelted iron with coke in 1713, a "coal rush" engulfed every part of Britain in which it was believed "black gold" was buried. The steam pump, designed by Savery and Newcomen to clear the flooded mines, prepared the way for Watts's steam engine. Hargreaves, Crompton and Arkwright invented machinery which changed the whole character of the textile industry and drove the poor into towns and factories. Benjamin Huntsman and Thomas Bolsover transformed the way in which steel was made and used. The restrictions on exports and the import of essential raw materials—a relic of mercantile, as distinct from merchant, England—were removed. By 1785 the nation was so confident that its future lay in industry and commerce that a General Chamber of Manufacturers of Great Britain was founded under the leadership of Josiah Wedgwood.

The idea on which Great Britain's nineteenth-century prosperity was built was an eighteenth-century theory. Adam Smith wrote *Inquiry into the Wealth of Nations* in 1776, as the culmination of his life's work on the nature of modern society. Hume and Joseph Priestley argued that religion and science went hand in hand. Perhaps Tom Paine, in prison and under sentence of death, meant to be ironic when he called his last great work *The Age of Reason*. But the eighteenth century was certainly the Enlightenment, even though the new view of the world did not come from England's ancient universities. Neither Oxford nor Cambridge was as supine as the institution by which they were dominated. The Established Church slept. It was left to John Wesley—in the revival which he came to lead—to perform for religion the defining duty of his time and bequeath a new view of the world to his successors. Although he lived and worked in the eighteenth century, it was the nineteenth which he helped to change.

Dissatisfaction with the Established Church began late and grew slowly. Much of eighteenth-century England was wholly neglected by clergy who were concerned for neither their parishioners' spiritual nor social welfare. Henry Fielding, in his *Proposal for Making an Effectual Provision for the Poor*, thought that prosperous England was ignorant of how dire the condition of parts of the country had become. "If we were to make progress through the outskirts of a town, and look into the habitations of the poor, we should there behold such pictures of human misery as must move the compassion of every heart. . . ." The church in general either did not know or did not care that such conditions existed—that only one child in four, born in London, survived and that infant mortality in the burgeoning towns of the Midlands and the north was even higher. Nor did it show much concern for the moral degradation which accompanied poverty. Religion was a matter of habit, not conviction. Christians were required to do little more than perform the rituals of formal observance under the supervision of priests who regarded the church as less of a calling than a profession for gentlemen.

The revolt against nominal Christianity was led by an unlikely revolutionary. John Wesley certainly did not look the part. He was, at most, five feet six inches tall, though some reports describe him as two inches smaller. There was a cast in one of his clear blue eyes, and his nose was long and bony. He never wore a wig and allowed his hair to grow unfashionably long—initially because he could not afford to employ a barber but, as he grew old and famous, because it was the appearance which his followers recognized. Nor did he seem, at least to passing acquaintances, a man who could move multitudes. His manner was invariably eager and intense, and his conversation almost always didactic. Aside from his core belief that faith offered the hope of universal redemption, he was disconcertingly inclined to make sudden adjustments to his theological position. Once he had changed his mind, he invariably denounced his opponents (who had often been his allies) with an unscrupulous determination never to admit that he had been wrong.

Yet there are innumerable, and carefully documented, stories of men who heard him preach for the first time or caught his eye and immediately determined to follow him wherever he might lead them. It was not because he was a great orator. George Whitefield, who, had he chosen, might himself have led the Great Revival, certainly preached with greater power and passion. But Wesley combined a genius for organization with an irresistible dynamism which came from the unswerving conviction and absolute confidence that he had been called to do God's work. The quality which enabled him to lead the Second Reformation was charisma, properly defined—"divinely conferred power or talent, capacity to inspire followers with devotion and enthusiasm." That characteristic made him irresistible to religiously inclined women, and he was as susceptible to them as they were attracted to him.

Women were his weakness; doctrinal promiscuity was his abiding sin. In other ways—moral, physical, intellectual—he was unreasonably strong, although profoundly (indeed often debilitatingly) introspective. Yet John Wesley was essentially a man of action who would ride a hundred miles in a day, stopping only to change horses and preach along the way. His capacity to conduct an almost continuous theological disputation (with himself as well as with his critics) at a time when he was creating—despite the risks to both person and reputation—a new Protestant denomination was a great tribute to his physical and intellectual stamina. Somehow he always managed to fight his way toward the final objective—first a revival, then an organization—despite distractions which would have diverted a weaker man. He was usually poor, often crossed in love, constantly reviled, regularly betrayed by false friends and in a permanent state of anxiety about his own fitness to answer his great calling. But he always struggled on. His character confirmed his mother's judgment that a stern upbringing would produce a strong man. She never even paused to think if her method of child rearing would also guarantee a happy life. But happiness, at least as the world understood it, was of no great consequence to John Wesley. He had been sent into the world to preach redemption. *Sola fide*, by faith alone. He created a new church through which that all-consuming belief could be preached to his universal parish. And in doing so he became one of the architects of the modern world.

2

AMONG OUR FOREFATHERS

The facts and the fables are difficult to distinguish. The most devoted and devout early Methodists—men and women whose
admiration came perilously close to idolatry—wanted to believe that
divine will guided John Wesley along every step of the way toward
the creation of a separate and independent church. And Wesley himself encouraged the mythmakers with dubious stories of his own.
Many of them concerned his forebears. For he had a reverence for
his ancestors which elevated them to the status of a holy family. Both
their politics and their theology were different from his. But at least
according to the folklore, even Bartholomew Wesley, his great-
grandfather and rector of Charmouth, bequeathed to his illustrious
descendant indomitable independence and unqualified love of God.
And Bartholomew Wesley was a Dissenter and supporter of
Cromwell's Commonwealth, while John Wesley forbade his followers to register as Dissenting ministers and was, from first to last, a
king's man loyal to the House of Hanover.

Bartholomew Wesley's story was almost certainly improved in the
Methodists' telling. But the facts on which it was based are beyond
dispute. In the autumn of 1651, King Charles II, defeated by Cromwell's army at the Battle of Worcester, fled southwest. The "proclamation for the apprehension of Charles Stuart and other traitors, his

adherents and abettors," offered a reward of one thousand pounds for the deposed king's capture. Charles was rightly doubtful about the loyalty of the retreating troops. Many of his soldiers were mercenaries, and virtually none of them had received their promised pay. So when he reached Bristol and found the streets crowded with the cold and hungry remnants of his dispirited army, he feared that he would be recognized and that the temptation to claim the bounty would be too strong to resist. Although badly prepared for the journey, he insisted that his party press on. They rode first west to Somerset and then south to Dorset.

Just before the fugitives arrived at Charmouth, where they planned to stay the night, the king's horse threw a shoe. The farrier to whom it was taken was surprised to discover that it had been shod in a fashion "common in the north of England," and the villagers, who trusted nobody they did not know, had their curiosity increased by the ostler at the inn at which the strangers stayed. The whole party had, he reported, insisted on occupying the top room and had "stayed up all night." Suspicion turned to fear, and it was decided to consult the rector—"the puny parson," as records called him in recognition of the diminutive stature which characterized all the Wesleys. How could they protect their property and families against the obviously dangerous intruders?

Bartholomew Wesley was at prayer, and his parishioners did not dare disturb him. By the time that his devotions were complete, Charles had left the village and turned east for Brighton, France and liberty. It was months before the people of Charmouth began to suspect that they had been hosts to the king. Then, an itinerant peddler told them that Charles II had passed that way. The effect was greatest on the rector. Throughout the years of the Commonwealth he constantly boasted that the long hours which the king spent on his knees was the result of the part that prayer had played in his narrow escape during his day in Dorset. And Bartholomew Wesley left no doubt as to either his loyalty or his intentions. He was a Commonwealth man. Had he not been on his knees when the king made his escape "he would surely have clept him."[1]

In his *History of the Rebellion in England*, Clarendon dismisses the story of near capture by "a fanatical minister" and attributes the alarm that was raised at Charmouth to "a weaver and ex-soldier." But whether or not Bartholomew Wesley narrowly missed a moment of destiny, he was a known Dissenter who would not use the authorized prayer book and was openly skeptical about the provenance of the Church of England's orthodox rites and rituals. After the Stuart Restoration he paid a terrible price for his heterodoxy. First he refused to swear that he accepted the Thirty-nine Articles of the Protestant faith and was, in consequence, expelled from his parish under the provisions of the 1662 Act of Uniformity. Then he defied the requirements of the 1665 Five Mile Act and refused to swear that he would "not at any time endeavour [any] alteration in Government either in Church or State" and was excluded from his living at Charmouth and the nearby parish of Charleston and required to leave the area. Fortunately, he had read medicine as well as theology at Oxford, so he could earn his keep as a free man and doctor. He died unrepentant and unreconciled to the Church of England.

Bartholomew Wesley became a central figure in early Methodist folklore. He had, the mythmakers claimed, established a pattern of moral independence from everything but the clear voice of personal conscience. That was a characteristic which they regarded as the hallmark of their leader.

Bartholomew's son, the first John Wesley, began his determined search for salvation when he was a schoolboy. From the age of twelve, he kept a diary in which—much like his grandson a hundred years later—he recorded his painful path to a holy life. A Puritan by instinct and, from the start of the Civil War, a passionate supporter of the parliamentary cause, he left Oxford at a time when Cromwell was the undisputed protector of England and four years before the deposed Charles II passed a troubled night in his father's parish. There is no doubt that Cromwell's Board of Commissioners would have gladly endorsed the ordination of so committed a follower. But he chose to join "the gathered church" in Weymouth and then formed a branch of that extreme Nonconformist sect in nearby Radipole. He remained with them for only a few months. When the vicar of Whitchurch died, the commissioners invited him to inherit the parish as pastor, and his acceptance of their patronage made him a hired man of the Commonwealth. It was a brief liaison. The Stuarts were restored to the throne, and he, like his father and almost a thousand other Dissenting ministers, was ejected from his living on St. Bartholomew's Day in 1662.[2]

The formal charges were that he had "neglected" the Book of Common Prayer, encouraged irregular preaching and "lacked proper ordination," accusations which cast their long shadow before them onto the whole life and work of his grandson. But he was also accused of treason, having "most diabolically railed in the pulpit against the late King and his posterity, extolled Cromwell and said that David and Solomon came far short of him."[3] He was convicted and imprisoned and eventually released, unrepentant, to live quietly in the nearby village of Preston. He died, at the age of forty, a year before his father. The new rector of his old parish refused permission for him to be buried in holy ground.

When the first John Wesley was invited to Radipole, he was offered an annual stipend of one hundred pounds. He never received more than thirty but, no doubt buoyed up by the hope of promised riches, married the year after his appointment. Matthew, his eldest son, became a doctor. Samuel—born in 1662, the year of his father's ejection—was intended for the Dissenting ministry, and perhaps, had his father lived, he would have followed the faith of his family. But during his formative years, the greatest influence on Samuel Wesley's life and beliefs was Henry Dolling, the headmaster of Dorchester Free School and the man to whom he later dedicated his first published work, *Maggots or Poems on Several Subjects Never Before Handled*. Dolling was a Church of England man first and last. But his enthusiasm for Anglican orthodoxy might not in itself have been enough to wean the young man away from the beliefs for which two generations of his family had suffered. He turned against Dissent because when he met Dissenters, he found them personally objectionable. The usual complaint was that they were too solemn. It may be a reflection on Samuel Wesley's character that he found them too frivolous.

He came to that stern conclusion during his years as a student in Mr. Veal's Dissenting academy in Stepney, where according to John Dunton, who married his sister, he was "educated upon charity"—more likely at the expense of his father's friends than of the parish. He found his fellow students shallow and insincere and their social conduct even less attractive than their attitude toward work and worship. At a supper held in Leadenhall Street, they "fell to railing at Monarchy and blaspheming the memory of King Charles the martyr . . . producing and repeating some verse on the subject." Samuel was an instinctive and ardent monarchist who would have resented any celebration of the Stuarts' exile. Jokes on the subject added profanity to treason. "One of the company told us of a design to have a cold pie served at table with either a live cat or hare, I forget which." The plan was to "get one of those who loved the monarchy and knew nothing of the matter to cut it up; whereupon, and on the leaping out of the hare or cat, they were to set up a shout and cry "Hello old puss!" to the honor of the good old cause and to show their affection for the Commonwealth."[4] It was not the sort of escapade that Samuel Wesley found amusing—or forgot. In his forty-second year—shortly after the birth of John, his second surviving son—he was still railing against the Dissenting academies.[5]

At the age of twenty-two, Samuel Wesley decided that he had done with Dissent and walked from London to Oxford and enrolled at Exeter College. Dissenters claimed that he cleared his debts with funds intended to educate their ministers. However the money was obtained, he arrived in Oxford with two pounds and sixteen shillings in his pocket.[6] The college register for 26 September 1684 describes him as a "Pauper Scholar," the fourth and lowest rank of undergraduate. He signed the register "Samuel Westley," the old form of the family name. The Dissenting past had been put firmly behind him.

Samuel Wesley almost certainly spent some months as a "servitor," waiting at table in the evenings on students with whom he had studied during the day. Later he may have earned his keep by giving instruction to more junior members of the college. He was ordained deacon in August 1688 and shortly afterward found a less humble source of income. John Dunton, his brother-in-law, was a publisher, and he managed to place several of Samuel's poems and articles in London magazines. By the time that he was ordained priest in February 1689, Samuel Wesley had accumulated ten pounds and fifteen shillings.[7]

It was at his sister's wedding to John Dunton in 1682 that Samuel Wesley met Susanna Annesley. They married on 12 December 1688, the year of the Glorious Revolution, which put William of Orange on the throne of England and, by exiling the Stuart James II, created both a constitutional monarchy and a constant source of friction within the Wesley marriage. Susanna was also was the child of a Dissenting minister. Her father, who had been ejected from the living of St. Giles in Cripplegate in 1662, was described by his more grandiloquent followers as "the Saint Paul of Nonconformity." He might well have been known as the Jacob of Dissent, for he fathered twenty-five children. Susanna, the twenty-fourth, chose to return to the Established Church. Her conversion took an even more extreme form than Samuel's. He was prepared to acknowledge as sovereign and supreme governor of the Church of England whoever received the support of people and Parliament. She retained a stubborn allegiance to James II, the Lord's Anointed, and, after his death, to his uncrowned son "Charles III." Susanna Annesley was very near to being a Jacobite. She was also, without apparently seeing any conflict in the two positions, a devout disciple of John Locke, the philosopher whose *Letter on Toleration* sought to justify the exclusion of Catholics from benefits under the Toleration Act of 1689 on the grounds that they were likely to retain allegiance to the deposed King James and, in consequence, sympathize with the foreign powers which plotted a Stuart restoration. Locke's theories became the bible on which she based the education of her children, a decision which, no matter how bizarre by modern standards, illustrated Susanna Wesley's most extraordinary characteristic. Almost alone among rectory wives of the period, she was an intellectual.

At the time of his marriage, Samuel Wesley was curate at St. Botolph, Aldersgate, a part of London which his son was to make one of Methodism's holy places. He remained there for about a year. Restless by nature, he then became a chaplain on board a man-of-war with the remarkably high salary of seventy pounds a year. However, after six months at sea, he decided that he must find employment more suitable for a married man, and shortly after Samuel (his eldest son) was born, he accepted the curacy at Newington Butts in Surrey even though it carried an annual stipend of only thirty pounds. He continued to write strange works of theology with even stranger titles—*The Tame Snake in the Box of Bran, The Grunting of a Hog, A Hat Broke at Cugels*—and became chaplain to the Athenian Society as well as a regular contributor to its gazette. The nature of his work did not change, but it marked him out as a staunch, if slightly indiscriminate, "king's man." Whoever sat on the throne—James or William—enjoyed his unswerving allegiance. His early years with Susanna must have taught her that her husband was unpredictable in all things except his intellectual pretensions and his loyalty to the crown.

Samuel Wesley's conspicuous loyalty attracted the attention of the marquis of Normanby. Under the marquis's patronage Wesley was appointed in 1691 to the living of South Ormsby, a parish of two hundred souls, ten miles south of Lincoln. It was a brief and turbulent incumbency. But recognition by a Tory grandee meant that he was also accepted by the church hierarchy as a man to watch and cultivate. Much to his delight, his preferment resulted in him being made a member of the convocation. That required, or perhaps only justified, frequent visits to London. Samuel rarely missed a session, whatever the turbulence he left behind at home.

Most of the trouble was the result of Samuel Wesley's autocratic character. But one of the unhappy incidents at Ormsby was—at least according to the account of the affair favored by his family—wholly to his credit. The story begins with an "intrusive visitant" imposing herself on Susanna Wesley. It continues with Samuel's return to the rectory during the unwelcome visitation and his discovery of the intruder's identity, whereupon he "went up to her, took her by the hand and very fairly handed her out!" The unwelcome guest who had forced her company upon his wife was (Samuel believed) the mistress of his patron, the marquis of Normanby.

Perhaps the story was an invention that initially was no more than an illustration of Samuel's general concern about loose aristocratic morals and was then gradually expanded and refined into an account of a specific and imaginary condemnation. But if the confrontation ever took place—and did, as John Wesley claimed, result in his father's being "forced" out of his parish—the erring nobleman was more likely to have been John Sanderson (later Earl Castleton) than Normanby. For Normanby remained an active advocate of Samuel Wesley's cause, patronage which he would have been unlikely to provide for an upstart clergyman who had insulted his mistress. In 1694 he unsuccessfully recommended Wesley for an Irish bishopric. And it was almost certainly Normanby who, a year later, suggested that the unbeneficed clergyman should be given the crown living at Epworth as a reward for his loyalty. The offer was made and accepted. John Wesley's father remained the rector of that parish until he died forty-eight years later, a beneficiary of the patronage on which eighteenth-century clergymen depended. The system which gave a lifetime's security to Samuel Wesley so offended his son John that it contributed to the latter's eventual defiance of the church's authority and the creation of the Methodist Church.

Epworth was a small market town on the Isle of Axholme, an inland island which was cut off from the rest of Lincolnshire and the world by five rivers—the Idle and Torr to the west and south, the Trent to the east and the Ouse and Don to the north. In the sixteenth century, it was submerged in water for most of the year. But in 1620 Cornelius Vermuyden was brought from Holland to drain the land and make it fit for agriculture. He did his job so well that the new fields and pastures were regarded as too good for the local peasantry. Much of the common land was enclosed. Some of it was given to Vermuyden as payment for his services. The rest was appropriated by the local gentry. The riots which first broke out in 1620 and erupted from time to time until the end of the century were interrupted only by the Great Civil War, when the isle raised a company for the parliamentary army. They were the protests of the landless farm laborers. Samuel Wesley became rector of a parish in which history and geography combined to make outsiders unwelcome. If the intruders were, like Samuel Wesley, onetime Dissenters who had recently acquired a passionate belief in the divine right of kings, their presence in the town was intolerable to local Nonconformists. To much of his parish, Samuel Wesley was a renegade and an apostate.

Samuel Wesley did nothing to ingratiate himself with his critics. He insisted on the strict observation of canon law and the acceptance of all the Church of England's traditional doctrine, ceremony and liturgy. He imposed a rigid penitential discipline on the whole parish. Communicants who offended against any one of the commandments were required to make public confessions of sin and perform public acts of atonement. Until the rituals of absolution had been performed they were denied the sacrament. It was a strict interpretation of the scriptures which, thirty years later, was to contribute to the first crisis in his second son's turbulent life. In John Wesley's *Advice to Young Clergymen* (1735), published as a manual for the guidance of young priests, he set out the disciplines which he believed should determine the course of parish life. There should be two services each Sunday, prayers in church on Wednesdays, Fridays and festival days and regular communion. The fact that it was necessary to assert a priest's obligation to perform such minimal duties illustrates the lassitude which engulfed the seventeenth-century Church of England. Epworth's influence on John Wesley never faded. When, in old age, he accused the Church of England bishops of gladly ordaining men "who knew something of Greek and Latin but who knew no more of saving souls than of catching whales,"[8] he was thinking of the clerical indifference of which he had first learned from his father's complaint about how other priests lived.

It was Samuel Wesley's belief in an active ministry, as much as his rigorous views on the implementation of orthodox liturgy and proper church "manners," which caused offense to his Dissenting parishioners. Isolated (he would have said "under siege") in his own rectory, he took increasing refuge in writing—journalism for his brother-in-law John Dunton, until the magazine he edited went out of business in 1696, and subacademic works of theology. *The Life of Christ in Verse* (published in 1693) was moderately popular. Before the turn of the century he had thought of, and perhaps even began to prepare, his *Commentary on the Book of Job,* a task which, since it took him more than thirty years to complete, was certainly his major work in terms of size, if not of quality. Two practical results flowed from his prodigious output of poetry and prose. A poem, written to celebrate the duke of Marlborough's victory at the Battle of Blenheim, so impressed His Grace that the rector of Epworth was appointed to the sinecure of the chaplaincy to Colonel Lepell's regiment. And whatever the merits of Samuel Wesley's own writing and the quality of his scholarship, his belief that he was a poet and theologian guaranteed that literature and theology were properly respected in the Epworth rectory—to the immense benefit of the rector's children, who, following their father's example and their mother's stern instruction, revered book learning.

It was not the only lesson which the young John Wesley learned at Epworth. By the time of his birth the religious society which his father had formed when he first arrived at the rectory was no longer a force within the parish. But the rector still believed in the importance of "bands," made up of the most devout Christians, acting as pathfinders to their less pious neighbors. The Epworth Society, which he formed from the "most sensible and well-disposed persons" in his parish, was created in the image of similar societies in London, most of them affiliated to, or loosely associated with, the Society for Promoting Christian Knowledge (SPCK).

Samuel Wesley had become a member of the SPCK during his brief curacy in London[9] and had found its theological position, as well as its form of organization, much to his liking. It was strongly (some of its critics would have said violently) antagonistic toward all things popish and actively supported the persecuted Protestant minorities of Europe. Samuel, who had once thought of becoming a missionary in America, applauded its hope of reforming the godless plantations of the New World. And as a literary figure he naturally welcomed the policy of spreading the joyous news of salvation by making books on theological and biblical subjects available to doubters at cut prices.

When Samuel Wesley wrote to the parent society in London, setting out the Epworth group's intention, he was careful to emphasize the priority which he gave to its various duties. "First to pray to God, secondly to read the Holy Scriptures and discourse upon religious matters for mutual edification and thirdly to deliberate on the edification of our neighbor." He enthusiastically agreed that the society must accept guidance and, if necessary, instruction from "a pious and learned divine of the Church"[10] since that was a role which he intended to perform. To ensure that the spiritual nature of the society was not debased, no one was admitted to membership "of whose solid piety" the rector or his associates "were not sufficiently appraised." As a result the numbers never rose above a dozen. But members acted in pairs to form satellite societies, though the "first society" retained control of policy toward the call for reform of church law and litany.

The rules of the Epworth Society were drawn up by Samuel Wesley himself on the basis of the constitutions of the London societies he had known. One of them was the obligation of miscreant members to correct their "disorderly walking." The correction of minor misdemeanors was a fashionable concept in eighteenth-century religious society. In 1735 the Society for the Reformation of Manners (SRM) boasted that in forty years it had promoted 99,380 prosecutions for debauchery and profanity in the London area alone.[11] But the Epworth group's constitution was as much based on the socially conscious Cripplegate Society as on the morally fastidious SRM. So as well as attempting to stamp out public profanity, it encouraged its members to succor the old, poor and sick. Whether or not his sons John and Charles learned of such obligations at their father's knee—an education which, for some strange reason, they were always anxious to deny—their Oxford Holy Club gradually developed the same rules and priorities as those which Samuel Wesley set out in his Lincolnshire parish. Epworth Society members believed that good Christians had social obligations to fulfill and did not concern themselves with the dispute about the heresy of salvation by good works which, thirty years later, was so violently to exercise the rector's sons.

Their "first care" was to "set schools for the poor, where children (or if need be adult persons) may be instructed in the fundamentals of Christianity." The fourth duty was "to take care of the sick and other poor and to afford them spiritual as well as corporal help."[12] Samuel Wesley thought that his society, and others like it all over England, followed the tradition of the monastic orders, which were "highly instrumental in the planting and propagating of Christianity amongst our forefathers."[13] Even though he was careful to add that Epworth was "reformed of the errors" which had afflicted the Franciscan and Carthusian houses, the comparison (as well as grossly exaggerating the importance of the Church of England societies) opened him to the accusation of Catholic, and therefore Jacobite, sympathies. But Samuel was not the man to allow the risk of unpopularity to stand in the way of a strongly held opinion—whether it was nostalgia for an earlier, more godly age or the importance of taking God's word to the unconverted. So the sanctity of the early Christian Fathers was an idea that was often expressed in the Epworth rectory. The notion that primitive Christianity was a model of piety to be envied and copied, picked up during his childhood, deeply influenced John Wesley's criticisms of the Established Church. It was only part of his spiritual inheritance. He believed himself to be guided by God. But often the Almighty acted through the agency of his parents. Often for good but sometimes for ill, the wishes and beliefs of Samuel and Susanna Wesley influenced their son's life long after they were dead and he had become the dominant figure in the Great English Revival.

Samuel and Susanna Wesley were an ill-matched couple. Susanna fulfilled her basic marital duties to the point of producing twelve children in as many years.* Remarkably, in an age when the infant mortality rate was three out of every four births, six of them survived. Six more children were born to Samuel and Susanna Wesley

---

* The following information is based on parish records quoted in Frank Baker's *Investigating Wesley Family Traditions*: Samuel, Jr. (1690), Susanna (1691), Emilia (1692), Annesley (unknown), Jedidiah (1694), Susanna II (1695), Mary (1696), Mehetabel (1697), unknown (1698), John I (1699), John II (1701), Anne (1701?), John III (1703), unknown (1705), Martha (1706), Charles (1707), unknown (1709), Kezziah (1709).

during the next seven years. Three of them reached the allotted span of threescore years and ten. Susanna Wesley was a conscientious wife and mother. But she found it impossible to share her husband's view that William of Orange was the legitimate king of England. So, one evening during the opening months of 1702, she failed to say "Amen" when, during family devotions, her husband prayed for the life and health of the sovereign. Susanna described what followed in a letter to Henrietta, Lady Yarborough, a local sympathizer with the Nonjuror clergy.*

> ... he retired to his study and calling me to him asked me the reason for not saying Amen. I was a little surprised by the question and don't well know what I answered, but too well remember what followed: He immediately kneeled down and imprecated the divine Vengeance upon himself and all his posterity if ever he touched me more or came into a bed with me before I had begged God's pardon and his.[14]

Susanna was a woman of unusual spirit, and she argued (highly impertinently by the standards of the time) that "since I'm willing to let him quietly enjoy his opinions he ought not to deprive me of my little liberty of conscience." She was also a woman of some learning. So she explained that she did not accept either the rebuke or the threat but "unsuccessfully represented to him the unlawfulness and unreasonableness of his oath." Samuel was neither convinced nor reconciled. But Susanna would not yield. Instead she looked for ways of justifying her rebellion. Men of piety, she told Lady Yarborough, "had advised her that she ought not to comply further, but persevere in following the dictates of my own conscience." Predictably Samuel did not share their view. He threatened, and perhaps even meant, to desert his wife and parish. Susanna certainly believed the threat to be real. "He is for London at Easter where he designs to try if he can get a Chaplain's place in a Man of War." Her

---

* Ordained priests of the Church of England who, as a matter of conscience, felt unable to swear the oath of allegiance to the new king.

anxiety was magnificently practical. "I have six very little children, which though he tells me he will provide for them, yet if anything should befall him at sea we should be in no very good condition."[15]

Samuel left home. Through either failure of will or lack of opportunity he never served on board a man-of-war. Susanna, in growing despair, sought advice from George Hickes, bishop of Thetford and the senior Nonjuror in the Church of England hierarchy.

> My Master will not be persuaded he has no power over the conscience of his Wife and though I believe he's somewhat troubled by his oath yet cannot be persuaded that it is not obligatory. He is now for referring the whole to the Archbishop of York and the Bishop of Lincoln and says that if I will not be determined by them, he will do anything rather than live with a person that is a declared enemy of his country.[16]

If, as we must assume, Susanna gave her friend and comforter an accurate account of her husband's attitude, Samuel's behavior (even by the standards of an eighteenth-century husband) was unreasonable to the point of madness. A modern marriage guidance counselor or divorce lawyer would have taken it for granted that his demands hid a more rational (if less elevated) reason for wanting to leave home. By the standards of the twenty-first century the rector of Epworth was demented in his devotion to King William. But in the context of the time, his loyalty, although excessive, was not altogether exceptional. Samuel Wesley was an ordained priest of what was not so much the Established Church as the state religion. Preferment depended on patronage, which was in turn determined by loyalty to monarch and court. Doctrinal position had an oblique influence on the prospects of promotion to dean, archdeacon and bishop. For High Churchmen were loosely associated with Tories—and, by their enemies, with Catholics, the Stuarts and, toward the end of the century, Jacobins. Whigs were Hanoverian and staunchly Protestant. So clergy who hoped for elevation had to make nimble adjustments to both their theology and politics as James II gave way to William and

Mary. William and Mary were succeeded by the Tory queen Anne, and Anne was followed by "German" George I and the Whigs. Samuel Wesley may be given credit for remaining consistent in his belief that whoever occupied the throne deserved his loyalty. But he was undoubtedly influenced by the spirit of the time, which made the Church of England a secular as well as a spiritual authority.

The eighteenth-century church was as much concerned with making men honest as with making them holy. Henry Fielding, the Dissenting author of *Tom Jones* and *Joseph Andrews*, explained in his pamphlet (ironically entitled *Proposals for an Effectual Provision for the Poor for Amending Their Morals and Making Them Useful Members of Society*) that "heaven and hell, when rung in the ears of those who have not yet learned that there is such a place . . . are by no means words of little significance." And Archbishop Tillotson, a traditional churchman, much revered for his ability to explain the word of God to man, judged that "magistrates have always thought themselves concerned to cherish religion and to maintain, in the minds of men, the belief in another life." That was "at first a politic device and it is still kept up in the world as a potent engine to awe men into obedience." The establishment and the Established Church could not be separated, and the characters of both institutions changed with the monarch and the shifting pattern of patronage. However sincere in his loyalty, a man of Samuel Wesley's temperament was incapable even of private rebellion against that consensus and gladly accepted the benefits which the system provided. Fifty years later even his son was careful to distinguish between those who accepted patronage and those who provided it.

The oppressive secular influence of the church, no less than its changing (although invariably intolerant) definitions of acceptable belief, made Susanna Wesley's courage in insisting that conscience prevented her from calling William her king remarkable for a woman of her time. She did not find it easy to be steadfast. In July 1702 she wrote again to George Hickes admitting that when Samuel briefly came home to Epworth, she had been on the point of forswearing her beliefs so as to avoid "the great many evils which would inevitably befall her"[17] if she refused to bend to his will.

Then, the letter explained, she had received the bishop's letter urging her to stand fast, and her courage was renewed. Samuel stayed at the rectory for two days and then left, vowing never to return. But Providence intervened. "He met a clergyman to whom he communicated his intentions and the reasons that induced him to leave his family . . . [who] extremely pitied him and condemned him but however, prevailed with him to return." However reluctantly he retraced his steps, Samuel Wesley must have quickly resumed married life. On 17 June 1703, a little more than ten months after Susanna sent George Hickes the news of reunion, she gave birth to a boy. He was christened John Benjamin in memory of two other Wesley children who had died in infancy.

THE SOUL OF THIS CHILD

The arrival of the Wesleys' fourteenth child did nothing either to reconcile the baby's parents to each other or to improve Susanna's failing spirits. Her letter to George Hickes, written to announce the grudging rapprochement with Samuel, ended with a passage of poignant speculation about the relationship between virtue and happiness, a subject which was to preoccupy her second son for much of his adult life. She concluded that "the end of virtue is peace and endless Felicity." But then she admitted that, virtuous woman though she was, she had rarely enjoyed the consequent tranquillity. Her husband's long absence had caused "abundance of trouble to him and his family." Nor did she anticipate that his return would herald a new age of peace and prosperity. Her only hope was that "heaven could grant the heavy curse that my Master has wished upon himself and Family may terminate in this life."[1] Whatever hopes Samuel Wesley entertained for heaven, he did not share his wife's aspiration for a quiet life on earth. His *Letter from a Country Divine*, published within months of John's birth, increased local antagonism by its attack on Dissent in general and Dissenting academies in particular. The people of Axholme turned against the Wesleys with a new severity. And Susanna accepted the consequences of their wrath with admirable fortitude. As she began the last paragraph of

21

the reunion letter to George Hickes she was told of a "new misfortune" which she reported to him with unaffected stoicism. "My house is now fired by one of my servants."[2]

The fire of 1702 was just one catastrophe in a decade of misfortune. The year before the barn had collapsed. Two years later the Wesleys' flax crop was ruined. Samuel Wesley believed he was the victim of the villagers' spite. He certainly encouraged their antagonism, as indeed he encouraged the antagonism of everyone with whom he did business. One cause of constant friction was his irresistible compulsion to draw attention to other people's errors. When William Wake, bishop of Lincoln, visited Epworth to confirm eight hundred candidates from the parishes of Coringham and Monlake, the rector, instead of rejoicing that his church had been chosen for the event, thought it necessary to draw the bishop's attention to what he believed to be a breach of church etiquette. It would, he said, have been better "for every parish to have come by themselves and none to have been confirmed but those whose name had been given by ministers."[3]

Samuel's preoccupation with church "manners"—the form of services and the respect for ritual—was rooted in obsessive fear and hatred of the Dissenters whose aims and beliefs he had once shared. His commitment to orthodoxy was so strong that his son John was convinced that he had written, or at least helped write, the notorious sermon which Henry Sacheverell preached to the lord mayor and aldermen of London in November 1709. It attacked Dissenters, latitudinarians and Low Churchmen in equal measure and denounced the ruling Whigs as the enemies of true religion. Sacheverell, at least as far as his attack on Dissent was concerned, did no more than articulate the views of the ultras within the Established Church. The Toleration Act of 1689 had made it possible for Dissenters to legalize their existence by registering their meetinghouses and licensing their preachers in the manner of felons on parole. But much of the Church of England was not even prepared to accept them on sufferance. The problem was Anglican insecurity. There were always suspicions of plots to subvert both church and state and fears that they might succeed. And the church was undiscriminating in its terror of opponents. Dissenters and Catholics were regarded with almost equal suspicion. Samuel Wesley was the embodiment of the Church of England's irrational anxieties. The neurosis caused him nothing but grief.

By his own account, Samuel Wesley's disastrous intervention in the county of Lincoln by-election of 1705 began with his "supposing there was a design to raise up Presbyterianism over the Church."[4] Consumed by the fantasy, he decided to support those candidates who were most opposed to Dissent. That in itself would have provoked much antagonism from the hundred or so Dissenters—Baptists and Quakers—in his parish. But the rector of Epworth pursued his cause with such a combination of irresponsibility and anti-Dissentient zeal that he turned enmity into hatred.

Four candidates mounted the Lincoln hustings. The sitting members, Sir John Thorold and Mr. Dymoke, were opposed by Colonel Whichcott and Mr. Bertie. Initially Samuel Wesley promised that he would not oppose Thorold, but instead of endorsing Dymoke, he announced his support for Whichcott because he was a local resident. However, on his return from one of his frequent visits to the convocation in London, Samuel discovered that both Whichcott and Bertie had canvassed the support of Dissenters while Thorold and Dymoke sought support only from members of the Established Church. Samuel Wesley immediately abandoned Whichcott and gave his support to both Thorold and Dymoke, with consequences that he reported to John Sharpe, the archbishop of Canterbury.

I went to Lincoln on Tuesday night May 29 and the election began on Wednesday the 30. A great part of the night our Isle people kept drumming, shouting and firing off pistols and guns under the window where my wife lay, who had been brought to bed not three weeks. A clergyman met me in the Castle-yard and told me to withdraw as the Isle men intended me mischief, another told me that he had heard near twenty of them say, if they got me in Castle-yard they would squeeze my guts out. When they heard I had gone home they sent the drum and mob with guns etc, as usual to compliment me till after midnight. One of them passing by on Friday evening and seeing my children in the yard cried out "O ye devils, we will come and turn you all out of doors a begging shortly."[5]

The rector's more respectable opponents took a different sort of revenge. Samuel Wesley had borrowed three pounds from a Mr. Pindar of Owston, principally to finance a visit to London to attend the convocation.[6] Pindar was a friend of Colonel Whichcott's and, infuriated by the rector's desertion of his candidate, called in the loan. Unable to make the repayment, Samuel Wesley was committed to Lincoln's debtors' jail.

Samuel Wesley's living at Epworth was worth £130 a year, far more than most parishes. But until the Wroot living (to which he was appointed in 1724) added £50 to his annual income, he was in perpetual debt. He had no idea how to manage money and survived, more or less solvent, by borrowing from friends. In his wife's words, he was "one of those who our Saviour saith are not wise in their generation as the children of this world."[7] That charitable explanation of her husband's incompetence was the excuse that Susanna gave her brother (a rich merchant living in India) for Samuel's mismanagement of funds entrusted to his care. Her letter of apology also contained a pathetic account of a conversation with the archbishop of York in the year of the county's by-election. "I freely own to Your Grace that strictly speaking I never did want for bread. But then I have had so much care to get it before 'twas eat and to pay for it after as has often made it very unpleasant for me."[8]

Samuel Wesley remained in jail for three months. Then the archbishop of York and some old Oxford friends convinced themselves and one another that he was a martyr to the church's cause and paid off his debts. "I am pretty confident," the released prisoner wrote, "that Your Grace neither reflects on nor imagines how much you have done for me by your bounty and favour."[9] Chastened, he vowed to live in at least comparative peace with his neighbors. Life in the rectory was uneventful, if never quite tranquil, for the next four years. Then there was yet another fire from which the whole family narrowly escaped. The early Methodist Church, by exaggerating the importance of coincidence, turned the near tragedy into an event of providential importance.

At some time between eleven o'clock and midnight on the evening of 9 February 1709 the roof of the Epworth rectory corn barn caught fire. We must assume that the Wesleys all slept the deep sleep of the just. For none of them woke until the whole house was ablaze and a burning timber fell on Mehetabel's bed. Even then, as she ran screaming from the room, her father (still half asleep) thought that her cries, combined with shouted warnings from the street below, were meant to raise the alarm about the destruction of a neighbor's house. As he rushed from the bedroom, ready to help in whatever way he could, Samuel Wesley was choked with smoke. Realizing at last that the rectory was on fire, he stumbled into the room where his wife, pregnant for the second time in barely a year, was still sleeping. There was, he told her, no time to dress. He then broke down the nursery door to release the nurse and the younger children and, after waking the rest of the family, led the way toward what he believed to be safety.

Susanna described the ordeal in letters to Samuel, her eldest son (by then an Oxford undergraduate), and to Joseph Hoole, her confidant from the days of her husband's desertion. Young Samuel was spared two embarrassing details of the escape which were confided in Hoole's letter. His mother and his siblings, having escaped the fire, stood in the garden "all naked and exposed to the inclemency of the air in a night which was so severely cold as perhaps anyone could remember."[10] And his father, having shepherded his family to the comparative safety of the rectory hall, discovered that he had left the keys in his bedroom and had to climb back up the blazing stairs to retrieve them before he could open the front door.

When the door was eventually opened, the sudden draft of air fed the flames, and the family was briefly beaten back. Two of the chil dren were led out through the garden door. Neighbors, who had rushed to the rescue, smashed the dining room window and pulled to safety the nurse and the infants in her care. Susanna, "not in a condition to stir like the rest nor climb a window or get to the garden door . . . endeavoured thrice to face a passage through the flames." Three times she was beaten back. Then, recalling Isaiah 43:2 ("when thou walkest through the fire, thou shall not be burned"), she "waded naked through the flames and suffered only a little scorching on the hands and face."[11]

It was then that Samuel and Susanna Wesley realized that John was still in the burning rectory. Twice Samuel attempted to return to the house and save his son, and twice he was forced back by the fire.[12] Then, certain that John was dead, he knelt in prayer for his son's departed soul. It is that, admittedly premature piety which encouraged critics of Samuel Wesley to claim that while his pregnant and distraught wife made valiant attempts to save the boy, he, overcome with panic and despair, prayed for an unlikely miracle.[13] Others simply believe that his prayers were answered. The truth is more prosaic than either of the more lurid accounts suggests.

When the nurse left the house, telling the children to follow her, she had assumed that John had responded to her call. But neither her cries nor the commotion caused by the fire had woken him. When he did wake and put his head outside the bed-curtains, he saw flames streaking across the bedroom ceiling. The landing outside his door was burning and about to collapse. So were the stairs below, which a few minutes earlier his father had tried to climb in a desperate attempt to rescue him. His mother gave the authentic account of his escape. "The child climbed up to the window and cried out to them in the yard. They got up on the casement and pulled him out just as the roof fell into the chamber."[14]

Almost seventy years later, when the letters were published, the aged John Wesley added the note "not exactly right with regard to me."[15] But there is no reason to believe the story (put about by Susanna's romantic biographers) that having started the fire by his carelessness, Samuel prayed for his children's souls while his wife affected a daring rescue.[16] The rector certainly prayed—prayed for the son who he thought was dead and then in thanks for John's rescue. "Let us give thanks to God! He has given me my eight children: let the house go, I am rich enough."[17] That much is certain. Less well documented is the story that became, as part of Methodist folklore, the proof that John Wesley had from the start been chosen to lead the Christian revival. The following morning, the anecdote goes, a charred page from the polyglot Bible was blown across the rectory garden by the winter wind. All that could be read from the scorched paper was "Give up all that you have and take up the cross and follow me."[18]

If the story is true, the Wesleys, living in an age when Christians, barely less than followers of other faiths, believed in signs and omens, must have been quite certain that God had sent His message to the whole family and perhaps to all the world. At the time of the fire, there was no reason for them to believe that it had been meant exclusively for their second son. The idea that John had been specially chosen to do God's work came gradually to his mother. But the drama of his rescue undoubtedly made her wonder if he had been saved in order that he could one day save others. When John was eight, and the trauma of the fire was two years behind her, Susanna promised God that she would be "more particularly careful of the soul of this child, that Thou hast so mercifully provided for, than ever I have been, that I may do my endeavours to instil into his mind the disciplines of true religion and virtue."[19] The syntax was confused, but the message was plain enough. John Wesley had been spared in order that he should do great work. He was a "brand plucked from the burning" and must offer others salvation from even fiercer flames.

For a time the Wesley family was so grateful for the deliverance that they were distracted from consideration of the plight in which the fire had left them. Then they had to face the hard reality. "No home, no money, food or raiment!" When they began to make an inventory of destruction and damage, it became clear how great their loss had been. They had, Susanna wrote to tell Mr. Hoole, "no time to recover anything." All the most valuable plate had been brought into the store chamber, a precaution which, for some reason, Susanna Wesley always took when she was pregnant.[20] In consequence much of it was melted down in the intense heat and only about twenty-five ounces were recovered in the days which followed the fire. What remained of the winter grain store was destroyed. "A considerable sum of money," which the rector had been paid the day before for the sale of his whole crop of flax, was lost amid the charred wood and rubble. But the "greatest almost inconceivable loss was . . . books and manuscripts," particularly a volume which Samuel Wesley "had just before prepared for the press upon the delivery of which he should have received £50."[21]

Two months after the fire, Kezziah, Susanna's nineteenth child and the tenth to survive infancy, was born prematurely.[22] Perhaps the risk and the rescue of February were not totally to blame for the April trauma, for two years earlier Charles had come into the world equally unexpectedly and had lain, as if dead, in his cradle until "the time when he should have been born according to the normal course of nature." He then had "opened his eyes and made himself heard." But the fire was responsible for what Susanna regarded as the temporary destruction of the rest of her family. Homeless, they were "kindly received into several families" in the village. But "they were allowed to do as other boys and girls did." They "talked to the servants; they ran about and played with other children both good and bad."[23] It was not Susanna's idea of a proper upbringing.

In 1732, at John Wesley's request, Susanna set out what she called "the principal rules which I observed in educating my family." The account of the precepts by which she had been guided—three thousand words in all—began with an apology for the disorderly state of her memory and the agreement that John should use her prescription in whatever way he chose. He used it—after suitable editing—as a guide to other parents and, most important, when it was published in his *Journal*, as proof that he was brought up to be a God-fearing man. One sentence sums up Susanna's philosophy of child care. "The parent who indulges it does the devil's work, makes religion impracticable, salvation unattainable and does all that in him lies to damn his child, body and soul for ever."[24] That rigorous rule was translated into regulations which covered almost every aspect of infant life.

The children were always put into a regular method of living in such things as they were capable from their birth as in dressing, undressing, changing their linen etc. . . . When turned a year old (and some before) they were taught to fear the rod and to cry softly, by

28

which means they escaped an abundance of correction. . . . Drinking or eating between meals was never allowed. They were so constantly used to eat and drink what was given them that when any of them was ill there was no difficulty in making them take the most unpleasant medicine.

The notion that a child should "have nothing it cries for, absolutely nothing" went out of fashion at the close of the Victorian era. And today the injunction "[M]ake him do as he is bid, if you whip him ten times running to effect it" would attract the attention of the police. Susanna ended her advice on the importance of corporal punishment with the footnote "whatever pain it costs you." But she was stern and unyielding by nature, and there is little doubt that she did what she believed to be her duty without much personal suffering. Her draconian inclinations were, she believed, supported by a theory of child rearing which gave them intellectual respectability. Susanna was so impressed by the philosophy of John Locke that she copied long passages from his *Essay Concerning Human Understanding* into her journal. And her views on the duty of Christian parents were, in their severe way, based on Locke's *Thoughts on Education*. Intellect and inclination combined to make the rules by which she governed stern and absolute. "The children of this family were taught, as soon as they could speak, the Lord's prayer. One day was allowed for the child to learn its letters and each of them did in that time know all its letters great and small except Molly and Nancy who were a day and a half."[25]

At first Susanna thought that the two girls must be "very dull." Then, having observed how long it took other people's children to learn the alphabet, she changed her opinion without altering her teaching methods. Perhaps she was unduly influenced by her eldest son's prodigious achievement. "Samuel, who was the first child I ever taught, learned the alphabet in a few hours. . . . I cannot remember ever to have told him the same word twice."[26]

The "same method was observed" with all the children. However, Susanna's letter does not reveal if John learned at the same prodigious speed as his elder brother. It concludes with a complaint against the neighbors who, despite their kindness in opening their houses to the homeless family after the fire, sent the children to the rebuilt rectory with "a clownish accent and many rude ways learned." Susanna corrected the faults by the application of "several by-laws." They included a provision to avoid "cowardice and fear of punishment" leading children into lying. To encourage respect for the truth, Susanna promised that "whoever was charged with a fault of which they were guilty, if they would ingenuously confess it and promise to amend should not be beaten." Other bylaws "stipulated that no child should ever be hit or beat twice for the same offence" and that "every signal act of obedience, especially when it crossed their own inclination, should always be rewarded and frequently commended." A "bylaw" on the education of women—"no girl be taught to work until she can read very well"—was remarkably progressive for an age in which only one woman in four could even write her own name. Indeed many of the rules which were made to restore the Wesley children's virtue—as distinct from improving their knowledge—sound positively liberal. But at the heart of Susanna Wesley's theory of education was the unyielding certainty that "in order to form the minds of children, the first thing to be done is conquer their will . . . whatever path it costs conquer their stubbornness." The theory worked—at least in terms of the tests of achievement which Susanna regarded as important. Samuel, John and Charles all grew up to be Christian scholars. And John remained—as the sincerest form of flattery—intellectually dependent on his mother's judgment for as long as she lived. And perhaps remembering what she believed about the education of his sisters, he often (unusually for the time) discussed theology with his women friends. When he consulted his mother as an authority on faith and morals, he always recognized that she was a paragon of fearless wisdom. Perhaps he admired her too much for his own good. And it might have been the awe in which he held his mother that prevented him from ever enjoying a satisfactory relationship with any other woman.

Unfortunately Samuel Wesley, an insensitive as well as a highly intelligent man, did not hold his wife in such high intellectual esteem.

In consequence, he was constantly surprised by her independence. So there can be little doubt that the letter which he received from the Reverend Mr. Inman while he was in London attending the 1712 Church of England convocation came as a shock to him. Mr. Inman, the curate at Epworth, complained that his authority was being undermined. Susanna was, at least according to the locum's judgment, holding "conventicles," acts of worship neither carried out in the manner prescribed by the Established Church nor registered as Dissenters' meetings. The Act of Toleration, which had made registered Dissent lawful, nevertheless proscribed unregistered conventicles as illegal gatherings.

The point at which private but collective prayers became a conventicle was a matter of dispute. And at least at first, Susanna Wesley believed that she was doing no more than providing her family with an opportunity for daily devotions, thereby fulfilling the spiritual gap which had been left in their lives by the cancellation of afternoon prayers when Samuel left for London. But after a week or two friends and neighbors were invited (or invited themselves) to join in. The curate reported that on one occasion in February 1712, more than two hundred people had crowded into the rectory kitchen.[27] Others were turned away because the room was full.

The suspicion that Susanna's behavior was unlawful was increased by her newfound enthusiasm for the work of Ziegenbalg and Plütschau, two young missionaries who had been sent by the king of Denmark to convert the Indians of Malabar. Susanna had found a collection of their sermons in her husband's study and, having read them herself, began to read them to her afternoon prayer meetings. The event grew so popular that the Epworth villagers began to attend the rectory kitchen in preference to the parish church. Once again life in the rectory was foreshadowing the disputes and dilemmas which one day John Wesley would face. Not surprisingly, Mr. Inman complained about the competition in exactly the tones which other Church of England clergymen used when Methodists arranged meetings which coincided with matins.

Susanna had a poor opinion of Inman, partly because he made a practice of preaching that debt was a sin and she believed that his texts were chosen as an implied criticism of her husband. Samuel was more forgiving and, in theological matters, was instinctively on the side of a clerk in holy orders rather than a woman who happened to be his wife. Inman convinced him that Susanna was breaking the laws of both church and state. He therefore wrote to his wife from his lodgings in St. Margaret's Churchyard, Westminster, telling her of his misgivings. The meeting looked "particular" (that is to say, unusual) to the outside world. It was improper for a woman to preside at such gatherings. Both offenses were compounded by Susanna's status as the wife of a clergyman "at present in a public station and character." Could she not, he asked, allow someone else to read from the collected works of the Danish evangelists? The letter reads like a genuine, if not very successful, attempt to be reasonable.

Susanna responded trenchantly to each point. Her rebuttal of the charges was couched in respectful language but carried an utterly uncompromising message. Her reply included an argument which reads like a passage from one of the sermons of John Wesley by which, thirty years later, her son defended his right to take the Word of God to the people rather than wait for the people to make their way to an unwelcoming church. "As to it looking particular, I grant it does. And so does everything that is serious or that may any way advance the glory of God or the salvation of souls if it be performed out of a pulpit, or in the way of common conversation, because in our corrupt age, the utmost care and diligence have to be used to banish all discourse of God or spiritual concerns out of our society."[28] The notion that it was unseemly for a woman to lead a prayer meeting was rejected in more conventional terms. The "superior charge of the souls" rests, she conceded, with the head of the family—especially so, if he was a minister. But the Wesley children had been left in her care, and she must therefore take responsibility for their religious education during their father's absence. How else could she answer at the seat of judgment, "when He shall command me to render an account of my stewardship"? The prayers and reading were family gatherings. A "few neighbors" asked to join the devotions, and since they wished to hear the Word of the Lord, she "dare refuse none that asked admittance"—even when more than two hundred people arrived at the rectory door. The idea that her husband's membership in the Convocation required her to act with especial restraint was dismissed out of hand. "If I and my children went a-visiting on Sunday nights, or admitted of impertinent visits as many do who think themselves good Christians, perhaps it would be thought no scandalous practice, though in truth it would be so." So that her husband clearly understood her absolute rejection of his second complaint, she added, "I value no censure on this account." The letter ended on an endearingly practical note. "As to your proposal of letting some other person read, alas you do not consider what people these are. I do not think one man among them could read a sermon without spelling a good part of it. And how that would edify the rest!"

Not surprisingly, Samuel Wesley regarded his wife's reaction as a refusal to respect his wishes. He responded at the end of the month with a letter which was less a request than an instruction backed up with the claim that "persons of influence" were demanding that the meetings end. It took Susanna nine days to compose her reply. Her letter began with an explanation of why she "had made no great haste to answer. . . . I judged it necessary for both of us to take some time to consider before you determine in a matter of such great importance." The implication that the rector had not examined the question with equal care was then confirmed with what must have been infuriating condescension: "I shall pass no censure upon the hasty and unexpected change of your judgement, neither shall I enquire how it was possible that you should be prevailed on by the senseless clamours of two or three of the worst of your parish." There was no question of her endorsing Samuel's judgment. Indeed she went on to argue, anticipating John's arguments for "field preaching," that her meetings were the best way to "change the hearts" of men and women who never attended formal services and make them "delight in public worship so as never to neglect it more." But she made it clear, by the end of the letter, that she accepted that her duty, as wife and mother, was to bow to the will of her husband—no matter how unreasonable his wishes might be. But despite her reluctant acquiescence, she made one thing clear. Susanna persisted in her belief that her husband was wrong.

> If you do, after all, think fit to dissolve this assembly, do not tell me any more that you desire me to do it, that will not satisfy my conscience; but send me your positive command in such full and express terms as may absolve me from all guilt and punishment for neglecting this opportunity of doing good to souls, when you and I shall appear before the great and awful tribunal of our Lord Jesus Christ.[29]

The elegance of that message—submission gracefully balanced against reproof—is matched by the courage it must have taken to send it. Susanna Wesley was, above all other things, a strong woman. And strong women make indelible marks on their sons. In John Wesley's case, the effect his stern and upright mother had on his character was compounded by the essentially female ambience of the Epworth rectory. His father was in London, separated from his family for long periods. Brother Samuel, his senior by seventeen years, was away at either school or university. Four older sisters shared the harsh lessons by which "self-will the root of all sin and misery" was conquered. It is not altogether surprising that when he got into the world beyond the rectory, his relationships with women were constantly compromised by conflicting anxieties about the relationship between instinct and duty.

The letter in which Susanna bowed to her husband's will ended with the pious hope that the rector would soon be home. Her wish was not granted. So she was left alone to deal with the smallpox which infected five of her children. Miraculously they all recovered. John, at least in the estimation of his mother, bore "his disease bravely like a man, and indeed like a Christian, without any complaint," though they could only guess that his spots were causing him pain, for he "looked sourly at them but he never said anything."[30] His demeanor was regarded—at least by the biographers who wrote shortly after his death—as proof of his contemplative, as well as stoical, nature. In a rare tender moment Samuel told his wife, "I confess sweetheart, I think our Jack would not attend to the most pressing necessities of nature unless he could give a reason for it."[31] The Wesleys were beginning to regard their second son as too much of an intellectual prodigy for his own good. The rector thought it necessary to warn him that not every problem could be solved by pure logic. "You think to carry everything by dint of argument, but you will find out how very little is done in the world by close reason."[32]

John Wesley's youthful belief in the universal sovereignty of reason did not remain with him into manhood. He constantly tested his faith against what he believed to be empirical evidence of God's redeeming love, but from time to time he lapsed into superstitions. He cut cards, drew lots and opened his Bible at random to determine God's will. And like so many aspects of John Wesley's character, his belief in the supernatural was nurtured at Epworth. He grew up in a household which, despite its dedication to Christian scholarship, was profoundly superstitious. A ghost walked at the Epworth rectory between December 1716 and February of the following year. Then, although not exorcised, it rested in peace. During its three-month visit, the family decided that it was the shade of Old Jeffrey, a local suicide.

It was the Wesleys' parlormaid who first heard Old Jeffrey's dismal groans. Susanna and her daughters attributed the story to girlish imagination. But only a few days later all the Wesley women heard repeated and methodical knocking on doors and paneling all over the house. For a time Susanna remained skeptical and, recalling that a neighbor had cleared his house of rats by playing on a trumpet, borrowed the instrument and attempted to blow away whatever made the noise. Her daughters begged her not to antagonize the ghost and felt that their warning had been vindicated when Old Jeffrey began to appear during the day as well as the night and extended his repertoire to include the sound of breaking glass and footsteps on the landings and a noise like a gobbling turkey-cock. The most balanced reaction came from a servant. When the handle of the corn-grinding machine began to turn of its own volition, Robert

Brown, the Wesleys' factotum, expressed his regret that Old Jeffrey never worked the grinder when it was full.

Old Jeffrey became such a regular and obtrusive visitor that Susanna was convinced of his supernatural origins. But even after he started gobbling, crashing and stamping, it was several weeks before the rector was conscious of his presence. The Wesley women kept Samuel innocent of all knowledge about the supernatural presence in his house—at first because they assumed that he would not believe them and then because they feared that the evidence being too strong to deny, he would draw a terrible conclusion from the presence, all about him, of an apparition which he could neither see nor hear. It was a common belief that spirits did not manifest themselves to the mortals whom they came on earth to harm. Susanna feared that her husband would be certain that he had not seen Old Jeffrey because the spirit revealed himself to the rest of the family as a sign that its head faced death and damnation.

Fortunately, after a couple of weeks, Samuel too heard the various improbable noises and, as his daughters had rightly predicted, first assumed that he was being harassed by unfriendly neighbors and dismissed his daughters' fears as girlish fancy. "Sukey," he said to the twenty-year-old Susanna, "I am ashamed of you. These boys and girls frighten one another, but you are a woman of sense and should know better."[33] He was reinforced in his rejection of the supernatural by Robert Brown's account of a badgerlike creature running out from under a bed. To destroy such intrusive vermin and to deter the hooligans who he believed were responsible for various invasions of his privacy, he bought a mastiff. But whenever the knocking began, the dog cringed, whined and attempted to take refuge in Robert Brown's bed. Then, as his family had predicted, Samuel began to believe that the house was haunted by a malign spirit. He fired his pistol in the direction of the ghostly noises and, calling Old Jeffrey a deaf and dumb devil, challenged him to join the rector in the study for some serious conversation about the afterlife. The specter did not accept the invitation, but it responded to Samuel's abuse by whistling, lifting latches, opening windows and brushing against the girls. As if to demonstrate the full depths of his evil, he was particularly active during prayers for the king and the royal family. The time had come to consider seriously what Old Jeffrey's purpose was.

Both Susanna and Samuel took it for granted that he was a harbinger of bad tidings. Susanna, reassured that his malice was not directed toward her husband, feared that her brother, a merchant in India who had mysteriously disappeared, had died. Samuel waited with dread for news of the death of one of his sons—probably Samuel, Jr., by then an usher at Westminster School. When he discovered that the young man was safe and well, he began to treat Old Jeffrey as a nuisance rather than as a threat. Then the noises ceased. By the time that the ghost disappeared, the whole family was calm about the brief manifestation—calm but absolutely fascinated. During the autumn of 1726 Samuel Jr., and John set out to document every detail of the supernatural occurrence in their parents' house: letters from their mother, extracts from their father's journal and statements from witnesses. The work went on haphazardly for some months. The Reverend Mr. Hoole, invited, as always in times of trouble, to offer his advice, gave a simple, and compelling, description of a single incident.

> One of the maids who went up to sheet a bed brought the alarm that Jeffrey was come above stairs. We all went up, and were standing round the fire in the east chamber. Something began knocking on the other side of the wall of the chimney piece as with a key. Presently the knocking was under our feet. Mr. Wesley and I went down, he with a great deal of hope and I with fear. As soon as we left the kitchen, the sound was above us in the room we had left.[34]

The Wesley brothers remained fascinated by Old Jeffrey for all of their lives. Years after they left the rectory, they still showed their account of the haunting to anyone who could read it. Joseph Priestley, being a scientist, judged the most likely cause was servants amusing themselves at their employers' expense or neighbors attempting to annoy the rector. But John Wesley retained his belief in Old Jeffrey's supernatural origins. Indeed he believed that he knew why the ghost had been sent to haunt Epworth. His father had sinned by vowing to ostracize his wife after she refused to pray for the life and health of King William in 1702. "I fear this vow was not forgotten before God." Sixty years later John Wesley was still sufficiently sure that Old Jeffrey was a supernatural messenger that he published the whole account of the Epworth haunting in the *Arminian Magazine*.[35]

John Wesley might have been more skeptical about Old Jeffrey's provenance had he been at the rectory to witness the strangely inappropriate manifestations of divine disapproval. But almost two years before the knocking and stamping began he was admitted to Charterhouse School as a foundation scholar on the nomination of the duke of Buckingham, lord chamberlain to King George and his father's patron in the living of Epworth. It was, by the standards of both church and state, an eventful year. Queen Anne died, and George, elector of Hanover, was offered the throne of England. Bolingbroke and the duke of Ormonde fled to France and conspired with Britannia's enemies for the return of a Catholic king. The threat was easily defeated in 1715, when the earl of Mar raised an abortive rebellion in the Highlands, but the treason enabled the Whigs to brand every Tory a traitor and, with their hegemony secured for almost a hundred years, launch an unexpected orgy of patronage and placemen. The result was a debased church which cared little for prayer and even less for its pastoral duties but was organized around absentee and plural benefices which were awarded to the ministry's favorites. It was a system which disgusted the adult John Wesley and did much to harden his heart against the Church of England. Ironically it was also the system which, having found his father a comfortable living, provided him with a place at Charterhouse.

At Charterhouse, foundation scholars—or "gown boys," as they were called—were the sons of gentlemen who, because their fathers could not afford an education proper to their station, were supported by the legacy of Thomas Sutton, at whose bequest the school and almshouses were founded in 1611. It was for this reason that John Wesley is described as "a poor scholar," a status which encouraged early biographers to exaggerate the hardship and humiliation which he suffered at the hands of more prosperous pupils. No doubt, as was the way with public schools, Wesley was treated badly by his seniors. But it seems unlikely that "for a considerable part of the five years that [he] spent at Charterhouse the only solid food he got was bread." So it must have been some other humiliation which he overcame ("without acquiring either the cringing of a slave or a despot's imperious temper") by "carrying out a strict command which his father gave him to run round the Charterhouse garden three times every morning."[36] Or, more likely, the whole story is the invention of Methodist mythmakers.

Not all the dubious anecdotes reflect as much credit on John Wesley as their narrators intended. A "Letter to Rev. Tooke LLD and Mr. H. Moore by an Old Member of the Society" describes an incident at Charterhouse which, although often quoted as proof that Wesley felt the call to greatness while still a schoolboy, illustrates an undoubted trait which not everyone found attractive. According to the "Old Member," the Charterhouse usher noticed that Wesley was in the habit of spending his time with boys much younger than himself, haranguing them about their faith and morals. The legend claims that when he was asked why he did not find friends among his contemporaries, he replied, "Better to rule in Hell than serve in Heaven,"[37] the one recorded instance of the founder of the Methodist Church quoting Satan (or at least John Milton's Satan) with approval. Twenty years later John Hampson (for a time one of his preachers) was to write that Wesley felt happiest in "tutorial relationships" with the young—especially young women. In old age he suffered greatly from the lack of a real friend. In early manhood he was almost destroyed by not being sure of the difference between a protégée and a prospective wife.

The prospects of painting an accurate picture of Wesley's time at Charterhouse are prejudiced by his own retrospective judgment about the years he spent there, judgments which were made during his penitential period when all his past life seemed seeped in sin.

Outward restraints being removed, I was much more negligent than ever before even of outward duties and almost certainly guilty of outward sins which I knew to be such though they were not scandalous in the eyes of the world. However, I still read the Scriptures and said my prayers morning and evening. And what I now hoped to be saved by was (1) not being so bad as other people (2) having still a kindness for religion and (3) reading the Bible, going to church and saying my prayers.[38]

That is not simply the gloomy hindsight of a forty-seven-year-old man who regretted even the minor follies of his youth. Nor is it the reverential memory of years spent under the moral guidance of his mother. Rather it is the conclusion of an introspective theologian who was feeling his tentative way toward satisfying definitions of sin and redemption and had come to the conclusion that true virtue, built on belief, required more than the avoidance of sin and the observance of religious ritual. It was in John Wesley's nature to see his whole life in the context of his current conviction. And at the time when he wrote the denunciation of his boyhood conduct, he had come to believe in the need to "imitate" Christ. What was more, the Charterhouse schoolboy had not felt "assured" of the love of God and the consequent certainty of salvation. So in introspective old age he designated himself an adolescent sinner.

The self-criticism was as inaccurate as it was unhealthy. If his brother Samuel was to be believed, young John was the epitome of scholarly virtue. Samuel, an usher at Westminster (where Charles, the rector's third son, had become a pupil in 1716), lived with his wife in Dean's Yard. So, with Epworth two hundred miles away, John spent his spare time with his brothers. It therefore fell to Samuel to report on his academic progress. As John approached sixteen and his last year at Charterhouse, the rector's eldest son sent his father a convoluted compliment to both his younger brothers. "Jack, I can faithfully assure you, gives you no manner of discouragement from breeding your third son a scholar." Three months later he added, perhaps a little ambiguously, "Jack is with me, and a brave boy, learning Hebrew as fast as he can."[39]

It is at least possible that Samuel was simply telling his father what he judged the rector wanted to hear. But we know for certain that John Wesley left Charterhouse with a fine command of Latin and Greek, and there is every reason to suppose that he also took with him many happy memories. That is the only explanation of the affection which he felt for the school throughout his life and the most likely explanation of why, until late middle age, he visited it at least once a year. In 1727 he was a steward at the Old Carthusians' Founder's Day Feast and helped to preside over a banquet of "roasted pike, fried whiting, venison pasties, pigeons, sirloin of beef, spitched eels, asparagus, roasted lobster, almond tarts, custards, Florentines, jellies and a great variety of other dainty and substantial dishes." It seems improbable that a boy who had lived for six years on bread would have wanted to celebrate his schooldays in so joyous a fashion or that he would have achieved the modest academic success which sent him on his way.

In June 1720, John Wesley, then aged seventeen, was elected an exhibitioner of Christ Church, Oxford. The award was limited to Old Carthusians, and he therefore made almost automatic progress from school to university. But, at least according to Alexander Knox, who knew him in old age, his father did all he could to guarantee his son both a place in the university's most socially prestigious college and a warm welcome when he got there. Samuel spoke to persons of influence, including Dr. Henry Sacheverell, Fellow of Magdalen, and—because of his denunciation of all Dissenters—a hero of all Tory Oxford. Sacheverell agreed to meet the young undergraduate. The meeting was not a success. Sacheverell was apparently taken aback by Wesley's diminutive stature.

"When I was introduced, I found him alone, as tall as a maypole and as fine as an archbishop. I was very little, not taller" (pointing to a very gentlemanly but very dwarfish clergyman who was in the company) "than Mr. Kennedy there. He said, "You are too young to go to University. You cannot know Greek and Latin yet. Go back to school." I looked at him as David looked at Goliath and despised him in my heart. I thought, If I do not know Greek and Latin better than you, I ought to go back to school indeed. I left him and neither entreaties nor commands could have brought me back to him."[40]

John Wesley, although God's humble servant, was—in matters concerning the vanities of the world—a proud man. He was also, as his life drew to a close, inclined to remember with advantage stories which contributed to his status as prophet and patriarch. But the tales which grew up around his boyhood are—fact or fable—at least consistent with a character which gave him the strength to seize and retain the leadership of the Methodist Connexion. And they make one other fact of his life transparently clear. Epworth—the sometimes complementary but often competing influences of his mother and father—remained in his mind and memory for all his life. The strength which made him the leader of the Second Reformation was forged in the country rectory.

4

BEAUTY AND VIRTUE

John Wesley entered Christ Church—then, as now, never called a college—in June 1720. Oxford, at the beginning of the eighteenth century, was not a seat of independent scholarship. It existed to justify, and therefore preserve, orthodoxy within the Established Church and to defend its doctrines and governance against the corrosive influence of both Roman Catholicism and Dissent. Orthodoxy was defined in a peculiarly Oxford way. Some dons were High Church and High Tory to a point at which they were suspected of Jacobite sympathies. A few were the remnants of earlier Whig patronage, and a minority remained outside the mainstream of Anglican opinion. But most senior members of the university held views on doctrine, litany and church "manners" with which the young John Wesley felt entirely at home.

The years at Charterhouse had taught self-reliance. But he wrote home with a frequency and in a manner which suggest that he both wanted and needed to test his developing opinions against his parents' judgment. The letters were addressed individually to either his father or his mother, never to both. That was because they were all written with a highly specific purpose. He asked his father for advice on matters of scholarship, texts to read and authorities to consult. His mother was consulted on faith and morals and the two personal pre-occupations of his first Oxford year, money and health.

Christ Church was the largest and the most aristocratic of the Oxford colleges. So a poor undergraduate did not feel at ease. But initially at least he visited local taverns to play cards—ombre—and backgammon, enjoyed a game of billiards, rowed on the river, attempted royal tennis and attended a race meeting on the meadow. Over his undergraduate years he gradually lost all interest in what he came to think of as frivolity. But at least until his ordination as deacon in September 1725 he played some part in the social life which surrounded him.[1] And his piety certainly did not prevent him from contemplating the desires of the flesh, a preoccupation which remained with him into old age. His translation (from the Latin) of *Chloe and the Flea*, the most quoted example of his mild erotica, was only one item in a series of pseudoclassical verses in which, slightly perversely, he related desire to infestation. At least the flea survived. "Now on her parting breasts he leaps / Now hides between his little head."[2] The bee, which featured in a second poem which he sent to his brother Samuel, did not.

> Drawn by the fragrance of her breath
> Her rosy lips he found
> There in full transport sucked to death
> And dropped upon the ground[3]

However, John Wesley, in the year of his ordination, envied the bee's fate. "Each god would quit his blissful state / To share a death like thine." Brother Samuel should have realized when he read the poem that John was going to have trouble with women. Fortunately emotional irresponsibility is incompatible with neither a serious mind nor an active conscience. John Wesley possessed both and the determination to be a scholar.

The Charterhouse exhibition paid Wesley twenty pounds a year, and his Christ Church exhibition paid about the same. It was not enough to live on. Henry Sherman, his tutor, kept his fees to an absolute

minimum and occasionally lent him cash. Various schemes were de-
vised to raise additional funds. His brother Samuel, still a student
(that is to say, Fellow) of Christ Church and therefore entitled to
rooms in the college, wrote to him from Westminster School to say
that if he found a tenant, he could keep the rent. Nothing came of
the idea. Back at Epworth, the rector, with desperate debts of his
own, could do little to help. For a while his mother hoped that her
brother Samuel Annesley would come to the rescue on his return
from service with the East India Company. But when she went to
London to meet him—principally to welcome him home but no
doubt also with his nephew's need in mind—he did not arrive on
the scheduled ship and was never seen again. So she was reduced to
sending the plaintive message "Dear Jacky, be not discouraged.
Perhaps notwithstanding all this we will provide a few crumbs for
you before the end of the year."[4]

John Wesley accepted his penury with good grace. After Oxford
was scandalized by stories of a footpad stealing an undergraduate's hat
and wig, he wrote to his mother with the reassurance "I am safe
from such gentlemen. For unless they carried me away, carcass and
all, they would have but a poor purchase."[5] For most of his undergraduate life, John Wesley chose not to wear a wig and allowed his
hair to grow long. Together with his prominent nose and piercing
blue eyes, it became one of the defining features of his appearance,
made famous in prints, on plates and pots. But the distinctive hair-
style was not part of a careful plan to be noticed. Nobody thought it
improved his looks, and his mother told him that a visit to a barber
would increase his energy. For once he doubted her judgment. "It
would doubtless mend my complexion and perhaps it might contribute to my making a more genteel appearance. But these, till ill
health is added to them, I cannot persuade myself to be sufficient
grounds for losing two or three pounds a year."[6]

Despite such minor economies, Susanna Wesley was still not sure
that her son was doing all he could to become solvent. "I wish," she
wrote to him, "that you would save all the money you can conve-
niently spare not to spend on a visit home but for a wiser and better
purpose to pay debts and make yourself easy."[7] By then Charles had

joined John in Oxford and begun to exhibit more extravagant tastes than his brother possessed. The ingenious Mr. Sherman suggested that he should let out his rooms and live in a garret on the edge of the city. Charles rejected the idea out of hand.[8] Susanna's mood of self-denial did not last. Six weeks after she wrote her plea for prudence, she changed her mind. "Your brother," she told John, "talks of coming hither at Whitsuntide; perhaps between this and that, something may occur or may happen that you may come with him."[9]

Money was not John Wesley's only cause for concern. His Oxford years—at least until he received the security of ordination and a fellowship—were prejudiced by constant minor illness. During his first year at Christ Church he contracted bilious catarrh. The condition persisted with such debilitating results that he decided he was dying of consumption. Hypochondria played some part in his diagnosis. But his fears were also based on what he reasonably took to be conclusive evidence of fatally damaged lungs. In 1723, while he walked in the woods near Oxford, his nose bled so severely that he thought it necessary to stanch the loss of blood by diving into the river.[10] The regular and frequent hemorrhages continued for years. But they gradually lost their terror. Then he discovered what he believed to be the secret of good health. Like the enthusiast that he was—in the common, if not the theological, sense of the word—once he had found a "sovereign cure" for all his maladies he followed the diagnosis and prescription without doubt or qualification.

In November 1724 he wrote to tell his mother that he had read Dr. Cheyne's *Book of Health and Long Life*. From then on he followed its instructions in every detail and attributed his improved strength and vitality to observation of its basic precept. Dr. Cheyne believed that the secret of good health was "temperance and exercise." John Wesley described the recommended diet with an unrestrained enthusiasm. "He entirely condemns eating anything salt or high seasoned, also pork, fish and stall-fed cattle, and recommends for drink two pints of water and one of wine in twenty-four hours, with eight ounces of animal or twelve of vegetable food in the same time."[11] Cheyne also recommended continual physical exertion—particularly riding, which "shakes the whole machine, promoting a universal perspiration and secretion of all the fluids"[12]—and early rising. "Those who live temperately . . . necessarily sleep but little." The rest "ought to go to bed by eight, nine or ten at latest and rise by four, five or six."[13]

Such a punishing lifestyle can hardly be described as convenient. But it fitted exactly with the discipline which John Wesley was forced to adopt when he began to evangelize throughout England. And because Cheyne had developed his pattern of guaranteed health as an antidote to the debilities caused by a debauched life in London, his remedy possessed a compelling spiritual quality which chimed with Wesley's fast-developing sense of vocation. As the early Oxford years passed, he grew more and more to a serious life.

The letters betray a naiveté—indeed a wonderment at the workings of the world—which confirms that for all his intellectual pretensions, the mark of a provincial rectory was still upon him. At twenty-one he was (at least according to the *Westminster* magazine of 1774) "the very sensible and acute collegian, baffling other men by the subtleties of his logic and laughing at them for being so easily routed; a young fellow of the finest classical taste and the most liberal and manly sentiments."[14] But he still wrote home in wide-eyed amazement to tell his parents of the extraordinary events which occupied the attention of his new acquaintances. Sometimes he was astounded by the supernatural. A fellow undergraduate called Barnsley claimed to have seen an apparition at the moment when as the young man later discovered, his mother died.[15] Wesley planned to visit a house which an acquaintance had assured him was haunted.[16] Perhaps most revealing of all, he set down in detail "the chief piece of news with us concerning the famous Jack Sheppard's escape from Newgate." For that story could not be related to anything even remotely spiritual. It was simply gossip. Sheppard, one of the most notorious criminals of the day, "was fettered, manacled and chained down to the ground by one chain round his wrist and another round his waist." Yet he managed "to force open his chains . . . break through the ceiling and pass six locked doors and get clear off without discovery."[17]

The endearing lack of sophistication in the letters home reveals only one small part of a highly complex personality. After less than a year at Oxford he began to worry about what Providence had designed for him. That led, naturally enough, to a desire to find a serious purpose in life and the fear that, even in his early twenties, too much time had already been wasted. His dissatisfaction—much exaggerated in old age when he wanted to renounce the years before his great conversion—was no doubt increased by what his later adherents identified as the first of the celestial signposts to point toward his destiny. The conversation with a college porter, which was said to illuminate the way in which God's spirit works in man, is the least well documented of all John Wesley's innumerable mystical experiences.

The porter was, we must assume, not one of the superior satraps who guard college gates but a mendicant who carried bags in the hope of earning a few coppers. According to the account of Wesley's meeting, the man had only one coat and nothing had passed his lips that day but water. Yet he gave praise to God. Wesley, in a rare moment of impiety, observed with apparent surprise, "You thank God when you have nothing to wear, nothing to eat and no bed to lie upon?" He then asked (with an irony which adds to the story's improbability), "What else do you thank Him for?" The porter answered, "I thank Him that He has given me life and being and a heart to love Him and a desire to serve Him."[18] If the story is true, it is not surprising that Wesley was impressed. It set a pattern of pious gratitude which Wesley tried to follow for the rest of his life—and did his best to impose on others.

When, on 17 June 1724—his twenty-first birthday—John Wesley sent his brother Samuel the verses on Chloe's flea, the real purpose of the letter was to express condolences on a broken leg. His message of sympathy is the first recorded example of a fortitude, in the face of others' misfortune, which grew, over the years, from insensitivity to what appeared to be an inability to understand normal human emotions. Samuel had broken a leg. But John thought the accident illustrated God's love and mercy. "If I understand you rightly, you have more reason to thank God that you did not break both than to repine because you have broken one." He went on to recount a story—told in a contemporary edition of the *Spectator*, of the Dutch seaman who, having suffered serious injuries after falling from the mainmast, "instead of condoling himself thanked God that he had not broken his neck."[19]

John Wesley's ability to recognize other people's tragedies as the expression of God's will—and therefore occasions for rejoicing rather than sorrow—grew with the years. Many of his condolences could have provided very little comfort for bereaved Methodists. It was common in eighteenth-century England for parents who had lost a baby to be told that the infant would be happier in heaven than on earth. But his message to his sister Martha, Mrs. Westley Hall, offered a novel consolation. "I believe that the death of your children is a great instance of the goodness of God towards you. You have often mentioned to me how much of your time they take up. Now that time is restored to you and you have nothing to do except serve the Lord till . . . you are sanctified."[20]

The message of sympathy to Christopher Hopper, a preacher whose wife had died in childbirth, was even more extraordinary. "The Lord hath given and the Lord hath taken away. . . . One thing is certain: He calls you to a more full and absolute dedication of your soul and body to Him. . . . Consider yourself more than ever married to Christ and His dear people. . . ."[21] It seems impossible that the recipients of such messages did not, at least at the moment of their grief, believe that Wesley was taking piety too far and that he was incapable of experiencing, or even understanding, normal human emotions.

Whether or not the mendicant porter played a crucial part in what came to be called "the change to piety," the significance of one other influence is beyond dispute. Bishop Jeremy Taylor—once a Fellow of All Souls on the nomination of Archbishop Laud, a Doctor of Divinity by royal decree of Charles I and the man to whom the martyred king had given his pocket watch a couple of days before his execution—was, no doubt, a favorite author of the Jacobites who still survived in Oxford's Senior Common Rooms. But his imprisonment during the interregnum also made him acceptable to the whole university community. Wesley read his great work, *The Rules of Holy Living and Dying*, as he prepared for graduation.

The book had been written to assist and comfort Church of England communicants who, during Cromwell's Commonwealth, were denied access to what they regarded as proper forms of worship. In consequence, it emphasized the importance of personal salvation and promised sanctification through purity of intention and argued that the state of grace could be achieved only by complete dedication to God. Wesley's reaction to Taylor's view of holiness was, as he remembered it in old age, swift and unequivocal. "I instantly decided to dedicate all my life to God, all my thoughts and actions being thoroughly convinced that there was no medium but that every part of my life (not some only) must either be sacrificed to God or myself, that is (in effect) the devil."[22] It was the beginning of a belief that haunted him for years. There were, he concluded, no degrees of faith. A man was either a "whole Christian" or not a Christian at all.

Taylor was a crucial influence—perhaps only second in importance to his mother—in convincing John Wesley that he should take holy orders and proceed to immediate ordination. He had considered the idea for over a year. An Oxford undergraduate could not escape the assumption that he was destined for the church. But he had been careful not to make any firm commitment. His reluctance had been only to a small degree related to a judgment about whether or not he would find the work congenial. For his temperament, which placed duty far above pleasure, did not allow such consideration. All he doubted was his fitness to become a priest. He had begun to agonize about the nature of true virtue and, in consequence, had become uncertain about the roots of his own faith.

As John Wesley became conscious of his destiny, he described, for the benefit of his followers, the traumas which had preceded the certainty of God's forgiveness. The doubts which the discovery of Taylor removed were dealt with in detail. He had been "early warned against laying, as Papists do, too much stress on outward works."[23] And he then briefly "fell among some Lutheran and Calvinist authors whose confused and undigested accounts magnified faith to such an amazing size that it quite hid all the rest of the commandments." As a result, briefly at least, he was "utterly lost, not being able to find out what the error was nor yet to reconcile his uncouth hypothesis either with Scripture or common sense."[24] Neither his mother nor Jeremy Taylor conclusively cleared John Wesley's mind about the relationship between faith and good works and the part each played in achieving true holiness. But they did convince him that the church was his vocation.

Soon after John's graduation in 1724, Susanna Wesley had told her son, "I heartily wish that you were in orders,"[25] and that she hoped he would come home and serve his father as a curate. Her motives were as much maternal as spiritual. "Then I could see you more often." Her son's doubts persisted. So Susanna advanced the theologically novel suggestion that he should take orders not *because* he had a vocation but in order to discover whether or not he had been called to serve the Lord. "I think that the sooner you are a deacon the better because it may be a greater inducement to greater study of practical divinity which of all others, I humbly conceive, is the best study for candidates for orders." It was, she believed, the best way of making his "calling and election secure."[26]

The Wesleys' preoccupation with their son's motive in seeking ordination was much to their credit and not at all in keeping with the period's usual judgment about the merit of taking holy orders. The ambition to become a member of a respected clerical profession was much more common among the clergy than the high concept of a priestly calling. Sons regularly followed fathers, hoping that benefices would pass down from one generation to another. In the eighteenth-century Church of England, preferment and patronage went hand in hand.

Queen Anne, much under the influence of Thomas Atterbury, bishop of Rochester, had packed the episcopate with Tories. Her Hanoverian successors worked assiduously to reverse that process. Queen Caroline, consort to George II, took a personal interest in ecclesiastical promotions. Benjamin Hoadly, successively bishop of Bangor, Hereford, Salisbury and Winchester, was a Whig pamphleteer. Edward Willes, bishop of Bath and Wells, deciphered intercepted dispatches from the papists as an agent of the Protestant court. The *Oxford History of England* concludes that "there were few Georgian bishops of whom the Church could be proud."

The duke of Newcastle, with more patronage at his disposal than any man in England, exercised his power according to his invariable rule for the appointment of bishops. "First to recommend none whom I did not think most sincerely affected to his majesty and his government and the principles on which it was founded. . . . The next rule has been to recommend none whose character as to virtue and regularity of life would not justify it." Some were absentees and used the obligation to be at Westminster for half the year in support of the government as an excuse for neglecting their dioceses. Others were simply gross. Leonard Blackburn did not conduct one confirmation service during his tenure as archbishop of York. Hoadly visited Bangor (his first diocese) once and Hereford (his second) not at all. When John Gilbert succeeded to the archdiocese of York, he insisted that tobacco and drink be made available in the vestry after services. It is hardly surprising that the high-minded John Wesley quickly grew disillusioned with the hierarchy, to which he was required to be obedient and respectful, and disenchanted about the prospect of life as a parish priest.

Parishes were allocated according to criteria which were similarly unrelated to either pastoral or evangelical ability. Many of them were gifted to absentee incumbents. In 1743, 393 livings within the gift of York were occupied by clergymen who did not live within the archdiocese, and another 335 were occupied by incumbents who held plural appointments. William Cobbett, surveying a different year in *Legacy to Parsons*, found "332 parsons shared 1496 parishes and another 500 clergymen held 1524 more livings." Bishops appointed their sons to lucrative livings. A relative of Lord North's, who became bishop of Winchester distributed thirty incumbencies among his sons and sons-in-law.

The minor clergy rarely enjoyed more than crumbs from the rich bishops' tables. The best livings were often occupied by the bishops themselves as an augmentation of their incomes. There were ten thousand beneficed clergy in England in the early eighteenth century. Six thousand had stipends of less than fifty pounds a year. Twelve hundred survived on twenty pounds. John Wesley did not take holy orders as the path to a life of luxury. He was "called." Like his father, he took the notion of vocation seriously. But his elevated attitude was not typical of his clerical generation.

In later life John Wesley argued that both his parents were enthusiastic for early ordination. The contemporary record argues differently. Samuel Wesley told his son, "I'm not for you going over hastily into orders."[27] And even when the decision was taken, Susanna sadly reported, " 'Tis an unhappiness almost peculiar to our family that your father and I seldom think alike. I approve the disposition of your mind."[28] The rector remained convinced that delay was desirable. If John was to make an informed, as well as an inspired, decision, it was necessary for him to continue his studies, particularly Latin and Greek. Being a practical man, he accepted that there was "no harm to desire getting into that office, even as Eli's sons did, to eat a piece of bread. But the principal spring and motive, to which all the former must be secondary, must certainly be the glory of God, the service of his Church and the education of our neighbors."[29] But Susanna dismissed her husband's call for more "critical learning," which, "though incidentally of use," was in "no way preferable" to entering the church as soon as possible.[30] As always with John Wesley, his mother's view prevailed.

Samuel was, however, left with the consolation that his son valued his academic judgment. John wrote to ask his advice on texts. His father replied in the best traditions of scholarship. "You ask me which is the best commentary on the Bible. I answer the Bible itself. The several Paraphrases and Translations of it in the Polyglot compared with the Original (and with one another) are in my opinion for an honest, devout, industrious and humble man, infinitely preferable to any comment I ever saw."[31] He added that if his son felt it necessary to read a secondary source, Grotius was probably the best choice. John Wesley read Grotius on the day of his "examination for orders." Next day he formally subscribed to the Thirty-nine Articles, and on 27 August 1725, the bishop of Oxford ordained him a deacon of the Church of England.

The works of Grotius, even combined with Taylor's *Holy Living and Dying*, needed a third element for them to work to bring about what John Wesley came to regard as a moral awakening and a spiritual milestone in his life. Sometime in the early months of 1725 Wesley met a "religious friend" who "set him in earnest upon a new life."[32] His more circumspect followers later claimed that the source of that inspiration was Robin Griffiths, the son of the rector of Broadway and a man who had already been the occasion of an incident which, in retrospect, was said also to have led up to the great spiritual awakening of 1725. The two young men had been together in St. Mary's Church, waiting for the funeral of a mutual acquaintance, when Wesley suddenly asked if Griffiths "really thought himself a friend." Being assured that Griffiths felt only affection for him, Wesley asked another Delphic question: "Why would he not do me all the good he could?" Griffiths "began to protest but was cut short." Wesley then set out his test of real friendship. If Griffiths was a real friend, he would provide Wesley with "the pleasure of making him a true Christian." The presumption of the suggestion—one undergraduate offering to "save" another—was an indication of Wesley's growing belief in his destiny. His demand was made even more impertinent by the implication that he was saved already, for he added that if his request were granted, "both of us would be fully convinced when we come to follow that young woman."[33]

According to the pious commentators who recorded John Wesley's early years, nobody ever resented, or was even startled by, his assumption that he could point the way to salvation. But the St. Mary's episode reveals more than an early belief in his vocation. He spoke in St. Mary's of being ready to meet his Maker "fully convinced," an indication that he was already beginning to consider the importance of "assurance," the certainty that God's redeeming love had saved the poor sinner who has faith in Him. The need for "full assurance" was an issue of theological principle with which he was to wrestle for most of his life.

Griffiths, although witness to the early indication of Wesley's gradually developing convictions, was a minor player in the drama of his first great awakening and almost certainly not the "religious friend" who "set him in earnest upon a new life." He was nominated by later Methodists for that distinction because some of the more austere devotees feared that the true begetter of the 1725 spiritual awakening was a woman—and one for whom their leader had feelings which were not entirely spiritual.

Sally Kirkham, daughter of the rector of Stanton, in the Cotswolds, was part of a complex emotional relationship which Wesley had with four women—Sally herself, her sisters, Elizabeth and Damaris, and their friend, Mary Pendarves. The evidence of infatuation is conclusive. On 26 March 1725 John Wesley began a new diary. Its primary object was not so much to record what had happened as to act as a charge sheet on which its author could register his failure to observe the general rules of life which he had set himself. One entry, dated 14 April but apparently entered some time after that date had passed, did not fulfill that purpose. It read, "First saw Varanese. Let it not be in vain." "Varanese" was Wesley's sobriquet for Sally Kirkham. Perhaps she did introduce him to a religious text which changed his life. But that diary entry is not a reference to theological scholarship.

The nickname, Varanese, itself has no significance. Wesley's circle, in common with a habit much practiced by the intellectual middle classes of the time, all called one another by names associated with the classics. Wesley was "Cyrus," his brother Charles was "Araspes." But the date of the entry, long after the event which it recorded had passed, combined with its obviously affectionate tone to raise romantic suspicions. Whatever the significance of those two enigmatic sentences, one thing is clear. Their interpretation as evidence of John Wesley's infatuation with Sally Kirkham, justified or not, is wholly consistent with his character. The founder of Methodism, eventual leader of the Great Revival and prophet of the Second Reformation was silly about women. He fell in love too often and too easily, and then he regretted that earthly affection had distracted him from his love of God. The result was emotional turmoil for him and the agony first of insecurity and then of repudiation for the women whose attention he encouraged and, when the relationship was weighed against his more spiritual obligations, rejected. Sally Kirkham was different from those who were to follow her in Wesley's affections in that she married another before the usual weeks of indecision began. So she escaped the protests of undying love followed by explanations that since his first duty was to God they could never marry. She was not, however, denied the close attention which she craved and encouraged.

It was Robin Griffiths, Wesley's companion at the St. Mary's funeral, who introduced John Wesley to Cotswold church society—the Tuckers, the Granvilles, the Kitchens and the Winningtons. But it was the Kirkham girls who drew him back to the area time after time. He was almost certainly in love—thought himself in love or pretended to be in love—with each of them in turn or possibly all three simultaneously. And they were undoubtedly, in their confused way, attracted by him. Damaris asked him to visit Stanton on weekends when her fiancé was not there. But she also called him her brother. By regarding Wesley as a lover one day and a platonic friend the next, she was reflecting the emotional ambivalence which characterized his relationships with all the women to whom he was attracted. The confusion always brought great pain to both parties in the unsatisfactory alliance. But the refusal to admit a consuming passion was essential to his conscience. The man who feared that he had "loved women and company more than God" needed to feel that he would not allow the pleasures of the world to divert him from the pursuit of holiness. Emotional masochism was part of his lifetime's penance.

After her marriage, Sally Kirkham, or Chapone, as she became, always insisted that her relationship with John Wesley was entirely spiritual, even though his diary contains coy accounts of hand holding and kisses. To emphasize the point, she explained that she loved him "more than any man except her father and husband"[34] and justified their obviously mutual regard on the grounds that it could be "neither expedient nor indeed lawful to break off that acquaintance which is one of the strongest incentives I have to virtue."[35] However, she was not above suggesting that if a little subterfuge were necessary to make their meetings possible, then a little subterfuge there would have to be. "If my husband should ever resent our freedom which I am satisfied he never will, such an accident would make it necessary to restrain the appearance of esteem I have for you. But the esteem as it is founded on reason and virtue and entirely agreeable to us both, no circumstances will ever make us alter."[36]

The theory that John Wesley had hoped to marry Sally Kirkham until, sometime in the summer of 1725, she told him (or he found out) that she was promised to another is supported by a letter from his sister Emily. It concerned her own unhappy love life. But one passage does suggest that she feared her brother was, or might become, similarly afflicted. "Whether you will be engaged before thirty or not I cannot determine, but if my advice is worth listening to, never engage your affections before your worldly affairs are in such a position that you may marry soon. . . . If you ever come to suffer the torments of hopeless love, all other afflictions will seem small in comparison to it."[37]

Sally Kirkham married Jack Chapone, a local schoolmaster. However, to Susanna Wesley's consternation, Sally remained scandalously close to John Wesley. "I heartily wish," his mother wrote, "that your converse with your friend may prove innocent. . . . I have had many thoughts of the friendship between V and thee and the more I think the less I approve. The tree is known by its fruits, but not always by its blossoms. What blossoms beautifully sometimes bears bitter fruit."[38] She went on to remind him of those who "seek to enter the kingdom of Heaven but are not able . . . because there is some Delilah, someone beloved of vice, they will not part with." Susanna's warning carried a highly offensive implication about the character of a woman who, according to her son, had been the herald of the good news of salvation which resulted in his absolute commitment to a life of holiness. Susanna must have known that they constantly told each other that the purity of their friendship was both absolute and a stimulus to holy living. Clearly she did not believe that interpretation of their affection. Her son, on the other hand, needed to convince himself that God sent women into his life to point the way to heaven.

Susanna's anxieties were increased by the knowledge that the Kirkham girls in general and Sally in particular competed for her son's attention with Mrs. Mary Pendarves, a widow of twenty who had been married for barely a year to a man forty years her senior. While visiting her mother and sister in the Cotswolds, she had become a friend of the Kirkham family—by then firmly established as Wesley's intimates—and she had assumed the sobriquet "Aspasia" as proof that she was part of their intellectual circle. John Wesley was immensely impressed by her knowledge of society, mostly gained as she prepared to succeed her aunt as maid of honor at the court. In one letter he asked her "to forgive the improprieties of behavior which inexperience of the world so frequently betrays."[39] His desire to impress her, or perhaps the insecurity he felt when he thought of her sophisticated habits, is clear from his letters—both their style, which was florid by even the standards of the eighteenth century, and their content, which was obsequious by the standards of any period. "I would fain imitate that generous spirit which, in spite of all the hinderances which surround you, so strongly inspire you to burst through all and redeem time to the noblest purpose."[40]

Mrs. Pendarves was used by John Wesley as a constant comfort and regular source of reassurance. Many of his letters to her include pleas for quick and lengthy replies. One, written after Oxford Methodism had come under attack, asked for her support against critics who accused him of being "too strict, with carrying things too far in religion and laying burdens on [himself] and if not on others which were neither necessary nor possible to be borne."[41] She responded by what amounted to return of post with absolute support of his judgment, total condemnation of his critics and a warning that since she was to spend three weeks in Dublin, he must not expect regular letters during the following month. Wesley, brought up in a household which consisted of a dominant mother and six sisters as well as his baby brother, needed the approbation of women, even though he could never find one whose character and judgment matched Susanna Wesley's. Mrs. Pendarves, three years younger but much more worldly-wise, provided sympathy and understanding to match Sally Kirkham's admiration and spiritual guidance.

It is because of the uplifting tone of her letters that Sally Kirkham is assumed to have provided the catalyst which fused John Wesley's search for truth into a metaphorical baptism. Perhaps her role has been exaggerated. But there is no doubt about what finally brought about the transformation. Whether or not Sally Kirkham—Varenese or Mrs. Chapone—introduced John Wesley to Thomas à Kempis, it was reading *The Imitation of Christ*, sometime during 1725, which marked what he regarded as a personal awakening more complete than the other Pentecosts which had preceded it.

John Wesley was explicit about the effect that à Kempis had upon him. "The nature and extent of inward religion, the religion of the heart, now appeared to me in a stronger light than ever it had done before. I saw that giving all my life to God (supposing it possible to do this and go no further) would profit me nothing, unless I gave my heart, yes all my heart, to Him." He had reservations about some of the à Kempis precepts. Reservations were in his nature. Taylor's pre-occupation with humility, which resulted in what seemed to be the constant hope of humiliation, had seemed inconsistent with the distinction of being made in God's image. To Wesley, à Kempis appeared to hold an equally perverse view, the expectation that Christians would find life a vale of tears. "I cannot think that when God sent us into the world, He had irreversibly decreed that we should be miserable. What is to become of all the innocent comforts and pleasures of life if it is the intention of our Creator that we should never taste them?"[42] The diary entries confirm that he was in a torment of indecision as he tried to balance his enjoyment of worldly joys with the fear that God wanted all humanity to live in ascetic self-denial. Time after time he asked the same question of his mother, his friends or himself. "If our taking up the Cross imply our bidding adieu to all joy and satisfaction, how is it reconcilable with what Solomon expressly affirms of religion—"that her ways are ways of pleasantness and all her paths are peace'?"[43] But, despite those doubts, à Kempis convinced him absolutely that the alternative to being a whole Christian was not being a Christian at all.

As John Wesley in old age looked back on those early years, he had no doubt that in youth he had not been a real Christian and that it was *The Imitation of Christ* which taught him "that true religion was seated in the heart and that God's law extended to all thoughts as well as to deeds and actions."[44] That judgment was influenced by a desire—perhaps, though not certainly, subconscious—to link the change of heart to the year of his ordination. Adjusting history to meet his theological needs became a habit. But in truth Taylor was the turning point, and à Kempis completed the work he had begun. It was *Holy Living and Dying* which inspired Wesley to become a "whole Christian," being like Christ in body and spirit rather than merely obeying his laws. *The Imitation of Christ* pointed the way to achieving that goal. But Wesley needed reassurance that he was pursuing his objective with proper academic rigor. He had absolute faith in the love of God but—at least in the early years of his quest—agonizing doubts about almost everything else, so he needed reassurance about the intellectual method by which his doubts could be resolved.

The memory of his mother's enthusiasm for John Locke's empiricism made him write to her with an assertion which revealed his uncertainty. The letter was written in the clear hope that his judgment would receive her approval and endorsement. "Faith is a species of belief and belief is defined as assent to a proposition on rational grounds. . . . I call faith an assent upon rational grounds because I hold divine testimony to be the most reasonable of all evidence whatever. Faith must necessarily be resolved into reason."[45] His mother was less than reassuring. Faith, she wrote, is "an assent to the truth of whatever God has revealed, because He has revealed it, not because we understand it." Her son capitulated at once. "I am at length," he replied, "come over entirely to your opinion."[46] Then he repeated verbatim her views that reason has a limited application to faith. He was groping his way toward the notion that only faith redeems and that redemption—obtained neither by piety nor by good works—was the uncovenanted gift of God.

Though still beset by doubts, John Wesley set about the work of a deacon with a determination which could not have been greater had he believed that he was working his way to heaven. For months after his ordination he did not return to Epworth. Instead he visited friends' parishes. The urge to preach was already upon him. He gave his first sermon at South Leigh, near Witney in Oxfordshire, on 24 September 1726. A funeral oration, made the following January at the committal of John Griffiths, an Epworth parishioner, gave a perfect résumé of what became his austere attitude to death. "It is no service to the dead to celebrate his actions since he has the applause of God, His holy angels and his own conscience. It is little use to the living since he who desires a pattern may find purposes enough in the sacred writings."[47] From then on Wesley was constantly in the pulpits of the Cotswolds. He wrote the names of seventeen "especial friends" in his diary and continued to meet them in coffee shops and for breakfast. But they were not frivolous social occasions. The friends discussed such topics as "Can the New Testament contradict the Old?" But even disputation was beginning to seem a waste of time. He was growing impatient of undergraduate habits. Knowledge, not argument, became his preoccupation.

His diary confirms that his reading was admirably eclectic. Watts on predestination, Fiddes on morality and Hutchison's *Enquiry into Ideas of Beauty and Virtue* were supplemented—some would say leavened—with Shakespeare, Milton, Spenser, Herbert and Rowe, a poet of less renown whose works included "The Ambitious Stepmother" and "The Fair Penitent." Wesley lived in an age which regarded science as complementary to philosophy and theology. Haley's *Magnetism and Geometry* and Boyle's *Chemistry* were on his reading list. So, slightly more surprising, was Nahum Tate's translation of Frascatoro's *Syphillis, a Poetical History of the French Disease*. Of one thing we can be certain. After his ordination almost everything was done with a purpose. For John Wesley had begun to change. His mother applauded his new seriousness. But it did not satisfy her. "The alteration in your temper has occasioned me much speculation. I who am apt to be sanguine hope it may proceed from the operation of God's Holy Spirit that, by taking off your relish for earthly enjoyment, He may prepare and dispose your mind for a more serious and close application to things of a more sublime and spiritual nature."[48]

Much to John Wesley's credit—and in proof, if proof were needed, of his filial piety—he did his best to meet his mother's wishes about a better organization of his time. Sometime during the summer of 1725 he wrote inside the cover of his first diary, begun three years earlier, his "General Rules for Employment of Time." In the autumn he augmented them with "General Rules of Intention." Detailed rules and regulations appealed to John Wesley's tidy mind and authoritarian character. Writing them—or commending others to write them for him—became a feature of his life. Those that he composed in middle age became a blueprint for the good life which he required others to follow. The first were guides to his own conduct.

In 1725 the rules were almost identical to those which he later required members of his Methodist Connexion to follow. He swore he would avoid boasting, greed of praise, curiosity, the useless employment of knowledge, all manner of passion and "intemperate sleep," which almost certainly meant staying in bed later than five o'clock in the morning. He also promised to eschew the company of drunkards and busybodies and to employ every spare hour in the study of religion. No action was to be taken before he reflected on its result, and all he did was to be "done in the name of the Father, Son and Holy Ghost." Every important decision was to be preceded by prayer. Duty was never to be neglected because of the temptation laid in his path by frivolous diversions. Having decided how he should behave, he decided that it was necessary to put in place some sort of audit of his conduct. On 20 September he resolved to review his life twice a day. On 24 October he felt it necessary to augment his daily reviews with a weekly assessment of the progress he was making towards improvement. And on 1 December he felt it vital to stiffen his resistance to evil by fasting every Wednesday. He was again approaching one of the turning points in his life when he decided that his past had been dominated by the devil.

His determination to be a whole Christian had made him impa-

tient with life in Christ Church before he had either graduated or
been ordained priest.

> When it pleased God to give me a settled resolution to be not a
> nominal, but a real Christian . . . my acquaintance were as ignorant
> of God as myself. I knew my own ignorance; they did not know
> theirs. I found that even their harmless conversation (so called)
> dampened my good resolution. But how to get rid of them was a
> question I resolved in my mind again and again. . . . I saw no
> possible way unless it should please God to remove me to another
> College.[49]

God, with only a little help from the rector of Epworth, gratified
that wish. The idea of an Oxford fellowship had come into John
Wesley's mind during the summer of 1725. Fellows of Oxford
Colleges were required to resign on marriage. So the date at which
he began to consider a collegiate (though in those days not necessarily an academic) career has been used by some biographers as proof
that his proposal had been rejected by Sally Kirkham. A more likely
explanation of the timing was a reluctance to spend his life in
Epworth, doubts about securing a living of his own and the happy
discovery that a fellowship, to which he might reasonably aspire, was
about to fall vacant.

Lincoln College awarded three fellowships which the statutes required to be occupied by natives of the county from which it took
its name. On 3 May 1725 one of the incumbents, John Thorold, resigned. By happy chance, he was the cousin of the member of
Parliament whose candidature Samuel Wesley had supported during
the riotous election of 1705. Thorold's father, the incumbent at
Scotton near Gainsborough, was also a friend of John Morley,
Lincoln's rector. Samuel began to canvass his son's claim with a
single-minded determination. He visited Thorold at Gainsborough,
wrote to the bishop of Lincoln and made formal representations to
the rector. When the two men met, Samuel's reception was "more
civil than ever he had expected it to be." At Morley's suggestion John
visited the college four times during August.

John Wesley's efforts on his own behalf did not prove a great success. He was, he feared, too solemn for the liking of the other fellows, who laughed at his earnest manner and pious habits. When he wrote to Epworth with the news that a more jovial aspirant was more to the college's liking, his father's reply aimed to bolster his courage. "As to the Gentleman Candidate you write of, does anyone think the Devil is dead or so much asleep or that he has no agents left? Surely virtue can bear being laughed at?" John's mother elaborated on the same theme. "It is a strong and well-confirmed virtue that can bear the test of buffooning." However, either to avoid the embarrassment of being a figure of fun or because he thought that the more he met the fellows, the more he damaged his cause, John Wesley did not visit Lincoln College between August and early December, when (as he then believed) the election was imminent.

The election was twice postponed, first until Candlemas and then until the early spring. As he waited, John Wesley made another assessment of his own conduct and character and laid down new rules to govern his future behavior. They included never rushing his prayers and always rising at daybreak. Three days before the decision was taken he called on the rector and three of the fellows. They could not have found his solemnity intolerable. For, on 17 March 1726, he was unanimously elected Fellow of Lincoln College.

Susanna Wesley responded to the good news in proper Christian fashion. "I think myself obliged to return great thanks to Almighty God for giving you good success. To Him and to Him alone the glory appertains." Samuel Wesley reacted in more temporal terms. "What will be my fate, God knows, before the summer is over, *sed passi graviora*. Wherever I am, my Jack is a Fellow of Lincoln College."[50]

John Wesley, who claimed to have hated life in Christ Church, found Lincoln wholly congenial. "I never knew a college besides ours whereof the members were so perfectly well satisfied with one another and so inoffensive to the other part of the university. All I have yet seen of the Fellows are both well natured and well bred; men admirably disposed as well to preserve peace and good neighborhood among themselves as to promote it wherever they have any acquaintance."[51] Whatever had changed his feelings about Lincoln, he was sure that it was the discovery of Taylor and Thomas à Kempis which had changed his life. "Leisure and I have taken leave of one another. I propose to be busy as long as I live if my health is so long indulged me."[52] The move to a new college helped him to keep that good resolution. "Shaking off at once my trifling acquaintances . . . I began to see more and more the value of time. I applied myself closer to study. I watched more carefully against sin."[53]

There was a second reason why John Wesley, at least while at Oxford, put all thought of worldly pleasure out of his mind. He had no money. The Lincoln fellowship entitled him to a variety of arcane emoluments which ranged from allowances for laundry to subsidies for salt. Until they were paid—perhaps a year after his election—he had to survive as best he could. Somehow his proud father raised another loan. A month after his fellowship election, John Wesley wrote to his brother Samuel with the news that "very unexpectedly" his father had "sent him a bill on Doctor Morley" (rector of Lincoln) for twelve pounds. Added to ten pounds already in his possession, it made ends just meet as long as he could "stay in the country until the College allowance commences."[54] So, devoted though he may have been to his new life, he left Lincoln College two days after his election as fellow and returned to Epworth. He could not afford the cost of a carriage, so he walked the whole distance and arrived at the rectory, more than a month later, on 23 April. His plan was to help with Samuel Wesley's commentary on the Book of Job and to lighten his father's load by acting as curate at Wroot. He performed both tasks with devotion—despite the many distractions of summer life in a rural rectory. He shot, he swam, he read "light books," including Restoration plays. And he visited neighboring families. Among them were a Mrs. Hargreaves, a widow, and her daughter, Kitty.

Kitty Hargreaves's name appears time after time in Wesley's diary entries for the summer of 1726. In June she was sent away by the rector "in suspicion of my courting her." His agony about the obligations of duty was clearly the result of guilt about both the time he was spending with Miss Hargreaves and the way in which it was spent. "As we would willingly suffer a little pain or forego [sic] some pleasure from others we really love, so if we really love God we should do it for Him." The promise of self-denial ended with a sentence in cipher. Decoded, it read, "Never touch Kitty again." On 13 August the entry was more general and more explicit. It was the resolution "Never again to touch a woman's breast."

John Wesley's difficulty in reconciling his interest in Miss Hargreaves with his obligation to live a sober life was an augury of traumas, of a far more serious nature, which were still to come. Four of his sisters—Mehetabel, Emilia, Susanna and Martha—all, to varying degrees, endured constantly unhappy marriages. Add to their sad histories John's unhappy record with women, and it seems that emotional irresponsibility was a family trait. But in the case of the tragic Mehetabel, the young woman's foolishness was compounded by her father's brutality.

During the autumn of 1725, when John Wesley was contemplating his prospects of a fellowship, Hetty, as she was known to her family, had married in haste and entirely against her own wishes. Hetty was very possibly the cleverest of all of Samuel and Susanna's children. At the age of eight she could read the Greek Testament at first sight. Unfortunately her intelligence was greater than her discretion. She had fallen in love with Will Atkins, a local lawyer. One night she had not returned to the rectory, and it was assumed by her father (and never either denied or confirmed by her) that she had spent the time with Atkins. Her father, scandalized by her behavior, may have forbidden her to see Atkins again. Or the lawyer may have been terrified by the rector into abandoning the woman it was assumed he had seduced. Samuel Wesley thought that an immediate marriage was essential, but he was not prepared for Atkins to become his son-in-law. The husband of his choice was William Wright, described in parish records as a plumber. The couple lived unhappily ever after.

Writing to her father, Hetty described the hopes of love which her forced marriage would shatter: "a mutual affection and desire of pleasing, something near equality of mind and person, either earthly or heavenly wisdom." She went on poignantly to suggest that when "all or most of these [are] wanting . . . [p]eople could not marry without sinning against God."[55] But the rector could not or would not be moved. So Hetty, more in despair than anger, told him, "I would rather have given at least one of my eyes for the liberty of throwing myself at your feet, before I would marry at all."[56]

Much to their credit, John and Anne (one of the Wesleys' youngest daughters) never disguised their sympathy for their unhappy sister. John was so frank in his disapproval of his father's behavior that he behaved in a way which his father regarded as "defiant and disrespectful." The rector wrote to his eldest son, Samuel, at Westminster School to complain "every day you hear how he contradicts me and takes your sister's part before my face. Nay he disputes with me, preaching . . ." Words then failed him.

The allegation was undoubtedly justified. On 28 August 1726 John Wesley had preached a sermon based on Allenbury's and Clarke's dissertations on charity. Later that Sunday his mother told him, "You preached that sermon for Hetty." John pleaded guilty and added, "I had, the same day, the pleasure of observing that my father, when Will Atkins was mentioned, did not speak so warmly or largely against him as usual."[57] But John Wesley was the eighteenth-century son of an Anglican churchman and knew that he had a duty to honor his father. So he apologized for any offense caused. Samuel, who did not forgive lightly, chose not to speak of filial obligation. Instead he invoked section fifty-three of canon law. "If any Preacher shall in the Pulpit particularly . . . of purpose, impugn, confute any doctrine delivered by any other Preacher in the same church, the churchwardens shall signify the matter to the Bishop." The lesson was not well learned. One of John Wesley's subsequent and persistent offenses against the Established Church was preaching against orthodox opinion, and without invitation, in other men's pulpits.

At least one happy event lightened the heavy Wesley summer of 1725. Anne, married to John Lambert, a land surveyor, gave birth to a son. The boy was christened by his grandfather with his uncle John as godfather. Sukey, the rector's daughter, and her husband, Richard Ellison, were in the congregation but were not entirely welcome at the rectory. The cultivated Wesleys thought Ellison "coarse and vulgar." They were just one more example of the Wesleys' matrimonial traumas. Emilia was absent. She was staying with her uncle in London. While she was there, she met and fell in love with Robert Leybourne, a Fellow of Brasenose College, Oxford. Emilia was already thirty-three and an old woman by the standards of the time who must have assumed that she would remain a spinster forever. Perhaps her parents feared that she had thrown herself at Leybourne in desperation, for when he did not move swiftly to a proposal, she was persuaded, after an intervention "in the ill-fated shape of a near relation," that she should refuse to see him. The near relation was almost certainly her mother. For some reason Emilia accepted Susanna's judgment. For ten years—until she met and married Robert Harper—Emilia Wesley found comfort in demonizing Leybourne. In six months "she never slept at night" and regarded death as a "consummation devoutly to be wished" because of her share in loving a man who never loved her, "though he had been rogue enough to pretend that he did."[58] Before she found consolation in Robert Harper, she took refuge in the composition of sentimental poetry. "Let Emma's helpless case be told / By the rash young and the ill-natured old." The Wesley family included both.

John Wesley, having proved his filial devotion and survived the months before receipt of his college income, returned on 21 October 1726 to Oxford, where he was Lincoln College's nominee to preach in St. Michael's Church. Before the end of the year he had become absorbed in college affairs and, as always, feared that he devoted too much of his time to worldly pursuits. He numbered secular learning among them, so while he could write in his diary "idleness slays" without fearing that he was predicting his own moral death, he did worry that his reading ranged over too wide a field of subjects and therefore bordered on the profane. When he asked his mother's advice, he was entitled to hope that she would endorse his wide (and sometimes self-indulgent) range of interests, for she had told him, "I would not have you leave off making verse, rather make poetry your diversion but not your business."[59] But during the months of uncertainty she was particularly critical of what she believed to be the fatal flaw of superficiality. "I am perfectly come over to your opinion that there are many truths which it is not worthwhile to know." As always, John Wesley accepted his mother's view and carried out her instructions. Two days after he received her admonitory letter he set out a scheme of daily studies which would, he hoped, concentrate his mind on essentials: Monday and Tuesday, Greek and Latin; Wednesday, logic and ethics; Thursday, Hebrew and Arabic; Friday, metaphysics and natural philosophy.

He was not certain how long he wanted to remain in Oxford as a Fellow of Lincoln College. But although he at least thought of applying to become headmaster of Skipton School in Yorkshire, an appointment which was within the gift of the college, he pressed on with preparations for the Master of Arts degree, which was a requirement of his tenure. It involved the preparation of three public lectures. Still eclectic in inclination, Wesley chose wild animals, Julius Caesar and love of God. He was, however, growing increasingly dissatisfied with life in Oxford. "I am so little at present in love with even company—the most elegant entertainment next to books—that unless they have a particular turn of thought, I am much better without them."[60] Although he complained that he was "experiencing the inconvenience of being almost necessarily exposed to much impatience and vanity,"[61] he was well enough thought of to be appointed lecturer in Greek and moderator of the classics. Absence from college being a habit of the fellows, his new responsibilities did not prevent him from returning to Epworth within weeks of his appointment. However, even allowing for the flattery and courtesies of the place and period, the message sent to him by another fellow in the summer of 1727 must have contained at least a grain of truth about his reputation at the university. "When I consider those shining qualities which I heard clearly mentioned in your praise, I cannot but lament the great exasperation we all feel in the absence of so agreeable a person."[62] Oxford was not, however, agreeable to Wesley. He was not sure what he wanted, but he knew it was not the life of a Lincoln fellow.

John Wesley was briefly back in Oxford in August 1727, but leave of absence was again granted in the following November and renewed in May and November 1728. Apart from the brief visit in that September, when he was ordained priest, he seems to have put Oxford out of his mind for well over a year. In early 1728 the prospect of preferment, or at least more profitable employment, had been dangled before him. "I believe that Gentlemen of your College would be glad to see you in Oxford and I have lately heard say that it would be much to your advantage to be here for they say that Mr. Tottenham wants very much an opportunity of resigning his pupils to you."[63] It was not an opportunity of which he wanted to take advantage. Perhaps he was simply enjoying himself too much in Lincolnshire even to contemplate a return to the university. He worked with his father in the morning, talked with his mother late into the night and, in between, visited neighbors. For a while his mood lightened. His diary records quadrilles with Mrs. Lambert, trips to York and one occasion, when he was a guest of Mrs. Hargreaves at Gainsborough, a meeting "with Miss Kitty in her closet." There was a brief return to Oxford in the early summer of 1729, but within days, he was on his way back to Epworth. But the days of home and ease were almost over.

In October 1729 the patience of the rector of Lincoln College was at an end. It was, he wrote, unreasonable that the junior fellow who had been performing Wesley's tutorial duties should be expected to deputize for so long. Moderators should discharge their duties in person. "Your father may certainly have another curate, though not so much to his satisfaction; yet we are persuaded that this will not move him to hinder your return to College since the interests of College and obligations of statute require it."[64] John Wesley returned on 22 November 1729 to Oxford, where his brother Charles (still an undergraduate of Christ Church) and his friend William Morgan were waiting with news of what they called the Holy Club.

5

EVERY WIND OF DOCTRINE

At first the Holy Club was no more than another Oxford society with ambitions as limited as its membership. John Wesley described its initial purpose in a letter to Richard Morgan, the father of an undergraduate whose death was initially blamed on what Wesley's critics called "pious excess." The description dates from 1731. So, unlike so many of the accounts of his early activities and beliefs, it does not suffer from the prejudice of hindsight. "In November 1729 . . . your son, my brother and myself and one more agreed to spend three or four evenings a week together. Our desire was to read over the classics (which we had before read in private) on common nights and on Sundays."[1] The implication that John Wesley had been one of the founding fathers of the club might have been an error of drafting or a desire to overstate his own role. Charles described the situation more accurately in a letter to Edward Chandler, bishop of Durham, in 1785. "In half a year [after the club's foundation] my brother left his curacy at Epworth and came to our assistance."

Charles Wesley's first year in Christ Church had been "lost to diversions." They included an attachment to Molly Buchanan, an actress appearing in *The Virgin Queen* at the Theatre Royal, Lincoln's Inn. It was more like an adolescent infatuation than a grown-up love affair, and the undergraduate saw very little of the object of his affection. However, the admission of his feeling had the predictable result. The man who was to become a pillar of Church of England respectability and a constant restraint on his brother's more irresponsible impulses incurred the deep displeasure of his family. John wrote to him asking the intriguing question "What company was in the York coach?" Because Charles replied that the answer was "fitter for private conference," we do not know why the journey created so much anxiety. Perhaps he was not the reprobate that the question implies, for his brother also insisted that "he pursued his studies diligently and led a regular, harmless life but, if I spoke to him about religion, he would warmly answer 'What would you have me to be a saint at once?' and would hear no more."[2] He also spoke of the "free tho' sharp air" of the college and found the "want of money as a great temptation to dullness." However, once he decided to change his ways, the determination was extreme and absolute. In common with all the Wesleys, his judgment on his own performance and moral status swung from hope of improvement to fear of spiritual failure. As soon as he decided to live a life of virtue, he found Christ Church the "worst place in the world to begin a reformation."

It is not surprising that his disillusion began at Oxford during the period which moved Edward Gibbon to write that the fourteen months he spent at the university were "the most idle and unprofitable of [his] whole life." Most of the fellows were ordained priests, and most of the undergraduates expected to take holy orders. But scholarship was not part of their preparation. Piety was encouraged by a variety of small religious societies which were devoted to holy living and (more controversially) good works. Only a minority of students felt moved to join. Sometime during 1729 Charles Wesley felt a compulsion to form a society of his own. The Holy Club—three members and no more than evening readings—was the result. It was his creation, but his brother's return to Oxford marked a gradual expansion in both numbers and activity. No doubt John's assumption of leadership owed something to his senior status as fellow and elder brother. But at least John Gambold, an early member of the club who was to become vicar of Stanton Harcourt, had no doubt that he "was always the chief manager." Gambold, in an unqualified encomium, explained why.

> He not only had more learning and experience than the rest, but was blest with such activity as to be always gaining ground and such steadiness that he lost none.... What supported this uniform vigour was the care he took to consider well of every affair before he engaged in it ... making all his decisions in the fear of God without passion, humour or self-confidence; for though he had naturally a very clear apprehension, yet his exact prudence depended more on humanity and singleness of heart. To this I may add that he had something of authority in his countenance.[3]

The Holy Club members were called Methodists before John Wesley joined them,[4] but the new recruit was reluctant to accept the name. That may be because, according to the speech he made to celebrate laying the foundation stone of London's New Chapel, he thought that it was an allusion to the stern techniques employed by a Roman physician at the time of Nero. His prescription for curing all ills—methodical diet and exercise—was identical to the regime which Wesley, and many other single-minded churchmen, favored. But it had to be disowned because it was associated with an emperor who was an Antichrist. Had he shared his brother's belief—that the title was a tribute to the Holy Club's "strict conformity with the statutes of the university,"[5]—he might not have taken so long to become reconciled to what Charles thought "a harmless name." Certainly, during the early years of its existence the Holy Club members were given far worse titles—Bible Moths, Supererogation Men, the Godly Men, Sacramentarians and Enthusiasts, a term intended not to suggest that they set about God's work with a will, but that they believed themselves to be "possessed by God." The presumption of a special relationship prejudiced the Established Church against John Wesley for the rest of his life. One of his few concessions to the antagonists was a permanent caution about names. In 1788, in his eighty-sixth year, he still spoke of "the preachers called

Methodists." The faith by which he wanted to be identified was Church of England.

The variety of names by which the Holy Club was known was not an indication of its fame or notoriety in Oxford. In fact, it was hardly known outside Christ Church before John Wesley joined and assumed its leadership. Many similar groups had been founded in other colleges,[6] and the Holy Club achieved a special status only during the winter of 1729–30, when it gained a sort of notoriety by working among the sick and the poor (not a usual feature of eighteenth-century Oxford Christianity) as well as expected its members to aspire to a level of piety which bordered on zealotry—another unfashionable habit among undergraduates.

John Wesley accepted that good works were a proper part of the Holy Club's activity. But to him they were not a means of salvation, but the result of striving for godliness. Whatever St. Paul might have said, John Wesley regarded charity—loving his fellowman—as an essentially supplementary virtue. He was searching for "the right state of soul" and hoped to achieve a "holiness of heart and life in himself and in others." That state was, he believed, most likely to be achieved by an application of the strict disciplines which the Holy Club promoted. It was more than a commitment to communion every week and the regular examination of the Scriptures. Holy Club members were expected to examine regularly both their conduct and their consciences to make sure that everything they did was at least an attempt to become a reflection of Almighty God. Thomas à Kempis still guided John Wesley's theology. "I take religion to be not the bare saying over so many prayers, morning and evening, public and private; not anything superimposed—added now and then to a careless worldly life; but a constant ruling habit of the soul; a renewal of our minds in the image of God. A recovery of the divine likeness; a still increasing conformity of heart and life to the pattern of our most holy Redeemer."[7] It was because he held that view of work and worship, and combined it with devotion to the discipline which he thought essential to the good life, that John Wesley was "charged with being too strict, with carrying things too far in religion and laying burdens on myself if not others which [are] neither necessary or possible to be born." That allegation, made by Richard Morgan (shortly after the premature death of his brother William), typified a criticism of Methodists which began to spread through the university.

A few months after the complaint was made, Wesley began to behave in a way which confirmed Morgan's complaint in every detail. The idea of formulating a personal catechism had first come to Wesley in 1732, when he set out his "General Questions" concerning good living. The questions did little more than check that prayers had been said, obligations fulfilled and the day's humble events carried out with the greater glory of God in mind. By 1733 they had taken on a more rigorous form and, at the turn of that year, they became the Exactor Diary.[8] The diary recorded "every hour in minute detail," the resolutions broken and kept, his "temper of devotion" (on a scale of one to nine) and his level of "simplicity" and "recollection," in addition to the usual record of his "reading, visiting, writing, conversing and other activities."[9] More "general questions" followed, some of them for his private contemplation. In 1734 the notion of celibacy was included in the thoughts of a good life, and a year later he was considering the possibility that because of woman's volatility, there was little virtue in female conversion. Then he began to wonder about the propriety of the whole exercise. John Clayton, a Brasenose undergraduate, had told him to steer between "scrupulosity" and "self-indulgence." Wesley was incapable of even making the attempt. His passionate commitment to living what he regarded as a virtuous existence was one of the secrets of his authority.

John Wesley intimidated (as well as influenced) those around him, but not because he held extreme views on the need to become "a whole" Christian. Extreme theological views were so common in eighteenth-century England that Wesley's opinions would in themselves have created very little stir. The problem contemporaries had with Wesley was that he not only believed that "heart and life" should conform to the "pattern of our most holy Redeemer" but actually tried to live according to that impossible aspiration.

The Holy Club reflected that conviction. Initially Sunday

evenings were passed casually in one of the member's rooms, and the conversation was no different from dozens of other undergraduate discussions. But the passion for piety grew. More meetings were organized—at first two a week and then on every weekday evening from six to nine. Sunday was always devoted to divinity. The rest of the week was divided between philosophy and the classics. Members fasted every Wednesday and Friday and took communion every week. But it was another of their observances which both frightened and infuriated less pious men. The Holy Club was obsessed with self-examination. Its members constantly confessed their own sins and shortcomings and expected others—in the hope of salvation—to do the same. The insistence that virtue requires the admission of vice is not a popular precept among the soi-disant godly.

Neither of the Wesleys worried about the antagonism which they encouraged. Both of them believed that followers of the true faith were, in this wicked and generally unredeemed world, likely to suffer for their convictions. Charles Wesley told John that when he argued against deism—the belief that reason alone could prove the existence of God as the Author of Nature and Moral Governor of the World without recourse to a highly unenlightened belief in revelation—he risked "being laughed out of his religion at the first setting out." But it did not prevent him from pursuing the argument. When Robert Kirkham, who had followed his old friend into the Holy Club, asked how to overcome the ridicule which it was attracting, John Wesley consulted his father. The rector sternly replied, "I question if a mortal can arrive at a greater degree of perfection than to steadily do good and, for that reason, patiently and meekly suffer evil." He then added, "Bear no more sail than is necessary, but steer a steady course." Bob Kirkham, who had "left his society in Merton" College to follow Wesley, was one of the new recruits who changed the Christ Church Methodists from a gathering of pious friends to an organized religious movement with members from all over the university. The roll call of members eventually included Benjamin Ingham, who was to travel with Wesley to Georgia as part of the doomed attempt to convert the natives to Christianity; John Broughton, a future secretary of the Society for Promoting Christian

Knowledge; John Gambold, who became a Moravian bishop, and, most important, George Whitefield, who was, for a time, to lead the Christian revival in England and remained—despite bitter disagreements over predestination—Wesley's friend to the last. One of the recruits, Westley Hall, married John's sister Martha after a secret courtship and an even more secret liaison with Kezziah Wesley. The result was the most tragic of all the Wesley marital disasters.

It was Robert Morgan, one of the original members, who persuaded the Wesleys to add a new obligation to the Holy Club's exacting duties. He had, for some time, visited prisoners in the city's debtors' jails and patients in the charity hospital. Supported by Kirkham, he argued that offering the hope of salvation to the afflicted was an essential part of the Methodists' work. On 24 August 1730 John and his brother Charles accompanied Morgan to Oxford's Castle Gaol. It was a small step from offering comfort to the inmates of the debtors' jail to collecting funds which could be used to discharge the debts of families who were lodged there not, in the Holy Club's estimation, because of sloth or profligacy but as a result of misfortune. In consequence, its members began to make a distinction between the deserving and undeserving poor. Because of their strict adherence to methodical good works, the Holy Club drew up a strict prison-visiting rota. John Wesley's name was written in against every Saturday afternoon.

It was John Wesley's habit to consult his mother on questions of faith and morals and his father on the subject of church governance. So he wrote to ask the rector if he approved of prison visiting. Samuel Wesley replied in his usual orotund English. On 21 September 1730 he wrote, "[A]s to your own designs and employment, what can I say less of them than *valde probo*; and that I have the highest reason to bless God that He has given me two sons together at Oxford, to whom He has given grace and courage to turn the war against the world and the Devil which is the best way to conquer them?"[10] If Samuel's convoluted syntax left his son in any doubt about the strength of his endorsement, the rest of the letter must have convinced Wesley that he had his father's approval. The rector had visited prison himself when he was an undergraduate. His experience suggested that it was wise to obtain the approval of the prison chaplain and the bishop in whose diocese the jail was situated.

The prison work met with mixed success. A year after it began, John Clayton, briefly in charge while John Wesley was in London, wrote to say that the prisoners in the Bocardo, Oxford's second debtors' jail, had done nothing but quarrel for several weeks. Progress in the Castle Gaol was, however, more encouraging. All the prisoners could read a little, most of them quite well. The more literate prisoners had been recruited to help the slower learners. In a proper spirit of Christian hope, Clayton had decided that the best way to face failure was to try even harder. He had applied for leave to visit St. Thomas's workhouse once a week.

From then on the Holy Club was unstinting in its determination to succor the poor. Morgan extended his activities to forming a "ragged school" for the children of the Oxford slums. When he became ill and left the university in the hope of recovery, the Holy Club raised enough money to employ a Mrs. Platt to take his place. John Wesley himself became notable for acts of declaratory compassion. During a visit to a church school he saw a girl who was shivering in her threadbare clothes and obviously suffering from malnutrition. Waving toward the holy pictures which were on all sides of the room, he said, "Thou hast adorned the walls with the money which might have saved this poor creature from the cold. Are not these pictures the blood of this poor creature?"[11]

John Wesley, with his Exactor Diary to guide him, almost always practiced what he preached. He "abridged himself of all superfluities and many that are called necessities of life."[12] His sermon. "The More Excellent Way" held up as an example of holy living "One of the Oxford Methodists [who] had thirty pounds a year. He lived on twenty-eight and gave away forty shillings. The next year, receiving sixty pounds he still lived on twenty eight and gave away two and thirty." Eventually the paragon's earnings rose to £129 a year and he gave £92 to the poor. Nineteenth-century Wesleyan Methodists had no doubt that the benefactor was John Wesley himself.

John Wesley's income during his years as a Fellow of Lincoln College is not easy to calculate. Theoretically a fellow was entitled to a share in college revenues. But the arcane way in which the entitlement was calculated left some of the recipients better off than others. "Provisions,"—a percentage of the fluctuating college revenues and the basis of every fellowship salary, was paid only to senior members of the college who were in residence. But while Wesley was in Epworth, he received a variety of improbable payments: eight shillings for laundry, four shillings for barbers, three shillings for vinegar and a shilling for brawn and oysters. There were also endowed inducements for preaching special sermons on feast days, as well as fees for tuition and special grants known as "obit" and "gaudy" money. In most years he received payment from Lord Crewe's Benefaction, a share of the deposits paid to secure the leases in land which the peer had given to the college. Only one thing is certain about his total income after he returned to residence. It was not enough to allow him to keep the horse which he had rashly bought to carry him to the Oxford churches in which he preached. In February 1730 he was offered a "curacy to continue a quarter or half a year." The salary was "thirty pounds a year, the Church eight miles from Oxford." It is not clear why, in his letter home, he did not tell his mother that the parish was Stanton Harcourt. Perhaps he was carried away with pleasure at the thought that he need not sell his horse, "since it is at least as cheap to keep one as to hire one every week."[13]

In Epworth, during his absences from the university John Wesley was always in debt to his college. After his permanent return to Oxford—thanks to the receipt of "provisions"—he began to make ends meet. He kept records of his spending which were as detailed and precise as the inventory of his time: fourpence for breakfast, one shilling and tenpence for pins, needles and ribbon, one shilling to the man who brought and erected a new bed. With so many accounts to keep, observances to perform and disciplines to respect, there must have been times when he found it hard to fulfill his academic obligations. Fortunately they were not onerous.

Fellows in residence were expected to lunch in hall at noon and attend the "gaudies" at which founders and benefactors were celebrated. The undergraduates were not required to sit an examination.

But to obtain a B.A. it was necessary for them to perform a number of supervised "exercises." There was formal instruction on every day (except Sunday) during the four weeks following November Chapter Day and from Ash Wednesday to the Commemoration of Benefactors in the third week of the Act (July) Term: Disputations on Mondays, Wednesdays and Fridays, Greek Testament on Tuesdays and Thursdays and declamations on Saturdays. Some fellows gave private tuition to studious undergraduates. But the whole sum of duties was never too exacting to prevent the performance of parish duties. Indeed it was more or less expected that fellows would hope for a parish and accept a curacy as second best.

Six weeks after he took up his fellowship, John Wesley had been nominated to preach the St. Michael's Day sermon, an early recognition of talent which, although unusual, was by no means unique. A month later he was appointed claviger, and again, although keeping the keys was a formal duty, the task and the title suggested that much was expected of him. However, he almost certainly spent more time on educating himself than teaching others.

Fellows of Lincoln were expected to take holy orders swiftly—ideally within a year. Wesley had bifurcated the obligation by being ordained deacon on 19 September 1725 (almost eight months before he became a fellow) and ordained priest, three years later, on 22 September 1728. He was also expected to be admitted M.A. and then, not more than seven years later, become a Bachelor of Divinity. The only exception to that rule applied to a fellowship in canon (later civil) law, which required the incumbent to prepare for a degree in that subject but did not set a date by which it had to be obtained. It became a contrivance by which senior members of the college could postpone their divinity examinations. Between 1703 and 1736 eight fellows took advantage of the escape route, holding the convenient fellowship for periods of between three and five years. Wesley, much to his colleagues' distress, held it for fifteen. Throughout that time, though rarely in residence, he received his complicated fellow's stipend. Together with his income from published sermons it sustained him until he was forty.

Whatever his distaste for the formalities of theological instruction and despite each day being carefully apportioned among the demands of the college, the Holy Club and his conscience, John Wesley's real work during the years of his Lincoln fellowship was, as it remained for the next ten years, a search for the road to personal salvation. He was beginning to examine some of the questions which were to preoccupy his mind until he achieved "a settled view" of "holiness." He had no doubt that virtue had to be absolute and built on the determination, as well as the desire, to live as Christ lived and think as Christ thought. All the books which he was later to claim marked significant moments in his "rebirth" and "awakening" carried the message that only the "whole Christian" could be saved. In 1730 a third essential text was added to *Rules of Holy Living and Dying* and *The Imitation of Christ*. It was William Law's *Serious Call to a Devout and Holy Life*. Two years later (probably after meeting the author) he read Law's *Christian Perfection*. It too profoundly affected him.

John Wesley was always susceptible to the idea of mystical moments when God changed his life. And reading one, or both, of Law's treatises was designated as another divinely inspired revelation—even though he was later to accuse Law of failing to teach him that the only way to salvation was to "strip oneself of one's own work and righteousness and fly to God." That complaint was made when his ideas of faith had been clarified. In 1730 the arguments about "justification by faith alone" were only beginning to rattle around inside his head. It was Law's work which he claimed had clarified his view on "Christian perfection." That judgment, made in his own work on the subject, *A Plain Account of Christian Perfection* (published in 1767, almost thirty years after his first reading of Law) has to be treated with caution. It was John Wesley's habit to treat every addition to his thought and understanding as a heaven-sent turning point in his life. And he also rewrote his own history. He read Law when he was obsessively concerned with his own salvation, but he described his reaction to what he had read much later, when he was under attack for capriciously varying the messages of salvation which he had preached to his followers. The notion of "Christian perfection"—the achievement of a sinless state—ran through all the other doctrines with which Wesley wrestled. And it was clearly intimately related to the concept of the "whole Christian," a condition to which à Kempis had taught him to aspire. In 1767, looking back to his Oxford years, he wanted to prove that his attitude toward perfection had always been consistent as well as coherent.[14]

In 1767 he had no doubt (or claimed that he had no doubt) that when, back in 1730, he read William Law, "The Light flowed so mightily upon my soul that" he was "convinced more than ever of the absolute impossibility of being half a Christian, and I determined, through His Grace (the absolute necessity of which I was deeply sensitive to) to be all-devoted to God, to give him all my soul, my body and my substance."[15]

The claim to absolute consistency is hard to sustain. The necessity of being cleansed from sin—from "all filthiness, both of flesh and spirit"—was a more absolute statement of the necessity to strive for perfection* than that which he had set out in earlier years. Adjustments—critics called them vacillations—about "perfection" clouded his clear view of sanctity and virtue for the rest of his life. But the second assertion on which Wesley's *Plain Account* was built—the "absolute necessity" of seeking redemption through "His Grace"—was the steadfast principle on which his whole belief was built. He certainly held that view in 1730, though with perhaps less certainty than he felt in 1767. But the intervening years saw his interpretation of divine forgiveness change time after time.

In the first decade of the seventeenth century, Jakob Hermandszoon—Jacobus Arminius in the Latinate world which he inhabited—had told his students in the University of Leyden that Luther's harsh interpretation of Augustine's work was wrong. Christ

---

* Christian perfection originates in St. Matthew's Gospel. Chapter 5:48 equates it to "walking with God,"—i.e., imitation of Him. Chapter 19:21 equates being perfect "with 'following Christ'"—i.e., having an assured faith. As a result, it can mean whatever we want it to mean. Early Christians thought sin impossible after baptism. Pelagianists believed in "earthly angels." In the Middle Ages Christians thought perfection meant no more than moral endeavor. Wesley, whose views on the subject constantly changed, consistently denied the possibility of "angelic perfection."

had died to redeem *all* our sins, not simply to guarantee the pre-destined place in heaven of an "elect" minority. From then on "Arminians" preached the gospel of universal redemption. The notion that all sinners could be redeemed divided followers in the Great Revival as it divided other Protestants. And it became inextricably linked with disagreement about how—if we all are capable of redemption—salvation is to be achieved. Some argued that granted free will, men and women could save their own souls by good works. John Wesley came firmly to the opposite view, though from time to time he found it necessary to nod in the direction of the importance of good works. He believed that redemption was possible *sola gratia*, by God's grace alone, and must be achieved *sola fide*, by faith alone.

An evangelist by nature since the days when he preached to the younger boys at Charterhouse School, John Wesley was psychologically antipathetic to the doctrine of predestination. If God has chosen to ordain the "elect," whose eventual salvation is inevitable no matter what they believe or how they behave, sermons, at least as an instrument of redemption, are a waste of time. Yet he accepted as a matter of simple logic that God, being omnipotent and omniscient, certainly *knows* who is destined for heaven and who is destined for damnation. The Protestant dilemma about how to reconcile His knowledge with man's freedom of choice was resolved for Wesley by the formula, evolved by Jacobus Arminius himself, that accommodated God's love and sacrifice and His willingness to see some of His children condemned to eternal damnation.

Arminians (or Remonstrants, as they were sometimes called) believed that Jesus died for all people—not just an "elect"—and that since divine sovereignty was compatible with free will, everyone who believed in Christ's redeeming mission could achieve salvation. Only those who rejected God's offer of redemption were damned. But since Arminius insisted that Christ died to save the whole world from sin, there was some doubt about how many people, if any, numbered in the ranks of the irrevocably doomed. The notion of predestination was qualified almost out of existence by making everyone *potentially* elect. But there was a second problem. Only

God could offer redemption. The power of original sin was, Arminius wrote, so great that even the elect might "fall from grace." So salvation depended on "final perseverance,"* the successful determination to maintain a state of grace to the very last. That final item of Arminian doctrine accounts for the obsession with "backsliding" which preoccupied John Wesley and a century of his followers. Although he was reluctant to set out his position in a sermon, Wesley increasingly came to believe that Christ's sacrifice meant that as he put it, "All may come." Everyone who completely accepted the gift of His grace and achieved "final perseverance" would take a place on the steps of the throne. Faith. Perseverance. Perfection. Assurance. One by one, the introspective Fellow of Lincoln College worked his way through the great theological disputes. And he came to firm conclusions. Unfortunately for his peace of mind, he did not hold on to them for long.

It is possible to argue, as some Methodist scholars do, that Wesley's theological vacillation was the working of an enquiring mind and that as "a child of the Enlightenment" he examined alternative doctrines in a search for truth. He was certainly influenced, as was his mother, by John Locke. But Locke's views on religion were less intellectually distinguished than his judgments on the social contract, political legitimacy and the rule of law. In his treatise *On the Reasonableness of Christianity* (published in 1695) Locke argued that skeptics were confounded by the way in which the Bible had brought together all moral teaching in one code and set out rules of conduct which were intelligible to (and accepted by) even the uneducated masses. That is empiricism gone mad. Wesley, believing he was following the same tradition, sought proof of God's existence and thought that he had found it when he heard stories of miraculous cures and mystical visitations.

* Final perseverance is achieved by those who live and die in a state of grace. The Catholic view is that it is possible only for those who receive God's special help. Calvin believed it was available only to the elect. Wesley, when he reached a settled position, thought that a few Christians did receive assurance of *final* salvation, but that everyone whose life justifies an assured *present* virtue could feel confident that God would maintain his state of grace.

The real religious enlightenment—William Paley's *The Failure of Complacent Belief* and Joseph Priestley's rational dissent—came long after Wesley began his undergraduate agonizing, and it is hard to imagine the founder of Methodism's accepting, at any time of his life, Priestley's Unitarian view that Jesus was "as much a creature of God as a loaf of bread." In many ways, the revival of which Wesley became part rejected the Enlightenment. Scripture was a greater guide than reason. Grace was more important than good works. Original sin denied the benevolent character of mankind. Belief in miracles was a rejection of the natural order. Hume's *Enquiry Concerning Human Nature* (one of the Enlightenment's standard texts) asserted that "no testimony of any kind of miracle has ever amounted to probability, much less to proof," of God's existence. Wesley believed the opposite. He used the language of the Enlightenment, not its methods. Bishop Joseph Butler, like William Berkeley an essential contributor to eighteenth-century religious thought, rebuked Wesley for his conduct, but there is little evidence to suggest that he influenced him by his writing. Wesley's doubts were temperamental, not intellectual.

Most of Wesley's doubts were a reflection of concern about his own conduct. So the search for truth did not bring John Wesley contentment. Indeed it increased his moral anxiety. Because he believed that the "whole Christian" accepted the assurance of salvation without doubt or qualification, he agonized about agonizing. Occasionally his doubts were expressed in the blasphemous language of resentment. "If God sees I sincerely desire devotion in prayer and that I can do no more than desire it, why does he not do the rest?"[15] He studied the works of theological authorities as diverse as Thomas Halyburton, a Presbyterian divine, and Gregory Lopez, a Mexican hermit. Sometimes he seemed to be edging away from the doctrine that only the "whole Christian" could be saved. "As we hate sin, grow in grace and arrive at the state of holiness—which is also a state of penitence and imperfection, but yet sincerity of the heart and diligent endeavour—in the same degree we are to be judge of the forgiveness of sins. . . . Forgiveness of sins is . . . a state of change effected upon us."[17] The Christian hope became "not to do well but to do our best," a surprisingly ambiguous statement which could be the advocacy of either perfection or improvement. He had no doubt that "without the Great Atonement there would be no remission of sin. . . . No man can qualify himself for heaven without the holy spirit which is given by God incarnate. . . . Christ is the propitiator of our sins."[18] Although there were some certainties, there was still much work to do before he could achieve the object of a note he set out in January 1733. It was headed "Not Tossed to and fro by Every Wind of Doctrine" and was (since the title described his theological inquiries exactly) at least a subconscious admission of fault. The note listed the influences which he hoped, once reconciled, would resolve all his dilemmas: "the Scriptures . . . The Papists (good work confounded) . . . Lutherans and Calvinists (faith done) . . . English Divines . . . Essential Non-Jurors . . . Mystics."[19] At least he was living up to the title of his favorite theological work, Law's *Serious Call*.

Law was not the only irresistible influence on John Wesley's theology during the years in which he consolidated his position as a Fellow of Lincoln College. In 1732, John Clayton abandoned the religious society in his own college and joined the Holy Club. He remained a member for barely six months. But in that time, as well as promoting the social dimension of the Holy Club, he introduced John Wesley to a group of Manchester Nonjurors, priests who had refused to swear an oath of allegiance to King William because they had already sworn fealty to the deposed king James and, in consequence, felt morally unable either to assert their loyalty to the temporal power of the crown or to accept what they regarded as the modern innovations of the Church of England. Under their influence Wesley began to wonder if the true model of virtue was to be found in the founding fathers. When he listed the Nonjurors among the theological authorities he must examine, he wrote "antiquity" next to their name. He had come to believe that the first Christians provided the model of true faith. He began to observe some of the rituals of the Primitive Church. Wednesday and Friday became obligatory fast days on which nothing was eaten before three o'clock in the afternoon.

Clayton's influence had practical as well as theological consequences. The son of a Manchester bookseller, he introduced Wesley to a literary circle which patronized the thriving London religious society movement. Sir John Phillips, already a substantial contributor to the funds of the Society for Promoting Christian Knowledge, became a patron of the Holy Club. His influence was at least as important as his money. Books and pamphlets were bought in London and distributed among members and the satellite societies which members were encouraged to form in their own colleges. At Clayton's suggestion Wesley "collected" prayers from members of the society and in 1733 published them as *Prayers for Every Day of the Week*. It was Clayton who persuaded him to extend the Holy Club's active ministry to the poor by visiting St. Thomas's workhouse twice a week. When Wesley left Oxford to visit his brother Samuel in London or his parents at Epworth, it was Clayton who was left in charge.

He was a faithful deputy. In August 1732 he wrote to Wesley in London to say, "Now you are gone we have in good part lost the honorable appellation of Methodists."[20] The Holy Club was swiftly to recover the title, though not in exactly the circumstances which Wesley would have chosen. *Fog's Weekly Journal*, a London Jacobite magazine, published a letter which accused the "Oxford Methodists" of the Holy Club of religious fanaticism. It was the beginning of a campaign against them which lasted for most of Wesley's remaining years in Oxford and one that stimulated him into an essential redefinition of Methodism's beliefs and objectives.

The attack on Oxford Methodism which appeared in *Fog's Weekly Journal* was very largely the result of the death of William Morgan and the suggestion, initially made by his father, that his fatal condition had probably been caused and was certainly exacerbated by the devotional excesses of the Holy Club. The story of Morgan's illness was more complicated than his grieving parents were prepared to concede.

When John Wesley returned to Oxford from the Cotswolds at the end of May 1731, he discovered that William Morgan was sick with a mysterious illness and had gone to Holt in the hope that his recovery would be accelerated by the clear Norfolk air. The "cure" was not a success. For almost a year Morgan moved in and out of Oxford searching for relief, if not remission. In February 1732 his condition had so deteriorated that John Wesley told his mother that the young man was obviously dying. "He can neither sleep, read, stand nor sit. . . . Surely now he is a burden to himself and almost useless in the world. His discharge cannot be far off."[21] At the time Morgan was said to be looking forward to an early death. But there was an improvement in both his health and spirits, and at the end of March, after the two men had eaten supper together, Morgan told Wesley that he had received a letter from his father which he was too weak to read, a surprisingly serious state of health for a young man who had just completed a hearty meal. Whatever the true reason, Morgan asked Wesley to read the letter aloud. It was a long complaint about William Morgan's relationship with Methodism. Morgan was no longer to be expected to live on a fixed allowance. But the money his father made available was for his use, not the Holy Club's.

> You can't conceive what a noise that ridiculous society you are engaged in has made here. Besides the particulars of the great follies of it at Oxford . . . it gave me sensible trouble to hear that you were noted for going into the villages about Holt, entering into poor people's homes, calling their children together, teaching them their prayers and catechism and giving them a shilling on your departure.[22]

Richard Morgan, the second remembrancer to the Exchequer in Dublin, wanted his son to enjoy "comfortable subsistence with reasonable and moderate recreations."[23] That was a view of life which John Wesley was pathologically incapable of understanding. Had he been more sensitive to the ways of the world beyond the Holy Club, he might have welcomed the letter as a warning. In the isolation of his moral arrogance, he paid no heed.

Morgan struggled on in Oxford until June. Then he left for Ireland in the hope that yet another change of scene would improve his prognosis. When again the hoped-for improvement did not come about, he determined to return to England, but his Irish doctor forbade him to travel. It is easy to understand why. "He was raving mad and three men set over him to watch him and hold him and by the direction of the physicians he was threatened with ropes and chains which were produced to him and rattled. . . . [He] used frequently to say that enthusiasm was his madness and repeated often 'Oh religious madness!' But, in the greatest rage, never cursed or swore or used any profane expression."[24]

William Morgan died on 26 August 1732, and although his father did not immediately make public his allegations against the Holy Club, most of Oxford society knew that he blamed his son's death on Methodism in general and John Wesley in particular. On Sunday, 15 October, Wesley learned of the rumor that Morgan had killed himself by continual fasting, a discipline which he was said to have learned from Holy Club members was essential to the Christian life. The time had come to meet the accusations head-on. Wesley's letter did not seek to refute the grieving father's calumnies one by one, but to lift the argument onto a higher plane by setting out boldly and clearly the principles on which Methodism was based. The "whole Christian," by "daily intercourse" with God, ensures that he is "more and more transformed into His likeness." As a result, God "assures our spirits that we have a title to eternal happiness." Wesley responded to the charge that he had encompassed the death of one of his followers not by refuting the obvious calumny but by setting out the doctrine of Christian perfection.

A more extensive definition was to follow. Like the letter to Richard Morgan, it was largely based on John Tilley's seventeenth-century sermon "On Grieving the Holy Spirit." Tilley's theology was the inspiration for the sermon which John Wesley preached in St. Mary's, Oxford, in 1733 called "The Circumcision of the Heart." The strange title was taken from the text for the day, St. Paul's Epistle to the Romans 2:29: "But he is a Jew which is one inwardly; and the circumcision is that of the heart in the spirit and not in the letter, whose praise is not of men but of God." The complicated metaphor was a call for complete moral cleanliness.

The language of the sermon was obscure even by the standards of eighteenth-century preaching, for its metaphysical message was conveyed by a series of complicated images, which matched both its title and St. Paul's mysticism. But the meaning is clear enough. More than thirty years later, in his *Plain Account of Christian Perfection,* Wesley described the sermon as containing "all that I now teach concerning salvation from all sin and loving God with an undivided heart." To succeed, the commitment to salvation had to be absolute.

> The circumcision of the heart is that habitual disposition of soul which, in the sacred writings, is termed holiness; and which directly implies the being cleansed from sin from all filthiness both of flesh and spirit; and by consequence, the being endowed with those virtues which were also in Christ Jesus; the being so renewed in the image of our mind as to be perfect as our Father in heaven is perfect.
>
> Only God can provide salvation. Indeed without the Spirit of God we can do nothing but add sin to sin: it being impossible to think a good thought without His supernatural assistance as to create ourselves or to renew our whole souls in righteousness and true holiness. He alone can quicken those who are dead unto God and breathe into them the breath of Christian life.

Wesley's description of Christian perfection as an attainable ideal was enough, even in the modified form which appeared in the letter to Richard Morgan, to convince the briefly outraged father that his son had not died the victim of half-crazy zealots. Indeed, he was so impressed by Wesley's obvious piety that he put his second son, also Richard, into the care of the man he had so recently denounced. Dr. John Morley, the dean of Lincoln, warned the young man that "Mr. Wesley's notion of religion . . . [and] the character of his Society, prevented several young men from entering the college." And since Wesley told Mrs. Pendarves that Morley was "one of the best friends I had in the world." we must at least assume that he was not biased against the fellow of his college. Perhaps his brother's account of the Holy Club's effect on the university prejudiced the young man against Wesley. For although the father was satisfied about Wesley's suitability to guide impressionable undergraduates, the son was not. His complaint that he was under the supervision of fanatics was complemented with a description of the Holy Club which was as convincing as it was incredulous.

> They imagine that they cannot be saved if they do not spend every hour, nay every minute of their lives in the service of God. And to that end they read prayers every day in the common gaol, preach every Sunday and administer the sacraments once a month. They almost starve themselves to be able to relieve the poor and buy books for their conversion. They attempt to reform notorious whores and allay spirits in haunted houses. They fast two days a week which has emaciated them to a degree which is a fearful sight. . . .[25]

Richard Morgan, Sr., began to wonder if he had been too easily re-assured. He wrote to Wesley to demand that his younger son should not be encouraged in those "over-zealous ways which contributed to the great misfortune which finished my other son." He wanted Richard to lead a "sober, virtuous and religious life but not to pre-tend to be more holy than the rest of mankind."[26] John Wesley replied that he shared exactly that aspiration. He had never at-tempted to make Richard Morgan a member of the Holy Club. He had, however, rebuked him for staying up until four o'clock in the morning and for keeping a dog in his room.

The facts, as described by a moderately objective observer, seem, more or less, to confirm John Wesley's version of events. John Gambold, long after he had ceased to be one of Wesley's intimates, de-scribed how Holy Club members had behaved toward new under-graduates. "They took great pains with younger members of the university to rescue them from bad company and encourage them to a serious and studious life." He listed the other help which was cer-tainly willingly, and probably gratuitously, provided: assistance with the "parts of learning that they were stuck at," introductions to other "well-disposed young men" and advice on "the rules of piety" when they would accept it. There was no suggestion of constant fasting, con-tinual prayer or the minute analyses of sins committed or imagined.

Richard Morgan, Sr., was convinced. Richard Morgan, Jr., was not. He half drafted another letter for dispatch to his father in Dublin. In it, Morgan made no direct accusation against Wesley's conduct—except for the allegation that he taught from too many religious texts and, in consequence, neglected the secular classics. Morgan's complaint was merely that by being associated with Wesley, he was held up to ridicule in the university. "I am as much laughed at and despised by the whole town as any [Holy Club member]. By becoming his pupil, I am stigmatized with the name of Methodist, the misfortune of which I cannot describe."[27] Morgan left the half-finished letter on his desk. Wesley, waiting to meet him in his room, read it—apparently without the slightest feeling of guilt or embarrassment. It was the first example of the flexible view of honorable conduct which so regularly characterized his theological disputes. His dubious conduct enabled him to reply to the accusations before they reached their destination. Again he chose not to deal with the allegations one by one but to set out his view of Christianity. He described it as "a constant ruling habit of the soul, a renewal in our minds of the image of God." Once again Richard Morgan, Sr., was won over. Wesley was thus spared the unpleasant duty of telling the father that his close supervision of the son was an attempt not to make him a Methodist but to make him a sober undergraduate. Wesley did not want to make the young man a saint, but conscious of the tragedy which had ended the life of his critic's brother, he was anxious to make sure that Richard Morgan, Jr., was not the victim of catastrophe brought on by high living and excess.

Although one Morgan was satisfied and another placated, Wesley's troubles were not over. The *Fog's Weekly Journal* had correctly predicted that William Morgan's death, and Methodism's part in it, would not be forgotten in the university. Critics of Methodism began to repeat the accusations which the Morgans had been persuaded to abandon. Happily help was at hand. A sympathetic pamphlet, *The Oxford Methodist, Being an Account of a Society of Young Gentlemen in That City, So Denominated,* was published in the summer of 1733. We must assume that Wesley was gratified but not surprised. The author had used material, including the correspondence between Wesley and Richard Morgan, Sr., which only he could have supplied. It might even have been William Law himself who drafted the encomium. The Holy Club had, he wrote, ennobled its members. "Religion is a cheerful thing and the Satisfaction they reaped from the sense of having performed what they took to be their Duty, however imperfectly, was greater and of a higher Nature than any they had ever before experienced." The pamphlet ended with the prophecy that "giving the Blessing of so long a life," the Oxford Methodists might be "the Means of reforming a vicious world."

John Wesley, while no doubt encouraging the grandiloquent defense, never thought of the Holy Club in such exalted terms. By 1733 he had discovered Oxford's limitations. Oxford itself, even with the associated living which was likely one day to come his way, was never enough for him. He was intellectually and theologically restless and, because of his unshakable confidence in the basic precepts of his religion, confident enough in his faith to speculate about all and every moral, liturgical and spiritual question which was incidental to it. As a result, he was susceptible to whatever influence was most recently focused upon him. The adjustments to his position were almost always entirely introspective. He considered his future in terms of his determination to take the most certain route to heaven. His loyalty was to God and his own soul. Nothing else was worthy of his unswerving allegiance.

In his early manhood John Wesley was in many ways intellectually footloose. The degree to which he was influenced by the latest authority he had read or met was illustrated by what his brother Charles called "The Jacobite Sermon." It was delivered on 11 June 1734 at a time when John Wesley was influenced by Clayton and William Law. Both men were Nonjurors and had declined to take the oath of allegiance to a monarch who they believed was not part of the ordained succession. Wesley's loyalty to the House of Hanover was beyond doubt, yet he delivered a sermon on the inviolability of God's anointed which he knew would outrage supporters of King George, a monarch who occupied the throne as the result of James II's ejection. There is no doubt that he anticipated their anger. For he took the precaution of showing the text to the vice-chancellor before the sermon was delivered and then, as he was "much mauled and threatened," defended himself with the less than heroic explanation that he was sanctioned by authority. He had not yet learned the lesson which all attention seekers are eventually taught. Fame and notoriety are easily confused.

The defense was necessary because in 1734 John Wesley had suddenly decided that remaining in Oxford might be the best way of spending his middle age. It was toward the end of that year that Samuel Wesley began to think of retirement from Epworth. Back in the January of the previous year he had suggested, at least tentatively, that John should succeed him, thus guaranteeing Susanna a home in old age. His son had been unenthusiastic. In the autumn of 1734 the suggestion was repeated in more urgent and more formal terms. John replied in November. He represented a return to Epworth as a desertion of duty. "Wherever I can be most truly myself, there I am assured I can most promote holiness in others. But I am equally sure that there is no place under heaven so fit for my improvement as Oxford."[28] His father replied with a reproof: "It is not our dear self, but the glory of God and the different degrees of promoting it which should be our main consideration and direction in the choice of any course of life."[29] And he persuaded his eldest son to make the same point in harsher language. Samuel, Jr., was not in a strong position to throw the first stone. He had become headmaster of Tiverton School and had already made it clear that he was not prepared to return to Epworth in any circumstances. That did not prevent him from reproving his younger brother. "I see your love of yourself, but your love of your neighbor I do not see."[30]

John Wesley consulted John Potter, the bishop of Oxford, who had ordained him. He received a most reassuring ecclesiastical opinion. "It does not seem to me that at your ordination you engaged yourself to undertake the care of any parish provided you can, as a clergyman, better serve God in your present or other station."[31] A copy of the bishop's judgment was sent to Samuel Wesley, Jr., in Tiverton. At the same time John wrote a letter to his father which set out twenty arguments why he should not return to Epworth. They revolved round the question of greater "holiness." By holiness I mean not fasting, or bodily austerity or any other external means

of improvement but that inward temper to which all these are subservient, a renewal of soul in the image of God. . . . And I believe
that in the state which I am I can most promote this holiness in myself because I now enjoy several advantages which are almost peculiar to it."

Wesley believed that he could maintain his hopes of holiness because his resolution was not undermined by "persons that have a
great concern for, but no sense of, religion." The implication that
Epworth was the home of inadequate Christians was as unflattering
to the parish as his determination not to live among them was in-
dicative of Wesley's strange combination of spiritual certainty and
moral doubt. But perhaps he himself realized how self-centered his
decision sounded. Or it might have been simply filial piety—always
a great element in his makeup—which made him change his mind.
Whatever the reason, he began seriously to consider applying for the
Epworth living.

It was while John Wesley was considering his moral obligation to
return to Epworth that he was approached by an "apple woman"
who told him that a female inmate of the Oxford workhouse had,
despairing of better times, attempted to cut her own throat. The
message about the pauper's despair had been sent by a servitor of
Pembroke College who had forbidden the messenger to reveal his
identity. His name was George Whitefield, and having admired the
Holy Club from afar for three years, he believed that the Oxford
Methodists were the people to give the woman the will to live.

Whitefield later claimed that he had sought to remain anonymous
out of modesty. A poor servitor could not aspire to friendship with
the exhibitioners and gentlemen commoners of Christ Church. But
he also had a second reason for hiding his enthusiasm. The members
of his college already mocked his piety, and he feared that involvement with the Holy Club would increase their persecution. So it
proved. The apple woman revealed his identity, and he was invited
to breakfast in Lincoln College. His formal association with the
Oxford Methodists resulted in abuse, assault and the withdrawal of
the patronage on which he depended.

If the young bloods of Pembroke hoped to deter Whitefield from close involvement with the Holy Club, they totally misunderstood his character. It was that attempted intimidation which convinced him that the Holy Club was his spiritual home. Once he had nothing to hide, he went to the extremes of piety, praying more, fasting more and indulging in more personal recrimination than any other member. His fanaticism helped to put Wesley's zealotry into proper perspective. The two men's theological disagreements were to become a feature of the Christian Revival in England, sometimes giving it vitality and sometimes blunting its cutting edge. But after those early days in Oxford, Whitefield rarely regarded himself as unworthy of his colleague's company.

Before John Wesley had finally decided what to do, news reached him from Epworth that his father was on the point of death. He hurried home, ready to accept Old Samuel's wishes and apply for the parish. But the last conversation concerned faith, not duty. "The inward witness, son. The inward witness. That is the proof, the strongest proof of Christianity."[32]

It has generally been assumed that once his father had died and a son's duty no longer called him home, John Wesley resumed his old determination to remain in Oxford. But a letter written at the time to Wesley by his friend John Broughton, and eventually published in the *Wesleyan Times*,[33] suggests that he might not have totally rejected the idea of securing the Epworth living and that he only abandoned the plan when soundings made clear that Edmund Gibson, the bishop of London, would block any plans for preferment. Broughton suggested that Wesley should canvass the support of the bishop of Oxford and, in order to gain the goodwill of the court, see if Queen Caroline would accept the personal presentation of his father's commentary on the Book of Job, a work of some scholarship which the rector had, rather inappropriately, dedicated to her.

Whether or not he persisted in his attempts to secure the Epworth living, we do know that John Wesley presented his father's work to the queen. She commented favorably on its binding. It is usually supposed that the visit to London was another mark of respect with no other motive than the fulfillment of Samuel Wesley's wishes. But the act of filial piety set off a chain of events which Wesley was later to regard as providential.

Because their brother Samuel had moved from Westminster to Tiverton, John and Charles, who had traveled south together, stayed with James Hutton, an Oxford contemporary and the son of a Nonjuror who, since he had been unable to take the oath of allegiance, had resigned his living and taken up schoolmastering. James Hutton took a great interest in the North American colonies and, while the Wesleys were with him, entertained John Burton of Corpus Christi College, Oxford, who had preached on the need to take the word of God to the settlement of Georgia. The meeting was not one of the miraculous events which, according to Wesley, so often pointed the way to salvation, but it did change Wesley's life.

6

THE FAITH OF A SERVANT

Even by the exotic standards of eighteenth-century adventurers, James Edward Oglethorpe was a colorful character. But his eccentricities were of the gentler kind. The scion of a Jacobite family, he had become sufficiently reconciled to the House of Orange to fight in the duke of Marlborough's army and, after serving as aide-de-camp to Prince Eugene, rose to the rank of general before he was elected to Parliament. Throughout his thirty years in the Commons he campaigned for prison reform. His Committee of Enquiry into Debtors' Gaols criticized the system which, by incarcerating defaulters, made it impossible for them ever to discharge their liabilities and denounced the conditions in which the debtors were held.

> The Committee saw in the women's sick ward many miserable objects lying, without beds, on the floor, perishing from extreme want; and in the sick men's ward much worse. For along the sides of the wall of that ward, boards were laid upon trestles and under them, between those trestles, were laid on the floor one tier of sick men, and upon [them] another tier and over them hung a third tier in hammocks.[1]

Outraged though Oglethorpe was by the conditions in the Fleet and Marshalsea prisons, he was, in the year of the report, unable to suggest an alternative for the discharge of debt. Then in 1730, ten months after the report was published, he heard that part of the American seaboard, a small strip of coastline between Carolina and Florida, was to be colonized and decided that it might provide the solution which had previously evaded him. The territory had not been formally established as a colony. But on 9 June 1732 Oglethorpe was granted a twenty-one-year lease to hold the land of the newly incorporated Georgia settlement "in trust for the poor." The House of Commons, encouraged by the thought that another barrier would be erected to Spanish, and therefore Catholic, encroachment on the Americas, voted Oglethorpe ten thousand pounds. The Bank of England did the same. Oglethorpe was made governor.

Oglethorpe was supported in his initiative by Percival, earl of Egmont, a generous patron of the SPCK and a man of conspicuous moral principle. The Georgia Trust, which he and Oglethorpe founded, determined that as well as succor the poor, protect trade and secure the boundaries of empire, the new colony would be the home of virtue. The territory which they were to govern was a land of small farmers, frontiersmen, planters and drunkards. Egmont and Oglethorpe determined to prohibit the sale of strong liquor, regulate trade with the Native Americans to ensure that they were not exploited by the settlers and end slavery. It was an ambitious program. Its achievement was not helped by the appointment as magistrate and storekeeper of Thomas Causton, a man who was certainly incompetent and probably corrupt.

During January 1733 the first new settlers—116 in all and mostly debtors—made immediate peace with the Creek nation. There were five tribes in all, and all of them were already well disposed toward any enemy of Spain because of the brutalities they had suffered during a previous brief occupation. When Oglethorpe returned to England in 1734, he took two chiefs, Tomo-Chichi and Sinarky, with him and presented them at court. It is not known if they were represented as savages come to repentance or zoological exhibits. Wesley, who met Tomo-Chichi during the visit, was not sufficiently impressed to record a distinct impression of the occasion in his diary.

From the start Georgia, under its new governor, attracted the persecuted minorities from far beyond Great Britain. The year before King George granted the royal charter, a sudden religious revival had swept through Salzburg. In the twenty-first century it would have been called mass hysteria. Twenty thousand followers of Augustus Francke took to the streets to read their Bibles aloud, denounce the pope and embrace the teachings of Martin Luther. After a year, news of their demonstrations reached London, and the Society for the Propagation of the Gospel in Foreign Parts arranged for their emigration to Georgia. They settled, together with two Pietist divines, Bolzius and Gromar, in a place they called Ebenezer. A party of Highlanders—probably what today would be called economic migrants—followed. In consequence, Parliament made a second grant. The Scots were joined by small group of Moravians, an advance party of what was to be a larger settlement in Savannah. Like the Salzburgers, they were Pietists, though followers of Count Zinzendorf rather than Augustus Francke of Halle. Both groups believed in variations of the theology which had convinced Wesley, after his meeting with the Manchester Nonjurors in 1732, that the church should return to the values and virtues of Primitive Christianity. If Providence sent John Wesley to Georgia so that he could test his faith against alternative interpretations of Christian living, it also seized the opportunity to examine how his beliefs helped him to overcome adversity.

The suggestion that he should devote the next period of his life to converting the heathen was made to John Wesley while he was in London, immediately after his father's death. It might have come from Charles Rimmington, the publisher of Samuel Wesley's commentary on the Book of Job, but the more likely source was John Burton. Burton, the Corpus Christi don who met Wesley at the Huttons', was helping Oglethorpe in his search for clergymen, to act both as missionaries to the Native Americans and pastors to the settlers. A retired priest who had acted as locum had died after a few months in the colony, and his successor, one Reverend Samuel

Quincey, had proved unsatisfactory for reasons about which we can only speculate, since the trustees agreed that their criticism should be omitted from the minutes. They did, however, record their decision to increase the number of clergymen in the colony. John Wesley, unsettled, doubtful about the future, but full of evangelical fervor, was an obvious recruit.

John Wesley was tempted by the suggestion that he could meet the colony's needs but, as always in his early years, uncertain about what God wanted him to do. Believing that "a man had no other way of knowing God's will but by consulting his own reason and his friends, and by observing the order of God's providence,"[2] he proceeded to apply that novel version of Locke's empiricism to the problem of unraveling the mysteries of faith. His brother Samuel, William Law and John Clayton were strongly in favor. His mother was passionate in her enthusiasm: "Had I twenty sons, I should rejoice that they were all so employed, though I should never see them more."[3] And he discovered, or was told, that his father supported him from the grave. During the previous autumn Samuel, Sr., had written to tell Oglethorpe, "Had it been but ten years ago, I would gladly have devoted the remainder of my life and labours to that place."[4] The discovery helped him to make up his mind and persuade his brother Charles that they should sail for Georgia together. He could not have been more frank about his motives. His object was self-improvement. The decision was taken in what he described as "the hope to learn the sense of the gospel by preaching it to the Indians."[5] Burton chose to describe Wesley's decision differently. He wrote to the Georgia trustees that "two gentlemen, one a clergyman, bred at the university and who have some substance, have resolved to go to Georgia out of pious design to convert the Indians. They are brothers and their name is Wesley." He was right to point out that Charles had yet to be ordained deacon. But his message did not adequately convey the difficulty with which Wesley's doubts about his duties had been resolved. Burton thought he was called to save the souls of Native Americans. Wesley himself was seeking personal salvation. The letter of appointment stipulated simple preaching. Wesley accepted the employment but ignored the advice.

A more significant description of the appointment was recorded by Egmont in his diary for 8 August 1735:

Appointment of Charles Westly [*sic*] to be Secretary of Indian Affairs. He being a good man and scholar will take orders and occasionally officiate at the church till we can get a settled minister. The elder Wesley is in orders and a Fellow of Lincoln College. The third gentleman (with £3000) yet seriously disposed goes with the elder Westly to assist him in the conversion of the Indians. Also one Mr. Hall of Oxford to replace Quincey.

The religious recruits were exactly as Egmont described them. So were their agreed duties. The significance of his description was that Oglethorpe did not, when the party arrived in Georgia, respect or act upon it.

Assembling the party of clergy had not been as easy as Egmont's note suggests. Wesley always realized that great spiritual endeavors need methodical preparation, and as soon as he decided on Georgia, he began to gather about him a group of fellow (though essentially subservient) missionaries. His brother Charles was apprehensive about both the journey and the job. But his doubts were overcome to such effect that he was ordained both deacon and priest within the space of nine days in preparation for his mission. Westley Hall, an Oxford Methodist, who had by then abandoned Kezziah Wesley and married Martha, was initially so enthusiastic that he sent Wesley a letter saying that he and his wife both were ready for the journey and a coach and horses waited outside his door. True to form, it was followed by a second message which said that he had been offered a parish and therefore could not sail. Matthew Salmon (another Oxford Methodist) also took orders in the expectation of sailing west. He too changed his mind and elected to stay in England. Benjamin Ingham was agreeable to accepting Wesley's invitation but needed a sign to show that God had chosen him to be a missionary. When Hall withdrew, barely a week before the departure date, Ingham believed that Providence had pointed him toward the West. Wesley was persuaded, with some difficulty, that Charles Delamotte, the son of a London merchant friend of Ingham's, should take up the fourth berth although he was not ordained. He was the "man worth £3000." His affluence certainly influenced the trustees' wish to interest him in the new territory.

The Society for Promoting Christian Knowledge provided John Wesley with thirteen pounds for "such books as he shall desire" and issued a statement to the London papers announcing that when the *Simmonds* set sail from Gravesend to Georgia on 14 October 1735, its passenger list would include "three clergymen, two of whom intend (after some stay at Savannah to learn the Indian language) to devote themselves to preaching the Gospel of our Saviour Jesus Christ to the Indian nations bordering on that colony." The notice ended (as such announcements often do) with a florid commendation of the endeavor which it publicized. "They seem to be extraordinarily well qualified for the undertaking and there is great reason to hope that God will in a peculiar manner assist the zealous endeavour of these pious persons."[6]

Before the *Simmonds* sailed, Wesley and John Burton exchanged correspondence concerning the fundamental purpose of the expedition. Burton assumed that Wesley was motivated by "the desire of doing good to the souls of others and, in consequence of that, to your own." Wesley's reply was admirably frank. "My chief motive is the hope of saving my own soul." But he modified that selfish ambition with an explanation of how his object was to be achieved. "I am assured that if I be once converted myself, He will then employ me both to strengthen my brethren and to preach his name to the Gentiles. . . . Nothing so convinces me of our own importance as a zealous attempt to convert our neighbor."[7]

The voyage of the *Simmonds* was the first event in Wesley's life to be described in his published *Journal*—not the private diary which recorded his thoughts as well as his actions, his supposed sins as well as his acknowledged achievements, but an account of his conduct which it seems he compiled, with remarkable prescience, as protection against future criticism. Extracts were later to be used as a public defense against allegations of misconduct in Georgia and as an explanation of why, having been briefly attracted to Moravian the-

103

ology, he had rejected the Church of the Brethren's teaching. Their initial appeal had been the result of what Wesley regarded as the application of Locke's empirical method, tangible proof of God's love. He saw how the Moravians behaved in times of danger and took their conduct as evidence of their closeness to God.

The Atlantic crossing took almost four months. At first the sea was rough but not perilous. Even then, the waves breaking over the ship's bows convinced Wesley, much to his shame, that he was "unwilling to die."[8] Willingness to meet God—indeed joy at the prospect—was regarded as a necessary characteristic of holiness. Wesley was incapable of rejoicing at the prospect of death. Then, in the New Year of 1736, the weather deteriorated, and on 17 January he recorded that "the sea broke over us from bow to stern, burst through the windows of the state cabin where three or four of us were and covered us all over though a bureau sheltered me from the main shock."[9] On 23 January another great storm buffeted the ship and Wesley wrote in his journal, "I could not but say to myself, 'How is it that thou hast no faith?' being still unwilling to die."[10] Worse weather was to come, bringing with it another of Wesley's many revelations. "The sea broke over, split the mainsail to pieces, covered the ship and poured in between the decks as if the great deep had already swallowed us up. A terrible screaming began amongst the English. The Germans [Moravians] calmly sang on."[11] When the storm had blown itself out, Wesley asked one of the Moravians, "Were you not afraid?" He replied, "Thank God, no." The women and children were equally composed. "Our women and children are not afraid to die," the Moravian explained. Much to his credit, instead of relapsing into the introspective guilt which often followed his discovery of other people's virtues, Wesley rejoiced to be in the presence of such complete Christians. "This was the most glorious day which I have ever hitherto seen."[12]

The Moravians' conduct seemed to confirm the strength of beliefs built on Primitive Christianity, and Georgia provided an opportunity to bring to God the local "Indians" who were untrammeled by the heresies, corruptions and distractions of second-millennium civilization. The Moravian idea of the good life which had been lost was essentially apostolic. And Wesley, who had just read Fleury's *Manners of the Ancient Churches* and had begun to convince himself that the age of the Fathers set the pattern of true Christianity, made no distinction between the two "primitive" ideas. So for most of the voyage he agonized about the best way to pursue the pattern of holiness which at the time he thought was the most certain road to redemption. But mental anguish was becoming a regular feature of his search for true faith. As usual he assuaged the agonies of doubt by following a detailed daily discipline that gave his life a social, if not spiritual, stability.

The missionaries rose at four o'clock and spent the first hour of the day in private prayer. They then read the Scriptures and commentaries on the Bible which were attributed (often without much provenance) to the early church. Breakfast was at seven, and public prayers at eight. Three hours of private study, from nine until twelve, were followed by a meeting to discuss their own deportment and the conduct of the other passengers during the voyage. And so the day went on in its methodical way, always allowing time for attendance at the Moravians' evening service.[13] John Wesley was by nature neither ecumenical nor latitudinarian, but Moravian theology was becoming increasingly attractive to him.

The *Simmonds* arrived at the mouth of the Savannah River on 5 February 1736 and anchored there. Oglethorpe sailed on, in one of the ship's boats, to the Savannah settlement and returned the next day with August Spangenberg, the Moravian minister. To Wesley's astonishment, Spangenberg immediately cross-examined him about his spiritual condition. "Does the Spirit of God bear witness with your spirit that you are the child of God?" Wesley was mortified that he "knew not what to answer." Spangenberg pressed on. "Do you know Jesus Christ?" Wesley, who had recovered his composure, replied, "I know He is the saviour of the world." Spangenberg was not satisfied. "True, but do you know He has saved you?" No doubt anxious not to seem certain about his own premature sanctity, Wesley explained, "I hope He has died to save me." Wesley feared that the conversation had exposed his spiritual inadequacy. But Spangenberg himself believed that the new minister had passed the test. "I observe that grace really dwells and reigns in him."

John Wesley took up his post in Savannah. Oglethorpe went on south to Great St. Simons Isle to inspect the new settlement of Frederica. Charles Wesley went with him. Travel between the settlements was to become a feature of the missionaries' lives in Georgia. It was both dangerous and exhausting. During one boat journey along the coast, a near-catatonic John Wesley fell asleep and went over the side into the Atlantic. He retained his composure. The Moravian influence had begun to make him a more confident Christian.

Everything the Moravians said or did increased Wesley's admiration for them. And it was to the Moravians that he turned when without either lodging or church, he needed a temporary home. If his description of the theologically, as well as physically, turbulent voyage was reliable, living with the Moravians should in any circumstances have been a welcome, calming influence. Add to that the turmoil of John Wesley's early weeks in Savannah, and it is clear that the pious serenity to which he returned each evening was bound to have a profound influence upon him.

On board the *Simmonds* Wesley had come to admire Oglethorpe. But soon after he landed, he and Charles were approached by Mrs. Hawkins and Mrs. Welch,[14] who told the brothers—we must assume by way of confession—that they both were, or had been, Oglethorpe's mistresses. More sophisticated confidants would have recognized the stories as obvious inventions. But the Wesleys believed them to be true, even though during the voyage across the Atlantic, Charles had formed a low opinion of Mrs. Hawkins, a woman of startling immodesty. There is no way of knowing if the women's slanders were the product of sexual fantasies or if, as early biographies suggest, Mrs. Hawkins was determined to cause trouble for Charles because he had imposed a strict religious discipline upon her. The second explanation is supported by the suggestion that, as well as telling Charles Wesley that she had slept with Oglethorpe, Mrs. Hawkins told Oglethorpe that she had slept with Charles

Wesley. That may be a story invented by Charles's friends to damn his tormentor. It is, however, certain that both women went to Oglethorpe to complain that the brothers were spreading the malicious rumor that each of them was in an adulterous relationship with the colony's new governor. Mrs. Hawkins helped to convince Oglethorpe of her genuine anger by attacking John Wesley with her scissors.

James Oglethorpe, apparently as gullible as the Wesleys, turned against Charles. Even when he realized that the stories of malicious gossip were invention, he still regarded the turmoil which they caused as the result of Charles's zealous determination to root out every form of evil. Oglethorpe's military training made him feel particular resentment that the colonists' unrest had been caused, or at least provoked, by one of his own subordinates. The governor decreed that Charles had been appointed secretary of Indian affairs and should confine himself to his official duties. Charles, remembering that Egmont had expected him to perform as occasional pastor, asked if that meant he was "forbidden to speak to the parishioners." Oglethorpe did not answer directly but complained that "it is much easier to govern a thousand than a score," meaning that a battalion of soldiers responds to orders and a colony of settlers does not.[15]

Oglethorpe began to tyrannize Charles. His behavior was so brutal that it might have been intended to drive the secretary of Indian affairs home. But as the colony was in desperate need of both clergy and administrators, a simple desire to persecute and punish is a more plausible explanation of his conduct. Charles had been told that he would live in the governor's house in Frederica. So he took no furniture to Georgia. Oglethorpe refused to provide him with any. For some weeks he slept on the floor of a bare room. When wood from the colonists' store was distributed to make primitive chairs and tables, Oglethorpe instructed that none should be given to the secretary of Indian affairs. Charles Wesley, because of the rejection by his employer as much as the physical hardship he had to endure, contracted what he called (because it released him from Oglethorpe's bullying) "a friendly fever." A well-wisher brought him a second-hand bed. Oglethorpe ordered that it be removed from the room and given to one of the settlers.[16] The torture continued until John Wesley sailed to Frederica to make peace. Several touching scenes ensued. They included Oglethorpe's prediction, inaccurate as it turned out, that he would die, during the next few days, while leading a reconnaissance expedition to determine the strength and location of Spanish marauders. Charles forgave him everything. But America, to which he had only come after much persuasion, had lost what enchantment it ever possessed. He left for home in July 1736, less than six months after he had arrived in Georgia.

On his arrival in England, he presented the Georgia trustees with a written report on the spiritual state of the colony. It was a perfect example of the attitude to life that made both Wesley brothers intolerable to some of their parishioners. Whatever their private doubts about their relationship with God, in public they were always right and their competitors, as well as their critics, always wrong. Charles Wesley's account of his brother's stewardship was a model of fraternal devotion. He told the trustees that "when he arrived at Savannah he found that the people had been miserably neglected by our late minister, Mr. Quincey. That but three persons partook of the Communion and that people diverted themselves with shooting on Sunday; but before he came away his brother (who is minister there now) had forty communicants every Sunday."[17]

John Wesley was made of sterner stuff than Charles. Georgia disappointed him from the start. Instead of becoming a missionary, as he believed the trustees intended, he was forced, by both circumstances and Oglethorpe's will, to become parish priest to the settlers. But he was determined to imprint his mark on the colony rather than let it force him to become a passive symbol of its Protestant allegiance. He preached his first sermon in Savannah on 7 March 1736. He then read a paper which set out the way in which he meant to run his parish. It amounted to a declaration of war on practices which he regarded as unorthodox but the settlers accepted as normal. He later described its purpose as a warning "that offences would come."[18] And come they did.

John Wesley proposed to celebrate Holy Communion every Sunday and on every feast day. But the sacrament would not be available to repentant sinners who had not been baptized in a manner of which the Church of England approved. Johann Martin Bolzius, the Salzburgers' pastor, was refused the sacrament because Wesley believed that he had not been christened by a legitimate authority. Twenty years later he repented and, remembering the incident, asked himself, "Can High Church bigotry go further than this?"[19] The Salzburgers asked themselves more or less the same question at the time of Bolzius's rejection.

Wesley was at least consistent in arguing that if he did not recognize baptism by other faiths, he was entitled, indeed he was obliged, to baptize members of other churches who saw the Anglican ceremony as their only path to receipt of the sacrament. Even then, no matter what form their baptism had taken, communicants were required to give notice of their intention to take the sacramental bread and wine, an impossible obligation in a colony where life could not be either predicted or planned. By baptizing a dozen Dissenters, he caused immense offense to the more self-assured Nonconformists who believed that they had been baptized already. Those he did baptize, children as well as adults, all had to submit to total (and triple) immersion, a practice which led Mrs. Parker, wife of the colony's second bailiff, to refuse Wesley's ministrations and have her child christened by another (unknown) minister. John Wesley was making powerful enemies. The antagonism was increased when he refused to read the burial service over a Dissenter. By June 1736 the criticisms of his conduct were being made in public. A Mr. Horton complained that his sermons were "satires of particular persons" and told him the parishioners "can't tell what religion you are at. They never heard of such a religion before."[20] Unfortunately some of Wesley's enemies thought that they had heard it during their time of persecution. The leader of the Second Reformation was said to be "a papist in disguise."[21] He was certainly rigid in his orthodoxy. At "the settlement of the Scotch Highlanders at Darien . . . I was surprised to hear an extempore prayer before a written sermon."[22] Had his scruples persisted, Methodism would never have prospered.

Wesley was a man who went from one extreme to another. It was not just his slightly arcane view of church "manners" which alienated John Wesley from an increasing number of the colonists. As always he chose to create a small group of especially devout Christians—the elite, if not the elect—who were encouraged to accept a particularly severe religious discipline in order to set an example to weaker flesh. Naturally enough, the weaker flesh was offended. The replication of the Oxford Holy Club was inspired by a religious society which had been formed in Savannah during the summer before John Wesley's arrival. Ingham discovered its existence while the Wesley brothers were in Frederica, during early April 1736.

In fact, in Savannah, as in Oxford, a society which existed before his arrival prospered without his influence. His diary (unlike the *Journal* published four years later to vindicate his years in Georgia) makes no mention of any close involvement in the meetings of the group to which Ingham introduced him.[23] In May 1736 Wesley did, however, draw up a plan which became the pattern for Methodist organization. It justified Wesley's later followers' calling the years in Georgia "the Second Rise of Methodism." The plan, Ingham explained, had two elements.

(1) To advise the more serious among (his parishioners) to form themselves into a sort of little society and to meet once or twice a week in order to reprove, instruct and exhort one another. (2) To select out of these a suitable number for an intimate union with each other, which might be forwarded, partly by our conversing singly with each and partly by inviting them all together to our house; and this, accordingly, we determined to do every Sunday in the afternoon.

The plan was first put into operation—at least by Wesley himself—in Frederica, though (perhaps because he was only rarely there) it did not meet with much success. The Savannah Society—no doubt as a result of its spontaneous creation—prospered, and after September 1736 Wesley assumed the leadership. A group of communicants met him every Saturday evening.

Wesley was not happy in Frederica, though he visited the settlement regularly for some time after Charles left for England in August 1736, in the "hope of doing some good." Then he decided that his prospects of bringing faith to that settlement would be permanently impeded by critics of his stern interpretation of the Christian obligation. They were, he said, in a mixture of admiration and complaint, "extremely zealous and indefatigably diligent"[24] in opposing him. But he persisted for five months in his attempt to confound his critics. Then he gave up. "After having beaten the air in this unhappy place for twenty days, on 26 January 1737 I took my final leave of Frederica. It was not only apprehension of my own danger, though my life had been threatened many times, but an utter despair of doing good there, which made me content with the thought of seeing it no more."[25] As a result, Wesley was no longer even minister to the whole colony but what Oglethorpe intended he should be, vicar of Savannah. All hope of converting the Native Americans was abandoned.

The hoped-for ministry to the "noble savages" had got off to a bad start. Before Wesley disembarked from the *Simmonds* in Savannah Sound, Tomo-Chichi and Sinarky came on board to express their people's wish to hear "the Great Word." But they also thought it necessary to explain that the behavior of the Christians they already knew—particularly the Spaniards who had killed Tomo-Chichi's father because of his refusal to be baptized—had prejudiced their people against a religion which appeared to be based on greed and violence. They were even more of a disappointment to Wesley than Wesley's religion had been to them. Shortly after the two chiefs visited the *Simmonds*, the brothers were rowed ashore in order to reciprocate the mark of respect. The meeting had been carefully arranged to meet the hosts' convenience. But when the Wesleys arrived at the village in which they had chosen to make camp, it was deserted. It was an augury of the relationship which was to follow.

John Wesley had set out for Georgia without beginning to understand how difficult the work of converting the Native Americns would be. The Choctaws, the most prolific of the tribes, lived beyond the impenetrable forest west of Savannah, the Chickasaws through almost equally difficult terrain farther to the west. The Cherokees inhabited the inland mountains, while the Uchees, who had set up a small town next to Savannah, were despised by the other tribes for their decadent imitation of the settlers' ways. The Creeks remained essentially nomadic and controlled some of the most fertile country in Georgia. Most of the Native Americans retained their instinctive suspicion of strangers and their primitive inclination to kill anyone they suspected of being a threat. All the tribes had, to some extent, been infected by the vices of earlier settlers, particularly drunkenness.

So Oglethorpe's determination that Savannah should not be left "destitute of a minister" was not, therefore, the only reason why John Wesley's mission to the Native Americans was never completed. Their inaccessibility combined with their character and habits to make the work of conversion impossible. Wesley found them such stony ground that not as indomitable in early manhood as he became in middle age, he chose not even to attempt to plant the seed of redemption among them. They were, in his judgment, "gluttons, drunkards, thieves, dissemblers and liars,"[26] and the Creeks in particular showed "no inclination to learn anything but least of all Christianity, being fully as opinionated of their own parts and wisdom as either modern Chinese or ancient Roman." So he abandoned them to darkness and left Ingham to visit Irene, an outpost near the Creek settlement, and attempt to learn their language and begin the construction of a Creek alphabet. Wesley's pessimism, if not his lack of evangelical zeal, was vindicated. Both endeavors were swiftly abandoned as failures.

The missionaries had not much more success with the task which had been set them by the Society for the Propagation of the Gospel in Foreign Parts, "the conversion of Negro slaves." Wesley was initially disheartened by the discovery that there had been "great neglect of their Christian education," but he was disappointed with the teachers, not those who should have been taught. Indeed he enjoyed a number of successes which were sufficiently spectacular to be recorded, individually, in his diaries. A young female slave, who was told that virtuous behavior would guarantee that after death her soul would get to live with God "above the sky," immediately asked for instruction in "how to be good."[27] When he found a young man "both very desirous and capable of instruction," Wesley worked, in his usual methodical fashion, on a scheme for replicating his success. "First to inquire and find out some of the most serious of the planters. Then, having inquired of them which of their slaves *were best inclined* and understood English, to go to them from plantation to plantation, staying as long as seemed necessary at each."[28] But the passion to become an itinerant evangelist had yet to stir within him. And the work among the African-American slaves never followed the proposed pattern. The man who would one day ride from Bristol to Newcastle, stopping only to preach and sleep along the way, decided that "a parish of above two hundred miles in length laughs at the labours of one man."[29]

So Wesley was obliged to concentrate his efforts and his energies on Savannah itself. And with his usual enthusiasm, he threw himself into the whole life of the settlement by learning German, in order to talk more freely with the Salzburgers and the Moravians. He also taught in the school which had been established by Charles Delamotte and maintained by the Society for the Propagation of the Gospel in Foreign Parts. The catechism competed with "how to read, write and cast accounts" for the teachers' time. When he discovered that the children who wore shoes openly despised their barefoot classmates, he taught in bare feet. The school occupied an increasing amount of his day. He took particular interest in the education of two young women, Miss Hopkey and Miss Bovey. Whatever the real reason for his particular devotion to their moral improvement and greater learning, it was to result in disaster and his flight, in disgrace, from Georgia.

John Wesley was afflicted by a susceptibility to young women which he recognized as both dangerous and wrong yet was unable to conquer. Perhaps it was the previous embarrassments, suffered in Oxford, Epworth and the Cotswolds, which made him realize how vulnerable he was. Whatever the reason, he described with remarkable candor the catastrophes which he was able to anticipate but not prevent. In March 1736 he wrote to tell his brother, "I am in danger every hour. There are one or two God-fearing young women. Pray I know none of them as to the flesh."[30]

For some months temptation was resisted and the danger averted as Wesley concentrated all his energies on improving his spiritual education, and Misses Hopkey and Bovey were kept at arm's length; he was as susceptible to new ideas as to young women. On board the *Simmonds*, Wesley had been deeply impressed by the Moravians' calm in the face of death. When he landed at Savannah, his conversation with Spangenberg had strengthened his view that the importance placed by Moravians on a personal relationship with God marked the true path to salvation. In July 1737 he had a second conversation with Spangenberg. It clarified, without providing any conclusive answers, a number of questions which were to haunt Wesley for the next ten years. It was easy enough for him to agree that conversion is "passing from darkness to light, from the power of Satan unto God." But he was encouraged to consider if the passing had to begin at a discernible moment, like Paul's sudden bolt of lightning, or could be spaced over many weeks, indeed months, of doubt and sorrow. Wesley, who also asked about the importance of good works, was told that "by works faith is made perfect." Once again the Moravians confirmed his belief that a love of one's fellowman was the consequence, not the cause, of salvation. He attended a Moravian ordination and certainly admired (as well as probably envied) "the great solemnity of the whole." It almost made him forget that seventeen hundred years had passed since Christ's crucifixion and imagine "that he was in one of those assemblies where form and state were not, but Paul the tentmaker and Peter the fisherman presided."[31] It all confirmed his affection for the Primitive Church.

His twenty months in Georgia did not, however, completely clarify John Wesley's mind. That was in part because he resolutely refused to understand the position of the Continental Pietists, either the Salzburgers or the Moravians, when it did not conform to his prejudices in their favor. The leaders of the two groups were in serious theological conflict with each other and, while constantly speaking of a reconciliation, regularly rebuffed attempts to arrange

even a working partnership. But Wesley chose to interpret their beliefs and behavior in the way which gave him most comfort and confidence. He was instinctively on the side of the Moravians, who
believed in the need to legitimize ordinations and baptisms by episcopal authority and therefore subscribed to what were then Wesley's
impeccably Church of England views. But in Georgia he was less in-
terested in their theology than in their conduct. The importance of
his Georgia experience was that had he not met and been impressed
by the Moravians during his time there, he would not have thought
even of inquiring about a faith which, by its example and influence,
was essential to his theological development. Savannah provided "an
opportunity, day by day of observing their whole behavior." During
the months before his mission house was built, Wesley and Delamotte "were in one room with them from morning to night, unless
for a little time spent in walking. They always employed themselves
and were in good humour with one and another. They had put away
all anger and strife, wrath and bitterness and clamour and evil speaking."[32] Wesley was always impressed by the practical manifestation of
virtue, the "imitation" of Christ.

Wesley's discovery of the Moravian religion had a practical by-
product. His new friends convinced him, by example, of the importance of incorporating hymns into the Sunday service. The Church
of England had historically rejected hymns as a violation of devotions
which should be based on sacred texts, not human invention. The
only deviation it allowed from the Book of Common Prayer, which
was constructed from the Bible itself, was metrical psalms. The
Moravians were calm in the storm as they sang their hymns. It was
enough to convince Wesley that mortal creations were acceptable to
God because they encouraged sinners to accept the reality of His
love. Thus the Methodist tradition of hymn singing was born. It was
a diametrical change in attitude from the insistence on constant
communion and the invariable use of the prayer book. Anglican orthodoxy was sacrosanct only when Wesley agreed with it.

It was the insistence on the strict observation of church "manners"—in order, it was generally believed, to suit his personal
needs—which brought about John Wesley's downfall in the Georgia

colony, although the immediate cause was Sophy Hopkey, a young woman who, at least for a time, hoped to marry him. When, despairing of a proposal or betrothal, she put him out of mind and married another, he denounced her marriage as a defiance of the church's ordinance because the banns had not been properly published. Accused of bias, he insisted that his judgment was no more than the particular application of his general rule to "observe every circumstance of the rubrics and canons." It was determination to respect and reinforce the rules with which he agreed that had made him so many enemies. Paradoxically, when the chance to damage him was presented to them, the aggrieved settlers' case was strengthened by the fact that in one particular, he had broken the rules for their convenience. Unfortunately for Wesley he had acknowledged, though he had not condoned, the settlers' habit of going through a form of marriage without the publication of the banns. It was that, together with the habit of arranging private baptism, which had made him write in his diary, "O discipline! Where art thou to be found? Not in England or (as yet) in America."[33] There is no doubt that he disapproved of the irregular unions which he could not prevent. But having let other technically illegal marriages pass with no more than an expression of regret, Wesley was foolish to make an example of a woman who had entered into an arguably illegal union after she had, according to Savannah gossip, refused his proposal of marriage. Indeed it was an act of such folly that it can be explained only by the blind jealousy of which John Wesley's detractors accused him.

Sophy Hopkey (niece of Thomas Causton, magistrate and storekeeper) was a young woman of a little under eighteen when she registered as a pupil in Delamotte's Savannah school. Observers claimed that John Wesley was immediately attracted to his protégée and made no attempt to hide his feelings. She, it seems, reciprocated his affection, for during a brief illness in August 1736 she nursed him back to health. That initial intimacy—the sick clergyman brought back to health by a young disciple—was to become the first stage in a pattern of emotional relationships which, for Wesley, almost always ended in disaster. Miss Hopkey, Wesley wrote in gratitude, "sat by my bed, read several prayers and prepared whatever I wanted with a diligence, care and tenderness not to be expressed." At first Ogle-thorpe welcomed the liaison. Indeed he encouraged it so enthusias-tically that Wesley was worried about the pace of its progress. Conscious that he was both vulnerable and susceptible, he had severe doubts about accepting Oglethorpe's suggestion that he should travel with Sophy to Frederica on 25 October 1736. He suspected, cor-rectly, that the governor was trying to make a match. The idea of marriage excited him but seemed out of the question for a man who had sworn to devote his life to God. The conflict between duty and desire was to become a regular feature of his emotional life.

The voyage to Frederica went ahead as Oglethorpe had planned after Wesley convinced himself that because the arrangements had been made by the governor, there could be no possible question of impropriety. And he felt protected from the threat of any long-term entanglement by the certainty that he intended to remain single and the belief "that Miss Hopkey meant to do the same."[34] Unfortu-nately, as they were crossing Dosay Sound, he thought it necessary to confirm her high moral status—faith as well as celibacy. He first sought reassurance by asking her the question which had haunted him since he had watched the brave Moravians face the storm on board the *Simmonds:* "Miss Sophy are you not afraid to die?" Her an-swer did not reflect any orthodox theology. "No, I don't deserve to live any longer. O that God would let me go now! Then I should be at rest. In this world I expect nothing but misery."[35]

Not surprisingly Wesley inquired about the cause of her despair. Her explanation seemed, at least to him, to answer his question about her wish and intention to marry. He discovered that Sophy Hopkey was engaged to a Mr. Mellichamp, who her uncle believed was mean and violent. One night, "lying by the fire," Wesley asked her if the commitment was irrevocable. He was later to claim that despite the obvious intimacy of the moment, he was initially moved solely by pastoral compassion but was then overcome by the sadness of her reply. "I have promised to marry him or none other." To comfort her, rather than because of any "forward design," he told her, "I should think myself happy if I was to spend my life with you." Miss Hopkey did not respond directly to the gallantry but repeated,

"I am very unhappy. I won't have Tony for he is a bad man. And I can't have none else." She then burst into tears and asked him never to speak of the subject again.

Wesley found it almost impossible to think of anything else for several weeks. The couple continued to meet as teacher and pupil. But despite constant protestation of his own intention never to marry, Wesley "could not avoid using some familiarity or other that was not needful." His *Journal* entries are remarkably frank about what took place. "I put my arm round her waist, sometimes took her by the hand and sometimes kissed her." Later he "resolved never to touch you more." The resolution was quickly broken. Throughout February 1737 he was in turmoil. On Thursday, the third, he was "in a great straight"[36] though he "still thought it best to live single . . . but felt the foundations [of that judgment] shaken more and more every day." Had Sophy "closed" with him, he "would have made but fair restraint." Fortunately, she told him that a clergyman should not marry, and he was convinced of the wisdom of her advice. So he congratulated himself "on a very narrow escape." But next day he went into Savannah, where he "groaned under the weight of unholy desires." On Monday, the fourteenth, he equivocated in a way which he must have known would revive Miss Hopkey's interest and hopes. "I am resolved . . . [i]f I marry at all not to do so till I have been among the Indians."

Those entries suggest, as does a letter written to his mother, that despite his personal inclinations, he always knew that marriage was impossible. Perhaps he did. But he could never bring himself to make this clear to Miss Hopkey. No doubt he spoke discouraging words. He might have even told her that he had consulted Delamotte and the Moravians as well as his conscience. But his behavior constantly suggested that he might one day choose love rather than duty. The fact was that although John Wesley could not have Sophy Hopkey, he could not bring himself to let her go. When she appeared to accept that the best she could hope for was platonic friendship, he immediately heightened the emotion of their meetings by announcing, without much precise reason, that he was thinking of leaving Georgia. Miss Hopkey was inconsolable. "What, are you going to England? Then I have no life in America left."

Either propriety or the hope of forcing his hand prompted Miss Hopkey to tell Wesley that she would no longer visit his house alone. She did, however, receive him when she was alone at her uncle's house, and he was again with her at the Caustons' on 26 February 1737. On that occasion Wesley, by great effort of will, avoided all physical contact, admitting (at least to his diary) that had he touched her, he did not know "what might have been the consequences." But next day, when they were alone again, they kissed and held hands. He left Miss Hopkey's company "swearing to be more wary in future."[37] The constant implication that Sophy was the serpent in his Eden is not to Wesley's credit. But she was certainly not the shy virgin that the Georgia elders were later to claim. On 16 February, at least according to the *Journal*, she told Wesley, "My uncle and aunt, as well as I, will be glad of your coming to our house as often as you please." He replied, "You know, Miss Sophy, I don't love a crowd and there is always one there." Her response was "But we needn't be in it." That dialogue is, in terms of Sophy's character, consistent with the account of her "consulting Oglethorpe on the dress which would be most pleasing to the young clergyman," a story which, since its source is John Telford, Wesley's sympathetic nineteenth-century biographer, has always been open to doubt.

John Wesley consulted Johanns Toltschig, the Moravian pastor, about what God required of him. But he could not bring himself to suggest that he had a real affection for Sophy Hopkey. So he asked if it was right to continue to meet her. Toltschig, reasonably enough, asked what would be the result of a prolonged friendship. Wesley later claimed to be astonished by the question. But it was his answer which was surprising. "I fear," he said, as if wedlock were a sin, "that I should marry her." Toltschig then told him, "I don't see why you should not."[38] Wesley took the answer to be equivocal and asked Ingham and Delamotte what they believed God, working through Toltschig, meant to recommend. They had no doubt that the Almighty wanted an end to the relationship. Telford, who wanted everything associated with Wesley to be sanctified, records that "the lady helped him to keep his holy promise of celibacy, by becoming engaged to a young man of substance." It is an interpretation of events which almost matched Wesley's account of the affair in old age. Forgetting, or choosing to overlook, the weakness of dalliance with the Kirkham girls, Wesley told the Reverend Henry Moore (one of the earliest biographers) that until he arrived in Georgia, he had never had a close relationship with a woman who was not a relative.[39]

The habit of drawing lots to determine God's will was common among even the most enlightened and educated eighteenth-century divines. So Wesley's reliance on pure chance to make up his mind was not confirmation of an adolescent infatuation but proof that he was struggling to do what was right. The lots were marked "Marry," "Think Not This Year" and "Think of It No More." No doubt to Wesley's disappointment, he drew "Think of It No More." A second lot told him that he should not see Miss Hopkey except in the presence of Charles Delamotte. That injunction he broke three days later, and it is hard to imagine that the first instruction—to put the idea of marriage to Miss Hopkey out of his mind—was ever obeyed. Even as he briefly succeeded in avoiding seeing Miss Hopkey alone, he wrote, "My resolutions remained. But how long? Yet a little longer, till another shock of temptation, and then I well knew they would break in sunder as a thread of tow that has touched the fire."[40]

The agonies of indecision were ended by Miss Hopkey herself when, on 9 March 1737, she announced that she wished to publish her banns of marriage to a Mr. Williamson, the "man of substance." Perhaps, had he chosen to grasp the moment, there would have still been an opportunity for Wesley to win her as his bride, for she added to the request for the banns to be published, "unless you have anything to object to."[41] John Wesley did consider the possibility that she was simply trying to force his hand. But he chose despair rather than action. "From the beginning of my life to this hour, I have not known one such as this. . . . God let loose my inordinate affection upon me and the passion thereof drank my spirit . . . to see her no more! That thought was as the piercing of a sword."[42] Perhaps she

thought that Wesley, mad with jealousy, would not fulfill his obligation to arrange a lawful marriage. Whatever her reasons, Sophy Hopkey decided to do without published banns, and on 12 March 1737 she married Mr. Williamson at Purrysburg in South Carolina. In consequence, she was guilty of an irregularity against which Wesley had specifically warned his parishioners but from time to time accepted. However, he did not regard her marriage, properly celebrated or not, as any bar to what could only be described as an intimate relationship—touching as well as teaching. It was the rule he had applied to Sally Kirkham after she became Mrs. Chapone, and he saw no reason to behave any differently with Sophy. But a more serious ambiguity complicated his relationship with the woman he had to call Mrs. Williamson. Perhaps as another manifestation of his emotional confusion, he began to believe that she had betrayed both him and her faith.

Following the behavior pattern common to rejected suitors, Wesley, who, during his inhibited courtship, had always spoken publicly and written of Miss Hopkey in entirely complimentary terms, began to discover faults in her character. At first they all related to neglect of her religious obligations and observances. She had not regularly taken communion. When, on 3 July, she began to rectify that omission, Wesley took her aside and listed several other faults. Thomas Causton rallied to his niece's defense. Wesley replied with what amounted to a threat as well as a justification. "Don't condemn me for doing in the execution of my office what I think it my duty to do. . . . What if I should . . . repel one of your family from Holy Communion?" Causton clearly did not take the warning seriously. "If you repel me or my wife, I require a legal reason. But I shall not trouble myself about none else."[43]

On 7 August 1737 John Wesley banned Sophy Williamson from communion. He wrote to her to explain why. His charge sheet began with her failure to follow proper church procedure. "So many as intend to be partakers of the Holy Communion shall signify their names to the Curate at least sometime the day before. This you did not do." But the indictment then became more general. "And if any of these . . . have done any wrong to his neighbors by word or

deed . . . the Curate shall advise him . . . not to come to the Lord's Table until he hath openly declared himself to have truly repented."[44] The wrong which Sophy Williamson had done was either to marry without published banns or to deceive her "neighbor" John Wesley about her intention to marry at all. In Savannah it was generally believed that her real offense was to reject John Wesley.

Mrs. Williamson, almost certainly under pressure from her husband, struck back. She swore an affidavit, asserting that Wesley had told her that she would save her soul only if she agreed to live with him and then, when she rejected the idea of an irregular union, proposed marriage. The accusations were sufficiently close to the truth to absolve her of the charge that she was prompted by malice. She was clearly bewildered by Wesley's ambivalence before her marriage and by his antagonism after it. Much of the blame for the scandal must fall on Wesley, who—as an indication of his emotional instability—was to behave in exactly the same equivocal fashion twenty years later.

Thomas Causton, chief magistrate of Georgia as well as storekeeper and Sophy Williamson's uncle and guardian, decided that his niece's honor could be restored only if Wesley stood trial in front of the colony's grand jury. The indictment listed ten offenses which the defendant set out in his diary. They included examples of every complaint that had been made against him since he landed in Savannah. "Refusing to baptize Mr. Parker's child by sprinkling, unless the parents would signify that it was weak. . . . Refusing to read the Burial Service over Nathaniel Polhill, an Anabaptist. Refusing to receive William Aglionby as a godfather because he was not a communicant." By comparison, "writing and speaking to Mrs. Sophy Williamson against her husband's consent"[45] seemed a minor misdemeanor.

The complaints were summarized in the indictment by the general allegation that Wesley had "deviated from principles and regulations of the Established Church, in many particulars inconsistent with the happiness of the Colony." Wesley described Causton's complaint against him in more dramatic language. The chief magistrate had accused him of being a "sly hypocrite, a seducer, a betrayer of trust, an

egregious liar and dissembler, an endeavourer to alienate the affections of married women from their husbands, a drunkard, the keeper of a bawdy house, an admirer of whores, whoremongers, drunkards and murderers . . . a refuser of Christian burial to Christians, a murderer of poor infants by plunging them into cold water."[46]

The grand jury, which Wesley claimed was packed with Dissenters, papists and infidels, intended to hear the indictment in two parts. In August it examined the charge that he had offended against the canons of the Church of England by altering the liturgy and introducing unauthorized hymns and practices into the act of worship. They were charges which were later also to be laid against Delamotte. But when they turned to the more personal items in the indictment, they chose also to examine Causton's conduct. Causton had made many enemies in Georgia, and his allegations against Wesley gave them an opportunity to take revenge for the injuries, real and imaginary, which he had inflicted upon them. The situation was regarded as so serious that William Stephens was sent to the colony by the Board of Trustees to inquire who was to blame for the turmoil. He blamed everybody a little and nobody very much. Wesley was accused of being the principal speaker at public gatherings of every sort where he "harangued the people though he had no business there." Stephens concluded that he had supported the rule of law but, in another personal interpretation of John Locke's philosophy, agreed that the settlers had the right to revolt against bad magistrates. The charge sheet was growing by the day.

Wesley's immediate reaction was that nothing should divert him from his duty, "thinking it more suitable to my calling still to commit myself to God." On 11 September he preached a wholly unrepentant sermon which repeated all the strictures he had made on the moral conduct and the church "manners" of the colony on the first Sunday after his arrival. His determination to stay and fight was reinforced by a memorandum, sent by a minority of the grand jury, to the trustees. It claimed that all the charges against Wesley had been trumped up by Causton. Wesley then attempted, at least according to his *Journal*, to make peace and believed that his overtures to the storekeeper had been accepted and that their quarrel was at an end.[47]

But he then realized that some of the colonists would never be reconciled to his ministry. So he decided to leave Georgia in the interests of public tranquillity and posted a notice in the town square announcing his intention. The magistrates forbade him to go. All the complainants, including Causton, insisted that their cases be answered. So on 2 December 1737 he fled.

The magistrates declared that anyone who assisted in his escape would be charged with contempt of court. But no one attempted to stop or hinder what was a very public flight from justice. Wesley attributed his easy passage to the support he had won among the people. Wiser friends believed that the magistrates wanted to see him go so that they could bring a swift end to the scandal, which, as Wesley himself had told Causton, was undermining the tranquillity of the colony. So Wesley left Georgia defeated but unrepentant. He set sail convinced that he had failed not because of any shortcoming on his part. "I shook off the dust of my feet and left Georgia after having preached the Gospel there not as I ought, but as I was able for a year and nearly nine months."[48]

At sea, in the early New Year of 1738, Wesley, with none of his usual confidants to console him, came very near to a nervous breakdown. "Finding the unaccountable apprehension of I know not what danger (the wind being small and the sea smooth) . . . I cried earnestly for help and it pleased God in a moment to restore peace to my soul." The irrational fear reawakened the doubts about his own beliefs that he had felt on the outward voyage during its great storm. "Whoever is uneasy on any account (bodily pain alone excepted) carries in himself his own conviction that he is an unbeliever." Anyone who is "uneasy of the apprehension of death . . . believeth not that to die is to gain."[49] There followed a prolonged period of introspection during which he wrote in his diary—and subsequently edited and published in his *Journal*—a litany of failure. He accused himself "of pride throughout my past life, in as much as I thought I had what I find I have not": real faith. He was equally guilty "of levity and luxuriancy of spirit . . . speaking words not tending to edify." It was a self-confessed doubter, unable to convince himself of God's love and mercy, who landed in Deal on 1 February

1738. The next day George Whitefield, who suffered no such doubts, set out on his own mission to Georgia.

On 18 February Wesley met Lord Egmont, the senior trustee of the Georgia colony in London, and gave an account of his suddenly abandoned stewardship. He admitted that he was "guilty of indiscretion but claimed that Causton our head bailiff was much more to blame."[50] The trustees accepted his explanation and decided, for reasons which they chose not to explain, to remove Causton from his post as storekeeper but retain him as magistrate. Wesley handed his documents of appointment to Egmont since "he had no more place in those parts." The Board of Trustees immediately revoked his commission. Not surprisingly, Egmont had no regrets about ending Wesley's mission to Georgia. The missionary had, in his view, turned out to be "a very odd mixture of a man, an enthusiast and at the same time a hypocrite, wholly distasteful to the greater part of the inhabitants and an incendiary of the people against the magistrates."[51]

Wesley interpreted his failure differently. He regarded whatever achievements he could claim in Savannah as vitiated by his lack of absolute faith. "It is now two years and four months since I left my native country in order to teach the Georgia Indians the nature of Christianity. But what have I found myself in the meantime? Why least of all what I expected, that I, who went to America to convert the Indians, was never myself converted to God."[52] Years later he was to qualify his self-criticism with a footnote, "the faith of a *servant*, though not of a *son*." The denunciation and the defense illustrate the real achievement of his American adventure. Thanks, in part to his personal experience and in part to the Moravians' example, he had at least begun to clarify the great questions which were to dominate his thinking for the next decade. He left Georgia still believing in justification by faith alone but agonizing about the stages in which sanctity could be achieved. He did not, however, remain consistent in one particular. He had set sail concerned about his own soul, not the Indians'. He returned with the same egocentric preoccupation.

7

Rites and Ceremonies

Methodism had prospered in England while John Wesley was away. After his return from Georgia in the autumn of 1736, Charles had urged his old associates to "resume all their rules of holy living"[1] and had then written to his brother with reports of the success of his injunction. "We see all about us in an amazing ferment. Surely Christianity is once more lifting up its head."[2] Most of the original Holy Club members had left Oxford for rural livings. They had become apostles of Methodism. Charles Kinchin was spreading the word in Lancashire. John Gambold had moved to Stanton Harcourt. Benjamin Ingham, his own mission to the Americas completed, went to Yorkshire. Charles Delamotte took a parish in Kent. In London Methodists met regularly in the Westminster home of James Hutton where they sang psalms "against the peace and quiet of the neighborhood." Hutton was the son of a Norfolk bookseller and had become one of Wesley's followers after reading the "One Thing Needful" sermon. Gambold, already attracted to the Moravian ideal, illustrated how broad a church the revival had become. In Wales, Griffiths Jones and Howel Harris, unconnected with Oxford Methodism, were leading an independent evangelical movement.

George Whitefield, associated with Wesley in Oxford and, for a time, a Holy Club member, had first moved to Gloucester (where he founded a religious society on the Oxford pattern) and then to London. In the two years of Wesley's absence, Whitefield had assumed the Methodist leadership. Before 1738 John Wesley was no more than part of the Great Revival—not leader but one of the led.

Whitefield's Oxford timidity (attributed by his followers to his origins as a potboy in a Gloucester inn) had been overcome by a personal revelation, an indispensable qualification for anyone who aspired to leadership of the Great Revival. At Easter 1735 he was suddenly consumed by "a great thirst." Then a voice within him spoke—"I thirst, I thirst," echoing the words of Christ on the cross—and he thirsted no more. His suffering at an end, George Whitefield knew himself to be saved. Certainty was not his only advantage. He had a second quality which, although not essential to effective evangelism, was regarded by those who possessed it as a gift direct from God and therefore proof of divine patronage. Whitefield was a natural phrasemaker and so much more effective a preacher than Wesley that Benjamin Franklin warned people who planned to meet him that they should empty their pockets before the introduction. Otherwise he would persuade them to give all that they had to the poor. It was said that he could bring tears to a congregation's eyes merely by whispering "Mesopotamia." It was largely due to him that the revival prospered in John Wesley's absence.

Good news traveled fast even in the eighteenth century. On his return to London, Wesley received a letter from James Hervey telling him of the "wonderful works of God" which Whitefield had performed. The whole nation, Hervey claimed, had heard of "the great evangelist." Wesley would, he had no doubt, react like the rest of the pious population who, on hearing of Whitefield's success, "could not but rejoice." This prediction of Wesley's reaction, which was a tribute to his generosity of spirit, was vindicated. In 1738, as throughout their lives, Wesley and Whitefield were able to disagree about both how the revival should be sustained and extended (as well as the theology on which it was based) without allowing their strong relationship to be permanently damaged by the pride which accompanies personal rivalry. However, when Wesley landed at Deal and heard that "the great evangelist" was about to set sail for Georgia to become the colony's new pastor, he was not sure if the colony was right for Whitefield or if Whitefield was right for the colony. Presumptuously he drew lots to determine if God approved of the appointment and concluded that the Almighty was against it. So he made God's will clear to his successor. Whitefield, offended by Wesley's interference in his relations with Providence but still a great admirer of his predecessor, left for America nevertheless. On his arrival in Georgia, he concluded that what "the good Mr. Wesley has done in America under God is inexpressible."[3]

The Georgia colony in which Mr. Wesley had done so much good was, in most ways, untypical of Protestant America. It was a new territory in which missionaries were needed for both natives and settlers. Farther north, second-generation Americans were redefining their religion. In Pennsylvania and the other middle colonies young Presbyterian preachers were challenging the cold Calvinism of the local churches. North in New England, still barely half a century away from the Puritan landings, an "awakening" which both exceeded and preceded the English revival was under way. The rediscovery of belief was usually spontaneous and local. For there was no torpid church against which to rebel or the feeling of landless exclusion which came with the enclosures and made many of the English new poor certain that God did not speak to them through parsons who were dependent on the gentry's favors. But there were evangelists whose work spread the word of new salvation. Typical among them was Jonathan Edwards of Massachusetts, whose lecture "God Glorified in the Work of Redemption by the Greatness of Man's Dependence upon Him" was so widely circulated that at the time of John Wesley's return to England half the northern seaboard of America knew that after it was first delivered in Northampton, "the town seemed to be full of the presence of God." The English and American revivals were very different in both nature and origin. But their parallel existence confirms that English-speaking Protestants were united in wanting something better and different. It did not need Edwards in America or Wesley and Whitefield in England to light the fire of evangelism. The revival, with different degrees of success, fanned smoldering dissatisfaction into flames.

In continental Europe, what would in England have been the Dissenting denominations were growing in confidence and numbers and were beginning to proselytize in new territories. Back in London, John Wesley lodged again at the Huttons', where John Hutton as a result of John Wesley's influence had begun to examine the teaching of the Moravian Church. When he heard that Peter Böhler, a Moravian minister, was passing through London on his way to America, Hutton invited him to attend a prayer meeting in his house. God had arranged for John Wesley's Moravian education to be completed.

Although he was nine years John Wesley's junior, Peter Böhler was a man of much more mature conviction. He had been converted to the Moravian faith by Count Zinzendorf, the religious movement's leader, and, after he was ordained minister, had acted as a missionary for his adopted religion by setting up Moravian "bands" as well as preaching the Moravian gospel. His belief that faith needed reinforcing with good organization matched Wesley's view exactly. He was a practical man who believed that his followers were more likely to retain their commitment if the societies in which they worshiped were divided into smaller groups reflecting the members' gender, marital status and degree of fervor. But he also had strong theological views. He complained that the Church of England was "even more churchy and liturgical than the Lutherans."[4] That view (like his criticism of the insistence that prayers were lawful only if they were read from printed books) anticipated Wesley's reservations about Anglican Church "manners." He seemed to realize at once that John Wesley needed his help. When Böhler learned that the brothers planned to ride to Oxford, he asked if he could travel with them. His account of the journey, written to Zinzendorf, suggests that he understood both the Wesleys' anxieties and the English character.

> I travelled with the two brothers John and Charles Wesley from London to Oxford. The elder, John, is a good-natured man. He knew that he did not properly believe in the Saviour and was willing to be taught. His brother, with whom you often conversed a

year ago, is at present much distressed in his mind, but does not know how he shall be acquainted with the Saviour. Our mode of believing is so easy to the Englishmen that they cannot reconcile themselves to it. If it were a little more artful, they would much sooner find their way to it.[5]

The three men set out on 17 February 1738. The following day Böhler began his attempt to resolve the doubts which he had rightly identified as disturbing John Wesley's piece of mind. Böhler's theology, which confirmed the conclusions to which the teaching of Law and à Kempis already pointed, allowed no compromise. So it was irresistible to a man who longed for certainty. He believed in "salvation by faith alone," and he defined faith in a way which must have added to Wesley's growing conviction that he must make a new beginning. There were, according to Böhler, no "degrees of faith." It was a grace which was possessed in full measure or not at all. In consequence, Wesley's problem was not that his faith was weak but that he totally "lacked the faith whereby alone we are saved." Wesley meekly accepted Böhler's diagnosis. Indeed he confirmed it. He could not claim the "full assurance" which was essential to true faith, and those who did not possess it had doubts about God's redeeming love. So he was not sure if in his spiritual inadequacy, he was fit to preach. Arguments about the propriety of preaching before certain redemption were, as Wesley would one day discover, agonizing the Moravians. But Böhler, less rigid in this particular than some members of that church, reassured him with an injunction which, although mystical, met Wesley's deep psychological need to evangelize. "Preach faith til you have it and then, *because* you have it you *will* preach faith."[6] Wesley was convinced of the path he should follow. Indeed he extended his belief in the efficacy of his ministry by taking the Word of God to a condemned man, an unheard-of ministry within the Church of England, since it was assumed that the prospect of hanging would concentrate the mind on false confession and bogus repentance. On 6 March 1738 he visited Oxford's Castle Prison, where he promised William Clifford (who was under sentence of death for assault, burglary and desertion from the army) that he could be saved—from damnation, if not the gallows—by faith alone. It was too late for good works.

Wesley, always during his early manhood dangerously susceptible to new ideas, was both convinced and disturbed by Böhler's analysis of his spiritual state. In times of doubt or difficulty he invariably consulted his friends, usually hoping that they would advise him to take the course which he preferred. So on 14 March he set off to Manchester, where he discussed the Böhler doctrine with Charles Kinchin and John Clayton. Clayton was by no means convinced that Böhler was a good influence on his old friend. Wesley therefore moved in with Kinchin for a period of quiet contemplation in the peaceful setting of a country parish. The peace did not last for long. After less than three weeks he returned to London to consult Böhler again. The Moravian minister had more disturbing news for him.

Wesley, exhibiting a remarkable humility, asked Böhler how he could acquire complete faith, adding, with rather less modesty, that he had not sinned as much as many other people he knew. Böhler would not concede that there were degrees of sin any more than he would believe that there were different levels of faith. The sin of not truly believing in the Savior transcended all other sins. True conversion would produce not a reformed man but a new man. And, said Böhler, that new man could be created—born again—in a moment.

The idea took hold. During April 1738 John Wesley became convinced that true conversion was likely to be instantaneous—not necessarily a sudden shift from Antichrist to true believer, but a definable, if not at the time recognized, moment at which true faith brought holiness (freedom from the power of sin) and happiness (the peace which follows the certainty of forgiveness). Wesley, at first uncertain about the notion of a miraculous moment, had consulted Thomas à Kempis's *The Imitation of Christ* in the hope that old beliefs had begun to coincide with new. Then he discussed the idea with "an old friend at Oxford," who both confirmed and complicated the doctrine with the explanation that "God can (at least if he does not always) give faith whereby cometh salvation, in a moment." Belatedly he looked to see what his Bible said on the subject. As a result, he wrote, with apparent surprise, that there were "scarce any instances there of other than *instantaneous* conversions—scarce any so slow as that of Saint Paul who was three days in the pangs of the New Birth." The combination of Oxford experience and biblical authority was conclusive. "Here ended my disputing. I could now only cry out 'Lord, help thou my unbelief.' "[7]

Robert Southey, whose biography is, by the standards of the nineteenth century, unusually skeptical, asked, "Is it possible that a man of Wesley's acuteness should have studied the Scriptures as he had studied them until the age of five and thirty without perceiving that the conversions which they record be instantaneous? And is it possible that he should not now have perceived that they were necessarily instantaneous because they were produced by plain miracles?"[8] Wesley's own explanation—that he had previously assumed that miraculous conversion was peculiar to the first age of the church—was ingenious but unconvincing. He was happy to accept that he had been mistaken. The most likely explanation of what, on face value, was an admission of remarkable ignorance is more psychological than either intellectual or spiritual. In early 1738 he wanted to be suffused in a sudden shaft of redeeming light. And the first step toward achieving that ambition was the acknowledgment (made all the more dramatic because it was new) that until the miracle had happened, he was unredeemed. Whether or not he was guilty of "enthusiasm," in the pejorative theological sense of that word, he was certainly an enthusiast by nature. The idea of instant conversion excited him.

Wesley's habit of suddenly changing his beliefs and holding the new conviction with the certainty with which he had held the old was a source of constant conflict with his friends. The turmoil which his Moravian period caused lasted for most of the spring of 1738. It began when his brother challenged his views on sudden revelation. Charles recorded the unhappy scene.

We sang and fell into a dispute—whether conversion was gradual or instantaneous. My brother was very positive for the latter and very shocking: mentioned some instances of gross sinners believing in a moment. I was much offended by his worse than unedifying discourse. . . . I insisted a man need not know when he first had faith. His obstinacy in favouring the contrary drove me at last out of the room.

Disputes between the brothers often ended with Charles's abandoning the fray in despair of ever changing John's mind. But the reconciliations were always swift. And the aims which they shared prospered because of their partnership. Success began to create its own problems.

What John described as Christians "of like mind, who seek fellowship with each other," had increased in number to a point where they could no longer be accommodated in James Hutton's house. So the London Society moved its headquarters to a meetinghouse in Fetter Lane, just off London's Fleet Street and was forever more known by the name of the street in which it planted the first seeds of the Methodist "Connexion." The move changed the nature, if not the theology, of the group. It was no longer a collection of family and friends but a congregation with distinct opinions about faith and redemption. Böhler, assisted by Wesley, took responsibility for its reorganization and ran it on strictly Moravian lines. Members met weekly in small groups "to confess their faith one to another and to pray for one another that they may be healed." On Wednesdays they came together for singing and prayer. A night of prayer and contemplation—so emotionally charged that it was called a love feast—was to be held each month. They were encouraged to find "others of whose sincerity they were well assured [and] meet with them" for the same purpose. Penitence and proselytizing were to go hand in hand.

Böhler left for America within days of Hutton's society's being reorganized, and John Wesley, in undisputed charge, began to spread the new gospel with energy and passion. His technique was not without its critics. Letters from the north arrived complaining about his conduct during the days he spent (in his own opinion) quietly contemplating the character of true religion. John Clayton wrote to him on behalf of his "Lancashire friends" to express doubts about the way he had behaved during the time before he had come fully under Böhler's influence. According to Clayton, "few or none were edified" by Wesley's preaching. They were "offended by his manner" and his extemporaneous style. Clayton was brutally candid. Wesley's behavior "established [his] reputation for self-sufficiency and ostentation." The first of these accusations was to be repeated by honest friends as well as enemies for the rest of John Wesley's life. The paradox of his character was that although he was "unwearied in the pursuit of good, unwearied in charity, unwearied in well doing and unwearied in saving souls . . . under God's province the real centre of his interest" was John Wesley.[9]

The allegation of self-absorption is, by its nature, unlikely to be accepted by the guilty party. And Clayton's criticism was ignored. Indeed John Wesley began to exhibit all the signs of religious megalomania. He turned his back on once-valued friends and previously accepted ideas. On 14 May 1738 he wrote to William Law to complain that his old mentor's earlier teaching had not put sufficient emphasis on redemption by faith alone. "Why," he asked, "did I scarce ever hear you name the name of Christ?"[10] and why had he not been told and taught that "faith, as well as the salvation it brings, is the free gift of God?" Law would have to "answer to our common Lord" for his failure to preach the true gospel of forgiveness. He went on to complain that Law overestimated him. "If you say . . . you knew I had faith already, verily you knew nothing of me, you discerned not my spirit at all. I know that I had no faith. Unless the faith of a devil, the faith of a Judas, that speculative, notional, airy, shadow which I was in the head not the heart."[11] Wesley expanded criticism of Law's teaching methods into doubts about the teacher's character. Law was invited to consider if his "extreme roughness" and "soreness of behaviour" could "possibly be the fruit of a living faith in Christ." John Wesley had become a zealot.

John Wesley's friends were alarmed by the new fervor. Initially Charles Wesley shared their concern. But he too had, for some time, been moving toward acceptance of Böhler's belief in a definable moment of conversion and had begun to castigate himself for not accepting the truth of that teaching from the start. After reading Martin Luther's commentary on Paul's Epistle to the Galatians he professed himself "astonished that I should ever think this a new doctrine."[12] He had told his sister Kezziah that he hoped to become "a new creature" and claimed to Hetty that he was beginning to experience an "inward change." The notion of being "born again" was taking shape. The discovery which he had made by careful study was reinforced by what he believed to be divine revelation. It came about on Friday, 21 May 1738.

Once again the Huttons were the agency of God's will. Staying with "old Mr. Hutton," Charles Wesley met a Mr. Bray, a poor ignorant mechanic whose simple faith much impressed him. Shortly after the meeting Charles was taken ill with pleurisy. Mrs. Turner, Bray's sister, told him that he would not recover until he truly believed. It was the sort of prophecy which Charles Wesley, for all his education, took seriously, but he took the precaution of testing the woman's sincerity by asking if she was willing and ready to meet her Maker. She replied, "I am and would be glad to die in a moment." Charles, we must assume, did not at that time feel the same, for he recorded the pleasure with which he heard a voice command him, "In the name of Jesus of Nazareth arise and believe and thou shalt be healed of all thy infirmities."[13] At first, he believed that the words were spoken by a Mrs. Musgrave, a friend who was helping to nurse him. Then he realized that she was downstairs. In fact, the benediction had been pronounced by Mrs. Turner herself, who later insisted it was inspired by a dream in which Christ instructed her to bring the good news of salvation. Charles Wesley, in a mood to receive such a message, felt his heart begin to beat faster but, although he took the palpitations to be a sign, was still unable to say, "I believe, I believe."[14]

Fortunately Bray, speaking with the authority of simple faith, assured him that he had experienced the moment of conversion. Charles Wesley found himself "at peace with God and rejoicing in the hope of Christ."[15] From then on he referred to 19 May 1738 as "My Day of Pentecost." In the true spirit of brotherhood he longed for John to experience the same benediction, a hope which was probably turned into anxiety by the knowledge that Kezziah, staying with the Clapton family at Stanton Harcourt, had also undergone a

135

profound religious experience. The future leader of Methodism was being left behind.

John Wesley had to wait only another five days. His published *Journal,* a much-revised version of the diary he wrote each day, sums up his spiritual development until the moment at which he accepted that he too had become a true believer. Böhler had convinced him of the need for full assurance. "A true living faith in Christ is inseparable from a sense of pardon for all past and freedom from all present sins. . . . The pure gift of God." That led to the rational assumption—at least for believers in universal redemption—that "He would surely bestow [that gift] upon every soul that earnestly and perseveringly sought it." So, "renouncing dependence, in whole or in part, upon my own works or righteousness," Wesley determined to give himself to God and swore to rely solely on "the blood of Christ shed for me" as his means of salvation. Christ had become his "sole justification, sanctification and redemption."[15] His own "moment of Pentecost" was approaching. It arrived on 24 May 1738.

Wesley's description of his state of mind before his next "conversion" and the state of grace which he enjoyed after he had been "redeemed" was published in his *Journal.* So it is important to judge the most famous passage in Methodist literature against the knowledge that it was composed with the intention of propagating the faith (and establishing Wesley's role as leader of the revival) rather than providing an objective description of the event.

> In the evening I went very unwillingly to a society in Aldersgate Street, where one was reading Luther's preface to St. Paul's Epistle to the Romans. At about a quarter before nine, while he was describing the change which God works in the heart through faith in Christ, I felt my heart strangely warmed. I felt I did trust in Christ, Christ alone for salvation; and an assurance was given to me that He had taken away my sins, even mine.[17]

The Aldersgate experience, or miracle, as some of Wesley's disciples called it, came in a moment like the blinding light which changed Paul's life on the road to Damascus and the voice of Providence which Augustine heard in the Milanese Gardens. It occurred very shortly after Wesley had, for the first time, been convinced that the sudden revelation was an acceptable (perhaps even essential) proof of redemption. Before then he believed, like the Puritans of the Commonwealth, that the divine will was expressed in omens, symbols and metaphors. After Aldersgate, belief in the mystical moment was never so strong again.

It is even possible that in his heart or on calmer reflection, John Wesley himself was not as convinced that Aldersgate was the turning point in his relationship with God as that first carefully drafted *Journal* entry suggests. What has been represented as the most important event in his life was the subject of only one other explicit reference in all that he wrote during the next fifty-three years, a letter to his brother Samuel, dated 30 November 1738. There are many references to 1738 as the *year* of assurance and many accounts of other spiritual experiences. One of them contributed to the certainty of Aldersgate Street's importance, for it was in November 1738 that "walking from London to Oxford," Wesley suddenly felt "the handwriting which was against me is blotted out."[18] But his long life was punctuated by such incidents. The pious Oxford porter was the first. The behavior of the Moravians on the journey to America was another. Still to come was the feeling of joy he experienced in Bristol on the first day he preached to the multitude. Then there were innumerable later revelations which were brought about by the example of holy men and the reading of their devotional work. John Wesley's life was changed by writing of every sort—by Henry Scougal's *Life of God in the Soul of Man* and Jonathan Edwards's *Faithful Narrative of the Surprising Works of God in the Conversion of Many Hundreds of Souls in Northampton New England* barely less than by Thomas à Kempis's *Imitation of Christ* or the works of Law and Taylor. Edwards's work even received the ultimate accolade of Wesley's approval. It was compressed into a tract, *A Treatise Concerning the Religious Affections*. He was, by nature, susceptible to divine guidance and, since he thought of himself as a scholar, particularly receptive when it was delivered in written form.

Even if the significance of 1738 is accepted as the influence of a whole year rather than the effects of a moment, it is still not the date which marks John Wesley's real spiritual turning point. That was 1725, the year of Taylor and à Kempis and the beginning of the life-long conviction that "perfection" must be pursued and might be achieved. Wesley's life was changed by what he came to believe about "inward holiness." The events of 1738 merely refined and confirmed the revelation of 1725.

In November 1738, worried by the apparent contradiction of be-lieving in redemption by faith alone but still insisting on the need for good works, he began to study the *Homilies* which Archbishop Cranmer had constructed for the education of those Catholic priests who, after the Reformation, agreed to be instructed in what, as re-cently accepted Church of England clergy, they must believe. Wesley was so impressed that he compressed the document's thirty-six pages into twelve. He called his précis the *Doctrine of Salvation, Faith and Good Works*. It became the standard text of Methodist belief, and Wesley regarded the work as a sure bulwark against the allegation that he was a heretic. Either natural insensitivity or blind zeal for his cause prevented him from understanding that by making his own edition of *Homilies*, he was, at best, committing an unforgivable act of lèse-majesté and, at worst, guilty of heretical presumption. The first four Methodist conferences (1744–47) used it as the basis of their statements of belief. It increased rather than diminished their alienation from the Established Church.

Whatever happened on 24 May 1738 or during the rest of that year, Wesley did not begin to enjoy the peace that passeth all under-standing. Despite the new feeling of assurance, he was still not a complete Christian and therefore perhaps not a Christian at all. His own inadequacy did not, however, prevent him from proclaiming what he called the "new gospel."

Not surprisingly, many of his close friends were deeply offended by this revision of his beliefs, particularly since his latest adjustment reflected badly on them. If he had not been a real Christian before his conversion, neither had they. And while his progress to redemp-tion had (according to his new analysis) accelerated, theirs had not moved forward at all. Mrs. Hutton (in one of the few contemporary references to the actual date) took particular exception to one sudden declaration and wrote a letter of complaint to Samuel Wesley. No doubt her outrage was increased by the circumstances of the outburst. John Wesley had interrupted her husband in mid-sentence. "Confine or convert Mr. John when he is with you. For after his behaviour on Sunday May 28th, when you hear it, you will think him not quite a right man. . . . John got up at our house and told the people that, five days before, he was not a Christian."[19]

Mrs. Hutton complained, reflecting the orthodox belief of the Church, that he was denying the blessing he had received from the sacraments. But Wesley repeated his admission and received a magisterial, if not wholly logical, rebuke. "If you have not been a Christian ever since I knew you, you have been a great hypocrite for you made us believe that you were one." Wesley was neither angry nor offended. He simply repeated his conviction that "When we renounce everything but faith and get into Christ, then, and not till then, have we any reason to believe that we are Christians."

If there was any ambiguity about John Wesley's position, he did not entertain hope that he had been a Christian for longer than he could confidently claim. Rather he feared that he was still in a state of total heathen unbelief. "My friends affirm that I am mad because I said that I was not a Christian a year ago. I affirm I am not a Christian now." Even the "Miracle" of Aldersgate Street was dismissed as an opportunity lost. "Indeed what I might have been I know not, had I been faithful to the grace given me (on 24 May) when expecting nothing less, I received such a sense of the forgiveness of my sins that I never knew." However, the sense that God had redeemed his sins had passed. "I feel this moment that I do not love God; which therefore I know because I feel it. The joy of the Holy Ghost I have not. Yet again I have not the Peace of God." True to the belief in redemption by faith alone, good works were dismissed as evidence of sanctity, not a path to salvation. "Though I have given all my goods to feed the poor, I am not a Christian."[20]

To John Wesley the alienation of his friends was a matter of little consequence. It was a constant feature of his ministry which he regularly experienced and bravely endured. But his sudden espousal of other dubious doctrines also offended the Established Church. In consequence, he was banned from preaching by two churches in Holborn, three in Bloomsbury and four in Wapping. The incumbents' complaint was not simply that in fine defiance of the principles he had once defended, he prayed extempore and that his sermons were spontaneous. His message offended against their doctrine. The *Homilies* required him to distinguish among justification (freedom from the guilt of sin), regeneration (freedom from the power of sin) and sanctification (absolute freedom from sin). His précis of them ignored the distinctions. Wesley, during his Moravian period, was not in a mood to believe in the stages of anything. So he preached the doctrine of complete, and probably instantaneous, conversion and claimed that those who became "whole Christians" were freed from sin "forever more." It was the complete faith for which he had longed during the storms that almost sank the *Simmonds* and about which he had written on his homeward voyage on the *Samuel*. Everything that he had learned and thought he had understood about the Moravians—from the conduct of the pilgrims on the journey to Georgia to the conversations with Böhler on the return to England—persuaded him that he was most likely to achieve "the sure trust and confidence in God" if he visited their headquarters in Herrnhut. He felt viscerally attached to the Moravians, but worldly considerations reinforced his determination to sit at the feet of Count Zinzendorf. Traveling to Germany was an alternative to making a real decision about his future. A return to Georgia was no longer either attractive or feasible. The Oxford fellowship had lost its charm.

On 7 June 1738, John Wesley "determined, if God should permit, to retire for a short time to Germany." The following day he visited his mother where she was staying in Salisbury and told her of his intentions. After reading her a prayer and describing his new theology, he asked for her blessing, which she denied him. His views were, she said, "extravagant and enthusiastic." For once he defied her wishes. On 13 June, together with Benjamin Ingham, he set out from Oxford for the Moravian settlement at Herrnhut, thirty miles east of Dresden. The journey was slow and arduous and did not end until 1 August. But his letters home confirm that the high hopes with which he began the enterprise increased with every mile which he traveled. On 6 July he wrote to his mother to tell her that, at Marienborn, he had met Count Zinzendorf, whose behavior "was not unlike that of his Master."[21] On the same day he told his brother that he was "with a Church whose conversation is in heaven in which is the mind that was in Christ and who so walked as he walked."[22] When he passed through Wrenor, a few days' ride from Herrnhut, the town gatekeeper challenged him and demanded to know his destination. He replied that he was "going to see the place where the Christians lived." At that moment John Wesley thought of the Moravians as the only true Christians in the world.

John Wesley was still living off the emoluments of his fellowship, supplemented by increasing earnings from his pamphlets and published sermons. His willingness to take the college's money raises questions about his probity, but the joy with which he described his meetings with the Moravians in Herrnhut is a great tribute to his humility. For while Ingham was admitted to Holy Communion, Wesley was not. According to Moravian doctrine, he was a *Homo perturbatus*. The Moravians subsequently claimed that he had been excluded for his own good, since he (unlike Ingham) intended to remain within the orthodoxy of the Church of England and would, by the Moravians' standards, have been impure (and possibly damned) at the moment when he received the sacrament. It was not the only alien doctrine with which he wrestled. At Herrnhut the habits, as well as the doctrine of the Established Church, were ignored. Wesley was set to work in the garden and, when he asked for time to change his clothes before visiting the local gentry, was told, "You must be simple my brother."

The subsequent examination of Moravian theology—the path toward salvation from "inward as well as outward sin"—did, however, reveal the disturbing fact that Böhler and Zinzendorf were in disagreement on fundamental issues. The justified man, the Moravian leader said, might have peace without joy as a promise that assurance would follow justification, a substantial relaxation of Böhler's "all or nothing at all" theology.[23] But Wesley possessed a unique facility for ignoring inconvenient truths. At that moment Moravians, in his mind, were united by truth and virtue.

Wesley left Herrnhut in good spirits, believing that he had met "many living witnesses to the reality of saving by faith," and his *nunc dimittis* confirmed at least his immediate commitment to the Moravian cause. "I would gladly have spent my life here but [for] my master calling me to labour in another part of his vineyard. . . . Oh when shall THIS Christianity cover the earth as the waters cover the sea."[24]

It is easy to understand why Wesley's friends grew increasingly impatient with the constant adjustments to his theological position. To Wesley, his vacillations seemed like a search for new truth and salvation. To others they seemed like self-indulgence. Not only did he deny the old "truths" on which his and their faith had previously been based and built, but he also constantly shifted or refined his position as new influences and new theories of perfection and redemption were put to him. Each marginal refinement was made with the zeal of a man who has suddenly discovered the only path to redemption. Typical of his constant adjustments, sometimes built on interpretation of terms and alternative meanings of religious language, was a letter which he wrote on 28 September 1738, after his return from Herrnhut, to the Reverend Arthur Bedford, chaplain to the prince of Wales and the Haberdashers' Hospital. Bedford asked him to clarify his views on assurance. The reply raised more questions than it answered. "By this one phrase 'assurance of salvation' we mean entirely different things. You understand thereby 'an assurance that we shall persevere in a state of salvation,' whereas I mean no more by the term than an assurance that we are now in such a state."[25] That sophistication of his view prompted a debate on "final perseverance," the vexed question of whether assurance and justification were, by their nature, permanent states or subject to what, in the Methodist vernacular, came to be called backsliding. As well as resentment about the certainty with which Wesley espoused each new idea, his friends felt, not unreasonably, that any ordained scholar of thirty-five should have worked out his position ten years earlier—and in private.

Samuel Wesley—West Country headmaster, orthodox Anglican and, since his father's death, head of the family—wrote to rebuke his young brother for raising doubts in the minds of the unthinking faithful. In his reply, John reiterated his position in what was perhaps the clearest exposition of his new faith as well as his only direct reference (the *Journal* account aside) to Aldersgate. "By Christian I mean one who so believes in Christ as that sin hath no domination over him. And in this obvious sense of the word, I was not a Christian until 24 May past. For till then, sin had dominion over me, although I fought with it continuously. But since then, from that time to this, it hath not. Such is the free grace of God in Christ."[26] Samuel replied with a combination of common sense and ruthless logic. "Have you ever since continued sinless? Do you never then fall? Or do you mean that you are free from presumptuous sin? If the former, I deny it. If the latter, who disputes?"[27]

If John Wesley was to the slightest degree perturbed by his brother's disapproval, he showed no outward or visible sign of his distress. He always welcomed advice which supported a position which he had already adopted and usually rejected criticism which confounded a judgment or theory which he had endorsed or adopted. In any event, he had practical duties to distract him from the arguments of his detractors. By the autumn of 1738 the Fetter Lane Society had sixty-four members. Wesley began to speak of their activities as a "general awakening." By November, when he spoke at Oxford, their activities had been elevated into the Great Awakening.

The general awakening, as its name implies, had been a series of more or less simultaneous revivals, all having common causes in the spirit of the age, the nature of society and the torpor of the church but separate from one another and innocent of any organization. Most of them had at least a loose connection with John Wesley either because he preached at their meetings or because the clergymen who supervised them were his Oxford contemporaries. Over the next ten years all the societies were welded into a "Connexion" as a result of Wesley's conviction that if they stood alone, they would wither and die. His genius was the way in which he matched organization to doctrine and made both reflect the needs of the essentially naive men and women who became his followers. On one hand, Holy Communion was gradually accepted not just as an occasion of the renewal of faith but—in order to meet the needs of simple Christians who wanted to mark the beginning of their compact with God—as the actual occasion of conversion. And at the same time rules were drawn up for the conduct of the societies. James Hutton was given the task of preparing them. Inevitably his Moravian leanings influenced their nature. But rules of any sort would have caused problems. Rules meant a church within the church.

Hutton proposed that within societies, bands should be organized in a way which separated the women from the men—according to Moravian practice. That caused John Wesley no difficulty. But he was doubtful about the proposals for the appointment of "monitors" to identify and suggest remedies for members' transgressions. The idea of "pastors appointed by the congregation" conflicted with what was then his strong belief in an apostolic ministry ordained by divine will. His doubts were an early example of the dilemma which was to increase with every extension of the Methodist Connexion. He was, and remained until his death, determined not to leave the Church of England. Yet he was increasingly attracted to ideas and activities which the Church of England found abhorrent. Usually he tried to reconcile the conflicting demands by minimizing, rather than avoiding, offense to either party. Often he accepted "pyrrhic defeats," pretending that his followers had forced upon him decisions which, in truth, he had always favored. Despite his strong views on the priestly vocation, he told Whitefield that in the matter of monitors, he would not insist on the acceptance of his "will and judgement against that of the whole society."[28] The inevitable result was criticism from both the conformists and the radicals.

Monitors were only the first step. In December 1738 James Hervey (another Oxford Methodist and old friend) accused him of attempting to turn "honest tradesmen" into preachers probably because he (like Samuel Wesley) had heard a rumor that John had allowed an Anabaptist to preach "from our pulpit." John Wesley made a tactical retreat. Tradesmen (honest or not) could not become "public preachers" unless "called" and properly ordained. But they could bear witness to their own conversion. No one asked him how a sermon differed from bearing witness to God's love. But there were other criticisms to answer. Samuel Wesley complained that his brother had preached in unconsecrated buildings and prayed extempore. John did not reply. He was guilty of both irregularities and intended to compound his sin time after time in the future. But in March 1739, when told not to interfere in other priests' parishes, he announced his unswerving intention to "instruct the ignorant, reform the wicked and confirm the virtuous."[29] Since he was unlikely ever to receive his own incumbency, he had no choice. He could preach in other men's parishes or not preach at all.

New offenses were committed against the Established Church. They included the sin of "enthusiasm." The Fetter Lane Society began to witness the manifestations of God's presence, the promise which the revival had made to true believers. On New Year's Eve 1739 Whitefield, Wesley, Ingham, Kinchin and about sixty other worshipers gathered for a "love feast." "About three in the morning, as we were continuing instant in prayer, the power of God came mightily upon us, insomuch that many cried out for exceeding joy and many fell to the ground. As soon as we recovered a little from that awe and amazement at the presence of His majesty, we broke out with one voice 'We praise Thee O God; We acknowledge Thee to be the Lord.' "[30]

It was Whitefield, not Wesley, who in effect began to believe that Methodism should consciously evolve from a collection of separate societies into a connection of like-minded Christians. Bristol and London should be partners in worship. As proof that he made no proprietary claim to the West Country, Whitefield invited Wesley to join him there. Wesley declined. Some of George Whitefield's supporters—as always in the case of rivalries, more partisan than the leader they followed—whispered that Wesley's refusal was prompted by unworthy motives. He was, they said, attracted to one of Hutton's sisters and would not forsake her company. Wesley himself increased the suspicion by offering several other conflicting explanations. He had still to make a final decision about returning to Oxford. He might be needed in Epworth. He doubted if his health would withstand the journey. To Whitefield himself Wesley pleaded prior commitments and reinforced his explanation with a detailed timetable of a typical week's work. On Sunday, 25 February 1740, he preached at St. Katherine's and then at Islington. Then he held meetings at two private houses and in Fetter Lane. On Tuesday evening he held meetings at four, six and eight o'clock. And so on for the whole week. Whitefield, who had worked with him in London until a few weeks before, must have known how Wesley filled his days. And the description of the heavy load must have roused suspicions that Wesley was no longer prepared to follow where others led. But Whitefield persisted. Wesley must visit Bristol.

This determination to see Wesley in Bristol illustrates Whitefield's spiritual arrogance and personal humility. When Lady Huntingdon, a patron of Nonconformist causes, spoke of a "new sect who call themselves Methodists," she added, "There is one George Whitefield at their head." Perhaps she was a little prejudiced in Whitefield's favor, for he, like her, was Calvinist by inclination. Had Whitefield wished it, he could, after his return from America, have reestablished himself as leader, the role he occupied while Wesley was in Georgia. He certainly led the way to Bristol and was, therefore, the pioneer of Methodism outside London and Oxford. But he had no real stomach for the onerous duties of leadership. And he certainly would not have spent long days publishing the carefully edited *Journal* which did so much to establish Wesley as the head of the new church. Whitefield wanted to preach, not organize. He *knew* that God demanded Wesley's presence in the West Country but did not presume to believe that the Almighty wanted to create a church in which George Whitefield was elevated above all others.

Whitefield had decided to go west when, like Wesley, he was denied the pulpits of London. He found Bristol fertile ground. His first letter to Wesley (written on 3 March 1739) described how "glorious doors opened among the colliers of Kingswood." Wesley was invited to "come and water what God has enabled me to plant." His second letter, written almost three weeks later, urged Wesley to leave London, "If the brethren, after prayer for direction, think it proper," and arrive in Bristol at "the latter end of next week." There were, he promised, "many ripe for bands," and Methodist societies had already been formed. John Wesley remained doubtful about the proposed enterprise, and Charles Wesley was strongly opposed. They took refuge in the Moravian custom of opening the Bible at random in the hope that the first verse they saw indicated God's will and wishes. The first half dozen passages they turned up predicted disaster. But it was not clear if the catastrophe would be caused by traveling to Bristol or staying at home. Then Charles Wesley opened his Bible at the words "Son of man, behold, I take from thee the desire of thine eyes with a stroke, yet shall thou not mourn nor weep, neither shall thy tears run down." For some reason that was taken to be an instruction to follow Whitefield. So John Wesley set out for Bristol. He met him there on 31 March and stood in the congregation while the great preacher addressed a gathering so large that its numbers could not be counted. Whitefield's voice carried as far as the farthest enraptured rank. Bolingbroke, High Tory foreign secretary and author of the Treaty of Utrecht, said that he possessed "the most commanding eloquence ever heard," and Benjamin Franklin, who had heard him in America, judged that "his voice could reach 30,000 people if the wind was favorable."

George Whitefield had believed that it was his Christian duty to answer Lady Huntingdon's call for him to tend the wandering flock in Bristol, "the sheep without a shepherd." So without hesitation or preparation he had ridden to the southwest. Welcome though his arrival was to the miners, the church establishment, led by Bishop Joseph Butler, was horrified to find such a man among them. He was banned from preaching within the diocese. So he took his gospel out into the streets of the city. The idea was not entirely novel. George Fox, the Quaker leader, had preached "out of doors" during the seventeenth century. Morgan, a Welsh Dissenter, had revived the practice a dozen years before Whitefield spoke in Bristol. So Whitefield neither chose nor invented "field preaching" but was forced to follow the practice out of necessity. Because of his oratorical powers, he made Bristol, at least for the moment, the center of the Great Revival. Wesley was pulled along by the irresistible tide. Having followed Whitefield to Bristol against his better judgment, he had to choose between preaching in the open air and not preaching at all.

There is hardly a marketplace or village green in England which does not now boast that John Wesley once preached within its boundaries. Field preaching became his life's work, and the itineracy, which enabled him to preach so frequently and in so many places, became the defining characteristic of both the Methodist Connexion and the man who led it. Yet at first Wesley reacted with horror to the thought of alfresco sermons and was, by his own admission, deeply reluctant to follow Whitefield's lead. "I could scarcely reconcile myself at first to this strange way of preaching in the fields of which [he] set me an example on Sunday. Having been all my life (till very lately) so tenacious of every point relating to decency and order that I should have thought the saving of souls almost a sin if it had not been done in a church."[31] Field preaching was, ironically, associated with the Lollards, a sect which Lincoln College had been founded to combat. It was "irregular," not "unlawful." And in Bristol it was immensely successful.

To Wesley, the size of the crowd at Whitefield's meeting seemed like an omen. It proved, at least to his satisfaction, that God wished the preaching conventions to be ignored. And the day after he arrived in Bristol he found biblical authority for adopting the "irregular practice." Preaching to the Nicholas Street Society, one of the several Methodist groups set up within the city, he took as his text the Sermon on the Mount and decided that he had stumbled on "a pretty remarkable precedent" for field preaching. Once again he was late in recognizing what now seems obvious. But although a late convert, he did not, as is so often the case, embrace his new belief with unquestioning vigor. He listened again to George Whitefield preach. On Rose Green, Bristol, his friend addressed the biggest crowd which he had ever seen. The sight of so many penitential faces overcame his inhibitions.

On 2 April 1739 John Wesley preached in the open air for the first time. According to his own account of the occasion, it was not, at least for him, an uplifting experience. "At four o'clock, I submitted to be more vile and proclaimed in the highways the glad tidings of salvation, speaking from a little eminence in the ground adjoining the city, to about three thousand people."[32] Then he preached at

Baptist Mill and the following Sunday to the miners of Kingswood at Hannam Mount. From then on he was preaching in the open air in and around Bristol without much sign of doubt about the propriety of his conduct. Perhaps his judgment about "decency and order" was influenced by the size of the congregations which he attracted. According to his *Journal*, Wesley preached, in total, to 47,500 souls during the first month in Bristol, averaging about 3,000 on each occasion. He did not describe how he calculated the totals but graciously conceded that Whitefield did better. Whitefield was equally generous and reaffirmed his belief that it was his job to break new ground, which Wesley subsequently cultivated. "Dear Mr. Wesley was left behind to teach them the way of God more perfectly . . . and to confirm those that were awakened."[33]

In Bristol, Mr. Wesley was assisted in that task by the Methodist societies which acted as the vanguard of the new evangelism. They were small groups of devotees who were never expected to encompass more than a tiny fraction of the congregations at services and meetings but acted as inspiration to the ministers and example to less committed followers. The two societies at Nicholas Street and Baldwin Street grew so confident in their continued success that they agreed the time had come to establish permanent premises. So they joined together in a united society to meet the cost of land and building. Even when they combined, the couple of dozen society members could not find the money that was needed. So they asked Wesley for help. George Whitefield urged caution. If the meeting room was owned and controlled by the board of lay trustees, it was at least possible that they would dictate how Wesley should pray and deny him the pulpit if he refused to accept their theological judgment. It was a sad, if necessary, precaution against what lay ahead. Whitefield had grown accustomed both to the intolerant Church of England's shutting its church doors to Methodist preachers and the Methodists' own inclination, natural enough in a nascent movement, to argue among themselves over liturgy, authority and doctrine. Wesley accepted Whitefield's advice and agreed to do all he could to support the new meeting room on condition that he held the lease and controlled its management. At first the members simply called it

Our Room, even though, legally speaking, it was John Wesley's. Then it became the New Room. John Wesley was deeply conscious of the attraction of that redeeming adjective. He also understood the power of property. As Methodism spread and developed, gaining and keeping control of the meetinghouses became a constant preoccupation and a major factor in creating a national connexion out of previously disparate societies.

Throughout the spring and summer of 1739, Wesley shared his time and energy between London and Bristol, riding east almost every week to supervise the work at Fetter Lane and back again to the West Country to cultivate the seeds that Whitefield had planted. Inevitably, the notion of field preaching having been established and accepted in Bristol, the practice was introduced to the capital. Wesley gave sermons on Blackheath and Kennington commons to crowds which were estimated as "not less than fifteen thousand." Once again, Charles Wesley felt and expressed instinctive doubts about the path his brother was to follow. For in his heart, as well as his mind, he was a true son of the Church of England—its canons and its liturgy, its homilies and its manners. Samuel was even more offended by his brother's behavior. He wrote to their mother to complain about what he regarded as her willful encouragement of his brother's irregular conduct. She was, he claimed, "spreading a delusion so far as to be one of Jack's congregation" when he had preached in the open air. Since the offending gathering had been held close to Bedlam lunatic asylum, Samuel emphasized his antipathy to the proceedings by ending his letter, "For my own part, I would much rather have seen them picking straws within the walls than preaching in the area of Moorfields."[34] He believed, with some justification, that the whole spirit and ambience of his brother's evangelism promoted hysteria. There were plenty of examples of abnormal behavior with which to prove his point. Meetings of a thousand people or more generated their own emotion. In consequence, the proceedings were frequently interrupted by what was called the gift of tongues.

The stories of strange happenings, some of them no doubt inventions or exaggerations, scandalized the Church of England. When

Wesley, perhaps rhetorically, called upon God to confirm the truth of his sermon, a woman rose in her place "apparently in the agonies of death." A Quaker, who had gone to express his strong disapproval of what he regarded as fake miracles, fell to the ground crying out, "Now I know thou art a prophet of the Lord." At Wapping in the late spring of 1739 "several persons were turning with a sort of convulsive motion in every part of their bodies and that so violently that often four or five persons could not hold one of them." Wesley had "seen many hysterical and epileptic fits but none of them were like these."[35] Samuel had no doubt what caused such unseemly incidents. Extempore field preaching was to blame. "Did these agitations ever begin during the use of any collect of the church? Or during the preaching of any sermon that had before been preached within consecrated walls?"[36] John met the criticism head-on. "How is it that we can't praise God for saving so many souls from death and covering such a multitude of sins unless we begin the work within consecrated walls? . . . I love the rites and ceremonies of the Church. But I also see, well pleased, that our Lord can work without them."[37]

Later that year John Wesley warmed to his theme. He told his brother, "God commands me to do good work unto all men, to instruct the ignorant, reform the wicked, confirm the virtuous. . . . Men command me not to do it in another man's parish. That is, in effect, not to do it at all."[38] Once more necessity and God's will combined to make him "ignore the works of the Church." And his unorthodoxy was sanctioned by the highest authority. "My ordinary call is ordination by the bishops. . . . My extraordinary call is witnessed by the works of God."[39] Perhaps in order to clear his own mind, Wesley set out his "principles in this matter" in a letter to his old friend James Hervey. He told him, in the most famous of all Methodist aphorisms, "I look upon the world as my parish." Three months later George Whitefield paid him the compliment of making exactly the same assertion.

The bishops were not impressed. The apparent claim that demons could be exorcised, inspiring a sudden explosion of faith, was added to the list of complaints which the Established Church made against Wesley and Whitefield. "Enthusiasm . . . pretending extraordinary

151

revelations and gifts of the Holy Ghost" was denounced by Joseph Butler, bishop of Bristol, as "a horrid thing, a very horrid thing." Charles Wesley, perhaps influenced by his brother's insistence that he was experiencing only "what every Christian may receive and ought to hope and pray for," was gradually reconciled to the new ways. After the initial agonizing, he began to preach in the open air with confidence and uncharacteristic wit. At Evesham he addressed the multitude from what he called Whitefield's pulpit. It was a rare attempt at humor. He was standing on a wall.

The Bristol clergy remained irrevocably opposed to the invasion of their parishes. The chancellor of the diocese argued that Whitefield, by preaching in other men's parishes without the incumbents' permission, was guilty of more than discourtesy. Extempore sermons, preached without license, were, he insisted, forbidden by both canon and civil law. The attack on the visiting Methodists was taken up by Josiah Tucker, the rector of All Saints, and immediately reinforced by Bishop Butler. John Wesley responded by repeating his belief that the world was his parish and added, for legal good measure, that, as a Fellow of Lincoln College, he was ordained to preach at large. That response, more ingenious than authoritative, was an adaptation of the advice given to him by the master of the college as a justification for refusing the Epworth incumbency. Then he added, for good measure, his countercharge against Tucker. The rector of All Saints was a heretic who denied the teaching of the church and the importance of Christ's sacrifice by claiming that sinful man could save himself by good works. Even if the allegation was justified, it was irrelevant to the complaint that Tucker had made against him. But sleight of hand deflected Tucker's assault. Diversion was a tactic which Wesley was to use time after time to confound his critics.

The success of field preaching, like the building of meetinghouses, created an irresistible momentum which obliged the Methodist societies to exploit their success in a way which caused even more offense to orthodox opinion. Indeed the popularity of the open-air meetings had an effect on Methodism which was simultaneously to divide it from the Church of England and draw it closer to workingmen and women. The clamor for outdoor sermons was so great that the handful of clergymen willing to respond to the call could not satisfy the needs of all the sinners who were desperate for conversion. The demand could be met only by laymen. And lay preaching led directly to eventual separation from the Established Church.

Lay preaching was not John Wesley's invention. In one form or another it had gone on since man thought it necessary to warn his brothers against sin and urge them to worship a force they could not understand. And like field preaching, it was pioneered as a feature of the revival by Howel Harris, a Welsh Calvinist, who, having been refused holy orders every time he applied for them, had the choice between preaching without episcopal authority or abandoning what he believed to be his vocation. In old age Wesley wrote that the first Methodist to follow Harris's example was Joseph Humphreys. In fact, it was probably Thomas Maxfield, about whom Wesley wrote that he "came and desired to help me as a son of the gospel," an early euphemism for lay preacher. "Soon after came a second, Thomas Richard, and then a third, Thomas Westall." Each of them demanded the right to "speak for the Lord," a claim Wesley dare not deny.[40]

John Wesley could have legitimately claimed that lay preaching began without his knowledge and continued against his wishes—had he been prepared to concede that in those early days, he exercised a limited authority over his followers. But it became one of Methodism's defining characteristics. So a variety of claims about the identity of the first lay preacher have littered Wesleyan history. Wesley's part in discouraging or promoting the practice remains unclear. All that can be said for sure is that there were three pioneers: Humphreys, John Cennick and Maxfield himself.

Joseph Humphreys was a Dissenter before he joined the Methodists, as part of the Whitefield faction, and a member of the Deptford Dissenters' Academy. For a while he rode both religious horses. He was expelled when his teachers discovered that he had begun to preach before ordination. John Cennick was the sort of man all Methodists admire. At the age of thirteen he had walked from Reading to London nine times in the hope of securing an apprenticeship. Failure had not embittered him. In 1735 he decided to "turn to the Lord" and give up singing and cardplaying. On 14 June 1739 he was in the crowd at a Bristol Methodist meeting which was about to be abandoned because the preacher was certainly late and possibly absent. A woman in the crowd who knew him suggested that he deliver the sermon. After drawing lots to determine God's wishes, he spoke with "boldness and a particular freedom in his heart," though he was careful "not to appear like a minister."

Thomas Maxfield was a pastoral helper with the London Methodists. He began preaching entirely on his own initiative and must have known that he was defying the wishes of his leaders. During the spring of 1739, Charles Wesley had supported George Whitefield in the castigation of two London members—Shaw and Wolf—who had claimed the rights of ordination, including the administration of the sacraments. And when they left the Church of England, he endorsed the decision to expel them from the London society. Charles still believed that the proper purpose of Methodism was the propagation of Methodist ideas and ideals among the ordained clergy. John, as always, shared the hope of harmony with the Established Church but was not prepared to jeopardize the future of his new societies or alienate their affection. So he responded to Maxfield's initiative less censoriously. His reaction, a combination of anxiety and irritation, made clear that he would not fight against what had become a popular demand for lay preaching. His letter to his mother, which reported that "Thomas Maxfield has turned preacher," did little more than make it plain that he did not approve of, and had not been party to, the breach of church law. It was not the response of a man who proposed to stamp out a practice which he abhorred.

Susanna chose to reinforce her son's decision to avoid a confrontation. She replied with what was probably an unnecessary warning. "Take care what you do in respect to that young man for he is surely called by God to preach as you are. Examine what have been the fruits of his preaching and hear him yourself."[41] John Wesley was notoriously susceptible to his mother's opinions. So he abandoned whatever thought he might have had of even censuring Maxfield. But to her and to the world, he justified his tolerance with the claim that he was "irresistibly led [to] go further than he at first designed" by pressure from the societies. He bowed before the force of their beliefs and could only say, "Let him do what seemeth to him good."[42] But he was still not sufficiently reconciled to the idea to defend it with any great conviction, even though the appointments of Richards and Westall as "sons of the gospel" a year later were indisputably made on his initiative.

In 1756, after fifteen years of lay preaching had made the innovation more commonplace than controversial within Methodism, he could still only find it in his heart to defend the practice in the most negative terms. "Is not a lay preacher preferable to a drunken preacher, a cursing preacher or a swearing preacher?" That feeble justification, based, as Wesley well knew, on an utterly false antithesis, confirmed his abiding, but sometimes obscured, devotion to the canons of the church.

8

THE ALMOST CHRISTIAN

The controversies over field preaching and lay preachers made Methodism and Methodists famous. On his way to Bristol in the spring of 1739, Wesley stopped at Bath, where he was accosted by Beau Nash, the professional gambler who made the Roman city the most fashionable spa in England. Nash, a great believer in discipline and orthodoxy in all matters except cards, accused Wesley of organizing a conventicle, an unlawful religious assembly. It was the crime for which old Samuel Wesley had denounced his wife when she held meetings in the rectory kitchen, though Nash added the allegation that her son's method of preaching "frightened people out of their wits."[1] Wesley replied with a question. "Did you ever hear me preach?" Nash admitted that he had not but added he did not need to. He had learned enough "by common report" to pass judgment on Wesley's conduct. Wesley responded with a reproof which allowed no further argument. "Sir, I dare not judge you by common report. I think it is not enough to judge by. You, Mr. Nash, take care of your body. We take care of our souls and for the food of our souls we come here."

The incident seems to have emboldened Wesley rather than either intimidated or embarrassed him, for he left the confrontation in an unusually bellicose mood. As he hurried through the streets, he was asked if he really was the great John Wesley and replied, "I am he." But when a group of ladies followed him to his lodgings, he proved less accommodating. As they awaited an audience, they explained that they longed to speak to so great a man. Wesley, told of their request, greeted them with a gratuitous insult. "I believe, ladies, the maid mistook. You only wanted to look at me. I do not expect that the rich and great should want to speak with me or hear me for I speak the plain truth—a thing you hear little of and do not desire to hear."[2] It was that sort of certainty in the righteousness of his cause which saw Wesley though the times of tribulation. When he returned to London, he needed the comfort of all the faith and confidence he possessed.

Until the summer of 1739 almost every influence on Wesley—from à Kempis's *Imitation of Christ* to the fearless behavior of the Moravians on board the *Simmonds*—had persuaded him of the need to be a whole rather than a part Christian. That, he believed, made him a Moravian, and that conviction had been confirmed in the spring of 1738 at Herrnhut, where he had received the confirming assurance from a preacher called Christian David that "many are children of God and heirs of the promises long before they are comforted by the abiding witness of the spirit." This enabled Wesley to believe that even though he was not a complete Christian, he could claim some credit for recognizing the need to struggle for improvement and for struggling on. As a result, he had in effect become a contented Moravian pastor supervising a Moravian meeting-house in Fetter Lane. The rules of the Fetter Lane Society ("in obedience to the command of God") were impeccably Moravian: weekly meetings to confess faults, members to be divided into bands for study and prayer, strict rules of conduct and worship. John Wesley, who instinctively believed in precise organization, might have remained a happy disciple of Count Zinzendorf had he not discovered that not all Moravians held identical views and that a faction, with different beliefs from those of Peter Böhler, who had introduced him to the complexities of the faith, preached a doctrine which he could not tolerate. It was called stillness.

Wesley's doubts about what, to him, was the new theology of

stillness had been preceded, by several months, by doubts about Moravian conduct. During the last week of September 1738, he had drafted a long, critical letter. It was an early indication that he would never be satisfied with any church which he did not dominate. The men and women whom he had so recently revered were accused of neglecting fasting, "levity of behaviour . . . failure to redeem time . . . Use of cunning guile and dissemination."[3] The letter was never sent. But sometime during October a similar list of complaints, couched in more emollient form, did go to Herrnhut.

Real trouble broke out in March 1739, when John Wesley was out of London visiting the Bristol Society and Charles was left in charge of Fetter Lane. The members challenged Charles's authority and pressed him to accept the propriety of lay preaching. John Wesley was still a month away from "submitting to be more vile," and Charles was then unequivocally against a breach in church "manners." As always, he expressed his view trenchantly and, in consequence, alienated society members who entered the argument with an open mind. Wesley returned to London to restore peace. For some months there was an uneasy truce. Then the more zealous among the Moravians began to argue for the extreme version of their faith. In the absence of both Wesleys they began to teach that "none has any justifying faith, who has ever had doubt or fear, which you know you have, or who has not a clean heart, which you know you have not, nor will you ever have it till you leave off running to church and sacrament . . . for you cannot use these things without trusting in them."[4] "Stillness" was anathema to Wesley.

On 18 October 1739, Philip Henry Molther arrived in London. Molther, a native of Alsace and a graduate of the University of Jena, was a member of the Moravian elite. He had been tutor to Zinzendorf's only son and, that assignment being satisfactorily completed, became a roving missionary. Molther was on his way to America when he paused to examine the prospects of spreading the Moravian faith within the Church of England. When he arrived, Böhler had left for Herrnhut, John Wesley was on another of his visits to Bristol and Charles Wesley, in temporary charge, was not a popular preacher. Naturally enough, the members asked Molther to address their Sunday meeting. Despite his habit of preaching in Latin, he became a favorite with the Fetter Lane congregation, a tribute to the members' scholarship or the emphasis they placed on the force rather than the content of a sermon. Molther did not reciprocate their admiration. The Fetter Lane Society, he complained, had "adopted many extraordinary habits." He particularly deplored "their sighing and groaning, their whining and howling, which strange proceedings they called the demonstration of Spirit Power."[5] His determination to stamp out such alien practices seems to have made him a hero among members whose high level of emotional commitment made them susceptible to high-handed authority.

Molther had spent two weeks in London by the time that John Wesley returned. In that brief time he had made stillness the society's accepted doctrine. The first person Wesely saw when he entered Fetter Lane was a woman whom "he had left strong in faith and zealous in good works: but who now told him that Molther had fully convinced her she never had any faith at all and had advised her, till she received faith, to be still, ceasing from outward works."[6] That, in itself, was enough to set Wesley irrevocably against Molther. But that was not his only objection to the regime which the Moravian had imposed on Fetter Lane. A dozen or so members, who were close to Molther, were taking decisions "as if they were the whole society."[7] That, in Wesley's view, offended against the Methodist belief in "Christian openness and plain speaking." It was an offense against Wesley's pride and authority, but it was also, in his opinion, damaging to Methodism's prospects in working-class England. The colliers of Kingswood, who had become the paragons and paradigm of Methodist evangelism, were well known "for neither fearing God nor regarding men." They could be encompassed only in an inclusive religion.

At the first meeting of the society which he attended after his return Wesley found that the Molther faction was not simply arguing for "stillness" but that it had imposed the doctrine on the whole membership, a fortnight's achievement which illustrated how dependent faith is on the emotional appeal of the moment. One man spoke "of the danger that attended doing outward works and the folly of people running about to church and sacrament."[8] After a long period of silence "some of the brethren" asserted the importance of the new doctrine. "Till they have true faith they ought to be still, that is to abstain from the means of grace, the Lord's Supper in particular."

Wesley was in a mood to challenge Molther. For he had acquired the confidence which came from the calm reassessment of beliefs that had once been held with an unsettling fervor. He remained certain that "to be saved," a man or woman had to become "a whole Christian." As late as 1741 he still spoke in the language of absolute change from potential damnation to sinless perfection. "Whosoever hath this faith which purifies the heart, by the power of God who dwelleth therein, from pride, anger, desire, from all unrighteousness, from filthiness of flesh and spirit is not almost but altogether a Christian."[9] But he was gradually coming to believe that "entire sanctification" might be approached in three stages: justification (which frees from the guilt of sin), regeneration (which frees from the power of sin) and sanctification (which frees from sin itself). In consequence, he had formed the comforting conclusion that "a man may have some degree [of faith] before all things in him have become new before he has the full advantage of faith."[10] When Wesley described his revised position at a meeting with Zinzendorf, it was dismissed out of hand. "Justification and sanctification are in the same instant." The convert "receives neither more nor less."[11] And there was an equally fundamental difference between the two men's theology. Wesley believed that worship was the path to salvation; Zinzendorf held that worship before redemption guaranteed damnation. John Wesley could not accept the notion that anyone who was not completely sanctified must be denied the sacraments. But it was not only the notion of stillness which disturbed him. He had begun to fear that the Moravian emphasis on redemption by faith alone, though undoubtedly right in itself, was, when combined with their other doctrines, dangerously close to antinomianism, the belief that faith so transcends all other virtues that once one is redeemed, behavior which might be sinful in others does nothing to diminish the sanctified state.

Antinomianism was, to both Wesley and the Church of England, the gospel of sinful living. It was also a challenge to priestly author-ity. For an antinomian could live in whatever way he chose, undis-turbed by the guidance or censure of the church. But the Moravian doctrine was setting the Fetter Lane Society alight with religious fer-vor. On his return to London after a few days in Bristol, he found that "scarce one in ten [members] retained his faith."[12] The society was in "utter confusion," and meetings ended (metaphorically we must hope) in "biting and devouring each other."[13]

Wesley's critics argued that the real objection to Molther's mission was more personal than theological and that Wesley was unable to serve in a society which he did not lead. In March 1740, James Hutton, who had become an out-and-out Moravian, wrote to Zinzendorf to say that Wesley, "being determined to do all things himself and having told many souls that they were justified who have since discovered themselves to be otherwise . . . is at enmity against the Brethren. Envy is not extinct in him." As the letter continued, at least Hutton's enmity toward his old friend became increasingly ob-vious, another sign of the high emotional level at which followers of the revival lived. "He seeks occasion against the Brethren but I hope he will find none in us. I desired him simply to keep to his office in the body of Christ and awaken souls in preaching but not pretend to lead them to Christ. But he will have the glory of doing all things. I fear, by and by, he will be an open enemy of Christ and his Church." He then went on to explain why Benjamin Ingham, to whom Wesley had written as a friend seeking advice and guidance, had replied in terms so vague that they added to the doubts rather than resolved them. "In Yorkshire," Hutton wrote, "Ingham and W. Delamotte are united to the Brethren. Some thousand souls are awakened." Wesley was losing adherents to both the Lutherans and the Moravians.[14] Hutton could not resist adding a personal note. "Both John Wesley and Charles are dangerous snares to many young women. Several are in love with them. I wish they were married to some good sisters, though I would not give them to one of mine, even if I had many."[15] Accurate though that opinion might have been, its inclusion in Hutton's letter illustrates how bitter the battle had become.

For a while there was an uneasy truce while Wesley and Molther held a series of desultory meetings at which minds rarely met. But whatever hopes of a reconciliation there might have been were extinguished by the behavior of the Moravian rank and file. Brother Ridley interpreted the doctrine of stillness in such extreme terms that he asserted, "You may as well go to hell for praying as for thieving," and John Browne told the Moravian Brethren, "If we read, the devil reads with us. If we pray, he prays with us. If we go to church or sacrament he goes with us."[16] Then the antinomianism, which Wesley feared, suddenly erupted. "We believers are no more bound to obey [the law of the land] than the subjects of the King of England are bound to obey the laws of the King of France." And one of Molther's adherents, who still qualified for the title Brother Bell, claimed that "the sacraments were like poison to a man who was not sanctified."

The battle was then taken up by one of the Brethren, contemptuously described by Charles Wesley as "poor perverted Mr. Simpson." He tried to resolve the dispute by converting Charles Wesley to the Moravian position. At their meeting he "laid down two postulates. (1) The ordinances are not commands. (2) It is impossible to doubt after justification." Had that not been enough to antagonize Charles, Simpson confirmed his undying animosity by announcing that "No unjustified person ought to receive the sacrament; for, doing so, he ate and drank his own damnation." Some members went to even more indefensible extremes. "It is," one of Simpson's associates declared, "impossible for any one to be a true Christian out of the Moravian Church." Simpson then suggested that John Wesley should return to London and make another attempt to find areas of agreement. Wesley agreed, and the two men met on 23 April 1740. Once again all Simpson could offer was a reassertion of the Moravian position. "Believers are not subject to ordinances and believers have nothing to do with them." All the hope of rapprochement which remained lay in a meeting between Molther and the Wesleys. "After a fruitless dispute of about two hours," John Wesley "returned home with a heavy heart."[17]

Two days later the Wesleys met Molther again. No one was in a mood to compromise. Molther was unwell. So sure was John Wesley of his own righteousness that he wrote, "I believe it was the hand of God that was upon him." Armed with this certainty, the Wesleys cross-examined the Moravian. Molther was unrepentant. Indeed he treated the brothers like moral inadequates. "He now explicitly confirmed that 1) there are *no degrees* in faith; that none has any faith who has any doubt or fear and that none is justified till he has a clean heart . . . 2) that every one who has not this ought, till he has it, to be *still*. . . . He also expressly asserted that to those who have a clean heart, the ordinances are not a matter of duty,"[18] John Wesley replied in similarly unyielding language. His next sermon took as its text "Thou fool, that which thou sawest is not quickened except to die." The longer the dispute went on, the more bitter the debate became. Then, after several weeks of acrimony, Molther decided to bring it to an end. On Wednesday, 16 July, the Fetter Lane Society was asked "whether they would suffer" Mr. Wesley to preach at Fetter Lane. After a short debate, the answer came "No." The society "continued in useless debate till about eleven."[19]

Two days later, after consulting his mother and other confidants, John Wesley decided how he should respond to the prohibition. He agreed to attend the love feast on the following Sunday, where although he could not preach, he could bear witness. In fact, he read a paper which summed up his arguments against Molther's theology. Its valediction was wholly uncompromising. "I have warned you, hereof again and again and besought you to turn back to the law and testimony. I have borne with you long, hoping you would turn. But as I find you more and more confused in the error of your ways nothing remains but I shall give you up to God you that are of the same."[20] On that dramatic note, he left Fetter Lane forever, followed by eighteen or nineteen members of the congregation. Fortunately another home awaited him at the Foundry.

John Wesley came to repent the years during which he had been captivated by the Moravians. Indeed he felt so guilty about his infatuation that he pretended it had ended long before the schism came to a head at the Fetter Lane meetinghouse. His account of his Moravian experience in his *Journal* is a classic example of history rewritten. Perhaps, in the certainty of his righteousness, Wesley was able to convince himself that the past was how he wished it to be. Whatever his success in deluding himself, he constantly sought to deceive others.

Despite its name, the *Journal* was not a record of Wesley's life and times written more or less contemporaneously with the events it described. The real story was told in the diaries, which were begun in 1725 and continued in an attenuated form (and often in code) until shortly before his death. The *Journal* was, at least initially, a response to attacks on John Wesley's integrity and intended as a public refutation of criticism of his conduct and character. In 1739 Robert Williams, a ship's captain who had done business in Georgia, published a sworn affidavit which described Wesley's "romance" with Sophy Hopkey and his consequent ignominious flight from the colony. It was, at the time, Wesley's habit to circulate handwritten notes and commentaries at the end of each meeting. Initially he judged that a reply to Williams in his Sunday night broadsheet was all that was needed. But as the story spread beyond Bristol, a more extensive refutation seemed necessary. In May 1740 Wesley published what was described as an "extract" from his *Journal*. It refuted Captain Williams's allegations. The notion of public vindication clearly appealed to him. He decided, just before publication, to add as a preface the letter which he had written in 1732 to Richard Morgan after the death of his son. It defended Oxford Methodism's strict rules of life and basic theology.

Five months later a second "extract" was published. It dealt with Wesley's "Moravian period" and was designed to demonstrate that although he had once seemed totally to accept their doctrine, he had recognized the shortcomings of some of their doctrines as early as his visit to Herrnhut. The allegation of theological inconsistency was anticipated and dismissed. According to the *Journal*'s highly selective accounts of Wesley's visit, some of the wiser elders of the church warned him against Moravian extremism during the summer of 1738. Chief among them was Christian David, who, it was claimed, described how easy it was for Moravians to fall into error. The clear implication of the account of David's criticisms was that Wesley accepted them but retained a sympathy for the views of the more moderate Brethren. "[A] great remissness of behaviour had crept among us . . . so insisting on faith as to forget, at least in practice, both holiness and good works . . . I saw that, least of all we ought to insist on the full assurance of faith, or the destruction of bodily sin and the destruction of all its motions as to exclude those who had not attained it from the Lord's Table or to deny that they had any faith at all."[21] The attempt to persuade his readers that he had always realized that there were two sorts of Moravian and that although he identified with the moderates, he had recognized and rejected the extremists from the start was more calculating than convincing. The dissembling confirmed that Wesley was beginning to develop a sense of history as well as destiny. Both feelings were encouraged by the increasingly clear identity of the connexion, which he led, a theological clarification which was as much forced upon him as chosen. If 1738 was the year of miracles, 1740 was the year of schisms.

Wesley had been advised, before he left for Bristol in March 1739, to "enter into no disputes, least of all concerning predestination, because the people were so deeply attached to it."[22] But he was incapable of suppressing the deepest of all his convictions: that Christ died to save all sinners. So he preached the doctrine of universal redemption in Bristol while Charles Wesley preached it in London. The result was, as Whitefield had predicted, divisions within the societies which had begun to spring up in London, Bristol and on the route Wesley and Whitefield covered in between. The first split came at Bradford-on-Avon, the second at Deptford. During the following year, the divisions deepened. Initially, Wesley and Whitefield hoped to minimize the damage. But Whitefield, growing tired of emollience, extended the argument to a denunciation of John Wesley's view of final perseverance, the belief that although only a *few* blessed souls receive earthly assurance of their final salvation, *everyone* can feel assured of present redemption and should be confident that God's love will continue until their salvation is guaranteed. And the doctrinal disputes intensified. Whitefield, on the other hand, found joy in believing in his certain salvation, even if he remained a poor sinner. So he rejected Wesley's promise of "sinless perfection." Imperfect though he was, he expected a place by the throne because he was one of the elect, a status to which many other sinners could not even aspire.

Whitefield's followers complained that the Wesleys' continual return to the contentious doctrines which divided Calvinists from the Arminians was proof of their desire to create "a Church within themselves and to give themselves the sacraments of bread and wine."[23] That was true of neither brother. Charles wanted to defend, if necessary to the death, the rites and ceremonies of the Church of England. John wanted to clarify his own beliefs. He could do it only through public argument.

Inevitably the revival involved the reexamination of long-held beliefs. Wesley, introspective and intellectual, was temperamentally incapable of holding a firm position for long. For a time he had respected the obligation which he had been instrumental in imposing in Bristol and London. Methodists in both cities had been prohibited from "discoursing on any controversial point of divinity." The laudable objective of the revival's leadership—Whitefield at least as much as Wesley—was to hold the revival together rather than stifle legitimate debate. But some of the deepest divisions were so fundamental that it was impossible to maintain the theological truce for long.

Until 1740 both men avoided a head-on collision over the great principle which divided them, the hope of universal redemption, which was the basis of Wesley's belief and a direct denial of Whitefield's conviction that only the preordained elect would find a place in heaven. The two priests admired as well as respected each other. So there was a personal element in the concordat, and even when it broke down, they remained friends. At the height of the controversy which brought about their effective separation, Wesley was still able to write about their disagreements in the most emollient terms. "For a time you are suffered to be of one opinion and I of another."[24] And Whitefield, discussing the leadership of the revival, was almost certainly sincere when he said, "Though you came after, I heartily wish that you may be preferred before me." For him the disciplines of leadership had no attraction. But as is so often the case with movements built on passionately held beliefs, the membership of both factions was less conciliatory than their leadership. And both Wesley and Whitefield felt a moral duty to defend their followers as well as their beliefs.

The great schism came about because in Whitefield's opinion, Wesley "did not act with a Catholic spirit" toward John Acourt after Charles had excluded him from the London society. Acourt claimed that he had been excluded because of a difference of opinion with the Wesley brothers. Asked which opinions he meant, he replied, "That of election. I hold a certain number is elected from eternity and these must and shall be saved; and the rest of mankind shall be damned."[25] Then he added, much to Charles's chagrin, "And many of your society hold the same." John Wesley always argued that Acourt's offense was less apostasy than troublemaking. The insistence that Acourt had not been denied membership because of his sympathy for Calvinism was plausible, if not totally convincing. Many existing members (including Joseph Humphreys and John Cennick, who had been given authority in Bristol) were Calvinists, and no one had objected to their membership in the societies. Acourt, however, was, Wesley claimed, guilty of "disputing" rather than respecting the injunction to "follow after holiness and things that make for peace."[26] If welcomed into full membership, he would, Wesley feared, damage Methodism's frail unity. His ruthless treatment of Acourt was clearly the result of his anxiety to hold the revival together. Then, apparently for no reason, on 29 April 1739 he willfully shattered the uneasy peace with a sermon titled "Free Grace."

Wesley's *Journal* records the event in matter-of-fact language. "I declared the free grace of God to about four thousand people from these words. 'He that spareth not His own son, but delivered Him up for us all, how shall he not, with Him, also freely give us all things?' "[27] But he must have realized the offense he would cause by his open assault on the idea of predestination. And he must have known that the anger would be immensely increased by the language he used to describe the doctrine. We can only assume that he was looking for trouble. "Call it by whatever name you please, election, preterition, predestination or reprobation, it comes in the end to the same thing. The sense of all is plainly this—by virtue of an eternal, unchangeable, irresistible decree of God, one part of mankind is infallibly saved and the rest infallibly damned."[28]

That analysis could be described as no more than a robust reiteration of the belief that Christ died to save all sinners, though it was hardly consistent with the promise to avoid theological controversy. However, what follows reads as if it were designed as a declaration of all-out war. "There is blasphemy clearly contained in the *horrible decree* of preordination. And here I fix my foot. And on this I take issue with every assertion to it. You represent God as worse than the Devil. But you say that you will prove by scripture. Hold! It cannot do."[29]

Whitefield's reaction, when the contents of the sermon were reported to him, was remarkably calm. Even when Wesley talked of publishing "Free Grace" as a pamphlet, Whitefield's principal concern still seemed to be the cohesion of the societies. Wesley consulted his friends and then drew lots to determine God's will. As was so often the case, God's will coincided with Wesley's own preference. The pamphlet was published on 29 May with what can only be described as a sanctimonious foreword. "Nothing but the strongest conviction . . . could have induced me openly to oppose the sentiments of those I esteem for their works' sake; at whose feet may I be found at the day of judgement."

The apologia ended with what, given the tone of the sermon, might be regarded as an impertinence. "Should any believe it is his duty to reply hereto, I have only one request to make—let whatever you do be done in charity, love and the spirit of meekness." Charles Wesley, at variance with his brother over some aspects of faith but equally opposed to the doctrine of preordination, composed a hymn on the same theme as the sermon. It was titled "Hymn on Universal Redemption," and its thirty-six verses were published as an appendix to *Free Grace*.

> And Shall I, Lord, confine Thy love
> As not to others free?
> And may not every sinner prove
> The grace that found out me?

Doom them an endless death to die
From which they could not flee
O Lord, Thine inmost bowels cry
Against this dire decree!

Whitefield left for America in November 1739, a month in which John was properly preoccupied with the death of his brother Samuel. Perhaps he was not preoccupied in quite the appropriate way. For although Samuel Wesley died wholly unreconciled to the Methodists' deviant theology, John (with an effrontery which often accompanies moral certainty) announced that at the last, the schoolmaster had accepted at least some of the tenets of the true faith. "My poor sister was sorrowing almost as one without hope. Yet we could not but rejoice at hearing from one who had attended my brother in all his weakness, that several days before he went hence, God had given him calm and full assurance. . . . Oh, may everyone who opposes it be thus convinced that this doctrine is of God."[30]

In the same month Methodism took a major step toward becoming an autonomous, if not an independent, church by the establishment of its own headquarters. Two men, unknown to John Wesley at the time and unknown to us still, suggested that he should preach on the site of the old, ruined Royal Foundry. With some reluctance (for he had other commitments that evening) he agreed and "preached on that day at eight o'clock to five or six thousand on the spirit of bondage, and the spirit of adoption and at five in the evening, to seven or eight thousand." Conscious of the warlike history of the place where he had preached, John Wesley ended the letter, which described his triumph, with a prayer to hasten the time "when nation shall not rise up against nation, neither shall they learn war any more." He made no mention of the satisfaction that he felt in attracting so large a gathering to a previously unknown meeting place.

Cannons had not been made at the Foundry since 1716, when an explosion, during the recasting of captured French ordnance, had so damaged the building that the armory and arsenal had been moved to Woolwich. The ruin was for sale at what the strangers believed to be a bargain price. They suggested that the Methodists should buy it. Wesley rashly agreed. The purchase price, £115, was borrowed in the belief that it would be repaid by Methodist members at the rate of four, six and ten shillings a year. But the Foundry was derelict. At least another £600 was needed to make it a habitable meeting place, particularly since Wesley wanted the new building to include "a board room" to be used for occasional prayer meetings, a school-room, a book room, a coach house and accommodation for himself and two other preachers. In three years the subscriptions totaled £480, leaving Wesley almost £300 in debt. But Methodism had acquired a permanent headquarters from which when the inevitable day came, both the Moravian and the Lutheran gospel could be rejected. And John Wesley had a home.

The new home, perhaps properly described as a refuge, was made all the more necessary by the belated response to Wesley's attack on predestination. For some time after he arrived in America, it seemed that Whitefield had decided to turn the other cheek. He sold copies of the Wesleys' *Hymns and Sacred Poems,* many of which were a contradiction of his most cherished articles of faith. But he also sent Wesley several reproachful letters. From Savannah on 26 March 1740 he wrote to "beseech" Wesley "by the mercies of God in Christ Jesus Our Lord" to "write no more about misrepresentations wherein we differ. . . . Dispute when there is no probability of convincing" would "only destroy brotherly love." When he arrived in Cape Lopen two months later, he declared, in something approaching anguish, "I think it best to stay here where we all think and say the same thing. The work goes on without division and with more success because all employed are of one mind." Back in Savannah in June he begged Wesley, "For Christ's sake let us not be divided amongst ourselves." In Charleston, on 25 August, he confessed, "I cannot bear the thought of opposing you, but how can I avoid it if you go about, as your brother once said, to drive John Calvin out of Bristol." In Boston at the end of September he included a mild rebuke in an otherwise emollient letter. "O that you would be more cautious in casting lots." It ended with the extraordinary assertion "I never read anything that Calvin wrote. My doctrines I had from

Christ and his Apostles."[31] All in all it seems that Whitefield wanted to avoid trouble. The same could not be said for Wesley.

However, both of the chief protagonists carried on their disputes with a degree of discretion. Their supporters felt no obligation to do the same. Whitefield's Boston letter of 25 September suggested that Wesley had wanted to cause a national controversy. But it also revealed a real concern for the abuse which was being heaped on his friend Wesley. "I find your sermon has had its expected success. It has set the nation a-disputing. You will have enough to do now to answer pamphlets. Two I have already seen."[32] One of them, *Free Grace Indeed!*, provoked Wesley beyond moderation. "I cannot answer the tract till it appears to be more in earnest. For I dare not speak of the deep things of God in the spirit of a prize fighter or stage player."[33] Supporters of the two causes took up arms. Howel Harris wrote to John Wesley telling him that belief in "elective love brings glory to God" and to John Cennick with the news that William Seward, Whitefield's friend and companion on his first American visit, was "dividing with brother Charles" Wesley and that he would do the same unless the Wesleys "receive further light and be silent and not oppose election and perseverance."

Despite the attractions of remaining among the united societies of America, George Whitefield arrived back in England in March 1741. It cannot have been long before he began to regret his decision to return to the land of controversy. In October, William Seward became Methodism's first martyr. Pelted with rotten eggs in Newport, blinded in Caerleon, Seward pressed on to Monmouth with the consolation "Better to endure this than hell." At Hay-on-Wye he was hit over the head and died of a fractured skull. John Wesley, asked to preach a memorial sermon, added outrage to grief by celebrating the life and work of the Calvinist hero with a passionate defense of universal redemption.

Debts of almost £1,000, all of them incurred by Seward, awaited Whitefield's return. One bill for £350 had been outstanding for so long that he was threatened with arrest and imprisoned in the Marshalsea. James Hutton, who had been his publisher, greeted him with the news that he could expect to earn no more from books and pamphlets; "dressing up election in such horrible colours"[34] had prejudiced Methodists against anything written by a Calvinist or in defense of preordination. Worse was to follow. The public confrontation which he had hoped to avoid was to be brought about by the malevolence of an unknown zealot.

During his stay in America, Whitefield had become "ten thousand times more convinced" that the elect were intended to go to heaven, irrespective of their conduct on earth. But he had come to realize that it was a conviction which he would have to defend with determination and courage, particularly against the charge of "antinomianism." St. Mark had asked in his gospel (2:1–3), "Were not the representatives of the law the chief enemies of Christ?" Such questions were open to sinful misinterpretation by the ignorant. Wesley had increased the temperature and lowered the tone of the argument by blurring the true interpretation of the passage with the suggestion that it sanctioned immorality. It was a debasement of his dispute with Whitefield which he probably came to regret. For he never included the "Free Grace" sermon in any of the published volumes of his collected works. Whitefield thought a reply was essential. During his last couple of months in America, his thoughts naturally turning toward home, he decided that on his return, it would be necessary to defend the doctrine of predestination against such charges. So in September 1740 he drafted, though he did not publish, his reply to the sermon on "Free Grace." Whitefield attacked Wesley at his weakest point, his willingness to make words mean what he wanted them to mean. "Free Grace" was based upon a "false definition of the word free" and an "equivocal definition of the word grace." He also questioned Wesley's biblical scholarship. St. Paul's Epistle to the Romans (8:32) did not, Whitefield insisted, mean what Wesley thought it meant. "He that spareth not his own Son, but delivereth him up for us all, how shall he not with him also freely give us all things?" was, he claimed, proof of election, not universal redemption.

However, Whitefield was still not ready for the final confrontation. During the voyage across the Atlantic he had written a clearly conciliatory, if conspicuously injured, letter to Charles Wesley. It referred to the poem which was printed at the end of *Free Grace.*

"How can you say you will not dispute with me about election but still print such hymns?" Perhaps he hoped that Charles would act as a mediator with John. But he must have known that were it to be published, the tone of his riposte to "Free Grace" would make reconciliation impossible. As well as questioning John Wesley's logic and theology, it cast doubts on his personal conduct, including what Whitefield claimed to be an extravagance in the use of the societies' funds. He attributed the profligacy to vanity rather than to greed. Perhaps even more divisive, it dismissed some of his most cherished beliefs as trivial. "What a fond conceit is it to cry up perfection and cry down the doctrine of final perseverance."[35] Wesley would undoubtedly have published such a pamphlet at once. Whitefield stayed his hand.

Immediate publication would have revealed that poor Whitefield was confused, as many other theologians have been, by Wesley's beliefs on the subject of perfection. Wesley's views were wholly consistent but hideously complicated. He rejected absolutely the Calvinistic notion of an elect who possessed "irresistible grace" that guaranteed them a preordained passage to heaven. But he did believe that a minority of true Christians received "absolute assurance" of their "final salvation" and that the rest could be confident that God's love—"expelling all sin"—offered "present salvation," which might well remain with them forever. Even the Christian who was so filled with the love of God that all sin "was excluded" would need, from time to time, to revive the holy state which he or she enjoyed. Methodism was a far more complicated faith than the emoting crowds at the prayer meetings realized.

Notwithstanding the aggressive tone and critical content of his pamphlet, George Whitefield showed it to Charles Wesley and asked for his reaction. Charles replied, "Put up again thy sword into its place,"[36] a suggestion which Whitefield took to mean that he should not defend his beliefs against the assault of *Free Grace*. Perhaps he was moved to reconciliation by Charles Wesley's metaphor. For he made no attempt to publish the pamphlet himself. Or although it would have been inconsistent with his character, he might have decided on surreptitious publication. However it came about, a copy of his letter was obtained by a member of the Methodists' London congregation, possibly John Cennick. It was printed in full and distributed during the morning service at the Foundry on 1 February 1741, without the formal permission of either writer or addressee. When a copy was passed to John Wesley, he related (after preaching) the naked fact to the congregation and told them, "I will do just what I believe. Mr. Whitefield would were he here himself."[37] He then made a great show of tearing up the offending document and "everyone who had received a copy did the same."[38] But the damage which had been done was irreparable. Wesley and Whitefield maintained their ambivalent friendship throughout their lives, writing to each other, sometimes sincerely, in the language of veneration. But Whitefield's response completed the work begun by the "Free Grace" sermon. A formal split of the members, if not the leaders, of the Methodist Connexion was unavoidable.

On 27 April, after a perfunctory meeting that resolved nothing, John Wesley set out his formal reply to Whitefield's accusations. The letter aimed at refuting all the charges in the broad indictment. Some of his points clarified questions of esoteric scholarship. It was wrong to accuse him of the Scotist heresy since the Scotists (far from believing in universal redemption) held that *Tota redemptionis nostrae Christium metaphora*.[39] He then moved on to repute allegations of extravagance by reminding Whitefield that the table in the Bristol meeting room was decorated with no more than "a piece of green cloth . . . and two sconces for eight candles in the middle." The banality to which the argument between the main proponents descended was relatively harmless—at least when compared with the way in which their supporters behaved.

One pamphlet written in support of Wesley described Whitefield as a man of heated imagination "who was full of himself. Very hot and impatient of contradiction." Aquila Smyth, a Whitefieldite, accused Wesley of "pride, envy and malice." The Reverend Alexander Gordon called Whitefield's pamphlet "arrogance and wicked slander" built on "false and poisoned insinuation." "The Error Expanded," by "R——ph J——psn of the Inner Temple," described Whitefield's position as "one of the greatest absurdities and impositions that folly or impudence could invent . . . a correspondence with evil." The Methodists began to divide. Lady Huntingdon, who had always regarded Whitefield as the true leader of the movement which she helped to support in Bristol, formed the Connexion of Calvinist Preachers. In Wales, the Calvinist Methodist Church was founded. Cennick and Humphreys broke their links with the Bristol and London societies.

John Wesley showed every outward sign of thriving on the controversies. But there is no doubt that he began to worry about being so isolated in his novel doctrinal position. When in April 1741, shortly after the Kingswood Society had revolted against his Arminian views and Joseph Humphreys had refused to help in a purge of the membership, Charles chided him for not defending the Established Church, his response to his brother was as near to self-pity as his resilient character allowed. "Five of us did stand together a few months since but two are gone to the right hand (poor Humphreys and Cennick) and two more are to the left (Mr. Hall and you)." A man of less robust constitution and conviction might have sought some kind of respite from the conflict in the quiet relaxation of a more gentle occupation. Wesley found comfort in work. In the summer of 1741 (despite all the other burdens upon him) he began the exercises required for his admission to the degree of Bachelor of Divinity, the qualification needed for preferment within the church and promotion within the university. And he did not choose dissertations on subjects which allowed him temporary escape from the theological turmoil. His *Genesis* examined predestination, means of grace and justification. The initial choice of text for his compulsory sermon was "How hath the city become a harlot?," a question probably provoked by the discovery that his Oxford Society had been "torn asunder and scattered abroad." But he was dissuaded from provoking the wrath of the whole university and turned his energies to preparing to preach before the university on "The Almost Christian." The idea of all or nothing was still haunting him.

9

ALL THINGS HIMSELF

By 1742 Wesley could speak—at least for the moment—with the voice of a man who possessed settled conviction. But he had arrived at that happy, if temporary, state after three years of turmoil. He had always believed in God's universal love and was, by nature, implacably opposed to the idea of stillness. So the three years leading up to 1742 were less concerned with the acquisition of new beliefs than with the abandonment of old friends who had accepted the novel heresy. But the process was painful. For he retained his respect and affection for the leaders of the Moravian Church and the Calvinist Methodists, with whom he had broken in the spring and summer of the same year. Long after each schism was irreparable, Wesley maintained relations of a sort with both Zinzendorf and Whitefield. But after the events of 1740 he was essentially dependent on his own spiritual resources. The only doctrine on which he could rely was Methodism. And because his theology was becoming more and more exclusive, he inevitably moved on (strode or stumbled according to rival judgments about his motivation) toward increasing independence. Doctrinal isolation and improved organization advanced side by side.

Wesley still really believed—or at least persuaded himself—that his behavior did not or should not bring him into conflict with the

Church of England establishment. And he adopted a tactic which has been favored by heretics down the ages, declarations of support for established doctrine, matched by practices which clearly flouted the rules he claimed to respect. In September 1739, when the campaign to brand him an apostate had barely begun, he had assured "a serious cleric" that "the doctrines we preach are the doctrines of the Church of England clearly laid down in Prayers, Articles and Homilies."[1] The following month he preached in Abergavenny on a text from chapter 28, verse 22 of the Acts of the Apostles. "But we desire to hear of thee what thou thinkest. For as concerning this sect we know everywhere it is spoken against." When it was demonstrated beyond dispute that he was in conflict with the church establishment, he began to adopt another favorite tactic of unrepentant dissidents. He claimed that he was the voice of the true religion. The heretics were the usurpers who had imposed their deviant views on the church. "The plain old religion of the Church of England . . . is now almost everywhere spoken against under the new name of Methodism."[2] His confidence was reinforced by Bishop Edmund Gibson, who, on hearing that Wesley's definition of perfection was no more than the hope of not committing sin, told him, in an absolution which must have been as deflating as it was reassuring, "If this is all you mean, publish it to all the world." Few other churchmen were so accommodating. And the mob, always ready, in eighteenth-century England, to take to the streets, had decided that he was both a heretic and a traitor.

The identification of Methodism as a distinct religion, with an independent theology and autonomous network of societies and meetinghouses, made the connexion vulnerable to assault from all those faithful Christians who despised and feared any change from the conventions of the Established Church. The assault was sometimes philosophical. Then it was usually led by the *Gospel Magazine*. More often it was physical and led by the mob. After 1739 Methodism and Methodists were under attack all over England. The mob's real objection was that Methodists were different, a minority that could be identified by both its habits and its self-righteous attitude. All sorts of explanations were invented to justify the physical assaults on preachers and congregations. Methodists were Antichrists who derided the true religion. They encouraged honest workmen to spend their days in prayer rather than in labor. The prejudice was influenced by hysteria. It was the Methodists' misfortune to come together at a time when every sort of association was suspect. The combination of workingmen was proscribed by the 1720 and 1740 acts of Parliament. Yet Wesley asked them to combine in a religious union. The rumors of the Wesleys' treacherous inclinations were particularly rife in Cornwall. In Yorkshire, Charles Wesley was accused of "treasonable words and exhortations in so much as he prayed for the soul of the banished Pretender." The Wesleys were accused of being Jacobite sympathizers who hoped to restore the Catholic Stuarts to the throne of England.

The accusation, based, at best, on Methodism's belief in disciplined worship which was easily confused with ritual, was bizarre but profoundly dangerous. During the Jacobite rebellion of 1715, Dissenters had demonstrated a passionate attachment to the House of Hanover—or at least an undying antagonism to the House of Stuart. Their loyalty had begun a process which eventually allowed Butler and Secker, originally Dissenters themselves, to become princes of the Church of England. That process had included the relaxation of the penal acts which prevented Dissenters from running their own schools and prohibited their membership in corporations unless they agreed to take the sacraments. In 1723 Walpole, reinforcing the Whig hegemony, asked Parliament to vote funds to provide grants for Dissenting ministers' widows. Their improved status was at least in part the result of their growing numbers. Daniel Defoe, himself a Dissenter, reported in his *Tour* of visiting Southwold, where a church which could "hold a congregation of five thousand" attracted twenty-seven parishioners to matins. Eight hundred worshipers packed the nearby Dissenters' chapel. But whatever the reason for the new tolerance, Dissenters were treated differently from Catholics. Associating Wesley with the popish threat against the state had the effect of encouraging the mob to attack Methodists.

In eighteenth-century England, poverty, increased by the pressures of landless peasants moving from the countryside into the new towns of the incipient Industrial Revolution, bred violence. It was a feature of the period's pastimes: bearbaiting, cockfighting and bare-fisted pugilism. It was reflected in a legal system which prescribed death by hanging for a child convicted of stealing a shilling handker-chief. And it was manifest in the mobs which were sometimes roused to action by politicians and sometimes came together sponta-neously to damage, destroy and tyrannize for sport. Methodism was an irresistible target.

The anti-Methodist riots had certainly begun by 1740, though it was three years before they became a regular feature of open-air meetings. No doubt John Wesley was briefly encouraged by the be-havior of the mayor of Bristol, who not only arrested the ringleaders of the anti-Methodist mob when they failed to disperse but refused to hear arguments about Methodist heresy as a mitigation of the offense. In the autumn of the same year Wesley was surrounded by angry pro-testers as he climbed down from his coach at the Foundry. According to his own account of the incident, after he addressed them on the subject of righteousness and the judgment to come, their mood changed. "They all showed me much love and dismissed me with many blessings."[3] But two days later they were back and actually in-vaded the meeting room. Again the lions lay down with the lamb, and Wesley reported, much to his own satisfaction, "I wonder that the Devil has not wisdom enough to discern that he is destroying his own kingdom. I believe he has never yet, at any one time, caused this open opposition to the truth of God without losing one of his own servants, who were found of God while they sought Him not."[4] And there was some reason to suppose that the popular mood had begun to change. In December 1741, Sir John Ganson, chairman of the Middlesex magistrates, visited Wesley to tell him, "So you have no need to suf-fer these riotous mobs to molest you, as they have done long. I and all the other Middlesex magistrates have orders from above to do you justice whenever you apply to us."[5] The Middlesex magistrates were as good as their chairman's word.

Henry Moore, one of the biographers who can claim to have dis-cussed his work with his subject, wrote that Wesley had told him who was the source of the "orders from above" which guaranteed

Ganson's offer of protection. According to Wesley's account, an Oxford merchant, who had moved to Kew, met King George while walking in the royal gardens. The two men fell into conversation, and their talk moved on from trade with the colonies to the state of religion in England. Their discussion turned to Methodism and the Wesleys, whom the king described as "making a great noise in the nation." The merchant, who had become a Quaker, rebuked his sovereign in the language of the Society of Friends. "I know them well, King George, and thou mayst be assured that thou hast not two better men in thy dominions, nor men that love thee better."[6] Wesley's conclusion to the story claimed that the king made clear to the Privy Council, "While I sit on the throne, no man shall be persecuted for his conscience' sake."[7] John Wesley's faith in the divine right of kings, and their invariable ability to be just and wise rulers, had—at least to his own satisfaction—been vindicated. Unfortunately the men and women who made up the mobs had less respect for the will and wishes of their sovereign.

With God and the king both intervening to keep the peace, John Wesley must have believed that he would be allowed to preach unhindered. Unfortunately holy writ did not extend beyond the jurisdiction of the Middlesex magistrates. Once outside the county boundaries meetings were so regularly disrupted that many disturbances were not even recorded. It was Wednesbury in Staffordshire that came to represent the risks that Wesley had to take and the dangers he faced. For it was the Wednesbury riots which he described in detail in his *Journal*. There were anti-Methodist demonstrations in Staffordshire throughout the spring and summer of 1743. John Wesley accused the local clergy of incitement. "I was not surprised at all. Neither should I have wondered if, after the advice they received from the pulpit as well as the Episcopal chair, the zealous high churchmen had rose and cut all that were Methodists to pieces." He decided that he must go to the aid of his beleaguered followers. When he arrived in Wednesbury, more than eighty houses in the town had been recently damaged by rioters.

A local magistrate judged that peace would be restored by a rigid application of the law. Wesley would have made the visit whatever the risks of assault and injury. But on the day of his arrival, having assumed the magistrate to be correct, he was "writing at Francis Ward's house in the afternoon when a cry arose that the mob had beset the house."[8] Wesley prayed that the mob be dispersed and the Lord hear his prayer. With the coast clear, he decided it was time to leave, but his hosts begged him to stay, and he agreed, "so as not to offend them," but "before five the mob surrounded the house again." Some of the leaders were brought to meet him, and they at least seemed pacified. Then Wesley, convinced that the Lord would provide, went into the street, where he addressed the crowd from a chair which one of the demonstrators had thoughtfully brought out from a nearby house. After he had spoken, it was clear that most of the mob were set on confrontation. A cry went up. "We want you to go with us to the Justice."

Wesley's *Journal* does not explain the reason for the request, but it cannot have been benign. The best Wesley could have hoped for was a desire to consult the local magistrates on the legality of Methodist meetings and preaching under the provisions of the Toleration Act. But he instantly and happily acquiesced to the invitation and in consequence (at least according to Wesley's own account of the events) precipitated the first of a series of mood swings in the mob. For the crowd responded to his agreement by shouting, "This gentleman is an honest gentleman and we will spill our blood in his defense." Since it was they who, until a minute earlier, had menaced Wesley, it is not clear against whom he needed to be defended. Nor is it certain that their conversion to his cause was complete. They still required him to visit the justice.

John Wesley and a crowd of almost three hundred therefore walked two miles in the pouring rain to Bentley Hall, the home of Mr. Lane, the local magistrate. The *Journal* records that "one or two had run before, telling him that Wesley was on his way." It also reports that Lane, wholly reasonably, asked them, "What have I to do with Mr. Wesley? Go and carry him back again." When the main body of rioters arrived, they were told that Mr. Lane was in bed. Perhaps the servant gave them that message in the hope they would disperse. Or the magistrate might have retired for the night after seeing the advance party. The mob would not be deflected from their determination to arrange a confrontation and waited, with growing impatience, for more than an hour. Then Lane's son came to the door and asked why they wished to see his father. The mood had changed again. Men who, two miles back, were prepared to die for Wesley, complained that Methodists "sing psalms all day; nay and make folk rise at four in the morning." Anticlimax followed bathos. The justice appeared in his nightshirt and, quite understandably, told his unwelcome visitors "to go home and be quiet."

Mr. Lane's good advice was rejected. Instead the mob decided to search for a more sympathetic justice, and one of their number suggested Justice Persehouse in Walsall. Persehouse was also in bed. So the whole enterprise was abandoned, and—in another strange shift of sentiment—forty members of the mob decided to see John Wesley safely home. But they had "not gone a hundred yards when the mob of Walsall came pouring in like a flood and bore down all before them."[9] Wesley's new friends "made what defence they could; but they were weary as well as outnumbered. So that in a short time, many being knocked down, the rest ran away and left [him] in their hands."

The Walsall mob made a noise "like the roaring of the sea." Perhaps because they could not hear John Wesley's emollient words, he was dragged into the town. He tried to escape by ducking into an open door. But the tenant, who was standing just inside, caught hold of him by the hair and flung him back into the road. Despite the manhandling, he "felt no pain or weariness." A second attempt to escape was frustrated by a shopkeeper who refused him refuge. He feared "they would pull the house down to the ground." Wesley continued to ask for the right to speak. The response was divided between "Knock his brains out" and "Hear him first," neither wholly encouraging.

According to the *Journal*, Wesley's "strength and voice then returned," a blessing which had to be reconciled with the earlier assertion that he felt neither pain nor weariness. The temper of the crowd changed too. The man who had led the first assault announced, "Sir, I will spend my life for you. Follow me and not one soul here shall touch a hair of your head." The mob attempted to ambush Wesley and his bodyguard as they crossed the bridge out of the town. But the escape was achieved. "God brought me safe to Wednesbury, having lost only one flap of my waistcoat and a little skin from one of my hands."[10] Wesley had no doubt that the deliverance was an act of God. He described the "particularly remarkable circumstances" which confirm the divine intervention. These combine the prosaic and providential in equal proportion.

> [M]any endeavoured to throw me down while we were going downhill on a slippery path to the town. . . . But I made no stumble at all nor the least slip till I was entirely out of their hands . . . a lusty mob just behind me struck me several times with a large oaken stick with which, if he had struck me once on the back of the head, it would have saved him all further trouble. But every time the blow was turned aside I know not how. . . . The very first men whose hearts were turned were the heroes of the town . . . one of them having been a prizefighter at the bear garden.[11]

The final proof that God was on his side was the comfort that came from the mob's inability, as Wesley saw it, to determine how to treat him. "None proposing any determinate thing; only 'Away with him! Kill him at once!'" What little comfort he drew from the general uncertainty about the preferred method of death must have been undermined by the facts revealed in the note which honesty compelled him to add to the account of his persecution. "Only one or two screamed out . . . 'Crucify the Dog.'"[12]

The famous story of Wesley's persecution in Staffordshire, designed to show how he could rise above adversity, should not obscure the fact that similar incidents were happening almost every day throughout the early 1740s. The result of the various antipathies were riots wherever the Methodists preached, the persecution made easy by the necessity of holding the meeting in the open. At Swindon the volunteer fire brigade drenched the meeting with its pump and hose, and when that did not make them disperse, shots were fired over the head of the crowd. At Hampton in Gloucestershire, hogwash was poured over the congregation for one and a half hours while the Methodists remained in silent prayer. In nearby Stratton a man was about to strike Wesley on the head with a club when a woman pulled the assailant away by his hair. Wesley was stoned in Southwark in 1741 and again in 1742. At Cowbridge in Wales, Methodists on their way to church were pelted with manure, and in Sheffield a Church of England clergyman encouraged and inflamed an already aggressive crowd and persuaded them to demolish the meetinghouse. At Pocklington in Yorkshire, churchwardens hired bell ringers to drown Wesley's voice. Indeed there was hardly a place in England during the whole decade where Methodists were free from assault.

The Church of England leadership was less concerned about the physical assaults on Methodists than the ripples of dissent which the disputes between the two leaders were causing in hundreds of parishes which had previously been untroubled by theology. John Wesley and George Whitefield were stimulating thought in otherwise quiescent parishes. The hierarchy was determined that their increasingly restless followers should not be encouraged to greater rebellion by the example of two turbulent priests. Edmund Gibson, the bishop of London, summoned the two men to appear before him and urged them to behave with proper clerical propriety. They ignored his injunction, argued again and were, time after time, called to his presence to receive the hierarchy's reproof. Neither man was in a mood to accept a reprimand. The meetings turned into disputations. The irony of the confrontations was that the warring factions which the bishop hoped to pacify were only united in their dispute with the church. The conflict intensified as the Methodist Connexion developed an existence which, for all Wesley's protestations, became increasingly independent of the church itself. But in the early days of Methodism, even when the connexion was genuine in its allegiance to the Church of England, the convocation had three legitimate complaints against both Whitefield and Wesley: doctrinal aberration, disregard for church order and "enthusiasm."

The doctrinal aberration, as seen by orthodox church opinion, included an unqualified belief in justification by faith and the consequent devaluation of good works, even though Wesley had always insisted that good works were an essential result (as distinct from agent) of salvation, if the sin of antinomianism were to be avoided. There was also some understandable confusion in episcopal minds between absolute perfection and final perseverance. Bishops who felt reluctant to pursue the arcane distinction, which Whitefield in some moods denied, found it convenient to accuse both men of believing in predestination.

Throughout all the early controversies, it was Whitefield who adopted the more radical position and was always willing to admit that he held doctrinal beliefs which were not identical to those of the Established Church. It was to him that Bishop Butler of Bristol issued the famous denunciation of "enthusiasm" in all its forms. "Sir, pretending to extraordinary revelations and gifts of the Holy Ghost is a horrid thing, a very horrid thing."[13] Wesley, far more anxious to respect the Church of England and determined to remain within it, always sought a legal justification for his irregularities or argued that they were forced on him by circumstances and the fervor of members whose love of God might be undermined if the clergy refused their wish to innovate for Christ. But although the two men had significantly different attitudes toward the church in which they were ordained, its almost identical antagonism toward them drove them together.

Despite the apparent bitterness of their disputes, always pursued more savagely by the followers than by the leaders, Arminians and Calvinists continued to cooperate for the greater glory of God. So Lady Huntingdon, although both patron and friend of George Whitefield's, had no hesitation in suggesting to John Wesley that he extend his activities to the northeast of England, where, she believed, the pitmen of Newcastle would be as receptive to his preaching as the colliers of the southwest had been.

John Wesley had already been invited north by John Nelson, a traveling stonemason, who had been inspired to become a preacher after attending a Methodist meeting in London in June 1739. It was devotion at first sight. Wesley "stroked back his hair and turned his face towards me where I stood and I thought fixed his eyes upon me." Nelson's heart "beat like a pendulum," and he sank to his knees with the words "Lord, thy will be done! Damn or save!"[14] The Lord willed that he should first help Ingham at Oxford and then move on to Birstall in Yorkshire. After Lady Huntingdon's intervention, John Wesley agreed to make his way north, first to visit the most loyal of his disciples and then to address the Methodists of Newcastle-upon-Tyne. His brother-in-law (described in Wesley's *Journal* as "one Mr. Hall") had been there "a year before but with no apparent fruit. Nor did anyone care to have him again." Westley Hall had already begun his descent into antinomianism and bigamy.

John Taylor, a servant of the earl of Huntingdon's and himself an occasional preacher, was waiting for John Wesley when he arrived at Donnington Park to comfort one of Lady Huntingdon's friends, who was preparing herself for a good Methodist death. Taylor, on Lady Huntingdon's suggestion, became the first of the traveling companions who, during the next half century, shared Wesley's life on the road. After a brief stop in Birstall, they arrived in Newcastle on 30 May 1742. The itinerancy had begun.

No preparations had been made for their arrival, for they knew no one who might prepare the way. So, with John Taylor at his side, John Wesley took up a position at the end of a street in Sandgate ("the poorest and most contemptible part of the town"), and the two men began to sing the doxology. A small crowd gathered, more curious than hopeful of conversion. Gradually it grew to several hundreds. Then, at least according to Wesley's own account, twelve or fifteen hundred people filled the street. He preached to them on the text "He was wounded for our transgression." When he had finished, he invited them to hear a second sermon which he proposed to preach that night on backsliding. The second crowd was bigger than the first, far larger than anything he had known in Moorfields or Kennington. Those at the back heard nothing, "although [his] voice was then strong and clear."[15] John Wesley had arrived in the north-east.

Within six months Wesley had bought land outside the City Gate on which to build his Orphan House, a name he chose in tribute to the Moravian children's crusade in Halle. The building was estimated to cost seven hundred pounds, toward which on the day of the inaugural sermon the Methodists of Newcastle had raised twenty-six shillings. As Wesley preached, the congregation broke into spontaneous prayers almost every time he paused for breath. Despite the evangelical success, the trustees were oppressed by the fear that their "clumsy ponderous pile" would never be completed. John Wesley was "of another mind: nothing doubting but, as it was begun for God's sake, He would provide what was needful to finish it."[16] And so it turned out. The Orphan House became the largest Methodist meetinghouse and the first Sunday school in England.

On his way south from that first visit to Newcastle, John Wesley visited Epworth for the first time in seven years. Uncertain of his reception, he stayed in the inn, and here he met a woman who had been in the service of the rectory during his boyhood. Assured that he was still remembered with affection, he offered his services—either to preach or to pray—to Mr. Romley, the new curate. The offer was rejected. However, the old servant and her friends had spread the news that he would be in church that night, and St. Andrew's was crowded from the chancel steps to the door. Romley chose as his text "Quench not the Spirit" and denounced "enthusiasm" as ungodly. Matins over, the crowd began to make its way home, but John Taylor stood at the churchyard gate and repeated as they passed, "Mr. Wesley, not being permitted to preach in the church, will preach here at six o'clock." At the appointed hour the churchyard was packed, and Wesley, who was developing a taste for the theatrical, addressed the alfresco congregation from his father's tomb and thus created one of the great images which in cheap print and lithograph inspired nineteenth-century Methodism. His valediction was usually omitted to protect the founder of the Methodist Church from the allegation that he had begun to enjoy being an outsider. After his third consecutive evening sermon in the bracing Lincolnshire air, legend has it that he announced, "I am well assured that I did far more good to them by preaching three days from my father's tomb that I did by preaching three years in his pulpit."[17]

The Newcastle Connexion had made travel, always the eventual consequence of a worldwide parish, an immediate necessity. It then became first an obsession and eventually a way of life into which John Wesley, in old age, settled, as if to journey twenty miles a day for five days a week were the usual habit of eighty-year-old men. "In his younger days he travelled on horseback. He was a hard but unskilful rider; and his seat was as ungraceful as it appeared unsteady. With a book in his hand and his hands up to his head . . . and a strange notion he had taken up of riding with the bridle on the horse's neck, many were the tumbles they had together." That description of John Wesley in and out of the saddle was written by one of his preachers, who, although he abandoned Methodism to become an ordained priest of the Established Church, retained his personal admiration for "the almost incredible degree of labour which nothing but the best constitution informed by the most active spirit could have enabled him to support."[18] He went on to estimate how many miles Wesley had traveled between 1739 and his death. "The lowest calculation we can make is four thousand miles annually which, in fifty-two years, will give two hundred and eighty thousand miles." Many of those miles were traveled through desolate countryside and along roads which were no more than muddy cart tracks, for although, by another of the calculations in which Methodist historians delighted, Wesley "paid more tolls than any man who ever bestrided a beast,"[19] even by the end of the itinerancy there were "but four good roads in England." The road between Preston and Wigan was typical: "Most Execrably Vile with Ruts Four Feet Deep."[20] All Wesley's journeys ended with, or were interrupted by, preaching wherever a congregation could be gathered together. "During fifty-two years he generally delivered two sermons a day; very frequently four or five. Calculating therefore at twice a day and allowing fifty sermons annually for extraordinary occasions (which is the lowest computation which can be made) the whole number in fifty-two years will be fifty-four thousand, four hundred and fifty." A note, added to the bottom of the calculation, reminds readers that "exhortations to Societies and other occasional meetings" to which John Wesley spoke were not included in the computation.[21]

It was in January 1743, with the foundation stone of the Newcastle Orphan House just laid, that the itinerancy really got under way. During that one month John Wesley preached in and around Doncaster, Epworth, Birdsall, Sheffield, Donnington Park, Wednesbury, Evesham, Stratford, Bath, Kingswood, Reading,

Windsor and Egham. For almost fifty years the routine and discipline were maintained. In October 1790, the month of the last substantial *Journal* entry, he visited Portsmouth, Cobham, Rye, Winchester, Sevenoaks, Colchester, Norwich, Yarmouth, Lowestoft, Lodder, Diss and Bury St. Edmunds before returning to London to preach at St Paul's, Shadwell on 24 October. He was eighty-seven, and he died five months later after collapsing, on his return home, from preaching at Leatherhead. He was an itinerant right to the end.

It was belief that sustained John Wesley, but both his willingness and his ability to drive himself on were increased by what can only be described as an almost mystical belief in riding itself. Occasionally he performed exceptional feats of endurance. On Wednesday, 13 June 1750, he was "on horseback with but an hour or two's intermission from five in the morning till within a quarter to eleven at night." Usually he survived the journey without incident. But sometime in late 1771, when he was sixty-eight, his horse stumbled and threw him against the pommel of his saddle. The bruising prevented him from riding for several days, and his friends seized the opportunity to suggest that he ride less on horseback and more in a carriage. He argued for several weeks, but by early March 1772, when he wrote a letter of thanks for the subscription which had been raised to cover the cost, he had reluctantly acquiesced to their wishes. But he still felt and expressed pleasure when, on his way to Ashton-in-Makerfield, he was able to "use [his] own feet and leave the poor horses to drag the chaise." Carriages did not appeal to him.

Sometime during 1773 he did agree to be driven on most of his journeys rather than ride. It was not a date which he chose to note in his *Journal*. But he did describe, with obvious schadenfreude, how a hired chaise fell into the river at Ballyrisy in Ireland. "I thought, however, it is well that my bags are on shore so my papers are not spoiled." Another post chaise was hired on 6 May of that year, but "In about five hours it could not drive twelve miles." So he "took horse and . . . just came at the time appointed." John Wesley accepted the need to abandon horse for coach neither willingly nor graciously.

That was in part because he honestly believed that regular riding was one of the reasons for his remarkably good health. He had no doubt that the same benefits could be enjoyed by others. In 1776 he suggested to John Fletcher, faithful friend and for a time his preferred successor, that they should travel together to northern England and Scotland. Fletcher was ill—as well as suspicious that Wesley wanted to use the occasion to persuade him to accept the unwanted succession. Wesley offered an inducement. "When you are tired, or like to be, you may come into my carriage: but remember that riding on horseback is the best of all exercises as far as your health permits."[22] Fletcher resisted the blandishments. On his return from the north, Wesley found Fletcher "a little better." He therefore suggested that his sovereign remedy might provide a complete cure. "I proposed his taking a journey with me to Cornwall, nothing being so likely to restore health as a journey of four or five hundred miles, but his physician would in no way consent."[23] John Wesley tried again and on his third attempt succeeded. On 13 November 1776 the two men set out together for Norwich in the hope, as Fletcher put it in a letter, that "the change of air and motion" would restore him to health. It was clear that he built his hopes in the Norfolk air while John Wesley relied on the beneficial effects of motion as provided by horse and carriage. Unfortunately neither remedy worked. Fletcher died of pulmonary consumption. But John Wesley's faith was undiminished. "I verily believe that if he had travelled with me . . . only a few months longer, he would have quite recovered his health."[24]

The near-obsessive enthusiasm for riding was intimately associated with his instinctive affection for horses—indeed for animals in general. He believed that although they were denied an understanding of God's love and therefore could not receive the redemption which was offered to men and women, they did have an afterlife of sorts. That entitled them at least to respect.

[Man] pursues [animals] over the widest plains, and through the thickest forests. He overtakes them in the fields of the air and finds them out in the depths of the sea. Nor are the mild and friendly creatures which still owe his sway and are duteous to his comments secured thereby from more than brutal violence, from outrage and abuse of various kinds. Is the generous horse that serves his master's necessity or pleasure with unswerved diligence . . . exempt from this?[25]

Wesley went on to complain that animals kill for food, man for pleasure. Whatever the merits of that distinction, it set him apart from his contemporaries, for whom bearbaiting and cockfighting were common entertainments. And his views on the "generous horse" induced him to include in his instructions to preachers the duty to feed their animals before they fed themselves. Preaching houses all over Britain were built to include a stable in which the itinerant's horse could be watered and groomed. It all added to the efficiency with which the work was carried out.

The equestrian statue of Wesley, outside the New Room in Bristol's Horse Fair, shows him riding with a "loose rein." It was, he claimed, that technique which had guaranteed so many trouble-free journeys.

> How is it that no horse ever stumbles while I am reading . . . No account can possibly be given except this: because then I throw the reins on his neck. I then set myself to observe; and I aver that in reading above a hundred thousand miles, I scarce ever remember any horse (except two that would fall head over heels anyway) to fall or make a considerable stumble, while I rode with a slack rein.[26]

The classic picture of John Wesley the evangelist is the image of a small man on a large horse. But there were travels by sea as well as land. The ill-fated adventure of 1735, when he had been terrified by the Atlantic storms on the way to Georgia and almost as afraid on the way back, was followed by three visits to continental Europe (the last to Holland when he was eighty-three) and twenty-one to Ireland. All the crossings were, by the nature of eighteenth-century ships and shipping, hideously uncomfortable, and many of them were dangerous, because of either weather or the disposition of other passengers. Wesley faithfully recorded his adventures: becalmed on his way from Liverpool to Dublin in 1758 and caught in a gale and rolling seas off Holyhead in 1773. Whether the passengers were bored by waiting or terrified of death, he invariably tried to turn their thoughts to God with an unsolicited sermon. He prided himself on being a good sailor, usually unaffected by wind and weather even when the other passengers were seasick. But then, he had developed a confidence which many of his traveling companions did not possess. Assurance—like the independent organization of Methodism—increased with the years.

The certainty that he was under God's protection was reinforced by the knowledge that God had given him both the temperament and the constitution to spend his whole life traveling the world, which was his parish. Early rising, which began as a penance for worldly thoughts, quickly became an ingrained habit. The eighteenth century rose and retired to bed with the light, but for most of his life Wesley was at work by five o'clock, even on the darkest mornings. The long days were sustained by a diet which was partly the result of early medical advice and partly the product of a determination to live simply in order to confirm his commitment to service and sacrifice. Whatever the causes, what he chose to eat conformed to what modern dietitians would call the recipe for healthy living. On his way to Georgia in 1735 he became a vegetarian. Two years later he began to eat meat again. But in 1740, for reasons which had everything to do with his attitude toward animals and nothing to do with a determination to lower his cholesterol levels, he became a vegetarian once more. And so he remained, to the undoubted benefit of his constitution, for the rest of his life.

John Wesley was a valetudinarian. He enjoyed ill health. And his preoccupation with his condition, combined with an inclination to anticipate death as well as exaggerate illness, made his willingness to punish himself on long and frequent journeys all the more remarkable. Fortunately he was obsessed with cures as well as symptoms. Often the sovereign remedies he prescribed for himself were as bizarre as the illnesses which he diagnosed. In July 1746 he decided that he was being gradually paralyzed by tea.

It was not until the early nineteenth century that the Methodists turned against alcohol. Throughout his life Wesley drank sherry, other wines and the several sorts of beer and porter which were the regular beverages of the working classes. Tea and coffee were the expensive affectations of the aristocracy and the intelligentsia. When tea was first imported into England in 1660, coffeehouses paid the revenue eightpence for every gallon they sold. In the year of Wesley's birth "dry tea" cost sixty shillings a pound in London. Methodists were discouraged, at first, from wasting money on a luxury which had no nutritional value. Then Wesley decided that it was slowly killing him.

At the height of his tea phobia, he claimed that at Oxford he had been in perfect health apart from what he described as an occasional paralytic disorder. In fact, he had suffered from—and presumably forgotten—a recurrent nasal catarrh which brought on nosebleeds, which were feared to be as a symptom of consumption. He spoke only of his trembling hands, which had often followed undergraduate breakfasts, when he turned against tea. For years he endured the condition, without thinking that he recognized the cause. Then, in September 1746, he noticed how many of his acquaintances suffered from the same affliction. The sufferers he knew best were questioned about their close acquaintance with alcohol. All of them insisted that they drank very little except tea. It seemed that the demands of health and economy were at one. "I considered what an advantage it would be to these poor enfeebled persons if I would leave off what so manifestly impairs their health and thereby hurts their business also. If they used English herbs instead of tea, they might hereby not only lessen their pain but in some degree their poverty."[27]

John Wesley's ideas on health, barely less than his views on faith, were, once established, pursued with the single-minded determination of a true zealot. The way in which he drove himself on with little thought for physical comfort, no apparent concern for worldly pleasures and infinite confidence in a variety of unfashionable causes, inevitably antagonized men and women with a more casual view of life. His eccentricities, from hatred of tea to love of animals, alienated him from conventional society. Increasingly he was driven to work and live within the narrow confines of his own connexion. In middle age everything conspired to make separation from the Church of England inevitable.

10

ASHAMED OF NOTHING

As John Wesley traveled the country, he left behind him Methodists who wanted the comfort and encouragement of knowing that men and women of similar beliefs joined them in a nationwide connexion. After the years of torpor, members of the near-moribund Church of England were excited and inspired by the discovery that some members of the clergy were sufficiently engaged by the business of belief to submit long-held doctrine to scrutiny. The religious societies—some Moravian, some following Whitefield and others Wesleyan in belief—began to take on new life. The societies, agencies of self-improvement and evangelism, had been founded by the Church of England in 1677[1] and in the early years of their existence had been held in deep suspicion by supporters of the Stuart monarchy, who suspected that they sympathized with the Puritans of Cromwell's Commonwealth. But after the Glorious Revolution at least the London societies, having proved their loyalty with public prayers at St. Clement Danes for the health and happiness of the sovereign, grew popular and prospered. The London Society for the Reformation of Manners got near to justifying the accusation that it had Puritan inclinations. In 1735 it announced that it had been so successful in its campaigns against brothels and drinking houses that it had promoted 99,380 prosecutions[2] since its creation in 1678. After the first flush of reforming zeal faded, the societies became little more than "a respectable pastime . . . by which, at small expense, [their members] could fancy themselves better than the rest of the world." So new evangelical societies, most of them without either the inspiration or initiative of either Wesley or Whitefield, were founded. But the leaders of the revival reorganized and reinvigorated them. In Bristol the amalgamation of the Baldwin Street and Nicholas Street societies and the building of a joint meetinghouse in the Horse Fair became the great example of Methodist initiative. The enterprise of Bristol's united societies was admired by Methodists all over the country and emulated by those who felt sufficient confidence to invest in bricks and mortar. Methodism was taking on a life of its own. It no longer needed a Wesley or a Whitefield to stimulate every expansion and innovation. Often societies created in the name of one denomination transferred their allegiance to another as membership changed. The Nottingham Society began Calvinist, became Moravian and was then taken over by associates of Charles Wesley. Like the Leicester Society (which remained loyal to Lady Huntingdon), it foundered. But more of the new societies succeeded than failed. The difference between the two often depended on whether or not the people were led by an eloquent preacher.

The most successful of the northern apostles was Benjamin Ingham, who had been with Wesley at Oxford and sailed with him to Georgia. By 1740 he had fifty regular "preaching stations" in Yorkshire. So many societies were formed out of his congregations that he held a monthly general meeting of leaders which, in its way, became a regional Methodist Connexion. It did not last. Ingham became a Moravian and handed his societies to the care of Fetter Lane. Across the Pennines in Lancashire, John Bennet was having more difficulty propagating the faith. A Methodist society was not formed in Manchester until 1747. But the north had begun to produce men who, when a national connexion was created, would lead and sustain Methodism in their region and contribute to its development throughout the country.

In the southwest a Methodist society of sorts was formed in St. Ives before either of the Wesley brothers visited the region. Joseph

Turner, a ship's captain from Bristol, asked the Wesleys to send a preacher to celebrate its foundation, and in July 1743 Charles decided to explore the new territory himself. He worked his way down the north Cornwall coast, preaching as he went, and John followed the same route a month later. There they promoted their work with Anglican evangelicals, clergymen whose "conversion" was independent of the Methodist impetus, but who became Wesley's natural allies. The tin miners of Cornwall, like the miners of Kingswood and Newcastle, proved particularly receptive to the new gospel.

In Wales the revival was initiated without the help of either John Wesley or George Whitefield. Its instigators were Daniel Rowland and Howel Harris, the pioneer of field preaching who (needing additional assistance) asked the leaders of English Methodism for help. Whitefield visited Wales in March 1739, and Wesley made the journey seven months later. Lady Huntingdon was beginning to exert the influence which was to culminate in the creation of the "school of the prophets," a theological college for Calvinist Methodist ministers at Trevecka. The college and the Calvinist connection survive to this day.

The Calvinist Methodists, uninhibited about creating an autonomous organization, were inaugurated at a meeting held near Cardiff during January 1743. Whitefield, encouraged by Howel Harris and supported by Joseph Humphreys and John Cennick, agreed on a plan for mass conversion. "Public exhorters" (assisted by "private exhorters") should be employed to supervise the work of the societies. Public exhorters were to be full-time and were required to supervise a dozen groups of Methodists. Private exhorters, who remained in their lay occupations, took responsibility for only two groups. Harris became "superintendent," and the associate priests agreed to combine their parochial duties with itinerant evangelism. The plans were made in admirable detail. Each society was to possess a box under the care of a steward in which weekly contributions were collected, and the exhorters were to meet in conference once or more a year. The Whitefield faction was a communicating network long before Wesley's connexion was any more than a handful of corresponding societies. Fortunately so many societies were formed in

England and Wales that both Whitefield and Wesley could feel confident of duty done. In 1750 there were 433 religious societies in Wales alone. Most were Calvinist, but Wesley had a foothold.

In Scotland, Methodism did not prosper. The influence of John Knox still hung over the kingdom, and Presbyterianism, which had become the Established Church in 1690, had not suffered the long torpor which incapacitated the Church of England. Nor was there any tradition of dissent on which Wesley and Whitefield could build. There were sudden, spectacular and localized revivals. Whitefield addressed a crowd of twenty or thirty thousand in Cambuslang during 1742, and the minister at Kilsyth preached the need for redemption to such effect that convulsions and possession, which were common in England, were observed north of the border. Indeed John Wesley's first contact with Scotland was a request from Edinburgh for information about "the possession by God" of members of his Bristol congregation. But there were no real foundations on which Methodism could be built.

John Wesley could rejoice that in England new societies were being formed in the counties as well as the towns—Somerset, Wiltshire, Gloucestershire and Warwickshire. The speed of Methodism's expansion meant that as the Wesley brothers moved on, there was often trouble among the members who were left behind. When John returned to Newcastle in February 1743, he found it necessary to "put away" persons who were not "walking according to the gospel." Sixty-four members were expelled, including seventeen for "drunkardness," twenty-nine for "lightness and carelessness," two for "cursing and swearing," one for wife beating and four for "railing and evil-speaking." Two days after the purge he decided that the societies needed a formal constitution. So he wrote *The Nature, Design and General Rules of the United Societies*—far more exacting regulations that those he had laid down in 1738, which had required little more than the rejection of sin.[3] The more precise and unified the connexion's rules became, the more difficult it was to distinguish the connexion from an independent church.

Regularizing the constitutions and organization of the societies was not an easy task. For they had grown haphazardly, often on the initiative of local members whose views were only vaguely related to Wesley's own doctrine. Their shape and size were more often the result of accident than conscious decision, and sometimes the Connexion could be held together only by Wesley's turning his back on his own regulations and insisting that there was no divinely ordained pattern of worship, but that brothers and sisters in Christ must tolerate one another's differences and work together for the God they all worshiped. As Wesley tried to impose a common pattern on the societies, he had to convince some of their members that they must accommodate variations from the principles which he laid down and the practices that he required. After 1742 he at least aspired to common rules. But like every other consideration, the aspiration gradually became second to the promotion of an ever-larger connexion.

The balance between rule and exception occupied John Wesley for most of 1742, a turbulent year, in which his mother died. Susanna Wesley, with nineteen pregnancies behind her, must have been as physically tough as she was morally strong, for she survived into her seventy-fourth year. The emphasis her children placed on the special importance of communion, which she received, in January 1740, from her son-in-law Westley Hall suggests her sons did not believe that before she "found Christ" during that event, she was either justified or sanctified. Since there is no doubt about the love and respect in which she was held by both John and Charles, their notion that she came late to repentance illustrates how strongly they believed in the necessity of being "born again." However, they had no doubt that she had a "good death" and went to meet her Maker with "no doubt or fear, nor any desire but to depart and be with Christ."[4] Wesley's comment on his loss confirms both her failure to come to early repentance and his own confidence in the path to heaven which he had prescribed. "My heart does not—and I am absolutely sure God does not—condemn me for any want of duty towards her in any kind, except only that I have not reproved her so plainly and fully as I should have done."

For some years Susanna Wesley had stayed with each of her children for months in turn. At the time of her death she was living in London in John's apartment at the Foundry. For most of her final visit both Charles and John were traveling the country. When John Wesley heard that the end was near, he hurried home from Bristol and arrived in time to hear her last words, "Children, sing a psalm in praise of God." She was buried in Bunhill Fields, and her eldest surviving son preached the sermon over her coffin. He took as his text Revelation 20:12, "and the dead were judged out of those things which were written in the books according to their works." Charles wrote her epitaph. It made no direct reference to the late date of assurance. However, its implication is clear.

> True daughter of affliction she.
> Inured to pain and misery
> Mourned a long night of grief and tears
> A legal night of seventy years.
> The Father then revealed his Son,
> Him in the broken bread made known.
> She knew and felt her sins forgiven
> And found the earnest of her heaven.[5]

The *United Society Rules*, published in 1743, would have accommodated her, even before she was born again. For they stipulated that those wishing to join need merely declare "a desire to flee from the wrath to come, to be saved from their sins," while to remain in membership required the demonstration that they were living up to their aspirations, "First by doing no harm . . . Secondly, by doing good . . . Thirdly by attending upon all the ordinances of God." The obligations were set out in detail. Evils to be avoided included swearing, profaning the Sabbath with business, drunkenness, fighting, going to law with brethren, buying or selling smuggled goods, usury, uncharitable conversations, speaking ill of magistrates, wearing costly jewelry or clothes, laying up treasures, extravagant purchases. "Doing good" was defined as encouraging care for the hungry, naked and sick, exhorting and improving the wicked and pursuing all other Methodist means of grace. At least the first obligation was fulfilled. In 1744 the United London Societies (with 2,000 members) raised £196 and used it to provide 360 paupers with needful clothing.

Within the societies, groups of pious Methodists were coming together (very often spontaneously) to live what they hoped would be sinless lives. They became the "bands" and were given an official status by the connexion during 1744. For band members the rules of holy living were even more stringent. They were required to eschew all spirituous liquor, never pawn their possessions, avoid "needless ornaments," snuff, tobacco and all forms of self-indulgence and marry only "believers." The obligations which the *Rules* imposed on Methodists were beyond the capabilities of some members and contrary to the tastes of others. So, a little more than a year after the Newcastle purge of 1742, seventy-six more members left the Newcastle Society. Fourteen Dissenters rejected Wesley's view on the sacraments. Nine husbands and wives were persuaded to leave by their skeptical spouses. And in an echo of John Wesley's own experiences at Oxford, nine members had grown tired of being laughed at by friends and family who thought the Methodists absurd. Nobody left, or at least admitted leaving, because he or she could not afford the subscription, which had been introduced in February of the previous year.

The subscription came about as an unhappy necessity, but like so many of Wesley's apparent detriments, it became the source of new Methodist strength. Wesley had accepted financial responsibility for both the Bristol New Room and the Newcastle Orphan House. However, in neither case did he know how to discharge the debt. His Lincoln College fellow's stipend of twenty-five to thirty-five pounds a year remained his only certain income, augmented from time to time by fees from the publication of pamphlets and sermons. It was enough to meet his bodily needs but no more. He was certainly incapable of even assisting in paying off the debts on the new meeting houses which had been built with his encouragement. On 15 February 1742 a group of prosperous Methodists met in Bristol to consider ways of paying off the mortgage on the Horse Fair Room. One of them, a Captain Foy, suggested that every member should subscribe a penny a week until the bill was paid. When it was pointed out that some Methodists were too poor to contribute, Foy offered to donate a shilling a week and take responsibility for collecting from eleven other members, paying the penny himself for anyone who was too poor to contribute. He suggested that other prosperous Methodists do the same. To encourage his colleagues, he asked for the names of the eleven poorest Methodists in Bristol, who would, he said, become his special care.

The idea, reinforced by the offer, was irresistible. The whole society was divided in "classes," meaning a ranking rather than groups of pupils. Wesley selected class leaders, who collected the pennies, not from his wealthiest followers but from Methodists he described as "those in whom I could most confide." The choice of leaders was based less on the assiduity with which they would count the pennies than the rigor with which they would supervise the behavior of their class members. From the start Wesley regarded Foy's scheme as a way of regulating his followers. When the collection system was extended to London, it was agreed that classes should come together in weekly meetings rather than be visited individually by their leaders. Wesley had no doubt about the principal advantage of the change. It had nothing to do with the collectors' convenience. The new arrangement meant that "a more full inquiry was made into the behavior of every person . . . advice or reproof was given as need required, quarrels made up, misunderstandings removed and, after an hour or two spent in this labour of love, they concluded with prayers and thanksgiving."[6]

The collection of subscriptions required the identification of members. So although the Foy scheme was seen by Wesley as a way of keeping Methodists on the path to true redemption, it also became an instrument for creating a register, itself a characteristic of a formal organization. Membership tickets, lasting for between two and three months, were issued, usually after the payment of a shilling entry fee. Absence from three consecutive meetings, without good cause, resulted in the withdrawal of the ticket. Class leaders were expected to take a benign interest in their members' welfare, advising them on, and helping them with, their family and personal problems. The result was what twentieth-century politicians would have described as a pattern of cadres, small cells of believers, locked into the hierarchy of the organization by the members' dependence on their leaders and the leaders' sense of duty to those they led. When John Wesley bought the New Room in Bristol to be the prayer house and meeting place of the United Society, he had neglected to provide the necessary finance because he believed that the Lord would provide. The Lord provided more than the cost of land and building. He inspired Bristol Methodists to create a system which enabled them to "live as the Christians of old, having things in common."[7] It also began to turn the several societies from local groups of devout Christians in search of personal salvation into branches of a national organization.

By the mid-1740s—with the connexion created, John Wesley's version of the homilies in circulation and the customs, if not the laws, of the Established Church consistently ignored—the foundations of an independent church had undoubtedly been laid. Charles Wesley realized the danger of drifting into separation and constantly warned against it. John Wesley vacillated wildly between promoting it, regarding it as regrettably both necessary and inevitable and pretending to himself and others that it could never come about. In fact he wanted to remain within the church. But he wanted far more to create a connexion. Indeed he believed he had a duty to create an institution which would make the revival permanent. Whenever he had to choose, he chose Methodism—and claimed that he had chosen to be true to what the Church of England ought to be.

Perhaps in early middle age both Wesleys still believed that Methodism's destiny to reinvigorate, not to challenge, the Established Church could be fulfilled in their lifetime. Whenever they were in conflict with either doctrine or rules of governance, they invariably claimed that the members had insisted that Methodism met legitimate spiritual needs that the Anglican hierarchy neglected. Sometimes the claim was justified. At others it could be defended only in terms of John Wesley's exclusive interpretation of the church's duties. Inevitably the prospects of schism were increased by the two doctrines—Wesleyan and Anglican—meeting in head-on collision.

Methodists were told that frequent communion, a confirming as well as a converting sacrament, was essential to continual redemption and were urged regularly to celebrate the Last Supper in their parish churches to guarantee final perseverance. Unfortunately much of the

Anglican priesthood regarded the Eucharist differently and held communion services only three or four times a year. John and Charles Wesley regarded it as their duty to make up for the deficiency of their colleagues. When the colliers of Kingswood were denied admission to communion in their parish church, Charles put aside his scruples and offered them the sacrament in the schoolroom,[8] claiming that like taking communion to the old and sick, it was not "private administration," a practice which the church prohibited. A dubious practice justified by semantics or casuistry always opened the way for an illegal practice which could not be justified by even the most convoluted logic. The distribution of the Eucharist in unconsecrated premises became a regular event.

Desperate measures were especially needed in London, where Methodists either found that communion was rarely administered or felt that they were unable to accept it from the hands of priests whose theology they rejected. John Wesley leased the old Huguenot chapel on West Street and claimed that because it was a consecrated place of worship, there could be no complaint if the sacraments were regularly celebrated there. So many Methodists took advantage of the opportunity that they had to be divided into phased groups who attended the chapel six hundred at a time. Confronted with such a demonstration of piety, the rector of St. James's, Piccadilly, complained to John Potter, recently elevated from the see of Oxford to the archdiocese of Canterbury. The archbishop found Wesley had neither broken regulations nor defied convention. Encouraged by such elevated approval, the Methodists accepted the offer of a chapel at Snowfields on the south bank of the Thames and extended the regular celebration of the Eucharist to a second site in London. It was all a sign of Methodism's success and increasing acceptance. But it was also a demonstration that Methodists, although still within the Church of England, increasingly thought of themselves as set apart from those who did not share their distinctive faith. Wesley rejected the allegation that he was promoting schism in the most aggressive language. He pleaded guilty to "gathering people out of buildings called churches" but he was not "dividing Christians from Christians and so destroying Christian fellowship." "These were not Christians before they were thus joined. Most of them were barefaced heathens. Neither are they Christians from whom you suppose them to be divided. You will not look at me and say they are. What, Drunken Christians? Cursing and swearing Christians? Lying Christians? Cheating Christians? If these are Christians at all, they are *devil Christians*."[9]

The mission to convert devil Christians into real Christians allowed no compromise with the sensibilities of an indolent church. Strengthening the alliance of his disparate societies, although close to the formal creation of a church within a church, was the natural next step. First the members of the connexion were grouped in "circuits" around which traveling preachers perambulated for two or three years, supervising their administration, confirming their financial probity and improving their theological education. Circuit preachers thus achieved a senior status. They became, as well as literal itinerants, the canons and archdeacons of Methodism. The officers of the circuit met at "quarterly meetings" to discuss and decide questions of mutual concern. The federal structure of Methodism was confirmed by the creation of an annual conference, as near to a governing body as John Wesley's personality would allow.

The notion of conference had first been discussed on 12 November 1739 at a casual meeting among John Wesley, John Gambold and John Robson, three Oxford Methodists who agreed to hold an annual reunion in London on the eve of Ascension Day. They were serious-minded men. So the reunions were intended to be occasions for spiritual renewal and rededication. They agreed to prepare for their meetings by sending one another accounts of their evangelical labors and constructed a list of potential recruits to what (at least at that stage) they thought of as an entirely spiritual gathering, entirely unrelated to territorial ambitions. The first conference would, they decided, be held in June 1740.

The 1740 conference did not take place. Most of its potential members were too involved in the day-to-day work of their parishes to spare the time to travel to London for an ill-defined meeting, which seemed increasingly pointless as the agreed date approached. And theological differences were beginning to separate the dozen or so delegates who had once been united by a common vision of redemption. But the idea remained attractive to John Wesley, and three years after the original plan collapsed, he decided to call a conference in London with the express purpose of examining the possibility of uniting the forces of the revival.

In what he called a "Triune conference," John Wesley planned to meet with "the heads of the Moravians and the predestinarians" in order to fulfill his "strong desire to unite with Mr. Whitefield and, as far as possible, cut off needless disputes." In the hope of at least clearing the ground, he set out the three areas of contention, "Unconditional Election, Irresistible Grace, Final Perseverance."[10] The description of disputed theology contained a concession of sorts, amended in later editions of the *Journal* to make his meaning more clear. "I do not deny that in some souls (in those eminently styled The Elect, if such there be) the grace of God is so irresistible that they cannot but believe and be finally saved. But I cannot believe that all those must be damned in whom it does not irresistibly work."[11]

Charles Wesley was (by his own description of events) "summoned" from Cornwall. John Nelson rode down from Yorkshire. But when they arrived in London, they heard that "the Moravians would not be there. Spangenberg indeed said he would be present, but immediately left England."[12] James Hutton excused his own absence with the explanation that Moravians "had orders not to confer at all unless the Archbishop of Canterbury and the Bishop of London were also present." The stipulation was not the exhibition of lèse-majeste that it at first seems. Zinzendorf still hoped that the Church of England would accept the Moravians as a parallel communion and was fearful of being associated with a dissenting faction. Whitefield was expected because John Cennick, by then firmly Calvinistic, was enthusiastic for the meeting. But he did not arrive. Although the meeting was confined to what the *Journal* calls the three "Arminian Methodists,"[13] Charles Wesley believed that 13 August 1743 was "used to good purpose." But the Methodists did not ennoble the occasion with the title of "conference." Because it did not fulfill its proper purpose, it was downgraded to "meeting." There would be a conference the following year, and it would be a success.

The conference of 1744 was designed to succeed. Moravians and Calvinists were invited, but they were not the leaders of those movements. Indeed they were men who, despite their theological differences with the Methodists, regarded Wesley as the leader of the revival. Their allegiance to the man, if not to his doctrines, was a guarantee against failure or collapse. They came together at the Foundry on Monday, 24 June. They discussed sanctification on Tuesday, church discipline on Wednesday, organization on Thursday, the rules of "assistants" on Friday and union with the Moravians on Saturday.[14]

The status and role of lay preachers were, in effect, decided at the beginning of the conference. The six ordained priests (who were the equivalent of a Methodist episcopate) met on the conference eve. They agreed that their lay brethren should play a full part in the following day's deliberation. That regulated their status and confirmed, at least by implication, that their preaching was authorized. The decision to embrace lay preachers was not taken after careful consideration of the apostolic succession or out of the conviction that every Christian had the right to serve God to the best of his or her ability. Nor were they accepted for no better reason than to avoid an embarrassing confrontation at the Foundry. Wesley had been considering how to elevate their station for months. His decision, like so many of the Methodist Connexion's developments, was the product of necessity.

The needs of the expanding movement, which believed in constant corporate worship, could not be met by half a dozen clergymen. And in June 1744 there was no way of knowing how many new recruits Methodism would attract. In any event, John Wesley had allowed (he was anxious to emphasize that he had not instructed) "sons of the gospel" to preach as long ago as 1738. Wesley wanted lay preachers, and his will prevailed.

Accepting that lay preachers were essential to the revival helped to establish the character of Methodism. The new church was reaching out for leadership and inspiration beyond the hierarchy of bishops and presbyters and was asserting that "unlettered mechanics" might receive "the extra-ordinary call." That inevitably attracted the antagonism of men who thought of following Christ as a gentleman's vocation. Laurence Sterne, a clergyman and grandson of an archbishop, thought Wesley's preachers "much fitter to make a pulpit than to get into one." Wesley, however, knew that they had been called by God. It was, however, still to be decided what, as well as preaching, the Lord called them to do. The first conference set out their duties in detail.

Their first duty was "to spread spiritual holiness," an objective they were encouraged to promote by forming societies wherever they preached.[15] But they were also to act as pastors, resolving disputes between members, advising leaders and stewards and examining their accounts. They were engaged to preach, whatever the inconvenience, where they judged the largest congregation could be assembled and to demonstrate their humility by being "ashamed of nothing" and therefore willing to carry wood, draw water and clean shoes. Doctrinal conformity was to be achieved by the constant recommendation of, and reference to, John Wesley's books. Their sermons, which were to be neither "awkward nor affected," were to condemn Sabbath breaking, dram drinking, unprofitable conversation, evil speaking and unsuitable debt. When "their preaching was done," they were to revive themselves on lemonade, candied orange peel or soft ale, but not late suppers, wine or eggs. The rules reflected almost all of John Wesley's prejudices. The connexion was being forged in his image.

It was the lay preachers who were most anxious that the conference should include theological debate. They wanted, and got, a reaffirmation of the doctrine of justification by faith. But the importance of repentance of sins and good works was also emphasized. All true Christians, they agreed, received full assurance. But degrees of faith were recognized as a common prelude to sanctification. Each item of belief was, the conference judged, confirmed by practical experience as well as ordained by the Scriptures. Methodism was becoming a "popular" religion. Indeed its primary purpose was to make the Church of England more acceptable to, as well as more sympathetic toward, the men and women it ignored and neglected. That required organization as well as exhortation. John Wesley believed that God had decreed that Christians should "watch over each other."

Membership remained open to everyone "who wished to flee from the wrath to come," the basic requirement for acceptance in a Methodist society from the start. But a fast-expanding connexion would, Wesley judged, disintegrate if it were built on such loose foundations. The structure of the Methodist Connexion, which was determined at the first conference and later incorporated in the published *The Nature, Design and General Rules of the United Societies in London, Bristol, Kingswood and Newcastle upon Tyne*, essentially reproduced the Moravian organization which Wesley had drawn up under the influence of Peter Böhler in 1738. Exclusive groups or "bands" were to exist within societies. They were to be composed of men and women who claimed to have obtained forgiveness of their sins. Members were to be admitted to bands only after highly intrusive cross-examinations which provoked the allegation that Methodism was acquiring the characteristics of a secret society. The questions (which justified, at least in part, the accusation) included, "Do you desire to be told your faults?" and "Do you desire we should tell you whatever we think, fear or hear concerning you?" Even membership in bands was not the ultimate accolade of Methodism. "Select Societies"—often groups of no more than four or five devout believers—were to encourage spiritual growth in those who "already walk in the light of God." To encourage "openness," men and women, married and single Methodists, were to meet in separate societies.

The conference made proper provision for dealing with backsliding and apostasy. Within each society, there had to be a "penitential band," which should consist of members "who have made a shipwreck of the faith." Sadly, some sinners would not even acknowledge their failings or accept the proper discipline of Methodism. They would have to be removed. Wesley had already "cleansed" the Newcastle Society. He determined to use the new rules which the conference had agreed to in London. He did not wait long to strike them down in righteous anger. "The next day [after the conference had ended] we endeavoured to purge the society of all that did not walk according to the gospel. By this method we reduced the number of members to under nineteen hundred. But numbers is an inconsiderable circumstance. May God increase them in faith and love."[16]

There was no doubt, at least in the formal discussions at the conference, that Methodism's future lay firmly within the Established Church, although some of the contributors at least implied that expulsion might be the unavoidable result of the essential refusal to compromise with their sincerely held beliefs. Indeed the new constitution, which was approved during the last two days of deliberation, required Methodists to defend, as well as respect, the doctrine of the Church of England, obey its bishops and observe its canon law "as far as individual conscience allowed."[17] Those obligations reflected the spirit of the conference, which had set out, at the very beginning, the need for final answers to all its dilemmas without wounding its members' consciences or breaking faith with its parent church. Field preaching, an initiative which particularly offended Church of England orthodoxy, was approved. But it should not be practiced at a time when church services were being held in regular places of worship. "Lay assistants," another contentious innovation, were to be allowed "only in cases of necessity." The general plan was to spread out slowly within the parishes, converting, without a thought of personal aggrandizement, both priests and people to the cause. Methodists worked "to save their own souls and those that hear them."[18]

The protestations of loyalty to the Church of England were for the most part genuine. But the men who wrote the Methodist constitution and constructed the rules for the governance of its constituent societies must have known, or should have known, that the construction of a formal connexion had taken them a step closer to schism. After 1744 at least some Methodists thought of themselves as actively creating a church within a church, not reluctantly allowing it to happen, but welcoming every move toward autonomy. The connexion had its own governance and dogma. The fact that it endorsed the doctrine of the Established Church barely reduced the risk of separation. For it was the priest's duty to accept the canons of the church, not to pass judgment on them either pro or con. Wesley was far too intelligent a man not to recognize the path on which he had set his foot.

Despite what John Wesley was pleased to call "settled beliefs," the annual conference, once established, persisted in refining doctrine. The constant reexamination of dogma was a distraction from the work of salvation. But Wesley, and his followers, felt a constant need to add extra precision to their convictions. The theological frontiers of Methodism were being established year by year. But the boundaries had to be constructed in a way which allowed the entry of new recruits.

The 1744 conference had agreed that "all true Christians have such a faith as implies an assurance of God's love."[19] That was soon adjudged to be too restrictive. So in 1745 the iron law was modified by a series of questions and replies, a method of communicating complicated ideas which was to become a standard Methodist technique. The answers were far from categoric.

Q.: Is a sense of God's pardoning love absolutely necessary to our being in his favour? Or may there be some excepted cases?
A.: We dare not say there are not.
Q.: Is it necessary to inward or outward holiness?
A.: We incline to think it is.[20]

Not surprisingly Wesley concluded that the replies, which had been drafted with the initial intention of allowing, without approving, doctrinal flexibility, needed clarification. So he began his "letters to John Smith." The true name of the recipient was probably Thomas Secker, bishop of Oxford and later archbishop of Canterbury, though there is at least the possibility that Wesley's correspondent was Thomas Herring, in turn archbishop of York and then of Canterbury. By either reckoning Wesley tested his ideas against the highest Anglican authority. His hope was that he could settle his own mind as well as establish the legitimacy of Methodism. Most of the letters were not requests for help but unqualified assertions. The second, written in December 1745, was categorical on the subject of assur-

ance. "No man can be a true Christian without such inspiration of
the Holy Ghost as fills his heart with peace and joy and love which
he who perceives not, has not. This is a point which I alone contend
and this I take to be the very foundation of Christianity."[21]

Assurance was a subject on which Wesley was to refine—some
would say change—his opinion time and time again during middle
age. There is no hard evidence that "Smith" helped him come to a
firm conclusion. But he did provoke Wesley into some much-needed
self-examination. "Smith" warned him that "Strict order once broken, confusion rushes in like a torrent at a trifling breach. You find
yourself going every day from the orderly paths. You are now come
to approve of lay preachers. Well, if they preach the gospel of peace
where is the harm? But order once broken, unsent persons take upon
themselves to preach all sorts of error, discord and confusion."
Wesley's response dealt less with the dangers which "Smith" described than with the critical implications about his character. "I sincerely thank you for endeavouring to help me herein, to guard me
from running into excess. I am always in danger of this and yet I daily
experience a far greater danger of the other extreme. To this day I
have abundantly more temptation to lukewarmness than impetuosity."[22] "Smith"'s reply was a compliment as well as a reproof. "The
son of a Wesley and an Annesley is in no danger of lukewarmness but
ought to take great care on the side of impetuosity and zeal."

John Wesley was right to insist that he rarely acted hastily. But he
felt a constant temptation to snatch at new ideas. Spiritual revelations
were rare, but intellectual revelations were frequent, and he always
accepted the new truth with a zealous determination that it should
govern his life and work. On 20 January 1746 he set out for Bristol
on a journey that was to end with a new belief, which, forty years
later, would be the occasion, if not the cause, of Methodism's final
breach with the Church of England.

On his way west John Wesley read *An Inquiry into the Constitution,
Discipline, Unity and Worship of the Primitive Church that Flourished the
Hundred Years After Christ*. Like most of the revelations, both intellectual and spiritual, it provided welcome news. The *Inquiry* had
been written in 1691 by Lord King, lord chancellor of England, to

establish the right of Dissenters within the church. But Wesley was not the man to allow a malign purpose to prevent the endorsement of a convenient conclusion. "In spite of the vehement prejudices of my education, I was ready to believe that this was a fair and impartial draft; but, if so, it would follow that bishops and presbyters are essentially of one order and that, originally, every Christian congregation was a church independent of all others."[23] The clear implication of his conclusion, at first not spoken but certainly understood, was that bishops had no exclusive right to ordination. Priest could ordain priest. The second conclusion was even more startling. The Church of England might well be the *best* church available to Wesley and his followers during the mid-eighteenth century, but it was not ordained to be the *only* acceptable church. During the years which followed, Wesley's reservation, spiritual and intellectual, always confirmed the convenient theories which justified his work and that of his connexion.

Lord King's work was to have a crucial effect on the future of Methodism. But it took time for it to be translated into Wesley's official theology. For the great issue of assurance was not yet resolved. The 1746 conference examined again the dogma of the previous year and then changed tack. First the notion that "sincerity"—the real desire to do God's will, as distinct from always following the blessed example—produced a "saving faith" was accepted into Methodist doctrine. Then the whole argument about salvation by faith or good works was dismissed to semantic quibbling. "In asserting salvation of faith we mean: that pardon (salvation begun) is received by faith producing works. That holiness (salvation continued) is faith working by love. That heaven (salvation finished) is the reward of this work." Methodism was still feeling its theological way, but it was determined to find a faith which was both intellectually consistent and compatible with the propriety of the connexion.

By 1747, Wesley (and therefore the conference) had changed their minds again and reverted to the old idea that assurance was essential. "This we know, if Christ is not revealed in them by the Holy Spirit, they are not yet Christian believers."[24] Once again, the "John Smith" device was used both to make his new meaning clear and to explain that it was no different from what he had meant ever since he first seriously considered these questions. "The sum of what I offered before concerning perceptible inspiration was this. *Every* Christian believer has a perceptible testimony of God's Spirit that he is a child of God."[25] The "John Smith" correspondence also examined Lord King's analysis of the Church of England's status as the one true vehicle for the expression of God's love. Naturally it accepted his conclusions as John Wesley had accepted them a year before. The doctrine was conveyed to society members in the usual question and answer form.

Q.: What instance or ground is there in the New Testament for a national Church?

A.: We know of none at all. We apprehend it to be a merely political institution.

Q.: In what age was the divine right of episcopacy first asserted in England?

A.: About the middle of Queen Elizabeth's reign. Till then all the bishops and clergy in England continually allowed and joined in the ministrations of those who were not episcopally ordained.[26]

Wesley continued, for almost forty years, to oppose the notion of Methodist ordination. But he must take the responsibility for convincing his connexion, long before then, that it would be a theologically respectable way for his followers to behave.

The progress of the Methodist Connexion can be measured in cycles in which periods of doctrinal reappraisal went hand in hand with renewed evangelical fervor. In the 1740s Wesley regularly preached to gatherings of thousands. But sermons preached to crowds in market squares and on commons could not be used to argue the complicated theology which Wesley employed as proof positive of his views on assurance, justification, universal salvation by faith and his right to preach independently of the Established Church. So he had added to all his other burdens the task of producing closely reasoned pamphlets on the great issues about which he had agonized for so long and which he believed he had at least begun to resolve in his own mind. Some of the pamphlets were classic tracts of three or four sheets. Others were virtually books of almost 150 pages. The longest works were often précis of other men's scholarship, a fact he never sought to disguise. The labors involved in abridgment and the discipline required to construct a commentary were so great that only a driven man would have added such a task to evangelizing in the great triangle of Newcastle, Bristol and London, as well as organizing what he increasingly regarded as a self-governing colony to the imperial church.

In 1745 alone John Wesley published thirteen titles. Some of them were responses and ripostes to attacks on himself and his societies. For as his connexion became more visible, it attracted the criticism which so often follows jealousy. Two criticisms, *A Serious Address to Lay Methodists to Beware of the False Pretences of Their Teachers* and *An Affectionate Address to the People Called Methodists*, were (to Wesley's chagrin) published by the Society for Promoting Christian Knowledge. The *Daily Advertiser* printed an advertisement, inspired by Count Zinzendorf and drafted by James Hutton, which declared that Methodists were a separate organization from the Moravians and should not, in any way, be associated with them. The Reverend Thomas Church, vicar of Battersea and prebendary of St. Paul's, set out the "Consequences of Methodism" in his *Remarks on Rev Mr. John Wesley's Last Journal when He Gives an Account of the Tenets and Proceedings of the Methodists*. According to Prebendary Church, they included "Enthusiasm, Antinomianism, Calvinism and a neglect and contempt of God's ordinances." As Methodism established both an organization and a doctrine, it was also developing a formidable body of enemies.

After the 1744 conference Methodism and Methodists attracted increasing antagonism, both from the church itself and from men who believed that Wesley's followers were a threat, not so much to established religion as to the accepted form of society in which priests and parishioners knew and maintained their proper places. The bishops shared an equal concern about doctrinal aberrations and the disruption of proper respect for the episcopate. *Observations upon the Conduct and Behaviour of a Certain Sect Usually Distinguished by the Name of Methodists* set out the complaints of the whole church hierarchy. It was almost certainly drafted by Edmund Gibson, bishop of London, who (if he was the author) had changed his view since he encouraged John Wesley to continue preaching his particular brand of faith in the way he chose. The pamphlet condemned the society meetings in private houses on the grounds that since they were public gatherings, those who attended them were Dissenters, and if they were not registered under the Toleration Act, the meetings were illegal conventicles. Registration was anathema to Wesley. For it was the formal concession that Methodism was outside the Church of England.

The disapproval of the establishment infected less illustrious strata of society. And soon mobs were renewing, with additional vigor, their attacks on Methodist prayer meetings in support of the archbishop of York's complaint that Wesley believed that "enthusiastic ardour" was the "true and only Christianity." Of course most of them were not quite sure what enthusiasm was or why it was an offense against the church. But they echoed the fear that long-held and respected values were under threat, as witness Methodism's elevation of men who were not ordained to something like the status of priest. The resentment increased as each of the subsequent conferences reinforced the organization and refined the dogma. There were also more personal objections to Methodism. The irritation which was caused by the exhibition of moral superiority was compounded by the fact that many of the men who urged sinners to change their ways were strangers who preached in towns and villages which, knowing little of what happened beyond their borders, were instinctively resentful of anyone from the world outside. Some of the practical concerns were justified, if not edifying. Methodism was a threat to the trades which the Puritans had once thought sinful: brewing, innkeeping and acting. Some Methodists even disapproved of music and musicians. But irrational fears were added to the reasonable apprehension. Methodists, it was said, persuaded men to neglect work in order to pray. And at a time when England again felt under threat from Catholic Europe's hope of returning the Stuarts to the throne, Methodists were once more suspected of being Jacobites in disguise. Charles Wesley had actually been heard to pray for "God's absent ones." He had meant sinners who, not having seen the light, were still outside the radiance of His love and forgiveness. But he was cross-examined by the magistrates on suspicion of having asked the Almighty to look kindly on the Old Pretender. The accusation of Stuart, and therefore Roman, sympathies was the hysterical product of the growing fear of invasion. In February 1744, when imminent invasion by France was rumored, all Roman Catholics were ordered to leave London. Charles Wesley wrote in his *Journal,* generally a more honest account of events than his brother's published memoir, that "the news of the threat from France only quickened us in our prayers, especially for His Majesty King George."[27] But John wanted a more public display of loyalty, not out of self-protection but as the result of his genuine feelings of loyalty to king and country.

John Wesley, in his allegiance to the ordained king more like his father than his mother, thought that it was necessary to send His Most Excellent Majesty "a humble Address of the Societies in England and Wales, in derision called Methodists." When he showed a draft of the text to Charles, he was warned that its wording "would constitute us as a sect—at least it would *seem to allow* that we are a body distinct from the national Church: whereas we are only a sound part of that Church." It was the sort of advice to which John Wesley was usually susceptible. But such was his concern to establish his fealty that he ignored the warning and, in a fit of patriotic fervor, portrayed the Methodists as the separated faith they were to become, though he took the precaution of denying that Methodism was outside the church.

> . . . we should not have presumed, even on this great occasion, to open our lips to your Majesty had we not been induced, indeed constrained, so to do by two considerations: the one is that despite all our remonstrances on that head we are constantly represented as a peculiar sect of men, separating ourselves from the Established Church: the other is that we are still traduced as inclined to Popery and consequently disaffected to your Majesty.

216

There followed an oath of allegiance which was intended to be absolute but was (almost certainly without Wesley's realizing it) equivocal. "We cannot, indeed, say or do either more or less than we apprehend [is] consistent with the written word of God: but we are ready to obey your Majesty to the uttermost in all things which we conceive to be agreeable thereto."[28]

The loyal address of 1744, written in the extreme circumstances of a likely Jacobite rebellion, reveals the essentially conventional element in John Wesley's character. Although he wanted to change the Established Church, he was a reformer, not a revolutionary. He wanted to respect, and be respected by, the hierarchy which he defied. This ambivalence in his character colored all that he did.

The allegation of papism, bizarre though it was, was no less absurd than the accusation that Methodists were instinctively subversive. Quite the opposite was true. Although John Wesley was prepared to challenge the authority of the Church of England in the name of God, he was a devout believer in the order which comes from a disciplined society. Methodists were not radicals. Charles Wesley prevented, by a combination of exhortation and threats of damnation, the Kingswood colliers from joining the corn riots of 1740.[29] Yet paradoxically, the popular movement against Methodism was prompted by the fear that it wanted to revolutionize a church which, although ineffectual, was comfortingly familiar. The rioters who broke up their meetings feared that if the Methodists had their way, the world would be stood on its head.

John Wesley had no wish to change the way in which society was organized—except where luxury at one extreme and poverty at the other stood between God and man. When he spoke of needing new men to build a new world, it was Christ's kingdom, inhabited by his saints, which he was offering to his followers. John Wesley believed that virtue must be built within the established order.

11

ALONG THE FLOWERY WAY

It took more than a decade for Methodism to become established in Ireland. George Whitefield had stopped briefly in Belfast on his way to Georgia in 1738. Where he stopped he preached. And John Cennick had visited Dublin at the invitation of the Society of Friends in 1746 and founded a Moravian society in the old Baptist meetinghouse in Skinners Alley. A year later Thomas Williams, a preacher who had fallen out with Wesley before he moved to Ireland, began independent preaching. He invited Wesley to join him, as both a gesture of reconciliation and the means of establishing Methodism in new territory. Wesley agreed at once and found the Irish "more teachable than the English."[1] He also discovered that the Irish were of an independent disposition. So a separate organization was formed with the promise of its own conference. By 1748 there were 350 "raw undisciplined soldiers" in Ireland who Wesley feared would "without great care desert their old master."[2]

At home in England John Wesley turned at least part of his attention to social questions. In 1746 he opened the People's Dispensary at the Foundry. Its purpose was to give "physic to the sick" according to his own prescriptions. The following year he published *Primitive Physick*, an "essay on easy and natural methods of curing most diseases." It was the natural result of an interest in science which, in the same year, prompted him to visit what his *Journal* calls "the electrical experiments." His medicine was less sophisticated than his physics. He claimed to "set down what appears in nature not the causes of the appearances." The practical remedies included placing the leaf of the celandine between the sole of the foot and the sole of the shoe as a cure for jaundice, and he prescribed a pound of mercury, taken in single-ounce doses, as a sovereign cure for twisted bowels. Twentieth-century historians have used the prescription as evidence of John Wesley's "anti-intellectual, philistine quality." But his view of medicine was no different from that of other eighteenth-century philanthropists who distributed medicine to the poor. At least, when he opened his dispensary at the Foundry in 1747,[3] he could claim, "I took into my assistance an apothecary and an experienced surgeon."

John Wesley's excursion into education was less philanthropic and more concerned with the greater success of the connexion. In 1746, George Whitefield had built a school in Kingswood with the primary purpose of educating the sons of colliers. It did not prosper even when it increased its numbers by adopting the sons of preachers from all over England. Wesley took over Whitefield's work and extended the building to include a large hall for preaching and accommodation for two full-time masters. The new school was opened on 24 June 1748. Its purpose was to teach the "poor to read, write and to draw accounts, but more especially (by God's assistance) to know God and Jesus Christ whom He had sent."[4] Wesley made sure that the task was properly accomplished by both setting the curriculum and composing the texts from which the lessons were taught, including an English grammar and primers for five other languages. As usual with Wesley, operating instructions were precise but capricious. The first class studied Wesley's *Instruction for Children*, which, he believed, provided the elements of a basic religious and secular education. In the second class the pupils studied Augustine's *Confessions*, in the third the works of Julius Caesar and in the fourth the *Iliad* and Greek verse. It was Wesley's firm view that the complete curriculum produced "better students than nine-tenths of Cambridge." It is not clear whether loyalty or caution prevented him from making the comparison with Oxford. The quality of the education was, he believed, improved by beginning each day with private prayers at four o'clock in the morning. Studies continued until eight in the evening. That timetable was based on Wesley's judgment that "He that plays when he is a child will play when he is a man."[5]

The character of the school changed—much to the dismay of Whitefield when he returned from America in 1749. What he had intended as a way of educating the sons of the deserving poor colliers of Kingswood had become an academy for the sons of preachers and extended to accommodate "lodgers" in the manner of Herrnhut. Wesley justified his new arrangements with the claim that men who traveled the country doing God's work needed to know that their sons were morally safe. Existing schools, although generally religious foundations, were, he believed, prepared to accept irreligious pupils and allow them to be taught by masters who were only nominal Christians.

By 1749 there were, in effect, four schools in Kingswood: separate day schools for boys and girls, a girls' orphanage and the "New House." Wesley's plan was becoming clear. "We design to train up children there, if God permits, in every branch of useful learning . . . till they are fit as to all the acquired qualification for the work of the ministry."[6] Wesley had chosen to build a theological forcing house in which boys were reared for eventual ordination and the Church of England ministry. The seminaries were to administer a stern regime. "Children of tender parents, so called (who are indeed offering up their sons and daughters unto devils), have no business here. For the rules will not be broken, in favour of any person whatsoever. Nor is any child to be received unless his parents agree that he shall observe the rules of the house and that they will not take him from the school, no not a day, until they take him for good and all."[7]

A man of such upright virtue and unyielding discipline must have found it immensely painful to discover, during the autumn of 1747, that his brother-in-law Westley Hall had become a practicing antinomian and therefore believed that true Christians (among whom he was sure he numbered) were released by the grace of God from observing either moral or temporal laws. He interpreted the dispensation as absolving him from the limitations of monogamy.

Hall, an Oxford Methodist, had provided early evidence of character defects. He had become secretly engaged to John Wesley's sister Martha and then abandoned her for Kezziah, one of the younger Wesley girls. Kezzy was abandoned in turn, and Hall took up again with Martha, who was then accused of stealing Kezzy's fiancé. Hall felt no obligation to explain the earlier relationship. Both Charles Wesley and his brother Samuel wrote poems lamenting Martha's decision to marry Hall and at once travel with him to Georgia, a fate from which she escaped as a result of her new husband's inconstancy toward the church as well as toward her. John, who had introduced the miscreant into the family, defended him even after Samuel wrote with evidence that Hall was a "smooth-tongued villain." The *Gentleman's Magazine* of September 1735, in an eighteenth-century version of the *Tatler*'s engagement notices, celebrated the union in misspelled verse.

> Such are Hall and Westley joining
> Kindred souls with plighting hands,
> Each to each entire resigning
> One become by nuptial bands.

The family did not disapprove to the extent that John Wesley was prepared to allow his new brother-in-law's conduct to stand in the way of loftier aspirations than human happiness. Hall was a potential disciple. So, no matter how badly he behaved toward Martha Wesley, Hall had to be encouraged. The marriage had taken place during the second week in September 1735, and Wesley had immediately invited his brother-in-law to join him on his mission to Georgia. Right up to 14 October, the day on which the brothers set sail, they expected Hall to join them. He had replied to their invitation with the news that both he and his wife were packed and ready and a carriage, with horses already in its shafts, waited in the yard. Then, in a further indication of his character, he sent another message to say that he had been offered a benefice in rural England which he proposed to accept.

Despite all the evidence to the contrary, for many years John Wesley continued to regard Westley Hall as "without question filled with the love of God. . . . The pattern of humility, meekness, seriousness and above all self-denial."[8] Disillusion came during the autumn of 1747. On 30 October Wesley wrote, from Salisbury, a letter which, when published in the *Gentleman's Magazine*, described Hall rather differently. "Many sober and judicious persons have often expressed their fears that the nocturnal meetings held at his house were scenes of debauchery: for now and then a bastard child was brought into the world by one of his devotees. . . . Last week he took formal leave of his flock and had the impudence to justify his infamous conduct from the case of Elkanah."

The precedent which Hall quoted was taken from the First Book of Samuel. Elkanah "had two wives. The name of the one was Hannah, and the name of the other was Penninah: and Penninah had children, but Hannah had no children." Under the pretense that his conduct was justified by the Old Testament, Hall, the *Gentleman's Magazine* reported, "set out for London, having first stripped his wife (a virtuous woman by whom he had seven children) of all her childbed linen and whatever he could readily convert into money. The flame of jealousy had broken out in many families where wives and daughters were his followers."[9]

Wesley rushed to see his sister and arrived in Salisbury on 1 December 1747. "From the concurring accounts of many witnesses" he learned the details "concerning the fall of poor Mr. Hall." The compassion which he felt for his sinful brother-in-law does him credit. But he was able to support his sister for only two days. His first duty was to consolidate his societies and the connexion by which they were bound together. At the time of Westley Hall's public espousal of antinomianism and his consequent polygamy Methodism was increasing in both number and strength, and Wesley was about to become its undisputed leader.

For more than twenty years, Wesley and Whitefield had been in uneasy partnership. They had argued, sometimes bitterly, about preordination. But they had worked together for the greater glory of God and the revival. In 1748, on his return from another visit to America, Whitefield became more closely associated with the countess of Huntingdon, a widow, and a member of the Ferres family, a noble house noted for its undoubted piety and probable insanity. Her critics claimed that it was "pride of birth" which attracted her to the "doctrine of the elect." Whatever her motives, she devoted her life to Calvinism, though during the early 1740s her approach to the revival had been sufficiently ecumenical to embrace Wesley's Arminianism and he had been an occasional visitor to her house at Donnington Park. She had also encouraged him to evangelize outside the Bristol–London axis. But her real loyalty was to George Whitefield and his theology of the elect. Lady Huntingdon chapels, which were built at her expense all over England, allowed Calvinistic Methodists to preach freely. Because they were called domestic chapels, they were exempt from the regulations which governed Dissenting public worship. Their existence formed a solid foundation for an independent connexion. It was when, because of her efforts, the number of chapels exceeded the number of preachers that she revised the constitution of Trevecka Theology College and gave it the task of training entrants into the Calvinist ministry.

Like Wesley, she was carried along by the impetus of her own enthusiasm and her supporters' determination to create a church in which they completely believed. The discovery that she had created, without quite realizing it, a Calvinist "movement" led her to believe that her followers needed a religious leader. When her opinion was reinforced by influential friends, she wrote to George Whitefield urging him to place himself at the head of a purely Calvinist Connexion. Whitefield, entirely unwilling to assume such a role, was concerned that Wesley might think him personally ambitious. So he wrote to explain that he could not be head of a party for he had "no party to be at the head of."[10] He explained that doctrine, as well as necessity, guided his judgment.

What have you thought about a union? I am afraid that an external one is impracticable. I find by your sermons that we differ in prin-

223

ciples more than I thought and I believe we are in two different places. My attachment to America will not permit me to abide very long in England: consequently I should weave a Penelope's web if I formed Societies; and, if I should form them, I have not proper assistants to take care of them. I intend, therefore, to go about preaching the gospel to every creature.[11]

Whitefield had always seen Wesley as the titular leader of Methodism and often said so. The declaration of 1748 was confirmation of that status. Almost since the earliest days together in Oxford, Whitefield had chosen to break the new ground which Wesley went on to cultivate. The division of labor suited Wesley's temperamental reluctance to spend time where success might not follow. He was always unwilling "to strike in any place where [he] could not follow the blow." Whitefield had successfully led the way in Bristol and in Ireland. His attempt to export the revival to Scotland in 1741 was a failure which Wesley was careful not to compound.

Whitefield's status as pioneer and pathfinder was confirmed by Wesley's reaction to the failed expedition north. The Scots' invitation had expressed unqualified confidence that Whitefield's theology corresponded exactly to theirs. On his arrival, they discovered that Whitefield did not adopt the extreme Calvinist position which the Presbyterians held, and he returned south to admit a failure.[12] Chastened by Whitefield's experience, Wesley did not venture north of the border until he felt certain of success.

It took years for John Wesley to convince himself that he might succeed where George Whitefield had failed. Encouraged by the invitation of Captain Gallatin, an army officer stationed at Musselburgh and, in consequence, a man unfamiliar with local attitudes, Wesley first rode north in the spring of 1751. On his arrival, he was warned by a local preacher, "You might just as well preach to the stones as to the Scotch," but the hope of leading a national connexion inspired the belief that Scotland could not be neglected. He determined at least to found societies in the large cities. By the time of Wesley's death, forty years later, there were still only eight chapels to show for his twenty visits. Failure was not the result of Scottish rejection of his Arminian doctrine. Thousands of Scots rejected the idea of predestination. But they were satisfied with the churches they already had. Religion in Scotland did not suffer from the torpor which infected England. There were doctrinal arguments within and about Presbyterian belief. But they were the result of Scotland's intellectual vitality and the healthy self-confidence of its churches. Combined with the diligence of a well-paid clergy, constant discussions created conditions in which it was difficult for Methodism to prosper.[13] There was no religious vacuum for John Wesley to fill.

Although Presbyterian Scotland was indifferent to John Wesley, John Wesley was far from indifferent to Catholic Scotland. A pamphlet, *A Word in Season or Advice to an Englishman*, set out the horrors which he anticipated would follow the restoration of the House of Stuart to the throne of England. His fear was that the pretender would "conquer England by the assistance of France" and "copy the French rules of government." His apprehension was increased by the certainty that England was "on the brink of utter destruction . . . because of our sins." He went on to list them: "sabbath breaking, thefts, cheating, fraud, extortion, violence, oppression, lying, robberies, sodomy and murder." Believing the list to be less than comprehensive, he added "and a thousand unnamed villainies." Twelve pages of what was as much a political polemic as a theological tract were devoted to the horrors which would follow the Old Pretender's usurping the throne of England. The passages were written with authority. Wesley had personal experience of the chaos which had been caused by no more than fear of invasion by James Stuart's son.

In 1745 Bonnie Prince Charlie advanced by forced march as far south as Derby. Had the Young Pretender not lost his nerve and turned back, London would have fallen to him and England would have been ruled by a Stuart monarchy. That tragedy was averted. But not without some inconvenience to John Wesley, who arrived in Newcastle for one of his regular visits on 18 September 1745, the same day that the Stuart army occupied all of Edinburgh except the invulnerable castle. Newcastle was in uproar. The mayor had summoned all householders in the borough to the town hall, where he required them to swear fealty to King George and prepare themselves to repel the invader. Eight hundred and thirty loyal burghers signed a declaration which "voluntarily obliged" them "to appear in person or to provide daily or when required an able man to act in concert with his majesty's forces."[14] The Orphan House was outside the town walls. So Wesley was not obliged to parade at the town hall. Indeed, as the Pilgrim Street Gate, through which he usually gained access, was bricked up to strengthen the fortifications, he might well have been physically incapable of doing so. Nevertheless, he thought it necessary to write to the mayor, explaining that his absence was not the result of "lack of reverence" for the municipal office and "much less was it owing to any disaffection to his Majesty King George."[15] The affirmation of fealty, written on the day that Charles Stuart's army defeated General Cope at Prestonpans, was also a plea to be excused service. His language was obsequious, even by the standards of the time. "I have no fortune at Newcastle: I have only the bread I eat, and the use of a little room for a few weeks in the year. All I can do for His Majesty, whom I honor and love (I think not less than I did my own father) is this: I cry unto God day by day in public and private, to put all his enemies to confusion."[16]

Three weeks later his affection was put to the test when he was required to make a sacrifice for the king's cause. The Orphan House stood in a position which would have made it a vantage point to Prince Charles's army as it advanced on Newcastle. General Husk, commander of the Hanoverian forces, instructed the Methodists that their property must be made less vulnerable to attack and capture. Wesley took less exception to the suggestion than to the way in which it was delivered. His complaint to General Husk illustrates that although the preachers were instructed to carry wood and clean shoes, their leader had a high regard for his own amour-propre. "A surly man came to me this evening, as he said from you. He would not deign to come upstairs to me, nor so much as into the house; but stood still in the yard till I came." The man, the complaint continued, then commanded, "You must pull down the battlements of your house, or tomorrow the General will pull them down for you." Like all such complaints, the letter emphasized that Wesley was entirely public-spirited. The demolition was of no consequence. "But

I humbly conceive it would not be proper for this man, whoever he is, to behave in such manner to any other of His Majesty's subjects at so critical a time as this."[17]

Neither the offense which had been caused by Husk's emissary nor the prospect of the Stuart invasion deflected Wesley from his real business in Newcastle. A couple of weeks after he had remonstrated with the general, he wrote to the mayor again. "My soul has been pained day by day, even in walking the streets of Newcastle at the senseless, shameless, wickedness, the ignorant profaneness of the poor men to whom our lives are entrusted. The continual cursing and swearing, the wanton blasphemy of the soldiers in general must needs be a torture to the sober ear." The letter concluded with a detailed and (the mayor must have thought) strangely gratuitous description of the Christian devotion displayed by British casualties during the Battle of Fontenoy. They had been supplied to Wesley by John Haime, a veteran of Marlborough's campaigns, who had become a traveling preacher.

A Word in Season, setting out the horrors which would follow a Stuart invasion, sold far better than Wesley's most important publication in the remarkable year of 1745. *A Further Appeal to Men of Reason and Religion* first summarized the doctrine on which he had settled and then, item by item, dealt with the many criticisms levelled at it. By then he had written enough "popular" books and pamphlets to guarantee him a steady income irrespective of how many serious works he sold. A sermon written in 1780 claimed that he had no idea of his earning power. "[H]aving a desire to furnish poor people with cheaper and plainer and shorter books than I had seen I wrote many small tracts, generally a penny a piece, and afterwards several larger. Some of these had such a sale as I never thought of, and by this means, unawares, I became rich. But I never desired or endeavoured after it."[18] That John Wesley did not seek riches or even aspire to be rich is a truth beyond doubt. But the idea that he did not realize the income that his pamphlets were generating is more difficult to believe. As early as 1749 he felt sufficiently confident of a steady income to promise that his brother Charles would, on marriage, be guaranteed a hundred pounds a year. It was a sign of John Wesley's fraternal devotion as well as his confidence in the continued popularity of his published work.

John Wesley, evangelizing around the "golden triangle," marked out by London, Bristol and Newcastle, as well as organizing his increasingly demanding connexion, left little time for anything except the remorseless demands of God's work. If not dead, the Cotswold friendships were certainly dormant. The reading had become less eclectic. No doubt he still thought of women, for he was temperamentally incapable of putting them out of his mind. But his instincts were suppressed and sublimated, and he no longer actively sought their company. Charles, perhaps because he thought himself a poet as well as a priest, had not completely put away worldly things. His attachment to the Church of England was stronger than his brother's, and his reluctance to break its rules far greater. Certainly the Wesleys were close. But while John was robust—the result, he claimed, of his rigid adherence to the rules of health and long life laid down by Dr. Cheyne—Charles was physically delicate and easily depressed. Henry Moore described Charles as "odd, eccentric and what is called *absent* to a high degree" and claimed that "despite their great love for each other," the obsessively neat and tidy John dreaded his brother's visits, "knowing well the disarrangement of books and papers which would probably follow!" However, in one particular they were damagingly similar. Both John and Charles were silly about women.

At Oxford Charles had become entangled with a London actress, and in Georgia his susceptibility had allowed him to be too easily duped by the women who claimed they were the mistresses of James Oglethorpe, the territory's governor. On his return to London, James Hutton had written that it would be best if both the Wesley brothers married and were thus kept out of trouble, though he added that he would not want his sister to marry either of them. And in 1745 a woman complained to the bishop of London that Charles had "committed or offered to commit lewdness with her." At the age of forty-two Charles decided to settle down with a woman nineteen years his junior.

During a mission to Wales he met Sally Gwynne, the daughter of a Welsh magistrate who had been converted to evangelical Christianity by Howel Harris. He used his skill with words, usually reserved for hymns, to write a love poem in praise of her:

> Two are far better than one
> For counsel or for fight
> How can one be warm alone
> Or serve his God aright?

Charles Wesley knew that he wanted to marry Sally Gwynne within weeks of their first meeting. However, on their return from Georgia the Wesleys had agreed never to marry without consulting each other, and Charles felt obliged to honor the agreement. So the proposal was delayed until the necessary consultation had taken place. John was not sure if Sally was suitable and, in an excess of fraternal concern, drew up a shortlist of names of other possible brides. Sally appeared on the list in last place. Charles talked to other friends. They too were doubtful about Sally's suitability. But Charles had one of the religious experiences which often pointed the Wesleys in the way they wanted to go. A feeling inside him prompted him to announce, "This is the Lord's doing. This is the Will of God concerning me." John was not completely reconciled. Would not marriage hinder the work of a traveling evangelist? Charles insisted that it would not and argued the case for married contentment so strongly that John changed his mind and became an enthusiastic supporter of the match. Marriage would bring his brother the peace he needed to continue and complete his work.

Sally's parents were not so enthusiastic. Even beneficed clergymen lived frugal lives. But Charles Wesley was a wandering evangelist with no fixed parish or income. Their daughter would, they feared, become a pauper. John quieted their anxieties by guaranteeing his brother an annual income of one hundred pounds for life. Charles was to have the first call on the profit made on the sale of John's books and pamphlets. It was a generous gesture, but one which makes it hard to believe that John "unawares became rich." All we can be sure of is that John Wesley did not spend his substantial income on himself.

Sally and Charles lived happily although in the bridegroom's words, the marriage ceremony was "cheerful without mirth" and looked "more like a funeral than a wedding."[19] The bride accepted from the start the demands of her husband's calling, about which she could hardly complain that she had not been warned. Charles spent the two weeks which followed the wedding preaching near his new home in Bristol. That was his only concession to his marital responsibilities. His *Journal* confirms that his priorities had not changed. "I then cheerfully left my partner for the Master's work."[20]

Despite his initial decision to put the Lord first, Charles Wesley gradually withdrew from the arduous work of an itinerant preacher. The demands of his family were in part responsible. His wife barely survived smallpox, three of his children died in infancy and the two sons who survived were musical prodigies.* So when it was no longer necessary to help his wife through the sadness of bereavement, he felt it necessary to share with her the joys of proud parenthood. But the gradual disenchantment was also, at least in part, the product of his fear that John Wesley, either by design or accident, was breaking away from the Church of England. The disengagement was gradual. But in 1753 John Wesley felt it necessary to complain that his brother was no more "in connexion" with him than George Whitefield. And he dated the disenchantment from the time of Charles's marriage in April 1749 and continued with the offensive injunction that it was necessary "either [to] act really in connexion with me or never pretend it." Then he laid down the rules by which the old relationship could be reestablished: "taking counsel with me once or twice a year as to the places where you will labor." The reproof revealed the real cause of offense. "At present you are so far from this that I do not even *know* when and where you intend to go."[21] John Wesley's authority was being ignored.

Yet the bond between the two men endured. And it was strong enough to survive in circumstances which would have ended forever a relationship which was not built on love as well as blood. Charles

---

* The eldest boy, named Charles after his father, was a fashionable, as well as brilliant, violinist and often entertained George III at Windsor Castle. He became music tutor to Princess Charlotte.

frustrated John Wesley's attempts to marry Grace Murray, almost certainly the only woman John Wesley ever really loved. And the nature of Charles Wesley's intervention, the virtual abduction of the prospective bride, might well have added profound moral condemnation to deep personal bitterness. Each brother, charged by high emotion, initially rejected the other. The emotion guaranteed swift reconciliation.

John Wesley must himself take some of the blame for the end of a courtship that might well have turned into a highly successful partnership. For in a bizarre repetition of his conduct with Sophy Hopkey in Georgia, he spoke of marriage in such ambiguous language that Grace Murray was never quite sure of his intention. Given time, he would have made his wishes clear. Charles made sure that time was denied him.

Grace Murray was born in Newcastle in 1716. In childhood "she was religiously disposed . . . but at the age of eight or nine she lost her religious impressions and began to attend dancing classes."[22] At eighteen she was on the point of marrying when she changed her mind and fled to London, where she became a servant in the house of an East India merchant. Her background, more the years in service than the dancing classes, was to have a profound effect on her prospects of marriage to John Wesley.

In London she met and married Alexander Murray, sometimes described as a sailor, more often as a ship's captain. She claimed that her husband's family had been associated with the Jacobite rebellion of 1715 and, in consequence, lost land and money, forcing Murray to sign on aboard a merchantman. Their only child died shortly after its first birthday, and Grace sought consolation in God. After hearing both Whitefield and Wesley preach, she was "converted" to Methodism. On his return from sea, her husband found her so obsessed with religion that he threatened to commit her to an asylum, but he was in time so impressed by the piety of her conduct and the strength of her conviction that he was converted to Methodism himself. Or so the Wesleyan legend goes.

Some facts are beyond doubt. Alexander Murray was drowned at sea in early 1742. The widow returned to her mother's house in

Newcastle. There was talk of her marrying again, but instead she moved to London, immediately joined the Foundry Methodists and took charge of the band which John Wesley had set up for the communion of pious women. In all probability she earned her living by returning to domestic service. The two qualifications, spiritual and temporal, were almost certainly the reason why, in the autumn of 1745, John Wesley suggested that she became housekeeper at the Orphan House in Newcastle. Her duties involved far more than the management of the property. She preached to classes of penitents, brought messages of cheer to the sick and visited Methodist societies in outlying parishes. Reunited with John Brydon, the man who it was thought would become her second husband, had he not lost his faith. A good Methodist could not become wife to a pagan. But Brydon reacted to rejection with the threat of suicide. "I was," she said, "afraid that his blood would be on my head because I did not marry him."[23] Fortunately he survived the ending of the relationship, and her feelings of guilt quickly passed.

Early in 1746 Grace Murray met "a gentleman dressed in black." It was John Bennet, the Methodist who had been instantly converted by a glance from John Wesley. Bennet came to the Orphan House in an advanced state of undiagnosed illness, but he recovered after Murray had prayed for both his body and his soul. Later, when he was fighting for her affection, Bennet claimed that he took her devotion to be a declaration of love and an indication of her hope that they would spend the rest of their lives together. John Wesley had been embarrassed by a similar conclusion. The inability to distinguish between compassion and infatuation was just one aspect of the emotional turmoil which afflicted many early Methodists. Murray and Bennet certainly corresponded for the next two years. But Grace insisted, "I never gave any answer concerning love affairs, for I thought that I would not marry again."[24] Like many Methodists, she had a relationship with religion that was emotionally indistinguishable from a love affair. The confusion often ended in disaster.

In August 1748 Wesley, visiting Newcastle, suffered a bilious attack. It could not have been very severe. For as well as preaching in the town, he addressed societies in Biddick, Pelton, Spen and

Horsley. But Grace Murray "nursed him back to health." On his recovery, at least according to his own account of events, he told her, "If ever I marry, I think you will be the person." It was, at best, a guarded proposal. But Grace Murray was entitled to believe that he was at least introducing the idea of marriage into their relationship. In fact Wesley treated her much as he had once treated Sophy Hopkey. He wished to think and talk about marriage but feared to become unequivocally committed to sharing his life with anyone but God.

Wesley was later to claim that he had proposed "more directly" and that Grace Murray gave him a "voluntary and express promise" to become his wife, thus entering into a contract of marriage *de futuro,* an arrangement about which the law of the time was ambiguous. Wesley's apologists claimed (as proof that his proposal was honestly meant and enthusiastically accepted) that Grace Murray's response to his overtures left no doubt about his intentions: "This is too great a blessing for me. I can't tell how to believe it. This is all I could have wished for under heaven."[25] It is just possible to argue that those sentiments do not amount to the acceptance of a proposal. But Grace Murray's subsequent conduct leaves little doubt about her wish to become Mrs. Wesley.

The relationship established, and his health restored, John Wesley prepared to set out from Newcastle to complete his tour of duty. It is not clear whether Wesley asked Grace Murray to travel with him or if she "begged that she might not lose him so soon."[26] In any event she accompanied him as he preached his way through Yorkshire and Derbyshire and was "unspeakably useful both to him and the societies."[27] The intimacy of the arrangement might in itself have been an indication of a formal agreement, with Wesley equivocating no more, had the excursion not ended with Wesley's leaving Grace Murray at Chorley in the care of John Bennet, his rival.

John Bennet had become a major figure in early Methodism. "Converted" in early 1742 after one beatific vision (the sight of John Wesley) had led to another, a vision of Christ, he had abandoned his merchant's business and created his own group of societies in the northwest of England. When Bennet threw in his lot with Wesley, he brought with him the whole "connexion." After he became a "son of the gospel," he attended as an invited lay preacher the 1744 conference, where he proposed the organization of quarterly meetings as a way of holding the connexion together and was welcomed as a man of practical ideas. Unfortunately, like Wesley's, his emotional relationship with God prejudiced his attitude toward women, though in his case divine intervention spurred him on rather than held him back.

In Bennet's view, his miraculous cure by Grace's healing hands meant that God had given her to him. This notion was confirmed by a dream in which Grace was told by Wesley, "I love thee as I did on the day when I first took thee," a clear suggestion that Bennet at least feared that Murray and Wesley's relationship had become intimate. Fortunately for his peace of mind, the dream continued with a rejection of the unwelcome advances. He decided that he had received a message from God which confirmed that Grace Murray should marry him. When he told her of what he regarded as a vision, he gave the solemn warning "Take care that you do not fight against God."

Fully awake next morning, Bennet approached the future more cautiously. He still believed that Grace Murray was his by divine decree, but he feared that Wesley stood in the way of God's will. "Is there," he asked, "not a contract between you and Mr. Wesley?" Grace Murray answered, "No," solely, she later claimed, to protect John Wesley's reputation. She then agreed that they should marry, if Wesley in his capacity as head of their church rather than as a rival suitor gave the union his blessing. She thus entered into a second contract *de futuro*.

Bennet wrote to Wesley with the less than gallant explanation that he proposed to marry Grace "although he did not want a woman," because he believed that God wished them to be united.[28] He added that he was prepared to overlook the damage which had been done to her reputation by the excursions to Yorkshire and Derbyshire. Wesley replied that Bennet had misunderstood God's intention and set off for Ireland. To confirm his intimate knowledge of the Almighty's wishes, he took Grace Murray with him. Letters were exchanged between Wesley and Bennet for several weeks. None of them mentioned Grace Murray's presence at Wesley's side. Bennet must have known that she was in Ireland, and Wesley knew that their relationship was about to undergo a radical change. In Dublin in July 1749 they signed a contract *de praesenti,* a form of private marriage which had legal force before the Marriage Act of 1753. It is not clear if Grace Murray thought that Bennet had deserted her or if she decided to desert him. Wesley, with some legal justification, convinced her that she need feel no guilt about reneging on the *de futuro* contract by which she had been committed to Bennet in Chorley. It was invalidated by the one she had earlier signed with him in Newcastle.

At the end of July the couple returned to Bristol, where Grace Murray, no doubt boasting about her forthcoming wedding, was told that Wesley was a notorious womanizer who had pursued other liaisons even during their brief courtship. Grace Murray's ardor cooled, and she began to think again about Bennet. For reasons which are inexplicable and unexplained, Wesley agreed to meet both her and Bennet at Epworth. Each party had a different account of what transpired after Bennet revealed that Grace had shown him every letter that Wesley had written to her. But it affected Wesley enough to make him announce that on reflection, he had decided that Murray's best interests would be served by marrying Bennet. According to Wesley, she then dissolved "in an agony of tears and begged him not to talk so unless he designed to kill her."[29] When he persisted in renouncing all claim to her hand, she ran to him, crying, "I love you a thousand times better than I ever loved John Bennet in my life. But I am afraid, if I don't marry him, he'll run mad." She had feared the same after she had rejected John Brydon, and the similarity between Mrs. Murray's protestations and Sophy Hopkey's fears for the sanity of Mr. Mellichamp (ten years earlier in Georgia) raise doubts about the accuracy with which Wesley described the Epworth meeting. But whatever the true facts of the encounter, Wesley's attitude veered wildly between the insistence (supported by Christopher Hopper, a preacher who had been called in to adjudicate) that propriety required Murray to marry Bennet and the assertion that she had been betrothed to him first and that Bennet must respect her earlier commitment and his undoubted seniority. After some vacillation Wesley endeavored to clarify the position by renewing the contract *de praesenti* with Hopper as witness. The law at the time was imprecise. The most accurate description of the relationship which resulted is "virtually married."

Accounts of what followed differ. In one version John Wesley wrote to his brother in Bristol with the news that a marriage had been arranged and Hopper was deputed to take the glad tidings to Bennet. In another, John Wesley wrote directly to Bennet and, despite the brothers' promise to consult each other before marriage, would have left Charles in ignorance of his decision had a copy of that letter not been sent to him by mistake. However he found out, as soon as Charles Wesley heard of the proposed wedding, he determined to do everything he could to prevent its taking place.

John Wesley began to vacillate again, and his doubts were confirmed by a dream reported in his diary entry for 1 October. "I dreamed I saw a man bring out G[race] M[urray] who told her that she was condemned to die and that all things were now in readiness for the execution of the sentence. She spoke not one word, nor showed any reluctance but walked up with him to the place. The sentence was executed without her stirring either hand or foot."[30] In a different mood, he would have regarded the dream as proof that she should submit to his will. In October 1749 he had begun to lose enthusiasm for the marriage. So the dream became an omen of doom.

Perhaps his brother Charles had already begun to convince him of the damage that marriage to Grace would do to the connexion. The problem, as Charles saw it, was her place in society. In an age when ordained priests were revered as persons of quality, John's marriage to a woman who had been a servant would, he feared, either split the Methodist Connexion or destroy it completely. And Charles was concerned about Grace Murray's legal status as well as her position in society. He set out "The case as it seems to me" in a letter which he hoped would make her realize the impossibility of the union with

John. "You promised J[ohn] B[ennet] to marry him—since which you engaged yourself to another. . . . And who is that other? One of such importance that in doing so dishonest an action would destroy both himself and me and the whole work of God."[31] Charles perhaps, not surprisingly, had got the events—*de praesenti* and *de futuro* agreements—out of sequence, but it is hard to understand why he feared that his own destruction might follow Grace's vacillation.

The stories again diverge. In one Charles and John Wesley decided—with or without Grace Murray's agreement is not clear—that Vincent Perronet, an increasingly influential figure in the connexion, should adjudicate on the legal status of the two suitors. In the other, John Wesley, preaching in Whitehaven, was persuaded by Perronet to go to Leeds and meet his brother for a reconciliation. He arrived in Leeds on the evening of 3 October 1749 but recorded, in dejection, "Here found, not my brother, but Mr. Whitefield," who told him that Charles had left for Newcastle and there he would remain "till J[ohn] B[ennet] and G[race] M(urray) were married." What was worse, Charles had taken Grace Murray with him. Whitefield's involvement in the unhappy affair confirms how personally close the Methodists remained even after their doctrines had irrevocably diverged. It also reveals the clear belief of the leadership that John Wesley had become such an important figure that his marriage was no longer a purely personal matter. Whitefield's legal judgment (for what it was worth) favored John Wesley. "It was his judgement that she was my wife and that he had said so to J[ohn] B[ennet]: that he would fain have persuaded them to wait and not to marry till they have seen me." But Charles was not a man to be diverted from what he believed to be the path of virtue. He decided on personal intervention, and his "impetuosity prevailed and bore down all before it."[32] His approach to his prospective sister-in-law left no doubt that he regarded his brother's affection for Mrs. Murray as a personal insult. "You have," he told her, "broken my heart."

Nehemiah Curnock, who edited Wesley's *Journal,* describes brother Charles as "capturing" Grace Murray and carrying her off. It is more likely that the impressionable woman was easily persuaded to ride with him, perched precariously behind him on his horse, to Newcastle. His plan seemed doomed when he discovered that Bennet did not want to see her, but Grace begged forgiveness, and Bennet relented. Charles Wesley seized the mood of the moment and on 3 October 1749 (the day on which his brother arrived in Leeds in the hope of meeting him) married Grace Murray to John Bennet in a ceremony which had none of the ambiguities of the previous contracts.

John Wesley received the news two days later. "At eight, one came to us from Newcastle and told us, 'They were married on Tuesday.' My brother came an hour after. I felt no anger but did not desire to see him." Whitefield told John that it was time for fraternal forgiveness. John did his best, but it was not reciprocated. Charles, exhibiting the difficulty of forgiving those we have wronged, told his brother, "I renounce all intercourse with you but what I would have with a heathen man or a publican," and it seemed to Whitefield and John Nelson, who were present at the failed reunion, that the two men could part forever. But they were wrong. First Wesley received his rival. "J[ohn] B[ennet] came in. Neither of us could speak, but we kissed each other and wept. Soon afterwards I talked with my brother alone. He seemed utterly amazed. He clearly saw I was not what he thought and now blamed her only; which confirmed me in believing that my presage was true and I should see her face no more."[33]

So poor Grace Murray was designated culprit for the emotional trauma which both the brothers, in their different ways, had suffered as a result of John Wesley's doomed courtship. The reconciliation with Charles was complete. John Wesley's published *Journal* for the following weeks and months records only a life of religious dedication, the itinerancy in no way disturbed by a broken heart.

That he loved her was not, however, in doubt. His feelings were accurately, if slightly sentimentally, described in his poem "Reflection upon Past Providence 1749."

> Oft, as through giddy youth I roved
> And danced along the flowery way,

By chance or thoughtless passion moved,
An easy, unresisting prey,
I fell, while Love's envenomed dart
Thrilled through my nerves, and tore my heart.

Borne on the wings of sacred hope,
Long had I soared, and spurned the ground,
When, panting for the mountain top,
My soul a kindred spirit found,
By Heaven entrusted to my care,
The Daughter of my faith and prayer.

In early dawn of life, serene,
Mild, sweet, and tender was her mood;
Her pleasing form spoke all within
Soft and compassionately good;
Listening to every wretch's care,
Mingling with each her friendly tear.

I saw her run, with winged speed,
In works of faith and labouring love;
I saw her glorious toil succeed,
And showers of blessing from above
Crowning her warm effectual prayer,
And glorified my God in her.

Despite the emotional reunion in Leeds, Bennet never quite forgave John Wesley. Indeed he continually feared and suspected that
despite his marriage, Wesley would persist in paying court to his
wife, a suspicion probably put in his mind by Charles, who knew of
his brother's previous record with married women. Quite independently of the Grace Murray affair Bennet was drifting away from
the Wesleyan view of Methodism and toward Whitefield and Calvin,
and his personal animosity toward Wesley must have accelerated the
alienation. By 1752 the breach was both formal and bitter. Bennet
attempted, fortunately for Wesley without much success, to swing

the whole northwest toward Whitefield. The Grace Murray affair damaged Wesley, not Wesleyanism.

The extent of John Wesley's pain was revealed the day after the reconciliation with Bennet in a letter to Thomas Bigg, a Newcastle Methodist. It reveals the anguish but not the equivocation.

> For ten years God has been preparing a fellow-labourer for me by a wonderful train of providences. Last year I was convinced of it; therefore I delayed not, but, as I thought, made all sure beyond a danger of disappointment. But we were soon after torn asunder by a whirlwind. . . . The whole world fought against me, but above all my own familiar friend. . . . Yesterday I saw my friend (that was) and him to whom she is sacrificed. I believe you never saw such a scene. But "why should a living man complain, a man for the punishment of his sins?"[34]

In a second letter, written to Charles, he set out how his views on marriage had changed over the years. As a child he had believed that he would "never find a woman such as my father had." Then (between roughly 1720 and 1730) he had put marriage out of his mind for more practical reasons. He could not afford to keep a wife. Moving from objection to objection, with what now appears a frenzied determination to justify his earlier rejection of marriage, he concluded that the Primitive Church believed that its priests should remain celibate. He then went on to explain that his objections had been refined from outright rejection of marriage to reservations about its propriety. The "taint upon the mind, necessarily attending the marriage bed" prevented a married man from concentrating his mind on God's will in the single-minded fashion which was possible for the unmarried. The need to keep a wife would also reduce a generous priest's ability to give to the poor. Finally he claimed that he had begun to revise all those views long before he met Grace Murray and that he had eventually come to the conclusion that marriage insulated the clergy from the social distractions of the single state.[35] And there was a second reason, at once more human and compelling, why marriage had become not so much acceptable as necessary, a reason so intimate that it had to be confided to his diary, not his brother. John Wesley needed to be protected from what he called "the ungodly desires and inordinate affections" which he "never did entirely conquer for six months together."[36] He then recanted the earlier view that the Primitive Church had demanded celibacy and defended his proposal to Grace Murray on the less than romantic grounds that it was "better to marry than to burn."

Marriage, which he had once thought certainly undesirable and possibly sinful, became an obligation. He decided to find a wife, and as always, he asked his friends to confirm the wisdom of the course on which he had already decided. He then responded to the needs of his public status with a statement on the subject. "Having reviewed a full answer from Mr. V[incent] P[erronet] I was clearly convinced that I ought to marry. For many years I had remained single because I believed that I could be more useful in a single state than in a married state." It was not quite true, but it served as a face-saving preamble to the recantation which followed. "I now fully believe that in my present circumstances I might be more useful in a married state." The *Journal* entry ends with an announcement which, for all its importance, is presented in the form of an aside. What sounds almost like an afterthought was added to the final reference to the married state: "into which upon this clear conviction and the advice of my friends, I entered a few days later."[37] Perhaps the casual announcement was meant to demonstrate that marriage was an obligation and that like George Whitefield, John Wesley "despised such vanities as love."

Mary Vazeille, a merchant's widow from Threadneedle Street, London, with a jointure of three hundred pounds per annum and a grown-up son,[38] came into John Wesley's life through the agency of his brother Charles, who met her at Edward Perronet's house in July 1749. It seems that she was seeking spiritual help, and it was, no doubt, to assist in its provision that Charles Wesley took her to stay with his wife's relations in Ludlow. When he and his wife returned with her to London, stopping in Oxford for a tour of the colleges, they stayed at the Vazeille house for more than a week. Although he clearly did not regard her company as intolerable, when he discovered that she might become his sister-in-law, he was horrified. Had any other name been put to him he would have been equally distressed.

The first meeting between John Wesley and his future wife was not recorded in his *Journal*. But by the summer of 1750, which was spent in Ireland, he wrote to her in terms which, although overtly pastoral and spiritual, were clearly meant to cement their relationship. By the autumn he had begun to think of Mrs. Vazeille as the woman who would protect him from worldly distractions. His letters began to reflect his admiration of her personal qualities. "I admire your indefatigable industry, your exact frugality, your uncommon neatness and the cleanness both of your person, your clothes and all things around you."[39] And the object of his admiration possessed another irresistible virtue. Mrs. Vazeille was well beyond childbearing age. She could become his wife without jeopardizing the itinerancy with the demands of fatherhood.

By 2 February 1751 John Wesley had told his brother that he was "resolved to marry." Charles, whose presumption knew no limits, was "thunderstruck and could only answer that he had given me the first blow and his marriage would come like the *coup de grâce*."[40] John, no doubt anxious that his bride was not carried off and married to someone else, did not reveal the future Mrs. Wesley's name.

It was "trusty Ned Perronet" who told Charles that the lucky lady was Mrs. Vazeille, "a woman of sorrowful countenance," of whom, up to that time, the younger brother "never had the least suspicion."[41] The fact that his attitude was one of suspicion and the fact that he had clearly suspected other women indicate that he knew his brother was dangerously susceptible and that he objected, in principle, to John's marrying anyone. Charles "groaned all the day and several of the following ones under [his] own and the people's burden," not because his new sister-in-law was unsuitable, but because his brother had accepted obligations which would hamper his work and had failed to keep the undertaking, made by both brothers long ago in Oxford, that neither of them would marry without the other's approval. Charles's judgment—questions of fraternal loyalty aside—was woefully wrong. Nothing could ever prevent John Wesley from giving absolute priority to Methodism. Certainly he was not distracted by domestic misery. And in the words of John Hampson, his onetime follower, "Had he searched the whole kingdom he would hardly have found a woman more unsuitable to the prospects of a happy marriage."[42]

John Wesley decided to break his promise to his brother by marrying without Charles's agreement at the climax of the wrong courtship. Had he been prepared to ignore that undertaking a year earlier he would have married Grace Murray. But he discovered the penalties of allowing others to veto his most personal plans only after his hope of happiness had been extinguished. So when he decided to share his life with Mrs. Vazeille without much thought or any advice, he broke both rule and promise and plunged into a marriage which began in acrimony and ended in disaster.

Shortly before his marriage—and we must presume in order to soften the effect of the announcement—Wesley wrote to all his preachers with the apparently perverse recommendation that "all those who are single should remain free from responsibility and encumbrance." But as always, he added a caveat to cover his own special case. Exceptions could be made to the general rule on the authority of divine guidance. If the marriage between Mary Vazeille and John Wesley was made in heaven, Providence was sadly lacking in imagination. For the courtship followed a familiar pattern. First spiritual advice. Then a more personal relationship. The period of doubt which inevitably followed was ended by the sudden need for the prospective bride to nurse her future husband through a temporary indisposition. Sophy Hopkey and Grace Murray had done the same. In the case of Mrs. Vazeille, her ministrations came at a time which guaranteed that Wesley's vague inclination to be translated into the reality of marriage.

A week after he told Vincent Perronet that he had become convinced that marriage was (at least for him) a blessing, John Wesley "after preaching at five . . . was hastening to take leave of the congregation . . . purportedly to set out in the morning for the North, when in the middle of London Bridge, both feet slipped on the ice."[43] His leg was "bound up by a surgeon," and he managed to

walk to the Seven Dials meetinghouse and climb, with great difficulty, into the pulpit. He was then carried by coach and sedan chair
to the Foundry. But he was in too much pain to preach. So he was
"removed to Threadneedle Street," to be in the care of Mary
Vazeille, who had become a pillar of London Methodism. Wesley
spent the rest of the week in prayer, study and work on two books,
Hebrew Children and *Lessons for Children.*

By Sunday, 17 February 1751, he was well enough to be carried
to the Foundry, but because he could not stand, he delivered the sermon on his knees. Wesley had hoped to set out for the north on the
following day but was still unable to walk. He occupied his time by
marrying Mrs. Vazeille. According to the *Gentleman's Magazine,* the
ceremony took place on 18 February. The *London Magazine* dated
the wedding as 19 February. Whatever the date, they lived unhappily ever after.

It took longer for Charles to be reconciled to John's marriage than
to accept the consequences of his brother's failed courtship of Grace
Murray. Even so, the acrimony lasted for less than a week. Then, after sacrament at the Foundry on Sunday, 24 February, an Ebenezer
Blackwell (in a well-meaning initiative) "fell upon" Charles and,
"beating, driving, dragging" him to his sister-in-law's house, demanded that the brothers become friends again.[44] Three days later
John and Mary visited the chapel where Charles was minister in
charge. Charles did his best to overcome his feelings and gave his full
blessing to the union. "I was glad to see him; saluted her; stayed to
hear him preach; but ran away when he began his apology."[45]

The apology was repeated wherever John preached for the next
month. It was not an expression of regret that he had chosen to
marry but a justification of his sudden change of view on the subject
of marriage in general. While Mrs. Wesley "sat open-eyed," he explained that at Oxford he had no more thought of a woman than for
any other being, that he married to break down the prejudice about
the world and him. Perhaps Grace found some consolation in the
certainty of his conclusion: "I am not more sure that God sent His
Son into the world than that it is His will I should marry."[46]

The wide-eyed bride herself was told that he hoped the marriage would "crown all your life with the work of faith and the labour of love,"[47] but he also warned that he had carefully considered the possibility that domestic obligations might hinder his work. She would, he was sure, be relieved to learn that he had decided that she would not be a burden. He expressed his confidence in language which she could not have found reassuring. His attitude to the obligations of marriage could not have been less equivocal. "If I thought that I should [preach] one sermon or travel one mile less on that account, my dear, as well as I love you, I would never see your face more."[48]

Wesley's "apology" to the society referred, as proof of the sincerity of his intentions, to the sacrifice of the "independent fellowship" which, according to the statutes of his college, he was obliged to resign on marrying. Mrs. Vazeille's fortune could have easily compensated for the loss, for in the days before the Married Women's Property Act, it passed automatically to her husband. However, to protect himself against the charge of fortune hunting, Wesley settled ten thousand pounds, the bulk of the late Mr. Vazeille's estate, on his wife and her children by her previous marriage.

At first it seemed that Charles Wesley's forebodings were misplaced. Ten days after the wedding, "being tolerably able to ride but not to walk," John Wesley set out for Bristol. Mary was left behind. She received regular affectionate letters. They were "helpmeets for each other," and the memory of her brought to mind two lines from Sappho. "And see and hear you all the while / Softly speak and softly smile."[49] He asked, "How is it absence does not lessen my affection? I feel you every day nearer to my heart. O that God may continue His unspeakable gift,"[50] and called her his "dearest earthly friend."[51] He returned home to Mary confident that he could fulfill the obligations which he had once believed were in conflict with each other. When he came to describe his early weeks of marriage in his *Journal,* he piously reiterated the warning he had given his wife on their wedding night. "I cannot understand how a Methodist preacher can answer it to God to preach one sermon or travel one day less in a married than in a single state."[52]

After a month at home Wesley set off for Newcastle. There were early hopes that Mary would travel with him. But she was not suited to the life of an itinerant preacher's wife, and soon her resentment at his absences began to show. By May 1751 she was sufficiently dissatisfied with her lot to tell Blackwell (the friend who had worked hard to reconcile her husband and his brother) that she "had many trials." By the end of the year she was so frustrated that she told her friends that John did not love her and that she suspected that he was at least seeing other women during his frequent absences. She provoked public disputes with the preachers and denounced John Bennet "in the gall of bitterness and bond of iniquity" in a way which made her husband wonder if she was mad. He eventually settled on a more prosaic explanation of her conduct. She had married him for money and had been disappointed by his modest standard of living. Not even the ten-thousand-pound settlement, which John Wesley regarded as a gift, had, he feared, reduced her resentment at the income from book sales, which he had settled on Charles, having been lost forever. That, he judged, was why she so disliked his brother. Her animosity was thoroughly reciprocated.

Most of the blame for the disaster which the marriage became must be heaped on John Wesley. He had proposed to a highly emotional recent convert, one who was flattered beyond common sense by the idea of becoming the wife of such a prominent figure. All he really wanted was a companion, a nurse and a gatekeeper against the intrusion of other susceptible women. And the constant protestations of love and devotion which were a feature of the early months of marriage made his later cold hostility all the more hard to bear. Yet the crisis, when it came, was caused by one of the acts of conspicuous affection which John Wesley thought it necessary to perform during the first days of his marriage. He told his wife, "If any letter comes to you directed to the Reverend John Wesley, open it: it is for yourself."[53] Unfortunately Mary Wesley took her husband at his word.

12

EXTRAORDINARY PROPHETS

When, after a month of marriage, John Wesley left his wife and traveled to Bristol, he told her that he was to have "urgent conversation" with his preachers. The conversations he had in mind, held as part of the 1751 Methodist conference, might have been more accurately described as cross-examinations. John Wesley had become so disturbed by what he had discovered about the behavior and the beliefs of some of his followers that he had decided that another purge was necessary. That decision was in direct opposition to the demands of the society members. Thirty preachers served nine circuits in England, Wales and Ireland, and Methodists had no doubt that the fast-expanding connexion needed more, not fewer. Wesley agreed. He was happy to encourage new recruits, but before he could take on new men, he wanted to make sure that his established lieutenants were not behaving in a way which he regarded as against the real interests of the connexion.

He accepted the inevitability, if not the desirability, of minor doctrinal differences as long as the preachers believed in salvation by faith with good works as redemption's consequences. His real objection was the espousal of beliefs—particularly unauthorized ordination and communion—which went further than acceptable, almost to the point of inviting expulsion. And he was even willing to accept the right to argue for both these heresies if the alternative was the loss of membership or the collapse of a society. However, he would not tolerate disreputable personal conduct, a cause of concern which he defined in different ways at different times. The constant rule changes which reflected his shifting views on propriety were as much intended to confirm his authority as to encourage and enforce propriety.

The Methodist membership saw the need for extra preachers in simpler terms. They wanted the new recruits to be available to perform additional duties. Chief among them were those extensions of their ministry which would have precipitated a formal break with the Church of England, particularly administering the Eucharist. Yet John Wesley had taught his followers that regular communion was a symbol of sanctity, and the ordained priests of the Church of England would not provide them with the frequent sacrament which they thought essential. The pressure on John Wesley to appoint more preachers and to give them an extended (and possibly heretical) authority grew daily harder to resist. But he was determined to avoid the heresies of both ordination and unauthorized communion. So he responded to the pressure by attempting to "purify" the preachers who had already been appointed and were, often in the interest of their own status, encouraging members to agitate for a relaxation on the rules governing the Eucharist. "Purify" was a euphemism for "expel."

John Wesley had decided, years before, that his preachers should not and could not be judged by the standards which defined the Anglican ministry. "Will you," he had asked, "condemn a preacher because he has not university learning or has not a university education? What then? He saves those sinners from their sins whom the man of learning and education cannot save."[1] But although he was not concerned about the absence of formal qualifications, Wesley was deeply worried about the personal disreputability of some of his followers and their willingness, indeed determination, to encourage demands for a head-on collision with the Church of England. Only half a dozen preachers were invited to Bristol for the 1751 conference. So, to complete the "conversations," three other confrontations were needed. Two were held in Leeds, and one was in Newcastle. Charles Wesley, who was certain to be robust in his defense of Church of England orthodoxy, was deputed to carry out the northern examinations. He announced his intention to judge the "grace, gifts and fruits" which each preacher had brought to Methodism.

Having agreed that his brother should deal with the northern heretics, John Wesley began to worry that Charles would be too exacting. So he urged him "not to check the young ones without strong necessity" and added a footnote on the qualities which new preachers were required to possess. "Of the two, prefer grace before gifts." To Charles it sounded dangerously like antinomianism. So Charles, warned by his brother that "we must have forty preachers or drop some of our Societies," pressed on with his purge.

The brothers had agreed on the principles by which Charles's purge should be guided. The criteria went far further than the identification of preachers who demanded to be regarded as priests and, true to John Wesley's character, were applied with a bewildering inconsistency. "Disorderly walkers," effeminate men, busybodies and "triflers" were not acceptable. Immorality was to be regarded as a reason for immediate expulsion. Charles would have defined "inadequacy" slightly more rigorously. He wanted to remove preachers with what he described as "insufficient gifts," a condition he thought to be endemic in the Irish.[2] John, exercising an authority which he had assumed rather than been granted, reminded Charles of the note he had added to the letter which commissioned him to smite the ungodly. Grace was the essential quality. However, the brothers were able to agree, without an argument, on the immediate expulsion of James Wheatley, a "wonderful self-deceiver and hypocrite" who had exhibited "obstinate wickedness" in his behavior toward women.[3] The charge sheet which was presented to other offenders was more controversial.

William Darney of Todmorden had already been accused of "stiff-neckness," by which John Wesley meant that he was reluctant to accept the authority of the conference. He was not, however, easily disciplined. He had brought into the connexion several independent societies and was a close friend of William Grimshaw, the perpetual curate of Haworth and, for a time, Wesley's nominated successor as chairman of the conference. However, Charles was determined that Darney would "bend or break" and, in effect, put him on probation after he had promised to publish no more of the doggerel verse which he claimed was divinely inspired. He went back on his word and was "laid aside" along with nine other miscreants.

Among them was Robert Gillespie, judged by Charles Wesley as "unworthy to preach the gospel," even though John believed he was doing God's work. The joy with which Charles overrode his brother is evident from the language in which he reported the laying aside of Grace Murray's husband, John Bennet. "A friend of ours (without God's counsel) made a preacher of a tailor. I, with God's help, will make him a tailor again." Charles was determined "to purge the Church, beginning with the labourers."[4] His criteria of acceptability included unqualified loyalty to the Church of England. He was also determined to illustrate his independence from his older brother, who, he feared, was not sufficiently ruthless in his opposition to "those preachers who felt neither love nor loyalty for the Church of England."

The purge, for purge it was, had, at least in the Wesleys' eyes, a theological justification. The Methodist preachers' duty was to "preach Christ,"[5] expounding both the law and the gospel. Too many preachers were following Wheatley's example and offering an "unconnected rhapsody of unmeaning words." Most of the preaching was not as bad as that. But it did—partly because of the untutored nature of the preachers—often stray from the classic interpretations of the Scriptures. The careful distinction which Charles Wesley chose to make between acceptable and unacceptable preachers was also a reflection of Methodist politics. Charles had very little sympathy for the preachers who complained of John's "rod of iron." But because he resented being ruled with it himself, he made common cause with some of his brother's critics.

Nobody disputes that from then on, John Wesley increasingly treated his preachers like the other ranks in the holy army which he commanded. The only argument is about what motivated his autocracy. Henry Moore, one of the biographers who actually knew

Wesley, set out what has become the classic defense of "Pope John." "The arbitrary power, so called, was exercised from first to last in keeping his associates to the work of God, that wholly religious design and employment which they all profess to embrace as their duty and calling when they joined him. And from this he certainly would not consent that any of them should swerve. In everything else he was, even by their own account, a father and a friend."[6] The father was stern, and the friend frank. Thomas Walsh was told that it was his preaching style—"violent straining of his voice added to frequent colds"—that brought on the consumption from which he died. John Cowmeadow was also a "martyr to loud and long preaching."

The mold in which John Wesley cast his preachers might, from the start, have been designed to attract applicants who would be difficult to manage. The requirements were set out in the question-and-answer form which he thought contributed to easy understanding. To the question "In what view may we and our *helpers* be considered?," he replied that they should be thought of as "extraordinary messengers" who were required "to provoke the regular ministers to jealousy" and to "supply their lack of service towards those who are perishing for lack of knowledge." The laws which governed preachers' official duties were supplemented by rules which guided their private conduct. "Never while away time, nor spend more time at any place than is strictly necessary. . . . Avoid all lightness and jesting. . . . Converse sparingly and cautiously with women. . . . Speak evil of no one. . . . Tell everyone what you think of him lovingly and plainly. . . . Do not affect the gentleman."

Wesley always insisted that he did not take the initiative in recruiting preachers but that volunteers insisted that they serve with and under him. The result was a motley army of Methodists who needed constant guidance about correct theology and the proper attitude toward the Church of England. Methodism was made up as it went along—very largely inside John Wesley's troubled mind. So authority was essential to cohesion, and John Wesley was the only authority Methodism possessed. There were always disagreements about both his interpretation of the Scriptures and his definition of holy living. But at least according to Wesley himself, the 1751 conference proved that "The more we conversed, the more the brotherly love increased. We seemed to be all of one mind as well as one heart." The unity was not as great as he believed or pretended. Nor was every brother quite as loving as he suggested. But there was just enough love and unity to keep the connexion more or less in one piece.

When Michael Fenwick was removed from the list of preachers, Charles Wesley gave or lent him the capital which he needed to set himself up as a barber, the trade he had left to follow God. That calculated distancing from his brother's criticism of Fenwick was part of his plan to help preachers into approved employment and thereby reduce their dependence on John. The plan was to "break his power . . . and reduce his authority within due bounds." Charles hoped to provide a more collegiate leadership and thereby "guard against his brother's rashness and credulity," qualities which Charles, much to his increasing resentment, said had kept him "in continual awe and bondage for many years."[7] Charles set out his intention in a letter to Lady Huntingdon, a dubious ally since because of her Calvinism, she owed her first allegiance to George Whitefield. The letter was intercepted by one of John Wesley's friends, letter opening being a constant practice in a connexion increasingly riddled with suspicion and fear. John retaliated in the manner of Tennyson, who complained about the quality of Balliol claret after the master of that college had criticized one of his recent poems. Why, he asked, had Charles collected money for the quarterly circuit fund to pay preachers' expenses when he was already allocated fifty pounds a year for that purpose *and* received the hundred pounds' annuity from the book fund? The calculated insult provoked another period of hostile silence.

Once again Vincent Perronet mediated and restored peace. With his assistance an agreement on preachers was drawn up. "None shall be permitted to preach in any of our Societies, till he be examined both as to grace and gifts . . . that no person shall be received as a travelling preacher or be taken from his trade by either of us alone, but by both of us conjointly, giving him a note under both our hands . . . Signed John Wesley, Charles Wesley."[8] One instruction was a matter of practical necessity. Even when approved and endorsed, "a preacher should not be immediately taken from his trade but be exhorted to follow it with all diligence." The Wesleys certainly wanted their preachers to remain part of the world they worked to save. But they also wanted them to pay for their own keep. In the early years there was no money for wages. And the remuneration of full-time preachers remained an issue until the late 1770s. Then what amounted to a wage structure was determined: twelve pounds a year for the preacher, twelve pounds for a wife, four pounds for a child and six pounds for the board and wages of a servant. If a society could not pay, the connexion accepted the responsibility. The scheme confirmed both the strength and independence of Methodism.

The agreement of 1751 held for the next five years, but the partnership was no longer a union of the hearts; had it been, the formal agreement would not have been necessary. It was even thought necessary to formulate a method of arbitration which could be employed when they were in dispute over the appointment of a preacher. "That if we should ever disagree in our judgement we will refer the matter to Mr. Perronet." New allegiances filled the vacuum left by the abandonment of old. Charles, although never a Calvinist, became increasingly close to Lady Huntingdon and visited her regularly to administer communion in her private chapel, a new loyalty which his brother deeply resented.

In May 1752 Whitefield returned from one of his regular visits to America, a mission made notable by his defense of Georgia's decision to allow slavery within its borders. There was, he argued, biblical precedent for the practice. He had barely landed when he began to complain about the contents of a tract which John Wesley had written and published the previous year. *Serious Thoughts upon the Perseverance of Saints* claimed to examine both sides of the question but was openly critical of the Calvinist position. At first Whitefield was only contemptuous. "Poor Mr. Wesley is striving against the stream. Strong assertions will not go for proofs with those who are sealed by the Holy Spirit even unto the day of redemption."[9] He might have been right to suggest that the growing emphasis on

Methodist orthodoxy was alienating some preachers as well as members. For during the early part of the year new and more strenuous efforts had been made to maintain Methodist unity around what John Wesley by then regarded as an established doctrine. On 29 January 1752 the Wesleys and eleven other itinerants had signed a concordat "not to listen or willingly inquire after any ill concerning each other" and when they heard "ill of each other . . . not to believe it." Promising not to believe information which has not yet been received must be as difficult as proving a negative. But at least the agreement assured the increasingly suspicious priests and preachers that when any of their colleagues heard a scurrilous rumor they would "as soon as possible communicate what [they] heard by speaking or writing to the person concerned" and until then "not write or speak a syllable of it, to any other person whatsoever."[10]

Seven weeks later six of the original signatories thought it necessary to subscribe to another declaration of collective loyalty. Rumors which "tend to weaken the union" and personal gossip had, in the name of God, to be avoided. The success of Methodism depended "in great measure . . . on the entire union of all labourers employed therein." But the new declaration defined union and promised unity in significantly different terms from the January statement. It ended with a promise which, although only a subclause, was the real purpose of the whole exercise. Charles and John Wesley, John Downey, William Spent, John Jones, and John Nelson all vowed "never to leave the communion of the Church of England without the consent" of one another.[11]

There was at that time no direct pressure for a break with the Church of England. But members continually demanded extensions to the connexion's work which, were they adopted, would—Charles Wesley in particular believed—inevitably lead to schism. He was dubious about his brother's ability to walk the theological tightrope between orthodoxy and heterodoxy, and he must have realized that John's ability to satisfy the societies without prejudice to the church was immensely hampered by his lifestyle. The continual itinerancy created the illusion that he was in constant communion with the societies. But in truth, he almost always saw them in circumstances which made a frank exchange of views impossible. He preached the Word of God and then passed on. And after the summer of 1751, he was either accompanied by a wife with whom he had little or nothing in common or anxiously anticipating news of the damage she had done to his reputation when she was left behind.

John Wesley set out from London on 15 May 1752, immediately after the concordat was signed and the day before it was circulated to the societies. He was on the road in England and Ireland for seven months and throughout that time in touch with London only by messages passed by word of mouth, letters carried by hand and the unreliable post, all of which took several days to cover the distance from the Midlands to London. It took him nine days, in snow and ice, to reach Manchester. In Birdsall, wind as well as weather was in his favor. When he preached, his voice carried for more than 140 yards. At Leeds he preached in the new chapel, and in Wakefield in the parish church, where—with the memory of the York riots still in mind—he was surprised, and perhaps relieved, to find so appreciative and attentive a congregation. In Sheffield too "all was at peace," and when Wesley moved east to his old home, the people of Epworth welcomed him as a returning hero. Unfortunately he found his brother-in-law Richard Ellison in abject poverty. His land was flooded, and his livestock were dead. There was in John Wesley's account of the disaster a note of disapproval which almost certainly means that he suspected Ellison of poor husbandry. But Sukey's welfare had to be protected, and Wesley attempted to make some provision for their rescue before he moved on to the coast. The welcome which he had received in south and west Yorkshire was not reproduced by the people of the East Riding. In Hull the mob began to turn on Methodism again. "Thousands gave serious attention," but hundreds pursued his coach and threw "whatever came to hand" at its windows. Wesley was protected from injury by "a large woman who sat on his lap" to act as a shield. The agitation spread. In York a magistrate tried to incite the citizens to break up the meeting by distributing copies of a scurrilous pamphlet, *Papists and Methodists Compared*. There was a small disturbance before the sermon was completed. It must, however, have been with some relief that on 30 April he arrived in Newcastle, the apex of the golden triangle.

When John Wesley turned south again, the mob at Barnard Castle dragged the town's fire engine out of its coach house and attempted to soak him and his congregation in water. Some of the worshipers were wet, but none was driven away. It should have been the last sermon before Whitehaven and Ireland. But when Wesley arrived at the port, his ship had already sailed. So he retraced his steps east. He had already witnessed a miracle at Wickham, where the sight of an eighty-year-old widow had been restored. At Todmorden there was a second manifestation of God's power and love. A clergyman, who had suffered violent fits of the palsy ever since he denounced Methodism from his pulpit, received John Wesley's forgiveness and began slowly to recover. It was on that joyous note that he returned to Whitehaven. On 13 July 1752 he set sail for Dublin.

Ireland was facing many of the problems which John Wesley had left behind in England. In mid-August he presided at what amounted to the first Irish conference. The formal business was setting up circuits and stationing preachers, but the discussion soon moved on to an examination of disagreement and dissatisfaction among the members. Methodism was reaching a stage in its development at which it must either close ranks around a precise doctrine and strictly enforced rules or risk disintegration into half a dozen factions. Wesley's temperament and his profound belief in Methodism's mission allowed only one response.

So the conference of 1753, held in Leeds, returned to the refinement of both dogma and discipline. First Wesley had to withstand "the corruptions of the Germans," the influence of the Moravians, who were so confident of their increasing appeal that they promoted a bill in Parliament to regularize their relationship with the Church of England and established, at the price of crippling indebtedness, national headquarters in Chelsea. The Methodists had also to resist the "taint of predestination and antinomianism." The increased influence of the Whitefield tendency owed something to the Wesleys' characteristic intellectual vacillation. Methodists had for a time readjusted their position to a point at which they accepted that the universal hope of salvation might be accompanied by what the Calvinists called the "unconditional election" of a chosen few. They then abandoned that amendment to their beliefs on the good and practical grounds that the acceptance of final perseverance was an agreement that a chosen few were guaranteed salvation, come what may, and therefore promoted antinomianism. Backsliding, an endemic disease of early Methodism, could be prevented only by the constant effort of priests and preachers. In consequence, assurance was final only if virtuous men and women struggled right to the end of the road. Lurches in belief played into the hands of the always certain George Whitefield.

So John Wesley, who had cooperated with the Calvinists even as he disputed their doctrine, decided that the time had come to do more than argue against preordination. Alien doctrines had to be purged from the connexion. The Leeds conference decided to overcome the threats from Calvinism and the Moravians by setting out more stringent rules of conduct. It resolved that what it called "predestination preachers' should be informed that "none of them shall preach any more at any of the Societies" and that "a loving and respectful letter should be written to Mr. Whitefield desiring him to advise his preachers not to reflect (as they had done continually and that both with great bitterness and rudeness) either upon the doctrine, discipline or person of Mr. Wesley." Whitefield replied to the letter with an insistence that the resolution "filled Mr. Wesley's people with needless jealousy." He wished that the Methodists would "talk less of persons and things and more of Him." The theological boundaries were gradually being drawn.

After a brief discussion on justification resolved that a true convert who could not identify "the exact time when he was justified" was the victim of poor preaching, the Leeds conference agreed that the preachers were not as strong for Christ as might be wished. That unhappy state they attributed in part to marriage with "unbelievers," defined not as women who were not Christians but as women who were not Christians of the right sort. It was agreed that in the future marriage to such a person would lead to immediate expulsion from the society. At the conclusion of the conference John Wesley wrote to Ebenezer Blackwell, "The harvest has not been so plenteous for very many years as it now is in the north of England; but the labourers are few." Methodism was still in desperate need of extra preachers. Yet the Wesleys constantly purged those who were already in place. The brothers had come to believe that their standards of conduct and character could not be compromised to the slightest degree. A consistency of belief (as defined by John Wesley at any one time) was essential to preachers in a unified and self-confident Methodist Connexion.

The pressures which led to the continual purges continued to build up. But John Wesley was never oppressed by the demands of leadership, and the itinerancy went on: the north and Scotland in the spring of 1753, back to London for the early summer, then on to the southwest before returning, through the Cotswolds, to London and the Home Counties. The work among the poor continued at the same time without interruption. In February he had visited the Marshalsea Prison (a "hell upon earth" and "a shame to those who bear the name of Christian") and then spent the next two days among the sick. According to his *Journal,* he witnessed scenes of suffering which were not to be found even in a pagan country. If one of the Native Americans in Georgia was sick ("which, indeed exceedingly rarely happened till they learned gluttony and drunkenness from the Christians"), those who were nearest gave the sufferer whatever was necessary for comfort and relief. No such compassion was to be found in England. His criticism was not, however, of all English society but of the prosperous middle classes. In the Marshalsea he found the paupers admirably industrious, "not one of them unemployed who was able to crawl about the room. So wickedly devilish false is that common objection, 'They are poor only because they are idle.' If you saw these things with your own eyes, could you lay out money on ornament or superfluities?"[12]

Time was even found for distractions appropriate to a son of the Enlightenment. In 1747 Wesley had witnessed what he called "the electricity experiments" and accepted their importance long before the significance of the discovery was recognized by the Royal Society. He regarded the experiments as a vindication of faith. "How must these also confound those poor half thinkers who will believe nothing but what they comprehend."[13] Benjamin Franklin's *Experiments and Observations of Electricity,* published in the *Gentleman's Magazine,* convinced the scientific establishment that "the species of fire, infinitely finer than any other yet known" was worth further examination and so excited John Wesley that he copied the main conclusions into his diary and then, as proof of his eclectic enthusiasms, published them in his *Journal.* In 1753 he was again intrigued by electricity's mysterious quality, particularly the way in which although "electrical fire discharged on rat or fowl will kill it instantly, discharged on one dipped in water, will slide off and do it no harm."[14] The pursuit of such questions was as close as John Wesley ever got to recreation.

From time to time attempts were made to lighten John Wesley's load. "A proposal was made for devolving temporal business, books and all, entirely on to the stewards; so that I might have no care upon me (in London at least) but that of the souls committed to my care."[15] Wesley, who was usually reluctant to delegate any of his power, seized on the idea with unqualified enthusiasm. Two sympathetic London businessmen, Thomas Butts and William Briggs, were appointed what he called book stewards, and a letter, almost certainly drafted by Wesley himself, was sent to all the societies in their name. It required each society to see that "a proper person be appointed to take charge and dispose of the books under your direction." It enjoined, "Let exact accounts be kept," and required all bills to be paid within three months. Most important of all, it stipulated that the two book stewards stationed at the Foundry should be "kept informed of books sold and profit made." Almost everything that Wesley did in mid-1753—revision of dogma and reorganization of the societies—had the result of concentrating power with the Wesleys at the heart of the connexion.

The book steward notion clearly attracted Wesley less because it lightened his load than because it increased his authority. Rest he found intolerable. And despite his hypochondria, he usually faced real illness with a reckless fortitude which usually complicated his condition. On Saturday, 20 October 1753, he felt what he described as "out of order" and on Sunday, the twenty-first "was considerably worse" but wrote, "I could not think of sparing myself that day." On the next day he was "extremely sick," yet he was "determined . . . to set out soon after four for Canterbury." For a month he continued his labors, sometimes feeling better, sometimes worse. Then, on 24 November, he felt so ill that he would have "stayed at home . . . had it not been advertised in the public papers" that he would preach a charity sermon that day. On Friday, the twenty-sixth, he was warned by his doctor that his only hope of cure was "country air, with rest, asses milk and riding daily." John Wesley took the advice but did not believe that the prescription would effect a cure. That night, believing that he was dying, he composed his own epitaph, "to prevent vile panegyric."[16]

<blockquote>
Here Lieth the Body
of
JOHN WESLEY
A brand plucked from the burning
Who died of a consumption in the fifty-first year of his age
Not leaving after his debts are paid
Ten pounds behind him.
God be merciful to me, an unprofitable servant
</blockquote>

Charles Wesley in his *Journal* quoted the epitaph in full. After the description "A brand plucked from the burning," he added, as a comment on his brother's many temptations, "not once only."

Although John Wesley had certainly overestimated the seriousness of his illness, the thought of his possible death concentrated Methodist minds on the succession. John Wesley himself had always assumed that his brother was next in line. So had most society members. But when the question became, or seemed to have become, a practical issue, Charles Wesley abdicated. "I neither could nor would stand in my brother's place (if God took him to Himself) for I had neither a body nor a mind nor talents nor grace for it." His removal from the succession, entirely a matter of his own choice, diminished his authority within the whole connexion. It might even have reduced his influence on his brother. Charles was the principal advocate of avoiding conflict with and separation from the Church of England. And at the end of 1753, just as John announced that he was dying of consumption and Charles renounced any desire to succeed him, the Methodist Connexion and the Established Church were only weeks away from a head-on collision.

Once again the casus belli was Holy Communion and the Church of England's unwillingness or inability to offer the sacrament as often or in the way that the Methodists were taught was essential to their salvation. The pressure for confrontation came, as was so often the case, from the rank-and-file members of the societies. As always, John Wesley wanted to remain in harmony with the Established Church but did not want it enough to risk the disintegration of his connexion.

Wesley was still adamant that unordained preachers should not administer the sacraments. The rock on which he built that stern conviction would not crumble. But there was a way of meeting the members' demands without violating Wesley's conscience. Unfortunately it offended the church more than unlawful communion. It was unlawful ordination.

Back in 1746 John Wesley had read Lord Peter King's *Inquiry into the Constitution, Discipline, Unity and Worship of the Primitive Church.* In 1755 he read Stillingfleet's *Irenicon.* Together the two books convinced him that the insistence on episcopal ordination was "an entire mistake,"[17] and Wesley concluded that the ancients, of whom he was still enamored, regarded the difference between bishops and presbyters as purely a matter of administrative convenience. If that were so, and if their judgment on the question remained valid, presbyters were entitled to ordain other presbyters, and the communion dilemma could be solved by the legitimate ordination of more priests. The doctrine was not so much disputed as dismissed by the Church of England. And at least in the early years of the controversy, John Wesley had not been prepared directly to challenge the Anglican establishment. But the idea took root in his mind. It blossomed and bore fruit when he thought the time had come both to break the power of the bishops and to justify his apostasy. In Georgia he had refused to administer communion to a parishioner who had been baptized by a priest whose ordination did not acknowledge "the apostolic succession." But the evangelical impulse had changed his mind. Arguments about who should administer the sacraments had become in Wesley's mind inextricably linked with his convictions about the preacher's sacred duty. He had written that the preacher's duty was to "save souls from death, reclaim sinners from their sins and that *every* Christian, if he is able to, has the authority to save a dying soul."[18] If that required the provision of Holy Communion, it was difficult to argue that the preacher should refuse to do his duty.

Wesley remained cautious but unyielding. His judgment, "If we cannot stop separation [from the Church of England] without stopping lay preachers, we cannot stop it at all,"[19] was typical of his determination to support his preachers, if necessary at the expense of the church. When the conflict was not with the church itself but with its apologists, he was totally uncompromising. Charles Wesley's threat to leave the conference if lay members were given the same status as ordained priests was met with the instruction "Give my brother his hat."[20]

For ten years the conflict about his position in the Church of England had raged on in John Wesley's mind. In 1748 his *A Word to Methodists* emphasized the importance of remaining part of the Established Church. But his critics accused him of advocating obedience while acting "contrary to the comments of [his] spiritual governors and stabbing the Church in the vitals."[21] The equivocation was, to a large degree, forced upon him as the only way to keep the connexion satisfied and still remain in the church. Robust defense of the need to obey the church's edicts offended the most militant preachers. While the church accused John Wesley of leading his flock into the wilderness—for no better reason than vanity and self-aggrandizement—the most committed Methodists complained of his reluctance to offend the bench of bishops.

In the high summer of 1751, Charles Skelton (who was soon to leave the Methodists because John Wesley would not leave the church) wrote to Wesley suggesting the creation of an "aristocracy" within the connexion to act as a cabinet or executive; it would have the power to ensure that all important decisions were taken, or at least endorsed, by the preachers. His letter complained with equal passion about John Wesley's autocracy and the tyranny of the church. Both arguments proved counterproductive. Perhaps, like all tyrants, John Wesley lived in perpetual fear of being overthrown and thus believed that calls for democracy must immediately be crushed. In 1752 yet another purge was begun. The new rules required all Methodists to make a declaration of loyalty to their new church. It was, John persuaded Charles, essential if Methodism was to be saved from becoming another irrelevant sect.

Yet Wesley could not altogether suppress the desire to speculate about the nature of the relationship between Methodism and the church. He did not "think either the Church of England or the People called Methodists or any other Society under Heaven to be the True Church of Christ. That Church is one and contains all true believers."[22] The notion of an indivisible church was a convenient justification for the continual detachment from Canterbury and York. But Wesley's temperamental inability to leave an idea alone led him into new areas of unorthodoxy. Eventually he followed the logic of the belief to the point at which (at least temporarily) he denied the need for baptism on the grounds that if it were essential to salvation, all Quakers would be bound for hell. And Quakers were, at that moment, regarded by Wesley as part of the indivisible church which he had just invented.

Charles Wesley continued to argue not so much for caution as for principled loyalty. In 1752 he had written a warning letter to his brother reminding him that the obligation of their ordination was "chiefly to members of the Church wherein we have been brought up." It was their duty "never knowingly or willingly to hear, speak, do or suffer anything which tends to weaken that union."[23] It was, John Wesley agreed, his duty to accept that injunction. But he continually failed to live up to the standards which he agreed were required of him—usually because conflicts with the church were forced upon him by Methodists who felt no allegiance to anything except Methodism. In June 1754, Thomas Sherlock, bishop of

London, excommunicated a Methodist named Gardiner for the sin of preaching without a license. The excommunication was a direct challenge to Wesley's authority as leader of the Methodist Connexion and a denial of the basic doctrine that Methodism was part of, not separate from, the Church of England. It was for that reason that he had forbidden his preachers to register as Dissenters. John Wesley's reaction to the bishop's initiative combined revolution with resignation. "It is probable the point will now speedily be determined concerning the Church. For if we must either dissent or be silent, *Actum est*." It is all over.[24]

The crisis heightened with the news that Charles Perronet, a man whom both Charles and John Wesley held in great esteem, had "given the sacrament to the preachers Walsh and Deaves and then to twelve at Sister Garder's." Charles was outraged by what he believed to be sacrilege and was mortified by his brother's response: "We have in effect ordained already." John's explanation that in his view, the commission to preach amounted to the same thing as allowing distribution of the sacraments did nothing to reduce his brother's fury. It increased when he discovered that a new ritual had been added to the preachers' commissioning ceremony. At his brother's suggestion, they knelt while John, one hand on their heads handed each a New Testament and told them, "Take this authority to preach the gospel."[25]

While Charles was urging John to avoid de facto separation, other, more strident voices were arguing that the crisis of unmet demand for communion could be ended only by outright separation. Thomas Walsh, a rare convert from Catholicism, told John Wesley that the people demanded the sacrament but would not receive it from ungodly priests. They would, however, "joyfully communicate with those by whom they have been brought to God."[26] The evidence from Haworth confirmed Walsh's judgment. When Whitefield visited the parish and assisted William Grimshaw at the communion service, the congregation was four times greater than the church could hold. They "sipped away thirty-five bottles of wine within a gill."[27]

Wesley was advised,
'preach faith 'til you have
it and then, *because* you
have faith you will
preach faith'
Hulton Getty

During the fifty-two years of
Wesley's itinerancy he preached
more than 40,000 sermons
Wesley & Methodist Studies Centre

Samuel Wesley dedicated his
Commentary on the Book of Job to
Queen Caroline. When John, his
son, presented it to Her Majesty
she was complimentary about the
binding
Wesley & Methodist Studies Centre

The Oxford Holy Club 'took
great pains with younger
members of the university to
rescue them from bad company'
Hulton Getty

General James Edward Oglethorpe – prison reformer and Governor of Georgia, a territory which he 'held in trust for the poor'
Wesley & Methodist Studies Centre

Thomas Maxfield – probably the first Methodist lay preacher. Susanna Wesley warned her son, 'Take care what you do in respect to that young man for he is surely called by God to preach as you are'
Wesley & Methodist Studies Centre

Wesley found the Creek Nation possessed 'no inclination to learn anything but least of all Christianity' *Hulton Getty*

August Spangenberg believed that 'grace really dwelt and reigned' in Wesley but advised him 'all good women avoid'
Eileen Tweedy / Thames & Hudson

Peter Böhler reinforced Wesley's belief that only faith could save and that faith must be complete and unqualified
Eileen Tweedy / Thames & Hudson

Prevented from preaching in Epworth parish church, John Wesley addressed the congregation from the graveyard. He wrote in his journal, 'I did far more good by preaching from my father's tomb that I did by preaching three years from his pulpit'
Hulton Getty

The City Road Chapel. New meeting houses were built all over the country without any regard for cost until Wesley insisted that they all came under his control
Wesley & Methodist Studies Centre

The Wednesbury mob complained that 'Methodists sing psalms all day and make folk rise at five o'clock in the morning.' Wesley claimed that God ensured that he survived the riots unharmed   *Hulton Getty*

Charles Wesley was 'odd, eccentric and what is called absent to a high degree'. But he was also a powerful intellectual force for at least postponing Methodism's eventual separation from the Church of England *Wesley & Methodist Studies Centre*

George Whitefield – a better preacher than Wesley but a man who had no desire to lead the Revival. Despite their theological differences, Wesley and Whitefield remained friends to the end *Wesley & Methodist Studies Centre*

Wesley preaching at the Connexion to an audience depicting the men who followed him
Eileen Tweedy / Thames & Hudson

Susanna Wesley told John, her
son, ''tis an unhappiness, almost
peculiar to our family, that your
father and I rarely think alike'
Eileen Tweedy / Thames & Hudson

Susanna Wesley's grave. Charles's epitaph referred to his mother enduring seventy years 'of grief and tears' – a comment on her acceptance of Methodist theology only at the end of her life
Private Collection/Bridgeman Art Library

The ordination of Bishop Asbury. 'Ordination meant separation' wrote Lord Acton. By consecrating its own bishops, Methodism made the breach with the Established Church inevitable   *Eileen Tweedy/Thames & Hudson*

The Methodists were doing no more than accepting Wesley's insistence that regular communion was essential to virtue. They were demanding that their spiritual needs be met. The seriousness with which the members took every opportunity to fulfill their spiritual obligation was illustrated by a letter written to the bishop of London by the vicar of Devlin, after more than fifty new communicants attended his Christmas Eucharist. His sympathetic account of the newcomers' piety confirmed that many priests who had little time for John Wesley nevertheless admired the devotion to God which he inspired in his followers. "It is a great tribute to the society that they wish more frequent opportunities to receive Communion. Some had come that morning . . . very near ten miles on foot, through weather very severe."[28]

As the pressure from the members built up, Charles Wesley began to fear that his brother's resolve to remain loyal to the church was weakening. "He is wavering, but willing to wait before he ordains or separates." Whether or not an antichurch faction was plotting to push the connexion into schism, Charles certainly believed that extremists were planning to demonstrate that unless it could guarantee regular communion from acceptable hands, it would dissolve. And the only practical way for that demand to be met was the ordination of priests by John Wesley and his acceptance, no matter how unwillingly, of excommunication from the Church of England. The issue had to be resolved one way or the other. Wisely, John Wesley agreed that the Leeds conference of 1755 should discuss a paper prepared by him and baldly titled "Ought We to Separate from the Church of England?"

Charles Wesley, who always feared the worst, had begun to believe that his brother either actively wanted separation or accepted it as inevitable and that the debate which he proposed was intended as a prelude to schism. For months he had warned friends whom he knew to be loyal to the church that the split was inevitable. He had congratulated Walter Sellon, a preacher and sometime master at Kingswood School, on "seeing through" those who continually urged separation on his brother. "Cursed pride had perverted them."[29] By the end of the year personal resentment had reinforced principled disagreement. "Since the Melchisedechians* have been taken in, I have been excluded from the cabinet council." His brother had evolved from dupe into villain. "He has come so far as to believe that separation is quite lawful, only not yet expedient."[30]

The brothers met to agonize about their differences on the day before the conference assembled. Charles wrote to tell his wife that the "preachers from the north" were unanimous for separation but that Grimshaw, "whom the separationists claimed for their own," had announced that "he would take his leave of us if we did of the Church." The debate went against separation. But Charles Wesley, who was determined to be dissatisfied, took exception to its tone, if not its result. Separation was rejected, less as a matter of principle than as a question of expediency. He left Leeds as soon as the separation debate was over without bidding his brother good-bye and after announcing, "I have done with conference for ever." On his way to London he composed his "Epistle to the Revd Mr. John Wesley." He read it to a "crowded audience" at the Foundry and paid for the printing of four thousand copies. He was particularly severe on "disloyal clergy."

> When first sent forth to minister the word
> Say, did we preach ourselves, or Christ the Lord?
> Was it our aim disciples to collect,
> To raise a party or to found a sect?[31]

John Wesley's approach to the continuing separation debate was offensive to his brother because it was, by necessity, pragmatic. Charles was offended because schism had been rejected for practical rather than theological reasons. But however pragmatic his reasons, John Wesley opposed separation during the 1755 debate in the most

---

* Melchisedech (usually spelled Melchizedek) gave bread to Abraham on his return from battle. Charles Wesley probably meant to refer to Methodists who were obsessed by the Eucharist, which, some scholars claim, Melchizedek originated.

robust language. Separation, he argued, would damage the societies by turning member against member, divert energies which should be used for saving souls into the sterile business of constitution making and lower Methodism's reputation with Christians who respected them without subscribing to their beliefs. His conclusion was that separation at that time would inevitably result in Methodism's becoming an unrepresentative and uninfluential sect. That had been the fate of earlier breakaway movements, and the connexion could hope for nothing better. His conclusion—that whether or not separation was lawful, it was certainly not expedient—was a less than a wholehearted proclamation of unity. But he followed his insistence on loyalty with a litany of rules setting out how loyal Methodists must behave. They must not deny or ignore Church of England doctrines, absent themselves from services or either resist or resent the laws and governances of the Established Church.

The arguments in favor of separation were set out less clearly in his speech to the conference than in a letter he wrote to Samuel Walker in Truro. The church, he said, was essentially "unscriptural" in its beliefs and liturgy. Its courts and customs were often "popish" or "heathen." There were problems with the liturgy—particularly the obligation to declare absolute consent to the whole contents of a "merely human composition." Many Church of England clergymen had not received "the inward call to save souls" and "neither lived the gospel nor knew it and taught it." The criticisms were represented as the views on the church expressed by rank-and-file Methodists. But he endorsed their judgment with the concession "I will freely admit that I cannot answer these arguments to my own satisfaction."[32] He could, however, repeat them with great clarity and conviction. Indeed he endorsed them with the admission that it was because of the failures of the Church of England that Methodists had "(1) preached abroad, (2) prayed extempore, (3) formed Societies and (4) permitted preachers who were not Episcopally ordained." He concluded his letter with what his brother would have regarded as a shameful admission. "Were there no alternative allowed, we should regard it as our bounden duty, rather to separate from the Church than to give up any one of these parts."[33] The carefully managed form of the debate was proof of both John Wesley's wish to remain within the church and the less than heroic fashion in which (to his brother's dismay) he ensured that the conference came to the same conclusion. "Lawfulness of separation" was debated first. "And it was only when we could not agree concerning this that we proceeded to discuss the expediency of it."[34] In a second letter written to Thomas Adams of Winteringham a month after the conference ended John Wesley confirmed how fragile the allegiance was. "We are fully convinced that to separate from the Established Church is never lawful but when it is absolutely necessary, and we do not see any such necessity yet."[35]

Charles Wesley naturally regarded the expediency argument as wholly unsatisfactory. To him church membership was a matter of principle. Clearly, to his brother, it was not a question of conscience. If circumstances changed, it might—on John Wesley's analysis—be expedient to leave. And Charles had no doubt what was meant by the frightening phrase "but when it is absolutely necessary." John Wesley would remain loyal to the church as long as it did not prevent him from acting like an independent force within it. He knew that none of the four essential freedoms which he set out in his letter to Samuel Walker was likely to be expressly forbidden. So at least schism had been avoided for the moment. Only if he claimed that the preachers were, in effect, ordained priests would a head-on collision be unavoidable.

Knowing that the powers of the preachers were the crucial issue, John Wesley had been careful to describe them to the 1755 conference in the most conciliatory language. Once again he drew a precise distinction between the preachers being "commissioned" by him, which might have seemed dangerously like unlawful ordination, and their enthusiasm to evangelize being rewarded with "permission" to preach in Methodism's name. He was explicit and emphatic in his insistence that a man who was "permitted" to become "an extraordinary preacher of repentance" was not authorized—by him or God—to administer communion. He claimed, with the support of biblical precedents, that the church had always accepted the existence of "extraordinary prophets" who were allowed to preach "when under extraordinary inspiration" but were never allowed to officiate at services which celebrated the Eucharist. In a remarkable (and intellectually discreditable) reversal of opinion, he even abandoned, or temporarily put aside, his earlier conviction that bishops and presbyters are members of one and the same order of priesthood. The suggestion that there was only one order of priests was, he said, "contrary to the New Testament and to all antiquity."[36] But although he seemed to be rejecting all the theories which offered his followers the hope of regular communion, he could not resist arguing that his "extraordinary prophets" were particularly blessed. Ordained priests had produced few converts before they embraced Methodism. "Can there be stronger proof that God is pleased with irregular even more than regular preaching?"[37]

In an attempt at reconciliation with his brother, John Wesley made a genuine attempt to be emollient. "I do tolerate unordained persons in preaching the gospel whereas I do not tolerate them administering the sacrament."[38] That was not the strongest possible endorsement even of lay preaching. But Charles was not impressed. He did not believe in his brother's sincerity. But he could not wholly resist his instinct to work with, rather than against, him. So he too attempted to be conciliatory and wrote, "The short remains of my life are devoted . . . to quench the flame of strife and division" which threatened to engulf Methodism.[39]

Charles began to fear separation by stealth. The preachers' attitude toward the Church of England worried him almost as much as the prospect of their usurping the sacred duties of ordained priests. They often either ignored the doctrine of the Church of England or treated it with contempt. In an attempt to hold back the tide of independence, he took to writing declarations of loyalty to both friends who shared his views and societies which opposed them. He told Grimshaw, "Nothing but grace can keep our children, after our departure, from running into a thousand sects and a thousand errors." The Leeds Society was urged to "[c]ontinue in the old ship. Jesus hath a favour for our Church and is wonderfully visiting and reviewing His work in Her." Rotherham, about to leave the church, was warned, "No salvation out of the Church."

The joint examination of preachers continued. Charles Wesley was still most concerned with their loyalty to the Church of England, John Wesley with their personal attributes and strength of calling. He was, throughout his life, dissatisfied with the performance and commitment of even his most devoted disciples. "No one I ever knew has all the talents which are needful for beginning, continuing and perfecting the work of grace in a whole Congregation."[40] But he thought 1755 a particularly disappointing year. "None of our itinerant preachers are so much alive as they were seven years ago . . . which of you is a pattern of denial in little things? Which of you drinks water? Why not? Who rises at four? Why not? Who fasts on Friday? Why not?"[41]

Charles Wesley did not keep his vow never to attend the annual conference again. He was duly in attendance in 1756, probably because he judged that his brother was in a mood to reaffirm his allegiance to the Church of England. Charles's campaign among the societies had built up opposition to secession. The activists wanted to leave, but the "silent majority" was determined to stay. Although Charles Wesley was absolutely loyal to the church, he was uninhibited in his disloyalty to his brother. Nine days before the conference met in Bristol he told Walker of Truro, "I should have broken from the Methodists and my brother in 1752, but for the agreement to remain in the Church and for us to act in concert with each other."[42] He described the plan which he, Grimshaw and others hoped to persuade John to accept. It amounted to a declaration of unity and the division of preachers into the "unrecoverable" (who would be expelled) and the "sound" (who would be prepared for ordination). Walker did not believe that Charles Wesley's solution would satisfy "regular clergy" who could not "in conscience work with lay preachers." He suggested a variation to Charles Wesley's scheme. "Unrecoverables" should certainly be expelled. But the "sound" should be confined to supervising duties in the societies and forbidden to preach.

Charles Wesley's reply reflected his understanding that the preachers' right to preach was not a principle on which his brother would compromise. Indeed it was the old issue which might make him abandon the Church of England.

Lay preaching, it is allowed, is a partial separation and may, but *need* not, end in a total one. The probability of it has made me tremble for years past and kept me from leaving the Methodists. I stay not so much to do good as to prevent evil. I stand in the way of my brother's violent counsellors. The object of both their fear and hate ... I know my brother will not hear of laying his lay preachers aside in so many words.[43]

So Charles Wesley sensibly decided to build on his brother's temporary emollience and at least ensure that the Methodists themselves did nothing that might lead to expulsion, provoke again the societies' enthusiasm for voluntary separation or encourage his brother to believe he had to make a choice between Methodism and the Established Church.

The "unrecoverables" were expelled. They included, as well as Roger Ball (openly antinomian) and John Edwards (a sheep stealer), John Toular, whose offense was "talking in his witty way against the Church." Plans were drawn up to attract a better class of recruit. Extra funds were provided for the Kingswood School so that more free places would be available to preachers' sons. The *Christian Library*, a présis of devotional and doctrinal texts on which Wesley had begun to work in 1749, completed by John Wesley the previous year, was made more easily and cheaply available. Fate, or divine will, made every new initiative, whatever its initial purpose, contribute to the creation of an increasingly independent and centrally controlled organization.

It was, however, (at least for a time) an organization which remained steadfast (at least in form) in its allegiance to the Church of England. A declaration of loyalty—exactly the words which were embodied in the agreement of 1752—was signed by all members of the conference. John Wesley's *Journal* records that on Saturday, 28 September 1756, "My brother and I closed the Conference by [*sic*] a solemn declaration of our purpose never to separate from the Church; and all our brethren concurred therein." To John Wesley's pleasure and relief, he was at peace with his brother. The fraternal tranquillity was not to last for long.

13

Things I Dislike

The obligation of celibacy was imposed on the Roman Catholic priesthood in the Late Middle Ages as a practical necessity. There was no suggestion that marriage was sinful, only that it was an impractical distraction. John Wesley was never distracted. He took it for granted that the wife of an itinerant minister, whose husband set out at four o'clock in the morning, changed horses at noon and rode on until midnight, stopping only to preach along the way, was obliged to be both saint and martyr. Mary Wesley found neither of those roles congenial. During the first three or four years after her sudden wedding, she accompanied her husband on most of his journeys around the golden triangle and seemed at least to accept her lot with fortitude. In 1752, John Wesley told the banker Ebenezer Blackwell, "My wife is at least as well as when we left London. The more she travels, the more she likes it."[1] He was surprised as well as gratified. At first he had feared that his wife would be frightened and perhaps even injured by the mobs that had attacked him during his early tours of England. In the spring of 1752 she had survived the assault in Hull, even though the large lady chose to shield husband rather than wife, and seemed to be positively enjoying the energetic notoriety of her state. By 1753 he consoled himself with the thought that "the Methodists are now at peace throughout the Kingdom."

He was optimistic enough to believe that he and his wife were at peace as well.

Mary Wesley was not, however, prepared to forget that her brother-in-law had opposed her marriage and, despite the formal reconciliation which immediately followed the wedding, continued to complain that Charles spoke disparagingly of her to the preachers. When John Wesley believed that he was dying of consumption, he begged Mary and Charles to become genuine friends. Both agreed, but his brother (doubting Mary's sincerity) told his wife, with clear apprehension, "I hope she will do as she says." A year later, after a visit to London, he wrote, we must assume in a rare moment of irony, "I called, two minutes before preaching, on Mrs. Wesley at the Foundry; and in all that time had not quarrelled once."[2]

However, there is no doubt that at least during the early months of marriage John Wesley exhibited all the signs of a passionate attachment. In March 1751 he wrote, "I can imagine that I am sitting just by you and see and hear you."[3] In April he celebrated the "pleasure of receiving two letters from [his] dearest earthly friend"[4] and asked, rhetorically, "How is it that absence does not lessen but increases my affection? I feel you every day nearer my heart. O that God may continue this unspeakable gift."[5] By May he was simultaneously apologetic and flirtatious. "Love is talkative. There[fore I can't] wait any longer since it is two w[eeks since] I wrote the former part of my last [letter] to you but [one]."[6] No doubt his new wife was pleased and flattered to receive such protestations of everlasting love, even though they were written in gibberish. But coming as they did from an itinerant minister of forty-eight—with a series of emotional catastrophes behind him—they do suggest infatuation rather than the deep affection which would have been appropriate to his age and station. The letters bear all the marks of emotional adolescence. John Wesley needed to be in love.

In his eighty-second year, *A Thought upon Marriage* more or less accepted that his various amorous attachments had been proof of a search for happiness and affection, though he attributed the longing to a fear that having lost God's love, he needed to find an earthly substitute. Mary Vazeille's motives for marrying Wesley were, we must assume, a combination of desire for the status that the match would bring and capitulation to the dangerous attraction that charismatic preachers invariably excite in unstable women. The arrangement was unsatisfactory from the start. Mrs. Wesley resented her husband's deeply emotional relationship with his brother and was deeply envious of John's close ties to his favorite preachers, particularly John Bennet, without whom her marriage would not have been possible. Her suspicions about women were no doubt often justified. It was because they grew so fierce and so frequent that John Wesley tried to reassure her by giving her permission to open his letters. She extended the invitation to include letters which he was sending as well as those which he received. In 1755, a packet, addressed to Charles Perronet, was discovered to include a note which the old friend was asked to pass on to a Mrs. Lefevre. Mary Wesley assumed the worst.

More provocation was to come. In February 1756 Mrs. Wesley went through her husband's pockets and found three letters from three women, Dorothy Furly, Sarah Crosby and Sarah Ryan. It was the relationship with Sarah Ryan which caused most offense. And if the tone of the correspondence reflected the nature of the relationship, Mary Wesley had every reason to complain.

Sarah Ryan was, when Wesley began his correspondence with her in 1754, a woman of thirty. Wesley's friends, quoting what they claimed was her own admission, describe her as "excessively vain and fond of praise." An anonymous acquaintance completes the picture: "As she grew in years, her ill tempers gathered strength; and she became artful, subtle, cunning and she had little regard either to justice, mercy or truth."[7] Whether or not that was an accurate description of her character, there is no doubt that Sarah Ryan was a strange confidante for an Anglican priest to choose as the recipient of his innermost thoughts on the blessings of religion and the curse of an unhappy marriage. She had emerged from poverty to become a domestic servant and then entered into a series of relationships: lawful marriage, bigamous marriage and casual liaison when one of her husbands was at sea.

Christian charity requires that Sarah Ryan should not be judged according to the company she kept. But it was at least unwise for Wesley to become embroiled with a woman who (at the age of nineteen) "married" a man who already had a wife, then became engaged to an Italian peddler and eventually settled down (albeit temporarily) with an Irish sailor, who, after some months of brutality, abandoned her and returned to sea.

For a while she returned to service. But she was too unwell (both physically and mentally) to satisfy her mistress. In 1754, deserted, alone and unemployed, she prayed in Christ Church, Spitalfields, for relief from the illness that had caused her dismissal from the position of lady's maid. Her prayers finished, she remained for the service and received the sacrament from John Wesley. At the moment of consecration of the elements she experienced a revelation. As a result, she became a Methodist and moved into lodgings in Moorfields with a group of pious women whose lives were devoted to the connexion. We know nothing of Wesley's attitude toward her, but in 1757, true to his habit of institutionalizing his relationships with the women to whom he was emotionally attached, John Wesley made Sarah Ryan his Bristol and Kingswood housekeeper. So the familiar pattern—conversion and infatuation followed by devotion to his health and welfare—was repeated. Previous relationships which had progressed from piety to at least sublimated passion had all ended in catastrophe of one sort or another. The Sarah Ryan affair was no exception. A dinner at which John Wesley presided during the Bristol conference of 1757 was interrupted by a furious Mary Wesley, who announced to the assembled guests, "The whore who is serving you has three husbands."[8] Whether or not the description of Sarah Ryan was correct, the impression which it created of her complicated marital state was undoubtedly true.

It was a relationship which Wesley never regretted. In 1782, in his eightieth year, he published nineteen of their letters—eleven from Sarah Ryan and eight from him—in the *Arminian Magazine*. Some of them were no more than notes on the proper running of the house. One was a warning that she must regard the establishment "as a city set upon a hill" and concluded with a less than complimentary explanation of why she would find it difficult to live up to the high standards which he expected. "You have no experience of these things; no knowledge of the people; no advantages of education; nor large natural abilities." But others were cries from his troubled heart. Life with Mary Wesley was becoming intolerable. "Your last letter was seasonable indeed. I was growing faint in my mind. The being constantly watched over for evil; the having every word I spoke, every action I did, small and great, watched with no friendly eye; the hearing of a thousand little, tart, unkind reflections in return for the kindest words I could devise."

As always, when enmeshed in his emotionally complicated relationships, John Wesley described his affection as a manifestation of God's will. "The conversing with you, either by speaking or writing, is an unspeakable blessing to me. I cannot think of you without thinking of God. Others lead me to Him, but it is (as it were) going round about: You bring me straight to his presence."[9]

It is impossible to know the true nature of John Wesley's relationship with Sarah Ryan or, for that matter, any of the other women whom he simultaneously encouraged and held at arm's length. Carnal desires at least flickered within him when he was young, for he recorded in his diaries various touchings and feelings which he regularly enjoyed and equally regularly promised never to repeat. Post-Freudian biographies have speculated about the possibility that his marriage was not even consummated. That suspicion built on his judgment that "Undoubtedly it is the will of God that we should be guardian angels to each other. O what a union is that whereby we are united, the resemblance even of that between Christ and His church"—an undoubtedly chaste union.[10] Explanations for Wesley's supposed celibacy have ranged from a fear that he might love a woman more than he loved God to certainty that he could never find a wife who matched his mother's purity and perfection. Impotence is not the sort of subject which the reverential Methodist biographies contemplated. It would, however, be entirely consistent with the juvenile pursuit of women in which John Wesley persisted well into middle age. Whether or not John Wesley remained celibate, he was able to rouse great passions of possession and jealousy in others. His wife reacted to the discovery—and continuation—of his relationship with Sarah Ryan with perhaps justifiable fury.

In January 1758 Mary Wesley left her husband. He described the circumstances of her departure in a letter to Sarah Ryan, thus continuing the correspondence which had caused the rift.

In the evening, while I was preaching at the chapel, she came into the chamber where I had left my clothes, searched my pockets and found a letter there which I had finished but had not sealed. While she read it, God broke her heart; and afterward I found her in such a temper as I have not seen her in for several years. She has continued in the same ever since. So I think God has given a sufficient answer with regard to our writing to each other.[11]

It is easier to understand Mary Wesley's fury than it is to justify her husband's belief that the rage, which his letters to Sarah Ryan provoked, was God's way of showing that the whole correspondence was blessed. Both God and Mary Wesley worked in mysterious ways. Under His guidance, wife returned to husband in less than a week. However, the relationship, which Charles Wesley thought could deteriorate no further, became violent as well as vindictive. John Hampson, a Methodist preacher as well as an early biographer, "went into a room and found Mrs. Wesley foaming with fury. Her husband was on the floor where she had been trailing him by the hair of his head; and she herself was still holding in her hand venerable locks which she had plucked up by the roots."[12] Other early witnesses claimed that although she refused to travel with her husband, she often preceded him to his next preaching place so she could see who accompanied him in his coach. She certainly sent copies of his more theological letters to his critics and enemies, and Richard Watson, another preacher and biographer, claimed that she sometimes altered them so as to suggest that John Wesley had suddenly become a heretic and sinner.

Mary Wesley's hatred of her brother-in-law grew with the years. Without the slightest justification she accused his wife of being John

Wesley's mistress, for no better reason than the hope that the allegation would distress both men. Finding the brothers in solemn conference, she locked them in the meeting room and shouted a catalog of their joint and several sins through the door. According to folklore, John Wesley secured release by quoting Latin verse until she could stand the sound of it no more. Since she could have easily moved out of earshot, the story is almost certainly apocryphal but does serve to illustrate the bizarre uncongeniality of the marriage. John Wesley himself set out his complaints against his wife in a letter which he wrote to her from Coleford on 23 October 1759. It began, "I will tell you simply and plainly the things which I dislike." His dislikes were numbered one to ten and included "sharing any one of my letters and private papers without my leave . . . being myself a prisoner in my own house . . . talking about me behind my back . . . laying to my charge things which you know to be false." It continued with ten pieces of advice. Each of them simply recommended that she abandon one of the "dislikes" which he had listed in his first paragraph. The letter ended with a protestation of affection: "These are the advices which I now give you in the fear of God and in tender love to your soul. Nor can I give you stronger proof that I am your affectionate husband."[13]

Perhaps John Wesley really believed that he was a good and loving husband. There is no doubt that Mary Wesley was a violent and vindictive wife. Their union confirmed his emotional irresponsibility and his unswerving devotion to the cause of the Methodist Connexion. For as he had prophesied on his wedding night, nothing ever diverted him from the task to which he believed he had been called. It was his tragedy that misery rather than joy was the distraction from devotion which he had to overcome. At least the great itinerant was spared the temptation to stay at home.

The marriage stumbled on, punctuated by frequent separations that were regularly heralded by Mary's announcing that she was leaving forever and followed by her brief and bitter reappearances. There were long partings, occasional meetings and much resentment on both sides until Mrs. Wesley died in the autumn of 1781. John Wesley was not suited to marriage. Although there is no reason to believe that he broke the Seventh Commandment, he was certainly not prepared to accept the discipline required to avoid the appearance of infidelity. And paradoxical though it may seem, his mind was too preoccupied with higher things to allow him to fulfill the obligations of care or attention. In his defense, it must be said that the twin (and sometimes apparently mutually incompatible) duties of holding the connexion together and keeping it inside the Church of England, combined with his determination to expand its influence and increase its membership, left him very little time for family life. Had he been the sort of man who allowed himself the luxury of contentment, the connexion would have died in infancy, for almost every year brought a new crisis.

Part of the problem was the inevitable result of rapid expansion and the swift promotion of new recruits. When, in 1758, moves were made to expel Mark Davis, a recent convert to Methodism who had quickly become a preacher, his reprieve was granted on the assumption that "objections to his phraseology will be soon done away with when he becomes more acquainted with the writings." Wesley made new Methodists first and explained to them what a Methodist was afterwards. There was no guarantee that they would accept what he regarded as the essential elements of belief. When Methodism was a string of unconnected societies, that was tolerable. When the connexion became a force in its own right, the Wesleys constantly had to choose between expansion and the conformity which they had come to believe was essential to its future.

Trouble was simultaneously caused and avoided by John Wesley's unwillingness, or inability, to contemplate original theological ideas. His tracts, pamphlets and sermons were invariably derivative: comments on the Bible or criticisms of other men's work and other denominations' interpretations of the Scriptures. Methodism, in consequence, became more defined by behavior than belief and was distinguished from the Established Church in which it sheltered—also divided between Arminians and Calvinists and trying to find the right balance between faith and good works—by conduct rather than conviction. Methodists joined a society as well as attended church services and submitted themselves to cross-examination about their personal morality. That loose definition of Methodism certainly helped with recruitment. But it also encouraged such a diversity of recruits that maintaining discipline was always difficult.

Despite what he regarded as an intellectual inclination, John Wesley was temperamentally incapable of breaking new intellectual ground. The Scriptures needed to be examined, but they could not be questioned. The Established Church, though sometimes straying from the path of true faith, remained the rock on which English Protestantism was built. All around him the Enlightenment was producing men who questioned the conventions of religion as well as science and philosophy. By 1760 Joseph Priestley—as well as "explaining" oxygen, defining the properties of iron, carbon, chloride and ammonia, inventing soda water (for use on long sea voyages) and advising Josiah Wedgwood on the scientific production of crockery—had developed what amounted to a new branch of Christianity. His special brand of Unitarianism proclaimed the certainty of God and salvation on the evidence of the constant increase in human happiness but had no time for mystical ideas of the Trinity and bodily resurrection. That sort of radical thinking was anathema to Wesley. Only in imperial England could the most influential religious figure of a whole intellectual age be a man who contented himself with refining rather than challenging doctrines of orthodoxy and created a new church by organization, not ideas.

The communion controversies, which always rumbled under Methodism's never very placid surface, erupted into another crisis in February 1760, when three laymen administered communion to members of the Norwich Society. Wesley could have argued that the circumstances of Norwich Methodism made them an exception which it was prudent to ignore. The ancient city's Methodists were in turmoil. It was there that James Wheatley had preached with such success before he had been expelled because of his lax morals. But he had repented his sins and, with the help of Lady Huntingdon, founded a tabernacle at which the Norfolk followers of George Whitefield worshiped. The tabernacle cooperated with both the Methodist Society and the Dissenting chapels. The Dissenters, being registered under the Toleration Act, lawfully administered communion to both their own followers and to the associated Methodists, whose preachers thought that both devotion and dignity required them to follow suit.

John Wesley, always selective in his views on the expulsion of troublemakers, was sure that they must be brought back into the fold rather than sent out into the darkness where they would almost certainly be captured by Calvinism. When he visited Norwich, he found the Methodists to be "the most ignorant, self-conceited, self-willed, fickle, intractable, disorderly, disjointed society that I knew in the three kingdoms."[14] But he judged that "many were profited by such chastisement and not one was offended. In fact, many stubborn hearts were melted down."[15] Charles was less convinced. He accused his brother of weakness and tolerating the Norwich irregularities for far too long. Waiting until the annual conference resolved the issue would, he feared, end with the Norwich apostates infecting other societies and putting together a majority for outright separation from the church.[16] In fact, he was more concerned with what he rightly believed to be a main threat to the whole basis of his new church. He had discovered, during his travels, that the "perfectionists" were gaining strength in the societies. It was only one, though the most popular and most dangerous, of the old heresies which were again beginning to gain popularity.

The reemergence of the perfection argument was, in part, the result of John Wesley's own equivocation on the subject, a weakness which must be attributed to his *wish* to believe in the notion of perfection on earth but his intellectual inability to accept that God could make living saints. Because of his hope to clarify his view on "holiness to the point of perfection," in 1760 he regarded the examination of that doctrine as a far more important use of his time than crushing the Norwich disobedience. And he was not in a mood to lose his Norwich societies, just because their members had defied the ordinances of the Established Church.

Charles Wesley, on the other hand, believed that nothing was more important than avoiding separation. The thought that Methodists were accepting communion administered under the provisions of the Toleration Act was absolute anathema to him, as witness his letter to John Nelson which warned "rather than see thee a Dissenting minister, I wish to see thee in thy coffin."[17] As always, he recruited Grimshaw to his cause, and the perpetual curate of Haworth obliged by threatening, in his usual violent language, to disown the heretical societies. "To thy tents O Israel! It is time for me to shift for myself, to disown all connections with the Methodists."[18] Charles Wesley read the letter to the London Society in the hope that it would deter them from supporting the dissidents. It did not have the desired effect. The members cheered, not out of loyalty to the old religion but because they were glad to see Grimshaw go.

At the Bristol conference of 1760 John Wesley, initially ignoring the demands to accept "perfection" reiterated the ideas and some of the words of his 1755 sermon "Ought We to Separate?" As always, when put to the test, he was firm in his insistence on continued union. Administration of the sacraments, as distinct from preaching, prophesying and evangelizing, was the preserve of ordained priests. To press for (or, more dangerous still, to declare unilaterally) the right of Methodists to turn their preachers into priests would bring a head-on collision with the bishops and make separation unavoidable. The more militant preachers remained unconvinced, claiming that they were already, in effect, Dissenting ministers and should be allowed to enjoy the benefits of that status. John Wesley, his authority challenged and the connexion's integrity in danger, decided that the time for emollience had passed. "He would not ordain and said that if [a preacher] was not ordained he would look upon it as murder if he administered the ordinance." Methodists who disputed that view were told that if they persisted in their disobedience, he would "renounce them in a quarter of an hour" as "the most foolish and ignorant [members] of the Conference."[19] The revolt subsided, and John Wesley wisely decided to let the Norwich dispute rest. Charles, however, remained determined to see the Norwich troublemakers punished. A year later he was still agitating for strong measures. But his brother would have none of it. "I told you before, with regard to Norwich, *dixi*. I have done at the last Conference all I can dare to do. Allow me the liberty of conscience as I allow you."[20]

That admission made clear that it was expediency, not conscience, by which John Wesley was guided. Despite his new enthusiasm for orthodoxy, he was still not prepared to impose it in a way that risked the defection of a whole society. Certain that the status of the preachers would one day have to be resolved, and that its resolution would precipitate the final break with the church, he chose to prevaricate and temporize in order to postpone the eventual schism. So although he was firm on the principle, he yielded when required to pass judgment on the practices of the Norwich disputants. His real attitude was revealed by his reaction to the conviction of sixteen Kent Methodists for the offense of holding a conventicle. The fine of forty-three pounds, imposed by the local justices, was confirmed by the quarter sessions, but quashed by the King's Bench. John Wesley gave thanks that the judge had bought him time by finding that the law had not been broken and, in consequence, that the Kent Society was not composed of Dissenters. "If we do not exert ourselves, it may drive us to that bad dilemma—leave preaching or leave the Church. We have reason to thank God it is not come to this yet. Perhaps it never will."[21] The final hope he knew to be vain.

Once again John Wesley chose to postpone what he must have known to be the eventually unavoidable confrontation with one of the two conflicting groups—separatists and loyalists—within his connexion. However, the need to clarify the Methodist view on perfection was urgent and immediate. That gospel, in its most extreme and heretical form, was being preached in the name of the connexion. Thomas Maxfield and George Bell had claimed that it was possible in life "to be like angels." Thomas Walsh and James Rouquet, looking at the other side of the coin, had told the Bristol Society that "a believer until perfect is under a curse of God and in a state of damnation." Grimshaw, who seems always to have been Methodism's lightning conductor, was told, in his own church, that anyone who repudiated the doctrine of perfection was a "son of the Devil." Repudiation, Wesley well knew, was the clear duty of a good son of the church. But as always the shepherd, fearful that he would lose some of his flock, he hesitated before he gave a clear lead. The doctrine of perfection was proving very popular with the fanatics who inhabited the wilder shores of Methodism. In the two years after the idea of perfection first began to enthuse Methodists, the London Society attracted five hundred new members. At Spitalfields a covenant of redemption, anticipating that perfection was most likely achieved in a gathering of like-minded potential saints, attracted two thousand worshipers to its Sunday service. Sometime after 1760 Wesley detected that the doctrine of perfection had begun "to spread through most of England, as well as Ireland and so the whole work of God increases."[22]

Wesley was not the man to turn his back lightly on anything which might add to the number of Methodists. But his reluctance to act was the result of more than his usual determination to protect and if possible to enlarge the connexion at all costs. He too believed in Christian perfection and believed that the spectacular blessing could be simultaneously granted to a whole congregation. He had seen it happen. The empirical evidence, which he thought respect for logic required, had been provided. Methodists had screamed as if they were suffering the pains of hell before they declared themselves "cleansed from all unrighteousness." He adjudged that they were sincere and their perfection genuine because "being poor illiterate creatures,"[23] they were unlikely to have heard or read about perfection and then counterfeited their apotheosis. He did, however, face one difficulty in dealing with the more outrageous claims about perfection. Although he was sure the condition existed, he was not sure how, apart from the occasional manifestation of divine intervention, it could be defined or recognized.

His solution—to both his own theological dilemma and the damage that disputes about perfection were doing to the societies—was to set out what he believed to be the moderate position of the doctrine. It was achieved by defining perfection in a way which, at least to simple souls, was absolutely meaningless. Human perfection was possible. But it did not mean that living human beings could be perfect. "Perfection in life" was not incompatible with a state in which "infirmities continue."

For years the paradox—literal contradiction to more rational minds—was the official and undisputed doctrine of Methodism. The 1758 conference endorsed the idea that perfection could be achieved while "imperfections and mistakes" remained. A year later that view was confirmed and extended with the publication of *Thoughts on Christian Perfection*. The notion that it was possible to achieve perfection without being perfect could not have satisfied the Methodists indefinitely. John Whitehead, Wesley's biographer and near contemporary, described the sophistry with which Wesley tried to rebut accusations of inconsistency as he adjusted his position during the early 1760s. "The doctrine of *perfection*, or *perfect* love, was undoubtedly taught among Methodists from the beginning, but the manner in which it was *now* preached—pressing people to expect what was called the destruction of the *root* of sin, in a moment—was most certainly new."

Wesley persisted in his careful (some would say) contrary definition of perfection partly out of belief and partly in the hope of keeping the peace. In 1763 his sermon "On Sin in Believers" set out the real meaning of perfection as he, pragmatic about the needs of the societies and mystical about the power of God, saw it. "The *guilt* is one thing, the *power* another and the *being* yet another. That Believers (true Christians who have been sanctified) are delivered from the *guilt*; and the *power* of sin we allow; that they are delivered from the *being* of sin we deny."[24] It was an explanation which satisfied no one. By its nature the Methodist Connexion attracted members who were looking for religious excitement. They wanted perfection, and they wanted it to be acquired in a visible moment. Thomas Maxfield and George Bell were happy to meet their needs.

Thomas Maxfield, a poor man who had married well, was one of Wesley's first preachers and so well thought of by the brothers that they persuaded the bishop of Derry—in Bath to take the waters—to ordain him. He was admitted to the priesthood with the injunction "to help that good man that he may not work himself to death."[25]

At first the instruction was obeyed. This meant that for a time Maxfield was Wesley's favoured lieutenant. He was, as a result, the subject of much criticism from the other preachers, who accused him of "setting himself up over them." John Wesley continually and strenuously defended him, thereby offending several of his preachers and a great number of his people.[26] In 1760 Wesley appointed Maxfield leader of a select band, all of whom claimed to have achieved Christian perfection of the sort which Wesley had specifically rejected. The more his views were opposed by the moderate preachers, the more extreme Maxfield became. He openly embraced "enthusiasm" in the worst sense of the word and, as a result, claimed to have regular visions and frequent conversations with God. The belief in his own unalterable perfection inevitably led to the sin of antinomianism. Civil laws, he claimed, could not restrain the godly. Methodism's reputation outside the connexion was cruelly damaged by comparisons between Maxfield's fanaticism and the behavior of the more extreme Puritan sects during the Interregnum.

Maxfield's associate in perfection was George Bell, a former corporal of horse in the Life Guards. He was "converted" in 1758 and claimed the ability to identify the exact minute of the exact day on which he was "sanctified." In March 1761 he wrote an account of the experience and declared that only he and his followers, among whom he included the disciples of Thomas Maxfield, were true Christians. The inclusion of Maxfieldites showed a remarkably generous spirit, since Bell clearly thought them inferior to his own disciples. The Bell faction was, Bell believed, immortal.

Before Maxfield and Bell began to disrupt the societies, the early 1760s seemed likely to be years of unique achievement for Methodism. Years later Wesley told the sad story of hopes dashed in his *Arminian Magazine*. "A great work of good was spread through three kingdoms. Numbers were justified and many truly cleansed from all filthiness of flesh and the spirit." The Methodists asked themselves, "Could these pillars fall?" and decided that "They thought not." They were wrong. For then "commenced the work of the Devil." The hopes of "eye and ear witnesses," who had confidently predicted an accelerating revival, were confounded by the excesses of "the perfection faction." They professed "to have the gift of healing, and in London did really attempt to heal the blind and to raise the dead." Worse sins were to follow. "After this they found fault with their ministers."[27]

John Wesley himself "made a particular enquiry into the case of Mary Spead, a young woman in the Tottenham Court Road," who, the evidence suggests, was suffering from the advanced stages of breast cancer. Mary Spead had been told by St. George's Hospital that her condition was beyond hope. When she met Bell, he asked her, "Have you the faith to be healed?" When she replied that she had, he touched her breast, she claimed, and the hemorrhage (which had been constant) stopped at once. Next day the pain returned. So she prayed, "Lord, if Thou wilt, Thou canst make me whole." Then, according to the Spead's account of the event, not only did the pain immediately end, but the previously ravaged breast returned to its youthful shape.

Even in an age when superstition had only begun to give way to reason, Mary Spead's testimony was greeted with total disbelief by most of the Methodist preachers. But not by Wesley. "Here," he wrote, "are the plain facts. (1) she *was* ill (2) she *is* well (3) she became so in a moment. Which of these can, with any modesty, be denied?"[28] There is no doubt that desperate to hold the connexion together, Wesley was willing to tolerate extravagances which his brother, and the more orthodox Methodists, would have denounced without hesitation. But his reluctance to deal decisively with Bell and Maxfield had another cause. He half believed, and wholly wanted to believe, the gospel which they taught. In conscience, he could do no more than redefine their idea of Christian perfection, and he could not deny the possibility of Bell's miraculously healing the sick because he had faith in miracles. He had witnessed them himself. They were proof of the living God.

However, theology aside, the claims of Bell and Maxfield were badly disrupting the London societies. Religious fanaticism attracts devoted followers among the weak, the lonely and the lost. So the mild rebuke, administered in October 1762, further enraged the extreme Maxfieldites. Society members began to resign. One returned her Methodist membership card with the promise "not to be brow-beaten any longer" and added, "Sir, we will have no more to do with you. Mr. Maxfield is our teacher."[29] Even then, with the imminent disintegration of the societies a real possibility, Wesley was unable to act decisively. Instead he made further inquiries into the nature of the apostates' beliefs and the depth of their treachery. On 24 November 1762 he stood, unknown and unnoticed, in the crowd at one of George Bell's meetings. "George Bell prayed, on the whole, pretty near an hour. His fervour of spirit I could not but admire. I afterwards told him what I did not admire; namely (1) his screaming, every now and then, in so strange a manner that no one could scarce tell what he said; (2) his thinking he had the miraculous discernment of spirits; and (3) his sharply condemning his opponents."[30]

A meeting was arranged among Maxfield, Bell and both the Wesleys. Maxfield was conciliatory to the point of convincing the brothers that "in some part he had been blamed without cause." John Wesley agreed to set out the points of persistent disagreement. The result was a letter of twenty-two paragraphs, thirteen of which began, "I dislike . . ." The basic criticism was doctrinal. "I dislike your supposing man may be as perfect as an angel: that he can be absolutely perfect . . . or that the moment he is pure, he cannot fall from it."[31] But the bitterest criticism was reserved for Maxfield's attitude toward the connexion: "What I most of all dislike, is your littleness of love to your brethren, to your own society; your want of union of heart with them and bowels of mercies towards them: your want of meekness, gentleness and long suffering towards them: your counting every man as your enemy; your bigotry and narrowness of spirit."[32]

The litany of objectionable qualities went on and on, leaving little doubt that Wesley's chief anxiety concerned the effect which Maxfield and his colleagues were having on the connexion. His concern was clearly justified. Some members supported Maxfield. Others supported Wesley. Rather more objected to the Methodist trumpet's not sounding a clear note. A Mrs. Coventry resigned her membership—and that of her husband, children and daughters—with the explanation that she "would hear two doctrines no longer."[33]

However, Wesley's letter of reproof did not convince Maxfield that he was wrong and must repent, and the problems with the societies continued into 1763. The Calvinists rejoiced. A Mr. Romaine wrote—with obvious satisfaction—to the countess of Huntingdon, "His societies are in a general confusion; and the point which brought them into the wilderness of rant and madness is still as much insisted upon."[34] John Downey, writing to Joseph Cownley, had no doubt who was to blame. John Wesley, he explained, had to fight new outbreaks of "enthusiasm" every day. "Why he suffers them we cannot tell. He threatens but cannot find it in his heart to put in execution. The consequence is, the talk of all the town, and entertainment for the newspapers."[35]

Charles Wesley was seriously worried about the "sad havoc Satan has made of the flock." He was not, however, sufficiently worried to leave Bristol and come to his brother's support. John wrote to him to say that Bell and his associates had "quitted the society and renounced all fellowship with us," and the letter began, "The sooner you could be here the better." A couple of weeks later he wrote again to assure him bitterly, "I say no more about your coming to London." He was in the mood to be both saint and martyr. "Here stood I; and I shall stand, with or without human help, if God is with us."[36]

The correspondence confirms Charles's growing detachment from the work of the connexion. It also illustrates the power which Maxfield had, or John Wesley thought he had, within the societies. Methodism attracted members who wanted their religion to be spectacular. Maxfield, offering more sensation than the orthodox connexion, inevitably became John's real rival in those societies which heard of his miracles at first hand. So instead of rejoicing at Maxfield's departure, he feared that it would alienate so many members that the future of the whole connexion would be put at risk. Even John Fletcher, vicar of Madeley and one of the Methodist priests who Wesley accepted was still his friend, told him that

Maxfield was "sincere and, though obstinate and suspicious . . . has a true desire to know the will and live the life of God."

John Wesley, despite his moments of self-pity, possessed the inner resources which came from unswerving conviction. He wanted a rapprochement with the Maxfieldites. But he wanted it on his own terms. Asked to think again about the true definition of perfection, he replied that he had nothing new to say on the subject. But he was prepared to repeat, in a slightly different tone, the truth which he had spoken so often before. "As to the word *perfection*, it is scriptural. Therefore neither you nor I can, in conscience, object to it unless we would send the Holy Ghost to school. . . . By *Christian* perfection I mean (as I have said again and again) the so loving God and our neighbor as to rejoice evermore, pray without ceasing and in everything give thanks."[37]

Once again perfection was defined in a way which bore little or no relationship to anything like the normal meaning of the word. To emphasize his consistency and to popularize his own strange definition, Wesley published *Further Thoughts on Christian Perfection*. It repeated that sanctification on earth would not save a man or woman from "unavoidable defects of understanding" and the inevitability of making "mistakes in many things" which "frequently occasion something wrong both in our tempers and words and actions." He pleaded with Methodists, "Let us not fight about words," an entirely understandable desire in someone who wanted to give words his own particular meaning. He then stood the whole argument on its head. Some believers in perfection lacked gentleness, long-suffering, meekness, fidelity and temperance. But to them he said, "You have not what I call perfection. If others will call it so, they may." Maxfield was unlikely to be brought back into the Methodist fold by being told that perfection, in the normal sense of the word, was not possible and, what was more, that he and his followers lacked what Wesley regarded as qualities essential to that condition.

Further Thoughts on Christian Perfection ended with instructions to believers which must have antagonized the Maxfieldites even more than John Wesley's catalog of their moral deficiencies. For it was a ragbag of uplifting advice which had very little to do with the subject under discussion. "Much grace does not imply much light. . . . Beware of the sins of omission. Lose no opportunity of doing good of any kind. . . . Do not talk much; neither long at a time. . . . Admit to no desire for pleasing food. . . . Avoid all magnificent, pompous words." It all helped to convince the bigots and fanatics that Wesley had no clear and consistent view of what perfection was or might be.

Fortunately for Wesley and the Methodist Connexion, George Bell, who had hovered on the brink of insanity for years, began to behave with such abundant belief in his own divinity that only zealots with comparable mental disorders were prepared to follow him. In Southey's view, he should have been "locked up in Bedlam for the sake of religion and decency and for the general good." One justification for that draconian prescription was Bell's announcement that the world would end on 28 February 1763. Wesley disowned him and denied that the prophecy had any Methodist authority. But some simple-minded citizens, remembering the earthquakes of 1750, took fright and fled London. Bell was imprisoned after a conviction for causing a public nuisance. On his release and recovery from his mental sickness, he abandoned Methodism forever and, according to Southey, finally embraced the ultimate degradation of becoming "a radical reformer."

John Wesley was left to explain why he had allowed the canker of a mad fanatic to grow within Methodism for so long. His explanation, although certainly an apology, was unconvincing. "I saw instantly from the beginning and at the beginning, what was wrong." Asked why he did not take action against the sin he had recognized, he replied with the biblical adage "I have many things to speak, but ye cannot hear them now."[38] In short, the societies would not have tolerated any denunciation of Bell and Maxfield. Luckily Bell disqualified himself from the competition for most compelling preacher and was no longer a threat. Maxfield, however, was a more serious contender.

On the day of Bell's promised apocalypse Wesley preached on the topical text "Prepare to meet thy God" and assured his congregation that the meeting was not imminent. He then set out for East Anglia where he spent "a few quiet and comfortable days" free from the turmoil of London apostasy. When he returned to London on 23 April, he was told that Maxfield "would not preach at the Foundry." He still felt only regret. "Some time after" the final breach, he wrote ("for the information of a friend") a letter which expressed his feelings. "So the breach is made; but I am clear. I have done all I possibly could do to prevent it."[39] He had done all he could to prevent it because he feared that Maxfield's defection would damage his connexion. The preservation and promotion of Methodism were becoming the whole object of John Wesley's existence.

The logic of the letter was impeccable. Bell's behavior had made it necessary for him to be prohibited from preaching on Methodist premises, and as a natural extension of that prohibition, Methodists (in good standing) could not share a pulpit with him even when he preached out of doors. Maxfield chose to ignore the edict.

One of our stewards, who, at my desire, took the chapel at Snowfields for my use was told by Mr. Maxfield that the chapel was his and that Mr. Bell should exhort there, whether I would or not . . . while things stood neither I nor any other of our preachers could, in conscience, preach there anymore. Nevertheless Mr. M. did preach there. On this I sent him a note, desiring him not to do it and adding, "If you do, you thereby renounce connection with me." Receiving this, he said, "I *will* preach at Snowfields." He did so and thereby renounced his connection with me.[40]

So Maxfield had not been expelled; he had expelled himself. The letter, addressed to a "friend" who probably did not exist, was published in the *Journal*. Its purpose was not to confirm Wesley's tolerance—for he regarded moderation in the pursuit of virtue as a sin in itself—but to portray Bell as the real villain while showing Maxfield to be guilty only of misplaced loyalty. There was no doctrinal reason why his followers should leave the connexion.

The breach with Maxfield was less damaging than Wesley feared but more personally acrimonious than he could have wished. The man who counted "everyone who did not follow him as an enemy" responded with characteristic ferocity. Fortunately some of his allegations against Wesley were too absurd (and too self-loving) to be taken seriously by anyone except his most rabid supporters. One allegation was that Wesley had glorified himself by quoting the epitaph which Philip of Macedon had written as an oblique compliment to Alexander the Great. "Yet if there's one who boasts he hath more done / To me he owes it, for he was my son." The thought that Wesley regarded himself as Maxfield's spiritual father was justified by the allegation that he had told the troublemaker, "Tommy, I will tell people that you are the greatest gospel preacher in England and you shall tell them I am the greatest." When Maxfield announced that he would not condescend to take part in the absurd exercise in self-promotion, Wesley "put him away."

Despite Wesley's forebodings, the breach with Maxfield had only a marginal effect on the membership of the Methodist Connexion. Records for November 1763 show that something between 175 and 200 members left the societies during that year, about 100 on Maxfield's account. The losses were quickly recouped, but the problem of the harm which Maxfield had done to Methodism's good name remained. And (much to John Wesley's regret) the controversy had, far from achieving Maxfield's aim, prejudiced the societies against the whole belief in Christian perfection in any form, even though it was a doctrine to which, at least in its limited form, Wesley subscribed without doubt or qualification. He certainly believed that deliverance from "the guilt and power of sin" might be an instantaneous gift from heaven. Yet Maxfield's fanaticism had caused the societies to shy away from both the idea of perfection itself and the hope that God might grant that state in a moment. All that was left for Wesley to do—both to secure the future of the societies and to dispel the demons of doubt and insecurity—was to strengthen the central organization of the connexion in a way which he believed reduced the risk of future apostasy. The conference in 1763 provided another occasion for tightening the ties which bound members together.

The proceedings did not go altogether as Wesley had intended. Two years earlier, the Methodists had created a "General Fund" by levying a subscription from every member. Debts on the chapels had risen to something like four thousand pounds, and every civil action in the King's Bench division (normally to demand justice's protection against the mobs) cost fifty or sixty pounds in lawyers' fees. Ready money was essential to the protection of the societies. However, since the connexion had become a national organization, it had, at least in the view of some conference members, developed other responsibilities which they were determined it should fulfill. They included what amounted to providing pensions for servants of the Lord who were too old or too frail to continue in His service. The decision was set out in the usual style of a positive answer to a question of the conference's construction. Minute twenty-one asked, "How may provision be made for old and worn-out preachers?"

Wesley would have replied, "Not at all." For he opposed the scheme in principle. His objection was based on the simple belief, which he practiced as well as preached, that service often required sacrifice and that the consequent suffering should be accepted as a badge of honor. But against his wishes, it was agreed that "every travelling preacher contribute ten shillings yearly" to be "lodged in the hands of three stewards, approved of by the majority of the preachers." The stewards were to have the duty of providing "what is needful . . . first for the old or sickly preachers and their families; then for the widows and children of those who are dead." The decision proved more than that Wesley's personal authority was less than absolute. It demonstrated that all the pressures on the connexion—the obligations imposed by an increasingly sophisticated organization, the demands of a fast-growing membership and the need to define a generally accepted doctrine—encouraged the concentration of power at the heart of Methodism. Even when the changes were imposed against John Wesley's will, they increased his authority. Whether or not he chose, or even approved of, the changes, every reform made Methodism more like an independent church with "Pope John" (as his critics had come to call him) at its head.

14

CHURCH OF ENGLAND MAN

As the years passed, John Wesley grew more and more single-minded in his preoccupation with the governance of Methodism. By his sixtieth birthday the connexion had become the vehicle for all his ambitions to revive the love of God in England. The difficulties of reconciling his theology with the demands of the followers for greater autonomy absorbed him. Increasingly he thought of little else but holding the connexion together and maintaining his absolute authority over both the management of the societies and the behavior of their individual members. There was little time for any of the old frivolities. Indeed the philistine, who had always lurked beneath the skin of the Lincoln fellow, came out of hiding. Persuaded to attend a performance of Thomas Arne's *Judith,* he found two aspects of the oratorio impossible "to reconcile with sense." "One," he wrote, "is singing the same words ten times over. The other is singing different words by different persons at one and the same time."[1]

Some of his natural instincts were too strong to suppress or ignore. He maintained his almost heathen interest in psychic phenomena. So he was momentarily distracted by the story of a man who "was in Lisbon during the great earthquake" and "while walking with his friend near Brightenstone," some months later, was overcome with the presentiment that Sussex was soon to be similarly torn asunder. He prayed "God grant the wind may rise," and his prayer was answered. "The clouds whirled to and fro . . . and brought an impetuous storm. . . . Some of the hailstones were larger than hen eggs." The storm "moved in a line about four miles broad, making strange havoc. . . . Wherever it passed it left hot sulphurous steam such as almost suffocated those it reached."[2]

Fascination with the inexplicable was not as potentially damaging as his continued attraction to young women. In his sixty-second year, John Wesley found himself called to be mentor to Margaret Lewen, "a remarkable monument to divine mercy." She was "about two and twenty and [had] about six hundred pounds a year in her own hands." The relationship began, as always, with advice about self-improvement and ripened to the point at which a clearly infatuated Miss Lewen gave Wesley a chaise and a pair of horses. It never, however, progressed to the point at which, in the usual pattern, she nursed him through injury or illness. She died two years after their first meeting, but through her Wesley met another young woman, Peggy Dale, Lewen's niece. Mrs. Dale was twenty when they met, and until she died, fourteen years later, she was the constant (and deeply grateful) recipient of the highly charged correspondence which Wesley always thought appropriate to the instruction of his female followers. Sometimes it took on a dangerously secular tone. "How far do you find power over your thoughts? Does not your imagination sometimes wander? Do these imaginations continue for any time? Or have you the power to check them immediately?"[3] About the same time Wesley met and established a close relationship with Lady Maxwell (aged twenty-one and widowed at nineteen), who, at his suggestion, opened a school in Edinburgh for poor children. Lady Glenorchy (widowed at twenty-one shortly after she met Wesley) bought a Catholic church and converted it into a Protestant chapel at which a Methodist sermon was delivered once a week and to which itinerant preachers could go for rest and inspiration. Charismatic preachers have always attracted admirers. Not all of them have either enjoyed or encouraged infatuation with Wesley's reckless piety. He remained, into old age, dangerously susceptible to every woman who seemed to admire him. His misfortune was that he felt able to express his emotions only in the form of uplifting moral advice.

However great the excitement that he found in saving young women from sin, the time that he spent on that indulgence never diverted him from the great work of promoting and protecting his connexion. At the beginning of the 1760s he must have known that it was fast becoming an independent church and that the race toward separation was gaining pace and could not be stopped. By then, although he did not approve of schism, he was certainly prepared—sooner or later—to accept it. At the 1763 conference his chief objectives were to create a Methodist constitution and to establish the Methodist articles of belief. Conformity was, in Wesley's view, essential to success. The changes which he made to the regulations during the turmoil of that year were thought, at least by Wesley, to encourage that essential result. They were incorporated into a new version of the *Published Minutes,* the statements of orthodox Methodist belief and connexion regulations. The articles of faith, doctrine and organization had been published (in the form of two pamphlets) in 1749 under the title *Minutes of Some Late Conversations.* In 1753 the two documents were revised and incorporated into a single pamphlet, *Minutes of Several Conversations.* In 1763 John Wesley expanded the published minutes into what amounted to a handbook. It was titled the *Large Minutes,* and it became the text which guided all Methodists' lives. The *Large Minutes* contained every noteworthy decision taken during the previous fifteen years and came to assume an almost mystical significance for the connexion. An inscribed copy was given by the conference to every preacher to mark his success in the annual examination. It became a symbol of his vocation and a guide to the rules of Methodist organization.

The decision to issue such a complete account of proper Methodist "manners" was another conscious attempt to promote conformity. Previously the canons of Methodism, laid down by Wesley or authorized by the conference, had been set out more by personal contact than by the published conclusions of the conferences. And they had rarely been enforced, more because of Wesley's fear of schism than as a result of his natural tolerance. In consequence, all sorts of heresies had attached themselves to Methodism. Arguments about the sacrament and perfection had not, as Wesley hoped, been submerged under a general desire for unity. New rumblings about "assurance," an old controversy, were heard in many of the provincial societies. The *Large Minutes* were meant to impose, or at least to encourage, uniformity by the power of the printed word.

The integrity of the societies had to be protected by the exclusion of those who might join to impose their heresies on Methodism. "In order to prevent strangers being present more than twice or thrice at society meetings, see that all in every meeting show their cards before they come in." The collective control of the whole connexion over Methodist property—with John Wesley laying down the rules of management—had to be reestablished by the universal application of a model trust deed. Love feasts were to be limited to members of the select bands. The sermon on evil speaking was to be read in each society every year. Preachers were "constantly to read the Scriptures, Wesley's tracts and his contributions to the *Christian Library* and to study the revised edition of John and Charles Wesley's *Explanatory Notes on the New Testament, Sermons on Several Occasions*. As always, the injunctions included petty regulations as well as great statements of principle. Eggs and wine were once again prohibited as "downright poison."

Extensive though the statement of aims was, the real importance of the *Large Minutes* was the codification of Methodist belief. The canon amounted to a distinct and comprehensive doctrine—distinct because it was set out like a body of independent belief. Whatever its context, its existence marked a step taken toward separation. In his sixtieth year Wesley continued to pay necessary respect to the Thirty-nine Articles and the Church of England's homilies. But he was laying down articles and homilies of his own. By choice and by design, year by year, Methodism was creating its own position within the spectrum of Protestant Christianity.

However, either because of his sentimental attachment to the faith in which he was brought up or because he regarded assertions of loyalty as essential to Methodism's success, he thought it right both to reiterate that he had no wish to separate from the Church of England and to instruct his preachers to behave in a way which confirmed their loyalty to the Established Church. So, when the *Large Minutes* boldly asked the question "What may we reasonably believe to be God's design in raising up the Preachers called Methodists?," the reply (although critical of the Church of England at least by implication) allowed no suggestion of schism. Methodism's purpose was "to reform the nation and, in particular, the Church; to spread scriptural holiness throughout the land." It was a more ambitious statement of Wesley's intention than anything which he had put in print before. But it was a statement which still bound Methodism to the Church of England. And the *Large Minutes* went on to demonstrate that the desire for unity, at least as defined by Wesley, was genuine. A subsequent item in the connexion's catechism, Wesley's favorite form of instruction, set out how preachers were to maintain good relations with the mother church.

> (1) Let all Preachers go to Church. (2) Let all our people go constantly. (3) Receive the sacraments at every opportunity. (4) Warn all against niceness in hearing a great and prevailing evil. (5) Warn them likewise against despising the prayers of the Church. (6) Against calling our society a church or the Church. (7) Against calling our Preachers, Ministers, our meeting houses churches (call them) plain preaching houses. (8) Do not licence them as such.

The "Advice to Preachers"—in reality it was an instruction—marked the culmination of a long campaign to strengthen Methodism by tying it more closely to those strands of Church of England belief which Wesley assumed were in sympathy with his ideas and beliefs. By 1763 he was set on colonizing a part of the Established Church.

John Wesley had long planned to gain at least the sympathy, and perhaps even the support, of evangelical clergymen who, it was reasonable to expect, shared his hopes of a revival within the Church of England. Back in 1755, in "Ought We to Separate?," he had been explicit about the proper Methodist attitude toward clergy who were the connexion's "friends." The response from the rectors of

England had been deeply disappointing. But the determination to build bridges had not faded with the years of rejection. It was essential to "do everything and omit everything we can with a safe conscience in order to continue, and, if it be possible, increase their good will."

For many years some evangelical clergy, Vincent Perronet and James Hervey among them, had behaved in a way which was almost indistinguishable from Methodism, principally by forming within their parishes societies which encouraged holiness and the study of theology. John Bagley had employed a lay assistant. Henry Venn, who was destined to provoke one of the great dilemmas of Methodist policy, had built a "chapel" in his parish, and John Berridge of Everton often set off from his rectory to follow an itinerant ministry. William Grimshaw, although passionately attached to the Church of England, followed every Methodist practice.[4] In 1750 Samuel Walker had formed a Parsons' Club in Cornwall at which the evangelical clergy of the county met to discuss their beliefs seven times a year. Five years later Risdon Darracutt had followed his example in Somerset, and John Fletcher set up the Worcester Society of Ministers of the Gospel in the Church of England. The call for a revival was not exclusive to Wesley, Whitefield and their followers. So it was heard in parishes which neither man had ever visited. But Wesley's genius was not the discovery of a new religious idea. It was the mobilization of the men and women who shared the beliefs of the connexion, which he led. Over the years he grew increasingly anxious that ordained clergy should be included in their ranks. Substantial recruitment would solve all the Methodists' problems.

Successive conferences issued invitations and promised warm welcomes. In 1757 John Wesley had written to Samuel Walker to say that the conference had "agreed that nothing could be more desirable" than "a closer union of the clergy who preached the truth."[5] He was particularly proud when young John Fletcher ran straight from his ordination to the Foundry and immediately began to assist at a communion service. But he needed more Church of England clergy, ideally men of standing and maturity, to rally to the Methodist banner. The way in which he pursued them down the years is a tribute to his determination. The eventual realization that allies could not be found in suitable numbers was one of the milestones on the road to separation.

In November 1761 John Wesley wrote to what he described as "fifty or sixty clergymen" to ask, "Ought not those who are united to one common Head and employed by Him in one common work be united to each other?"[6] He then listed fourteen ministers—himself and his brother among them—who "agree on essentials: (1) Original Sin, (2) Justification by Faith, (3) Holiness of Heart and Life, provided their life be answerable to their doctrine." Those fourteen, together with "other clergymen who agree on these essentials," should, Wesley suggested, come together in a holy union. There would be no obligation to agree on everything but an agreement "in love . . . to each help the other in his work and enlarge his influence by all the honest means he can." The result was so disappointing that two and a half years later, the 1761 letter was copied out and sent again with a sad little covering note. "I propose no more than . . . the bounden duty of every Christian. . . . I myself have endeavoured so to do for many years, though I have been almost alone therein." The second letter was no more successful than the first, but Wesley struggled on for five more years to find those "who preach those fundamental truths, original sin and justification by faith producing inward and outward holiness."

Sympathetic clergymen, together with the countess of Huntingdon and George Whitefield, whose Calvinism was again being overlooked, were invited to the 1762 conference. Two or three turned up, but neither their numbers nor their attitude suggested that a wholesale union was possible. Nevertheless, encouraged by the influential Howel Harris, John Wesley invited the full list of suspected sympathizers to meet him on the last day of the 1763 conference. The attendance was an improvement on the previous year, and the Church of England visitors were accompanied by two Moravian bishops. But again very little progress was made even toward real cooperation. Harris and Wesley toured England looking for allies without much success. For the next six years he continued to make advances to sympathetic clergy. Then, at Leeds in 1769, he told the conference, "Out of fifty or sixty to whom I wrote, only three vouchsafed me an answer. So I give up." His contempt for the reluctant clergy was absolute. "They are a rope of sand; and such they will continue."

John Wesley's failure to recruit ordained priests to the Methodist cause was interpreted by his followers as proof that the Church of England clergy lacked reforming zeal. In fact, a revival, parallel to that which Whitefield and Wesley led, had been going on within the Established Church for twenty years. However, most of its members wanted to pursue their evangelical missions without either accepting John Wesley's leadership or incurring the wrath of the bishops. John Berridge experienced a personal revelation comparable with those which made John and Charles Wesley "whole Christians." "As I was sitting in my house one morning and musing upon a text of the scriptures, the following words darted into my mind with a wonderful power and seemed indeed like a voice from heaven. Cease from thine own works. The tears flowed from my eyes like a torrent. The scales fell from my eyes immediately." As well as burning all his old sermons, he composed this epitaph: "I was born in Sin 1716. Remained ignorant of my fallen state till 1730. Lived proudly on faith and works for salvation till 1752. . . . Fled to Jesus alone for refuge 1756."

It was not only a reluctance to accept Wesley's leadership which kept the evangelical clergy separate from Methodism. The firm rejection of Calvinism alienated some potential recruits. The Reverend Augustus Toplady, speaking as always for the ultras of the church, could "discern no medium between absolute predestination and black atheism." But William Grimshaw, a Wesley ally and, at one time, possible successor, regarded Arminianism as "the great religious evil of the age." Wesley's doctrine, as well as his autocratic nature, divided him from other evangelicals. But they certainly existed within the Church of England. Methodism was just the most important part of a general Protestant trend.

The failure to recruit ordained clergymen was a problem for the connexion, which was complicated by the difficulty of deciding how Methodists should behave toward Church of England priests who were sympathetic yet not absolutely committed to Wesley and his particular view of evangelism. Should Methodists leave the field to them or should men of almost identical beliefs compete in their propagation of evangelical Christianity? When the conflict first arose, Samuel Walker had suggested from Truro that the Methodist Society of St. Agnes should be handed over to the care of the curate of that parish, James Vonter, "who preaches and lives the gospel."[7] Whatever Vonter's virtues, Wesley was not prepared to lose an outpost of his empire. In 1761 the appointment of Henry Venn as rector of Huddersfield had raised an even more delicate problem. Venn was associated with Wesley and much respected by local Methodists. But simply to worship with him would have been to lose their identity by becoming no more than evangelical Anglicans. So a typically convoluted formula was invented to balance the connexion between independence and cooperation. "Where there is gospel ministry already, we do not desire to preach. But whether we can leave off preaching because such a one comes after is another question, especially when those who are awakened and convinced by us beg and require the continuation of our assistance." After some pressure from Charles Wesley, it was agreed that although the Huddersfield Society should not be disbanded, preachers would visit it only once a month. A year later the visits were abandoned completely.

The relationship with the ordained clergy was slightly tenuously associated in Charles Wesley's mind with the whole secession controversy and the demand that preachers be allowed to officiate at Holy Communion. The letter in which he sought protection for Venn also raised again the question of the self-ordained preachers of Norwich. He believed that a pattern of disobedience was building up. Each item was in itself not enough to provoke a schism. Added together, they demonstrated a willingness, if not a wish, to separate. It was not only Charles who feared that his brother was becoming a subversive influence within the Church of England. The earl of Dartmouth, a supporter of Methodism, was sufficiently worried by his chaplain's analysis of Wesley's heresy—recruiting his own preachers and organizing ordained clergy to act as agents of Methodism—to ask a complicated rhetorical question. The chaplain repeated it, almost verbatim, to John Wesley. "Is it a law of the Church and State that none of her ministers shall 'gather congregations' but by the appointment of the bishop? If any do, does she not forbid her people to attend them? Are they not subversive of the good order of the Church. Do you judge there is anything sinful in such a law?"[8]

Wesley, having offered a variety of theological justifications for his connexion's behavior, ended with a hypothesis which he no doubt believed would be particularly persuasive to a peer of the realm whose duty it was to defend England's matchless constitution. The letters between Wesley and the chaplain, written sometime between 1759 and 1761, were not published by Wesley until twenty years later.

> Suppose one had asked a German nobleman to hear Martin Luther preach, might not his priest have said, "My Lord, in every nation there must be *some settled order* of government, ecclesiastical and civil. There is an ecclesiastic order established in Germany. You are born under this establishment and your very rank and station constitutes [sic] you a formal and eminent guardian of it. How then can it consist with the duty arising from all these to give encouragement, countenance and support to principles and practices which are a direct renunciation of the established constitution. Had the force of this reasoning been allowed, what had become of the Reformation."[9]

Despite the continual justification of Methodism as a legitimate part of the Established Church, Wesley had begun to feel that the church would never embrace his societies or recognize that he did God's work. Fearful that continual attempts at cooperation—without a matching statement of its theological integrity—might damage the connexion's confidence, he decided that the time had come at least to define the boundaries of what, by 1764, had become a substantial organization with thirty separate circuits in the United Kingdom and almost one hundred traveling preachers. However, to the rest of the Church of England, apart from the handful of ministers who associated with Wesley or accepted the description, Methodism was a mystery. The definition was complicated by Whitefield's use of the term to describe his Calvinism and the even more damaging habit of some registered Dissenters who appropriated the name for themselves. Wesley discovered that in parts of Ireland, Methodists were men who "place all religion in wearing long beards."[10]

The determination to defend the connexion's theological integrity did not prevent Wesley from resorting to highly dubious expedients in the hope of extending provision of the all-important sacraments. One was the employment, in 1763, of Erasmus, introduced to John Wesley as the Greek Orthodox bishop of Arcadia, a diocese which a classical education should have taught him was, as well as a province in the central Peloponnese, Virgil's ideal of pastoral simplicity and the home of Pan. Wesley had inquiries made about the bishop's authenticity and was assured, by no less an authority than the patriarch of Smyrna, that the man was genuine. He was invited to ordain Dr. John Jones, an itinerant preacher for seventeen years and the man who had initially vouched for the bishop's respectability. Not surprisingly, Erasmus obliged.

Other preachers immediately claimed the same improvement in their status. *Lloyd's Evening Post* reported, "To the article in the papers relating to three tradesmen being ordained by a Greek bishop another may be added, a master baker."[11] It also claimed that two preachers had asked to be made bishops, but Erasmus had declined. Charles Wesley was scandalized and complained so publicly that Jones left the connexion. The ordinations did little to solve Methodism's problems. Samson Stanforth, convinced that if he was a priest at all, he was a priest of the Greek Orthodox Church, refused to perform the offices which Wesley had hoped his ordination would make more accessible. Thomas Bryant persisted in the belief that he was a clerk in holy orders. As a result, the Sheffield Society split in two. The need to define what exactly the connexion stood for grew increasingly urgent.

John Wesley decided that the essential definition would best be set out in *A Short History of Methodism*. It was published in 1764 and included a bold assertion of loyalty. "Real Methodists," wrote Wesley, were "Church of England men." They "love her Articles, her

Homilies, her Liturgy, her discipline." But, as always, the description of Methodist practice which followed made clear that very often the love which Wesley felt for the Established Church had to be denied in the interests of his societies. Charles Wesley, describing the difference in attitude between him and his brother, explained how John dealt with the unavoidable conflict he clearly felt. "His first object was to the Methodists, then to the Church. Mine was first to the Church, then to the Methodists."[12] The injunction which followed the history urged preachers "to live according to what they preach" and to be "plain Bible Christians." The implication was clear. Where Methodism and the church disagreed, the church was wrong.

There followed an avalanche of advice offered in sermons or laid down in pamphlets. Wesley's work covered every aspect of the preacher's life. A sermon, "On the Use of Money," reiterated the gospel of true charity which he had first proclaimed in Oxford. "Earn all you can. Save all you can. Give all you can." A pamphlet, *Advice to People Called Methodists with Regard to Dress*, concluded that although it was a Methodist's duty to sell any "costly apparel" which he might possess and donate the proceeds to the poor, it would be better to burn extravagant clothes than to wear them.

A précis of the *Short History* was read into the minutes of the 1765 conference, thus making it the Methodist equivalent of Holy Writ. The extract gave a special importance to the paragraph which dealt with the connexion's early failures. Preoccupation with doctrinal disputes with Calvinists, antinomianists and Dissenters had deflected the societies from their social duties, particularly the Christian education of children. Moving to the present tense, Wesley concluded, "This is not cured by the Preachers. Either they have not weight or light enough. But the weight of these may be in some measure supplied by public readings of sermons everywhere, especially the fourth volume, which supplies them with remedies suited to a disease."[13] It was, as well as another indication of Wesley's confidence in his special ability to reflect the will and Word of God, further proof of the low esteem in which he held his preachers. When defending them against bishops, he always insisted that what they lacked in learning they more than made up in piety. But he was rarely fully confident of their command of the Scriptures. His sermons met a desperate need. Inadequate preachers could make up for their deficiencies by preaching the gospel according to John Wesley.

To reinforce the demand for a common theology, Wesley began to add new sermons to the old. "The Scripture Way of Salvation" reiterated the doctrine of salvation by faith. He had preached on the same subject on innumerable occasions. But the defining principle of his belief had been constantly challenged by preachers who, despite their deviation, claimed Methodist affiliation. "The Lord Our Righteousness" refined Wesley's view on justification and sanctity. The argument sounds, to the uninitiated, more about words than theology. But the dispute about the true source of salvation—Christ's passive or active righteousness—divided Calvinists from those Protestants who held that God's love and forgiveness were available to all who believed and repented their sins. The disagreement had always centered on two verbs which qualified and explained the righteousness which mortals might achieve. Was grace "implanted" by faith or "imputed" as a result of an irreversible gift from God. Calvinists insisted that "imputation" was an essential item of belief, the only protection against the presumption that man could save himself by good works. Wesley traditionally regarded imputation as a denial of *sola fide*—and another aspect of the claim that some men and women were ordained for salvation while others were irrevocably beyond hope of either justification or eventual sanctity.

John Wesley remained unflinchingly opposed to every aspect of the notion that some men and women were "preordained" to take a place in heaven. But his attitude toward the imputation/implantation dispute was unusually emollient. It was often his habit to claim that words meant what he wanted them to mean and that disagreements within the church were really the result of confusion and ignorance rather than fundamental and irreconcilable differences in doctrine. But his reconciliation of the two doctrines of righteousness was particularly bland. "God implants righteousness in everyone to whom He has imputed it." The glib refusal to stand firm on what had always been his previous position marked another change not in belief but in his assessment of where the future of Methodism lay.

Reliance on members drawn from a narrow segment of the Church of England—attracted to its ranks by its Arminian theology—would no longer sustain an expanding connexion. Methodism had to become a "popular" religion which attracted its own recruits and neither intimidated nor deterred them with scholarly disputations. Sometimes the theological lines had to be blurred, and sometimes theology had to be forgotten in order to attract men and women who were frightened by long words and complicated ideas. Methodism was taking on a separate identity, but its definition was not as sharp as John Wesley had once intended. It was the only way truly to make the whole world his parish.

John Wesley's remedy for all the societies' problems and his prescription for increasing their success was always a combination of intensified discipline and redefined doctrine—even if the redefinition was the agreement to accommodate a greater diversity of theological opinion balanced by sterner rules covering personal conduct. And so it was in 1765. A *Short History* and *The Sermons* refined the theology. A series of published minutes from the annual conference—formally called *Minutes of Some Late Conversations Between Rev. Mr. Wesley and Others* but known colloquially as the Penny Minutes—dealt with the conduct of preachers and members.

The Penny Minutes became the Methodist directory, containing lists of preachers (classified as admitted, on trial and assistants) and the stations to which they had been sent, as well as the financial statement which the various subscriptions, collected locally but distributed from London, made necessary. But the real importance of the Penny Minutes lay in the detailed instructions which they contained. John Wesley aspired to govern every aspect of the preachers' lives and work. The preaching houses, which were never to be called churches, must have sash windows which opened downward. There should be no arms on the seats and no tub pulpits. Those economy measures, necessitated by the societies' habit of spending more on building than they could afford, were supplemented by rules for the work within the preaching houses themselves. They were prompted by Wesley's instinct for propriety. Men and women were to sit separately, divided by an aisle.

Societies which, because of their new preaching house, had abandoned outdoor preaching were to resume the practice at once. Only at harvesttime was preaching to begin later than seven o'clock in the evening, and love feasts must be finished in time for the congregation to be home at nine. Singing was to be taught in all societies. Members might "tenderly and prudently call each other brother and sister," but most of them talked too much and should learn to converse with restraint. Preachers were never to "take drams" or snuff. Many members were "absolutely enslaved" to both vices and needed to be set a good example. "Little oaths as upon my life, my faith, my honor" were to be discouraged.

Any preacher who published a pamphlet or sermon without permission would be immediately expelled. No one should be admitted into one society on the basis of a certificate which claimed membership in another, unless it was accompanied by proof that it was genuine. It was important that the preachers should be "merciful to their beasts." Hard riding was an offense against God's creatures. A preacher should "see with his own eyes his horse, rubbed, fed and bedded." Inspectors would be sent to inspect the deeds of every preaching house to guarantee that both ownership and use conformed to the prescribed pattern.

Although the first set of Penny Minutes set out such comprehensive rules of conduct and further tightened John Wesley's grip on the societies, they were never mentioned in his *Journal*. Indeed the event at which they were approved is dismissed in two lines in the entry for 19 September. "Our conference began on Tuesday the 20th and ended on Friday 23rd." The reason for John Wesley's reticence when the *Journal* was printed—as always, long after the events it described—was almost certainly the way in which the preachers reacted to the regulation of their lives.

The edicts of the Penny Minutes were attacked during their discussion at the 1765 conference and again in 1766, after they had been tested for a year. The preachers' complaint was not, in fact, if not in form, about the existence of the rules but rather about what the rules required. They objected to John Wesley's authoritarianism and his presumption that he had been set in power over them. He defended himself to the 1766 conference with his usual claim that he had never asked to rule the societies but that the members had asked him to lead them and he could not refuse. "It was merely in obedience to the Providence of God and for the good of the people that I first accepted this power which I never sought, nay a hundred times laboured to throw off." However, the speech continued with a passage which was not wholly consistent with the claim that he sought no authority.

> Some of the helpers say "This is shackling free-born Englishmen" and demand a free conference, that is a meeting of all the preachers wherein all things shall be determined by most votes. I answer it is possible after my death something of this kind may take place; but not while I live. To me the preachers have engaged themselves to submit to serve me as sons of the gospel. . . . Every preacher and every member may leave me when he pleases, but when he chooses to stay it is on the same terms as he joined me at first.[14]

Urgency and poignancy were added to John Wesley's statement by his sudden conviction that, at the age of sixty-three, he was facing his last year on earth and preparing for his final conference. And he felt wholly unprepared to meet his Maker. In June 1766 he was consumed by another crisis of conscience. His letter to his brother confessed, "I do not love God. I never did. Therefore I never believed in the Christian sense of the word. Therefore I am only an honest heathen, a proselyte of the Temple. . . . And yet to be employed of God! . . . surely there was never such an instance before from the beginning of the world."[15] John Wesley quickly recovered from both the premonition that he would soon die and the fear that he was still only a "half Christian." He often felt forebodings of death and damnation, and they usually passed as swiftly as they came. In 1766 the brief despondency provoked (as well as a slightly perverse statement of his undiminished authority) innumerable sermons, pamphlets and books.

Perhaps the most important among them was *A Plain Account of Christian Perfection*, though its importance was not the originality of the ideas which it contained. Indeed it was written for quite the opposite purpose. It described Wesley's views in the form of a historical résumé of his spiritual progress since 1725. His description of those early beliefs concludes, "This was the view of religion I then had. . . . This is the view I have of it now, without any material addition or diminution. . . . This is the very same doctrine which I believe and teach today without adding one point." In large part the book's purpose was to show that Wesley's beliefs had been constant. Luke Tyerman, Wesley's nineteenth-century biographer and the least severe of his critics, made the best of Wesley's sophistry by describing the assertion as "unquestionably true with the one exception of his new teaching that Christian perfection is attainable in *an instant* and by *faith only*." Despite the size and importance of the change in doctrine which some commentators admitted Wesley chose to overlook, the adjustment to history was greater than they, or Wesley, acknowledged. Wesley claimed that he had taught instant perfection through faith in 1741. But the best that can be found to support that version of events was a hymn which included the lines:

> Oh that I now the rest might know
> *Believe* and enter in.
> *Now* Sorrow, *now* the power bestow
> And let me cease from sin.
>
> Remove this hardness from my heart
> This unbelief remove.
> To me the rest of *faith* impart
> The sabbath of thy love.

Within days of *A Plain Account of Christian Perfection*'s being published, Wesley's claim of consistency was challenged by Thomas Rutherford, the Regius professor of divinity at the University of Cambridge. That was, in itself, proof that Wesley had become a figure in theology and church politics. Uncharacteristically, Wesley admitted that Rutherford was right. He had "relinquished several former sentiments," a confession which he regarded as immensely to his credit when compared with his critics, who never conceded errors. Others might have amended their views without observing it. But Wesley wanted the world to know that he had the intellectual honesty both to recognize and to admit his inconsistency. However, his explanation for his theological adjustments did little credit to his intellectual self-confidence. The adjustments to his theology were the result of the necessity to respond, simultaneously, to so many varied critics "one pushing this way, another that." He then went on to admit that long ago he had given up the idea that assurance was the *only* proof of justification. The concession marked the point at which theological purity took second place to the pragmatic demands of leading the connexion. The claim that he had never changed was meant to hide not so much a change in his doctrine as a major revision in his attitude toward the importance of doctrine itself. The former Fellow of Lincoln who once agonized about both the nature of belief and his own capacity to believe (and had suffered a sudden crisis of conscience only weeks earlier) had decided, "We must get rid of long words and simply fall back on the truth that he that feareth God and doeth righteousness is accepted of Him."[16]

Lord Acton, historian and author of the aphorism on the inevitable relationship between power and corruption, believed that 1 December 1767, the day on which Wesley's statement was made, "marks the separation of Methodism from the Church of England." That judgment was based on what Acton believed he had identified as the rejection of fundamental Church of England doctrine, not a refusal to accept its liturgy and laws. The apostasy, which always took the form of a dilution of once-absolute doctrine, had developed over years. Its origins can be traced back to 1750, when Wesley first modified his previously inflexible judgment that "full assurance" was an essential characteristic of true faith.

Wesley himself continued to agonize about true faith. In a sermon which he delivered in Bristol during 1740 he reproached those who believed themselves to be "the elect of God." Because it was intended as a fundamental statement of theological principle, it was published as a pamphlet with the title *Free Grace*. "This, otherwise termed 'the full assurances of faith' is the true ground of a Christian's happiness. And it does indeed imply a full assurance that all your past sins are forgiven and that you are now a child of God."[17] The sermon went on to make clear that the condition he described did "not necessarily imply a full assurance of our future perseverance." Only Calvinists could feel assured of indefinite forgiveness, and they were in error. But to be a complete Christian, it was essential to doubt neither the love of God nor His intention to keep the promise that all who believed would be saved. Salvation depended on acquiring that confidence in His mercy and maintaining it by the regular observance of the devotional disciplines which Wesley advocated. Belief in the absolute doctrine lasted for about ten years.

As early as 1750 Wesley had expressed the view that although assurance was essential to "saving faith," there was an interim condition in which men and women, although not assured that their sins were forgiven, have a "degree of faith." He then qualified his clarification with the assertion that "faith necessarily implies an assurance . . . that Christ loved me and gave himself for me."[18] To reconcile the two positions, he accepted that there were "exemptions" to the assurance rule. In February 1756 he adjusted his position. "Can a man who has not a clear assurance that his sins are forgiven be in a state of justification? I believe there are some instances of it."[19] Christians qualified for exemption because of "disorder of body or ignorance of the gospel."[20] The confusion, Wesley scholars now claim, was because he used one of his favorite phrases, "faith of a servant"—as distinct from "the faith of a son"—in two different ways. The first described believers who, lacking assurance, were not yet justified. The second covered "the exempt cases" who were justified but still, because of ignorance, lacked assurance. Either way, it is a denial of the basic Anglican belief that justification comes from faith alone and the assurance which it provides. Accepting that interpretation of true faith began the process which, by 1767, culminated in the judgment that a "desire to flee from the wrath which is to come" was the only qualification for Methodist membership. Once Wesley began to commend a life spent "fearing God and working righteousness" (without being certain that Christ died to save all Christians) he had come perilously close to tolerating the once-reviled "half Christians" and accepting that "good works" might offer an alternative path to salvation.

Theologians who have written about Wesley in 1767 have invariably chosen to follow his reasoning in the terms in which he presented it to the societies, the constant search for scriptural truth. But there is a second, more worldly explanation, which is supported by a sermon he gave to the society at Redruth which "explained at large the rise and nature of Methodism." It also set out Wesley's analysis of the connexion's success. "I have never read or heard of, either in ancient or modern history, any other Church which builds on so broad a foundation as the Methodists do: which requires of its members no conformity either in opinions or modes of worship, but barely this one thing to fear God and work righteousness."[21]

The significance of that statement is not its erosion of the *sola fide* or even the half suggestion that there was room in heaven for sinners who hoped for redemption by popish good works. Methodism had become a broad church. It was looking for recruits outside the Church of England and offering a place in the societies to new members who did not understand, and therefore could not be expected to accept, the complicated theological formulations of the Oxford Methodists. Lord Acton might have been wrong to identify 1 December 1767 as the moment of separation. The idea of one crucial moment is itself a delusion. But the significance of the period of which that day is symbolic is clear. Church of England doctrine was no longer sacrosanct. Like established liturgy and governance, it had been sacrificed in the interests of the connexion. As a result, Methodism, which had once been notorious for the inflexibility of its doctrine, gradually became, at least by popular reputation, a church which accepted into its membership anyone who claimed to be a Christian.

A less prescriptive view of Methodist doctrine had become essential to the future development of the connexion. For the rules of conduct and the regulation of membership, which were begun by the publication of the *Large Minutes* in 1763 and continued with the circulation of Penny Minutes for the rest of the decade, had made Methodism a national organization. An attempt to impose a single view of faith or dogma could have shattered the fragile unity of a movement which, by 1767, Wesley had decided should be more tightly controlled and supervised by a new bureaucracy. After that year the Methodists kept national membership records. It is therefore possible to calculate the success of the more relaxed approach to doctrine. In 1767 its rolls registered 25,911 members. By the time of Wesley's death, in 1791, membership had almost tripled to 72,468. The growth rate, of about 4 percent a year (with occasional and usually inexplicable reductions) continued into the middle of the nineteenth century. Wesley, as faith required, welcomed the new recruits to the army of the saved. But expansion was to carry its own inevitable penalties.

The societies were particularly afflicted by the sin of disobedience, particularly in their reaction to Wesley's constant instructions to obey the laws, if not the doctrine, of the Church of England and to avoid offending its clergy by competing with their services or openly challenging their authority. The Norwich Society continued to behave so badly that Wesley thought it necessary to issue a formal warning: "For many years I have had more trouble with this society than with half the societies in England put together. I will try one year longer and hope you will bring forth better truth."[22] The society's crime was to hold meetings at the time of Sunday services. Members of other societies were guilty of more worldly trespass.

According to Charles Wesley, the colliers of Kingswood, although forced by intimidation and class loyalty to follow their workmates, had conducted themselves during the Bristol grain riots of 1740 and 1753 with commendable restraint.[23] The good behavior did not persist into the 1760s. Although John Wesley claimed that wrecking, "the scandal of Cornwall," was unknown among Methodists, the evidence suggests that he was wrong. The best that can be realistically said for the reforming influence was that society members abstained from luring sailors to their deaths on Sundays.[24] Certainly there are examples of local preachers defending wreckers in the courts, and, in Ireland, members were formally expelled for robbing wrecks and bodies washed to shore.

Smuggling was even more difficult to stamp out. Members were expelled after conviction in Sunderland. Preachers reported that the habit was too ingrained to be prevented on the Isle of Man and so endemic in the coastal towns of Norfolk that preachers escaped prosecution for offenses committed on Sundays. In 1767 Wesley condemned the practice in *Word to a Smuggler*. The frequency with which he repeated the stern rebuke to the coastal societies confirms that he was not simply addressing a social evil. He was condemning the behavior of his own members.

More prevalent and more dangerous were members who offended against the Pauline view that love was the greatest of all Christian virtues. Although faith alone saved, faith also made Methodists their brothers' keepers. That, more than the message that abstinence is good for the soul, was the moral of both *On the Use of Money* and *Advice to People Called Methodists with Regard to Dress*. The last paragraph of a pamphlet ostensibly devoted to such esoteric subjects as "cleanliness as a great branch of frugality" concludes: "After providing for those of thine own household things needful for life and godliness, feed the hungry, clothe the naked, relieve the sick, the prisoner, the stranger, with all thou hast. Then shall God clothe thee with glory and honor in the presence of men and angels."[25]

Calls to assist the poor are usually addressed to those who are assumed to be in a position to help. Wesley certainly demanded sacrifice from every stratum of society, but he also knew that there were men of substance among his members. One estimate suggests that in 1760 Methodists could be divided into six rough categories: peers and gentlemen, 1.2 percent; professionals, military and naval officers, 4.4 percent; freeholders and farmers, 24.8 percent; merchants, tradesmen and innkeepers, 12.1 percent; manufacturers (men as well as masters), 20.9 percent; and laborers, husbandmen, cottagers, seamen, fishermen and common soldiers, 26.6 percent.* The comparatively high figure for members in urban occupations, in a society which was still basically agrarian, is a reflection of the Church of England's neglect of the new industrial poor and Methodism's mission to fill the spiritual vacuum. An analysis of the Methodist lead-

---

* The missing 10 percent are classified "unknown."

ership, based on the occupations of the 347 who were society trustees in the West Riding of Yorkshire, emphasizes the point even more strongly. Only 14 percent were employed (as either owners or workers) on the land, but 13 percent were tradesmen and 66 percent manufacturers. Only 3 (a little less than 1 percent) were laborers.

The terms "agriculturalist" and "manufacturer" cover so wide a social spectrum that they reveal virtually nothing about the class, as distinct from the occupational, composition of the Methodist leadership. A miscellaneous sample of local preachers, made as part of the same survey, provides a clearer picture. Of the 111 in the survey, 63 percent were artisans, 12 percent members of professions, 9 percent farmers, 11 percent shopkeepers, 3 percent gentlefolk and 3 percent unskilled. Methodism met the needs of the new industrial working class, but they were its members, not its leaders.

For years the societies had collected from members to finance what amounted to alms for the poor. As early as 1746 some societies had begun to offer elementary medical care, supported by *Primitive Physick*, the manual written by Wesley himself. Some societies formed what were, in effect, credit unions and, as well as lend their members small sums, tried to find jobs for those who were unemployed. In 1767 all those activities were extended and expanded. "The loan fund was increased to 120 pounds and the number of borrowers multiplied."[27] Methodism was on the march. But Wesley was not sure how many years were left for him to lead it.

His mind again turned to thoughts of death, not merely to "dying well," which to Methodists meant retaining faith in redemption to the end, but to leaving his affairs in the good order that was to be expected of a man whose love of God required financial as well as moral discipline. As always, he extended his decision on personal morality into advice to the whole connexion. "From these words 'Set thy house in order' I strongly exhort all who have not done it already to settle their temporal affairs without delay. It is a strange madness which still possesses many, that are in other respects men of understanding, who put off from day to day, till death comes in an hour when they looked not for it."[28]

The will with which he set his house in order during 1768 shows how little he had to leave. Charles Wesley was to inherit all of his brother's books apart from those which were actually being used in Kingswood School. James Morgan, a preacher he commended for "always doing his best," was to receive his pocket watch, Ann Smith (his housekeeper) a ring and Peter Jaco (a virtually unknown preacher) his bureau. Any traveling preacher who did not possess a full set of his sermons was to receive one. The rights to his works still in publication were to be held in trust, first to honor the promise of a regular income which he had made to his brother, then "for the continual relief of the Poor of the United Society of London." Everything of substance being distributed, he left "the residue of books and goods" to his wife. When the end came, more than twenty years later, he still had very little to leave. In some years he gave away as much as a thousand pounds, a fortune by the standards of the eighteenth century. In total he probably donated, in his life-time, more than thirty thousand pounds to the causes, religious and social, which he thought contributed to the works of God.

Wesley knew that his real legacy to the world was Methodism, which, by the late 1760s, was organized in a complicated network of societies and controlled by a conference which imposed enough discipline to qualify the connexion as an autonomous church. So in 1769 he began to consider how he could guarantee the success of his creation after his death. His first instinct had been immediately to consult the ordained ministers who supported the Methodist cause. Each of them received a letter asking for advice about how the future could be secured. But few, if any, responded to his invitation. He turned for advice to the traveling preachers. But he did not ask for their unprompted opinions. Instead he set out his plan.

On notice of my death let all the preachers in England and Ireland repair to London within six weeks. Let them seek God by solemn fasting and prayer. Let them draw up articles of agreement for those who choose to act in concert. Let those be dismissed who do not choose it, in the most friendly manner possible. Let them choose by votes a committee of three, five or seven each of whom is to be moderator in his turn. Let the committee do what I do now; propose preachers to be tried, admitted or excluded, fix the place of each preacher for the ensuing year and the time of next conference.[29]

The future was, he hoped, secured. But it was secured in such a way that Wesley would continue to influence Methodism from beyond the grave.

15

THROW AWAY THE SCABBARD

John Wesley did God's work in many different ways. As he approached old age, one of the obligations which he accepted most willingly was his mission to young women. The letters which he wrote during the mid-1760s reveal a commitment to that particular evangelistic endeavor which was both personal and emotional. Time after time he complained that his special charges had not written to him as often or in the length that was appropriate to the relationship between pastor and protégée. The tone changed, but the message was always a desire for a closer association.

Lady Maxwell was sternly rebuked. "Your silence is not enough. I will not believe you are tired of my correspondence unless I have it under your own hand. But when I have heard nothing from you for six or eight weeks I begin to be full of tears."[1] Mrs. Moon was reminded of her responsibilities. "I am persuaded your heart is as my heart. . . . What is always in your power is to bear me before the throne of grace."[2] Peggy Dale was urged to remember the beneficial effects of their friendship. "I feel it does me good to converse with you even at a distance."[3] Jane Hutton received a half-jocular reproof. "Indeed, you hardly deserve to hear from me, what, put me off with a letter of two lines!"[4] And Ann Bolton was reassured of the wisdom which she had shown in accepting Wesley's advice not to be "yoked to an unbeliever." God was given credit for the "deliverance [from] being joined to one who was not what he seemed." John Wesley believed it would be better if the spinster remained single. But he realized that might not be possible. "If you should do otherwise, will you not consult *me* before you engage?"[5] No doubt his description of Ann Foard as "one I sincerely loved"[6] was a statement of purely platonic affection. But the letters express that emotion in a style which would be entirely appropriate to a less spiritual relationship than that of priest and parishioner. It reveals something more important than John Wesley's continual susceptibility. His love of God both sublimated, and in some ways reflected, more earthly passions.

The letters to his young acolytes were written in a style which was quite different from that which he employed when writing to his wife, even when his purpose was to comfort her after she had barely survived an illness which was at first thought fatal. The letter, beginning "My Dear Love" and ending "Your ever affectionate husband," was a model of formal propriety. A reference to the gratitude he felt to God for making her "the chief instrument of restoring [his] health"[7] fifteen years earlier was followed by the advice that she should not be discouraged if her vigor was restored less quickly than she had hoped. Slow progress was common "at this time of year." In any event, a temporary incapacity might contribute to her salvation by allowing time for her to be "more entirely devoted to Him whose favour is better than strength or health itself." The cold detachment could not have done much to reduce the sick woman's fever. For she must have known that by nature, her husband was not a cold man. But after years of rarely broken separation he could not show her the warmth of feeling which he exhibited without inhibition to his young devotees. At the end he did his duty—no less and certainly no more.

When the news of her illness reached him in the early hours of Sunday, 14 August 1768, shortly after his arrival in Bristol, he "took chaise immediately and before one in the morning"[8] reached the Foundry, where he found "the fever was turned and the danger over." His *Journal* does not reveal if he spoke to, or even saw, his presumably sleeping wife. But he set out again back to Bristol barely an hour later. Having made the journey of 228 miles in rather less than seventeen hours, he presided over the annual conference and then set out on a preaching tour of the southwest. He found time to write to express his hope of a complete recovery on 5 September, three weeks later. Wesley's conduct could not properly be described as neglect, though it was hardly a model of concern. His explanation—he would not have condescended to call it an excuse—was that there could be no truce in the war against the devil. The campaign against Calvinism, as well as ungodliness, had to be fought night and day. He had made that plain to his wife on the night of their wedding. What Mary Wesley could not have been expected either to anticipate or to understand was that her husband never lost his zest for battle or his willingness to fight by whatever means were available—fair or foul—for the triumph of his cause.

John Wesley had struck out so often and so wildly that it often seemed as though his love of battle clothed his thinking about the cause for which he fought. So the campaigns of the 1760s were mounted in order to vindicate his reputation for theological consistency as well as in the hope of finally confounding old enemies. Dr. William Dodd, prebendary of Brecon and chaplain in ordinary to the king, reflected the criticism which Wesley had to overcome. "Wesley fights against everybody. Indeed not only is his hand against every man's and every man's against his but his own hand is also against himself. His writings abundantly contradict themselves; and it would be no hard matter to set *John* against *Wesley* and *Wesley* against *John*."[9] Unfortunately, Wesley's attempts to demonstrate intellectual moderation usually only illustrated his theological intemperance.

The great controversies of the 1760s—the decade in which Wesley approached his allotted span—had begun in 1765, shortly after the death of James Hervey, an Oxford Methodist and Holy Club member who had become a clergyman of evangelical persuasion. Ten years earlier Hervey had written a devotional work titled *Theron and Aspasio*. Hervey had asked for Wesley's comments on his work and received, instead of the constructive criticism for which he had hoped, a scathing denunciation. There is no doubt that Hervey asked for confidential advice, but Wesley, without warning, published his assault on *Theron and Aspasio* in a book of essays, *Preservative Against*

Unsettled Notions of Religion. As was the habit of the time, Hervey wrote a long refutation of Wesley's polemic. A draft was sent to several like-minded clergymen. Before they had time to reply, Hervey (a consumptive) died. A few hours before his death he was asked if he wanted the vindication to be published. He replied, "It's not a finished piece. I desire you will think no more about it."

Moved by his brother's death and by the belief that Wesley had never paid the proper penalty for his intemperate assault, William Hervey published what he described as *Eleven Letters . . . Containing an Answer to Remarks on Theron and Aspasio*. The letters alleged that many of the views which Wesley had condemned were identical to opinions which he had expressed in past years. Cut to the quick by the allegation of inconsistency, a regular and usually justified charge which always moved him to great passion, Wesley decided to attack on intellectually dubious ground. Ignoring the merits of the arguments, he claimed that some of the letters were the work not of James Hervey but of John Cusworth, a regular adversary who had certainly been consulted by Hervey during his preparation of the "letters."[10] He also published—under an offensive title—a series of letters which he had written to James Hervey. He called it *A Treatise of Justification, Extracted from Mr. John Goodwin, with a Preface Wherein All That Material in Letters, Just Published under the Name of Rev. Mr. Hervey Is Answered*. John Wesley, knowing that God was on his side, thought that he was entitled to use whatever weapons were to hand.

It was an age in which the religious tract flourished and theology was taken seriously. But Wesley's closely argued reply to Hervey was hard work even for eighteenth-century theologians. However, it did bring its rewards. The author was invited to Scotland to preach before the countess of Buchan. The countess was deeply impressed by the performance. As a result, Wesley was appointed her chaplain, and his sermon "The Good Steward," which argued that we hold our whole life in trust and must account for how it has been used on the day of reckoning, was published at her expense. Its message—dangerously like the promise of redemption by good works—was, again, entirely anti-Calvinistic. The campaign against the idea of election was being fought all over again. Wesley assiduously preached the doctrine of final perseverance and sudden grace for the next three years. In 1766, fearing that the pupils of Kingswood School were attracted to the heresy of election, he "told [his] whole mind to the masters and servants [and] spoke to the children in far stronger manner that I ever did before." He emphasized his strength of feeling by vowing, "I will kill or cure—I will have one or the other—a Christian school or none at all."[11]

In early 1767 he locked horns with Dr. Dodd again. Like many other divines before him, the Brecon prebendary had made the mistake of assuming that the perfection of which Wesley spoke was perfection as a normal man would understand it. Dodd had written that a "Methodist according to Mr. Wesley is one who is perfect and sinneth not in thought or deed." Impatient at his adversary's lack of subtlety, or reluctant to reveal the sophistry on which his theory depended, Wesley replied that despite Dodd's "passionate desire to measure swords with him," he did not intend to reply. "I can employ the short remainder of my life to better purpose."

In 1768 there was a brief respite in the Methodist civil war while Lady Huntingdon and Wesley combined forces in face of the common enemy. St. Edmund Hall, Oxford—in a sudden fit of orthodoxy—expelled all of its students who admitted to being Methodists. Most of them were Calvinist by inclination. But from then on, followers of both Whitefield and Wesley found it hard to gain admission to Oxford. Dr. Johnson managed to support both the Dissidents and the master of the college, as well as polish the image of his wit, by observing that "a cow is a very good animal in a field, but we turn her out of a garden." Neither Wesley nor Lady Huntingdon was amused. Both of them decided to set up rival institutions of their own. An "academical" course was instituted at Kingswood, and Lady Huntingdon set up her college at Trevecka. John Fletcher, vicar of Madeley and an enthusiastic Wesleyite, became president. Joseph Benson, a Kingswood master, was appointed head of the institution.

With two Wesleyans in charge, Trevecka, founded as a Calvinist college, should have been a focal point for harmony. But Wesley, perhaps sensitive about the success of the college and offended by its employment of his adherents, took exception to what he regarded as

Fletcher's apostasy from belief in salvation by faith alone. Fletcher defended himself, and Wesley, who knew Fletcher to be a true friend, changed tack. His objection to Trevecka was, he said, its management by what he described as "genteel" Christians. In case anyone doubted to whom he referred, he denounced Lady Huntingdon's alleged habit of speaking about "my college, my masters and my students."

There then began what was to amount to a long war of pamphlets and sermons which Wesley pursued by yet another stratagem far too disreputable to be called dubious. He himself constructed a criticism of Calvinism based on what he claimed to be a summary of that faith as it had been set out by one of its most energetic proponents, Augustus Toplady, a Church of England curate and author of the hymn "Rock of Ages." Wesley must have known that the text, which he recklessly and wrongly attributed to Toplady, did not do his adversary's Calvinism full justice. "One in twenty (supposed) of mankind are elected; nineteen in twenty are reprobated. The elect shall be saved, do what they will, the reprobate shall be damned, do what they can. Reader believe this or be damned. Witness my hand A.T."[12]

Unfortunately Toplady had never seen the précis which Wesley claimed summarized his view, and he would certainly not have endorsed it if he had. Much to the credit of his scholarship, the letter in which he refuted Wesley's interpretation of his views dealt more with the crudity of Wesley's criticisms of Calvinism than with their corrupt misattribution. But it did conclude on a personal note. Wesley, he wrote, had descended "into his costermongering of false quotations, despicable invective and unsupported dogmatism. . . . An opponent who thinks to add weight to his arguments by scurrility and abuse resembles the insane person who rolled himself in mud in order to make himself feel fine."

Wesley did not reply. Instead he wrote from York on 24 June 1770 to tell the Methodists of Yarn (following Toplady's metaphor) that he "did not fight with chimney sweepers" and concluded, "He is too dirty a writer for me to meddle with. I should only foul my fingers."[13] He then, perhaps wisely, announced his intention to leave the correction of Toplady to others. From then on the real intellectual battle against Calvinism was principally carried on by Walter Sedon, a traveling preacher, and John Fletcher, ironically the president of Lady Huntingdon's Calvinist Trevecka College. However, Wesley could not resist entering the lists from time to time. It was because of his habit of mounting sudden raids on his enemies and then running for cover behind his colleagues that Toplady called him an "old fox," a description which gave more offense than all the other juvenile abuse.

The result of the disputations was an end to the period of cooperation which had followed the St. Edmund Hall expulsions and confirmed the need, at least in Wesley's mind, for true Methodists to restate their Arminian belief in redemption by faith. He decided that the 1770 conference must reaffirm the articles which he rightly claimed had first become the binding principle of Methodism in 1744 and had been redefined, but never diminished (whatever other doctrines had been diluted), at every conference since. However, when he considered the terms in which the old religion should be revived, his mood led him to express the established theology in more intemperate language than had been employed in previous and less agitated conferences.

The 1744 conference had concluded that Methodism, in its excitement over the doctrine of justification by faith alone, had come far too close to endorsing the hated antinomianism. In December 1767, while he sat in his coach as he prepared to set out on one of his journeys, a number of precepts "came into his head." One of them concluded:

> That a pious churchman who has not clear conceptions even of Justification by Faith may be saved. . . . That a Mystic who denies Justification by Faith (Mr. Law for instance) may be saved. But if so what becomes of *articulus stantis vel cadentis ecclesiae* [the article by which the church stands or falls]. . . . Is it not time for us to return to the plain word, He that feareth God, and worketh righteousness is accepted by him?[14]

The sentiments represented another breach of orthodox theology. But Wesley was careful to express his unorthodox thoughts in language which made his new notion more or less acceptable to the

Church of England. They were based on the Scriptures and denounced doctrines which were anathema to the church. So although mildly heretical, they provoked no outcry. The ideas rattled around his head for nearly two years. Then in 1769 he felt ready to set out the revised doctrine in detail. It was included in the minutes of the 1770 conference. They made no concessions to Wesley's critics inside or outside the connexion.

The conference, which began in Bristol on Tuesday, 7 August, lasted for five days. Some of the delegates initially feared that Wesley was too preoccupied with thoughts of a second visit to America to concentrate on doctrinal disputation. But on the fourth day he began to set out his restatement of theology and announced that it was to be included in the conference minutes. In consequence, it would come to represent official Methodist doctrine, even though it had been determined by John Wesley alone and could not be amended in any way by the assembled priests and preachers. As always, the precepts were carefully numbered. They came to be called the Eight Propositions. Number three summarized them all: "We have received it as a maxim that a man is to do nothing in order to [find] justification. Nothing can be more false. Whoever desires to find favour with God should 'cease from evil and learn to do well.' Whoever repents should do 'works meet for repentance.' And if this is not in order to find favour, what should he do them for?"[15]

To Calvinists, what seemed to them the unqualified endorsement of salvation by good works was absolute heresy. Lady Huntingdon condemned it as "popery unmasked." She forbade Wesley to preach in any of her chapels. Joseph Benson, the principal of Trevecka College, thought that loyalty required him to resign, but Wesley persuaded him to stay in the hope of bridging the gap. Lady Huntingdon took a different view and dismissed him. John Fletcher then tried to mediate but, on being told that support for the 1770 minutes was treachery, relinquished the college presidency.

Wesley, like most men of conviction, reacted to assault by restating his position with renewed clarity. Attacked in the *Gospel Magazine,* he announced that he had reviewed the Eight Propositions and "the more I consider them, the more I like them, the more fully I am convinced not only that they are true, agreeable both to Scripture and to sound experience but they contain fruits of the deepest importance."[16] It was a reiteration, in unusually strong language, of the old beliefs. Faith, only faith, redeems. Good works are the fruit, not the cause, of redemption. Redemption is a gift of God, not a boon which man could obtain by his own exertions. Whatever his feelings about the need to hold the Methodist movement together, Wesley was not in a mood to be represented as diminishing the importance of *sola fide*. So he wrote, in near anguish, to John Fletcher, "Who is there in England that has asserted these things—blood and righteousness of Christ as sole cause of salvation—more strongly than I have done?"[17]

Feelings ran strongly on both sides of the controversy. And it seemed that fate was determined to cooperate with human malice in deepening the bitterness. On 29 September 1770, George Whitefield, who had hoped that Wesley would soon succeed him in his mission to the British colony in North America, delivered a two-hour sermon in Exeter, Massachusetts, even though his doctor told him that he was "more fit to go to bed than preach." He replied, "True," and then, looking to heaven, added, "Lord I am weary *in* thy work, but not *of* thy work." He died at six o'clock the following morning.

Whitefield was buried in New England. Later it was discovered in his will that he had hoped for a grave in the cemetery of his Tottenham Court chapel because of his wish that the Wesley brothers would take their eternal rest beside him. "We will," he had once told the congregation, "all lie together. You refuse them entrance here while living. They can do you no harm when they are dead." Chastened by their lost leader's magnanimity, the Tottenham Court ministers asked John Wesley to preach a memorial sermon. The service was due to begin at half past five, but the chapel was full at three o'clock, and it was agreed that to avoid illness and injury among the congregation, it would begin an hour early. Wesley took as his text "Let me die the death of the righteous and let my end be like his." He preached the same sermon again that evening at Whitefield's Moorfields tabernacle.

John Wesley knew that there was the risk, perhaps the likelihood, that whatever he said would cause offense. "It was," he said, "an awful season. Everything as still as night." He first dealt with Whitefield's character: "unparalleled zeal, indefatigable activity, tender-heartedness to the afflicted, charitableness towards the poor, the most generous friendship and unblemished modesty, frailness, openness of conversation, unflinching courage, and steadfastness in whatever he undertook for the Master's sake."[18] Nobody could possibly object to that. But he moved on to an encomium of Whitefield's theology. And it was impossible to deal with that subject without enraging the dead man's most devoted followers, even though he chose to emphasize the beliefs about which they agreed. "These are the fundamental doctrines which he everywhere insisted on: and may they not be summed up in two words—the new birth and justification by faith? These let us insist upon with all boldness at all times and in all places."[19]

John Wesley's Whitefield memorial sermon was, in the manner of the time, published and sold in pamphlet form. It was immediately attacked for failing to mention those doctrines which, although held dear by Whitefield, were not endorsed by Wesley. There had been no mention of election. Wesley was unrepentant. His certainty that he had always done his duty by his old friend was confirmed by the bequest of a mourning ring which, slightly quaintly, was to be shared by both the Wesley brothers. It is a token of the "indissoluble union with them, in heart and Christian affection, notwithstanding our differences in judgement about some particular points of doctrine."

Others found it more difficult to accept that equally sincere Christians might disagree and yet retain their mutual affection and respect. They believed that by Wesley's ignoring the doctrines which separated his beliefs from Whitefield's, the memory of a good man had been slighted in what should have been a tribute to his virtue. Walter Shirley, a cousin of Lady Huntingdon's, and the man who had first raised the idea of purging Trevecka College, sent out a "circular letter" to all known Calvinists within the Methodist movement. It proposed that "real Protestants . . . who disapprove of the [1770 conference] minutes, go in a body to the [1771] conference and insist upon a formal recantation . . . and, in the case of refusal, that they sign and publish their protest against them."[20]

One of the circulars was shown to John Fletcher, who immediately took up arms in defense of the 1770 position. His first duty, he wrote, was to give Wesley "the earliest intelligence of the bold onset" and assure him that he had many friends in the societies. But the message of support also promised that he would "write to Mr. Shirley to expostulate with him" and ended with a promise: "If my letters have not the desired effect, I shall probably, if you approve of them and correct them, make them public for your justification."[21] Wesley approved but did not make any significant corrections. Fletcher's criticisms of Shirley were expressed in trenchant language. But strength of feeling was the mood of the moment. Lady Glenorchy, another titled recruit to Methodism, banned all of Wesley's preachers from the chapels under her patronage.

There are two similar, but different in significant detail, accounts of the eventual confrontation. One derides the failure of Shirley's enterprise. The delegation which arrived in Bristol to demand Wesley's recantation was "less than half a score . . . and included at least two young men still preparing for the ministry."[22] Shirley asked if his circular letter had been read to the conference. It had not, but Wesley agreed that it should be on the following day. The delegation then presented Wesley with a declaration which it requested or demanded that the fifty-three preachers who were attending the conference should sign. It represented Wesley's view in every particular. "Whereas the doctrinal points of the Minutes of a Conference held in London on 7 August 1770 have been said to favour Justification by Works; now the Rev. John Wesley and others assembled at the Conference do declare that we had no such meaning and that we abhor the doctrine of Justification by Works as a most perilous and abominable doctrine." Wesley made some minor alterations to the text and agreed to sign. After some show of reluctance, Shirley accepted that he should "make some public acknowledgement that he had mistaken the meaning of the [1770] minutes." Honor was served.

However, according to *The Life of the Countess of Huntingdon*, an anonymous work which it is generally assumed was written by Shirley himself, Wesley—without any prompting from his critics—presented the delegation with a statement which he had drafted in preparation for the meeting and already persuaded the fifty-three preachers to sign. It included the declaration that the Huntingdon faction had misjudged the meaning of the 1770 conference minutes but was, in every other particular, conciliatory. Wesley's *Journal* confirms that the meeting ended harmoniously. After he and Shirley had "conversed for about two hours," there seemed to be general agreement on doctrine. "I believe," he wrote, "that they were satisfied that we were not dreadful heretics, as they imagined, but tolerably sound in faith."[23]

There the matter might have ended—at least for a time—with Wesley either agreeing to a concordat or, in the alternative version of events, positively promoting the new accord. However, he was not in a mood for genuine conciliation, and he had in his possession the five letters which John Fletcher had addressed to Walter Shirley. They had been redrafted in the form of a pamphlet with the title *Vindication of the Rev. Mr. Wesley's Last Minutes*. It concluded that "zeal against those principles [set out in the 1770 minutes] is no less than zeal against the truth and against the honor of our Lord." Fletcher had been clear that the pamphlet was to be published only if Shirley and his supporters continued the fight. Their acquiescence to a tentative agreement, no matter how reluctant, should have meant that the letters remained private. But Wesley, desperate not to give the impression that he had retreated in the face of Shirley's advance, once again betrayed a friend by publishing his work against the author's will and without his knowledge. Despite Fletcher's clear intention that the manuscript should be destroyed "if matters should end peaceably," the *Vindication* was sent to the printers on the day after the meeting with Shirley had ended in apparent agreement. In a letter to Lady Huntingdon, Wesley explained that continuing the dispute was his sacred duty. "Till Mr. Fletcher's Letters are answered I must think that everything spoken against these minutes is totally destructive to His honor and a palpable affront to Him."[24] That view could only be justified by the belief that an attack on John Wesley was an attack on the Almighty Himself. That explanation, although certainly an example of his "enthusiasm" and probably blasphemous, was a sign of grace in that it at least attempted a justification for breaking the truce which he had negotiated. The way in which he accounted for his action to his brother was more blunt and even less to Wesley's credit. "They have drawn the sword," he told Charles. So he had decided "to throw away the scabbard." Fletcher, though inclined to forgive Wesley everything, was mortified. "I feel for poor dear Mr. Shirley whom I have [considering the present circumstances] treated too severely in my vindication of the minutes. I am ready to defray, by selling my last shirt, the expense of printing my *Vindication* and suppress it."[25]

The *Vindication* was published in August 1771. In September Shirley replied, revealing in his *Narrative* that Fletcher had not wished to continue the dispute in public but had been overruled by Wesley. So the pamphlet war grew more bitter, with at least John Fletcher struggling to keep the fierce debate on the subject of doctrine rather than motives and personalities. The result was the publication, in rapid succession, of his first two *Checks to Antinomianism*. There followed a series of theological texts which, because of both their number and their quality, made Fletcher the authentic theologian of Methodism.

In the *First Check* Fletcher defended Wesley against the accusation of Pelagianism, the denial of original sin and the consequent belief that earthly virtue rather than divine grace was the path to salvation. The *Second Check* attempted to reconcile Wesley's reliance on *sola fide* with his obvious attraction to good works. Faith, Fletcher wrote, was the "first justification." Repentance of sin and determination to observe God's laws was the second. To reject the "second justification" completely was to embrace antinomianism. Richard Hill, a young man on the point of ordination, published "a conversation" between several clergy of different denominations which claimed to prove that Shirley's charge of Pelagianism was justified. So Fletcher produced a *Third Check* which offered a more sophisticated explanation of how justification was achieved. The irresistible grace, in which the Calvinists believed, denied free will. Salvation, he wrote, undoubtedly *begins* with, and depends upon, God's grace. But for it to be completed, it needs sinful men and women to accept the gift which God has offered them. Gradually Methodism was beginning to establish its defining theology and balance the importance of faith and works.

Fletcher had clearly been wise to hope that the controversy would be ended amicably. For the debate, although conducted in baroque language and dependent on classical mythology almost as much as the Scriptures, was too vicious to allow an easy reconciliation once the dispute was over. The *Gospel Magazine* for August 1771 declared that Wesley was the "employer and dictator" of everything that had been written to clarify Methodism's position on the relationship between faith and works. That made him responsible for the pamphlet *The Church of England Vindicated from the Charge of Absolute Predestination*, which the magazine described as "a composition of low scurrility and illiberal abuse" written by a man who had "horribly blasphemed and daringly given the lie to the God of truth, by asserting that any justified soul may at last perish in hell." The nearest it got to serious criticism was the assertion that "Arminianism is made up of grace and works so blended together as to destroy the true meaning of both." The same issue included a poem which was dedicated to providing "proof that evil men and seducers wax coarse and worse."

> In vain for worse may Wesley search the globe,
> A viper hatched beneath the harlot's robe.
> Rome, in her glory, has no greater boast
> Than Wesley aims—to all conviction lost.

John Wesley was at least entitled to claim that he had been wholly consistent in his opposition to Calvinism, most notably in his sermons in Bristol (on free grace) in 1739, to the Fetter Lane Society in 1740 and to the University of Oxford in 1744. But none of the earlier declarations had sparked a reaction to compare with the reception of the 1770 minutes. So the argument dragged bitterly on with Fletcher and Wesley both increasingly convinced that they had to challenge the doctrines of preordination and antinomianism whenever they were expounded. They were certain that "Lady Huntingdon's preachers will do little good wherever they go." For they were "swallowed up in the detestable doctrine of predestination and can talk of nothing else."[26] Wesley's hostility lasted throughout the decade. In 1774 he wrote that he saw "more and more clearly that there is a great gulf fixed between us and all those who, by denying [universal redemption] sap the very foundation of both inward and outward holiness."[27]

Fletcher continued to preach his sermons against preordination and write his pamphlets denouncing Calvinism and, as proof of his philosophic rather than polemical character, to engage in scholarly rather than scurrilous correspondence with theologians of a different persuasion. However, in early 1773 he produced his *Fourth Check on Antinomianism*, titled *Logica Genevensus*. It reopened the controversy in its most violent form. Perhaps that was not Fletcher's wish. For the competition in mutual abuse only began after Richard Hill accused him of "unfair quotation . . . shocking misrepresentations and calumnies," a practice which, he might have added, was in the best traditions of Wesleyanism. If the Protestant Church had been sleeping before the revival, the civil war among the Methodists certainly confirmed that it had awakened—unfortunately in a bad temper.

Then toward the end of 1773 there was a lull in hostilities. It seemed that both sides had waited for the other to show signs of wanting peace, and somehow Fletcher passed the word to Hill that he "wishes to have done with controversy." On the assumption that the news of Fletcher's hopes for peace was correct, Hill instructed his London bookseller that all his polemical works should be removed from the shelves. He wrote to Wesley to tell him of the action that he had taken and to apologize for "whatever may have savored too much of his own spirit."[28] He then suggested a reciprocal gesture. "If I stop the sale of my books, I hope that the *Four Checks* will be stopped also." He also asked that the Wesleyan preachers, who so regularly attacked him, should be instructed to end their campaign of vilification, adding, it is hard to say with what justification, "particularly one Perronet of whose superlatively abusive and insolent little piece Charles Wesley had testified his abhorrence from the pulpit."

John Wesley, in possession of private papers which might be published to his advantage, was incorrigible. Once again letters which were intended to be entirely confidential were made public. The whispers did not reveal the actual contents or quote passages verbatim but they did create the clear—and it is reasonable to suppose intentional—impression that Hill had recanted his Calvinism and sued for peace. So, not unreasonably, Hill published the entire correspondence with a preface that made clear that whatever hopes of unity he had once harbored, the doctrinal war must go on. Wesley once more failed to rise to the occasion with the apology which Hill was due. Instead he replied in an article contentiously titled *Some Remarks on Mr. Hill's Farrago, Double Distilled.*[29] It dealt with neither the theology of Hill's pamphlet nor the complaint that his confidence had been abused but offered various items of patronizing advice. "Be courteous. Show good manners as well as good nature to your opponent of whatever kind." It ended with an enraged and emphatic denial that he had made the letters public, a claim to absolute probity which was undermined by the knowledge that he had in the past regularly committed the offense which he insisted was beneath him.

The controversy continued. Fletcher published his *Last Check to Antinomianism* in 1775. Toplady responded with the allegation that work produced on Wesley's behalf was made up of "an equal portion of gross heathenism, Pelagianism, Mahometism, popery, Manichaeism and Antinomianism culled, dried and pulverized *secundum artem* and above all mingled with as much palpable atheism as could be possibly scraped together." Attacks of that savagery drew Wesley and Fletcher even closer together at a time when Wesley was in need of a friend rather than a follower.

During October 1773 a Bristol Methodist preacher had written to colleagues in Wales with worrying news. "Mr. Wesley has been with us for some time. He seems to be declining fast and I think that there is great reason to fear that he will not be with us long." In his *Journal* for 4 January 1774 Wesley himself described the nature of his indisposition, preserving his modesty by recourse to Latin. Some years earlier his horse had stumbled and jarred his testicles against the pommel of his saddle. The immediate pain was considerable, but it passed and was forgotten. Then he "observed *testiculum alterum altero duplo majorem esse. . . .* In twelve months it was grown nearly as large as a hen's egg." Fortunately he noticed the deterioration while at the home of a physician in Edinburgh. A hydrocele was diagnosed, and what the patient called "a radical remedy" was recommended. London doctors cautioned him against surgery while "he remained easy." Recovery would require sixteen days of rest, which they knew he would not take. But the swelling increased, and with it the pain. So the operation was performed "and drew off something more than half a pint of thin, yellow, transparent water. With it came out . . . a pearl the size of a small shot." John Wesley was back in the saddle within a week, visiting members of the London societies.

The reckless return to the itinerancy was typical of Wesley's confidence that God, who notices the fall of a sparrow, would spare and protect a servant who labored in His vineyard. In his youth he had followed Dr. Cheyne's prescription for "health and long life" and maintained both a strict diet and a vigorous regime of daily exercise. In his seventies he ate with care. But a life of constant physical and emotional stress was beginning to take its toll. He had no one regularly to look after him, and he made not the slightest attempt to look after himself.

In 1775, during one of his occasional tours of Ireland, he had stayed in Castle Caulfield in lodgings so dilapidated that "the rain came plentifully through the thatch" into his room. However, he "found no present inconvenience and was careful for the morrow." A week later, after seven days continual traveling and preaching, he was almost overcome with what he called "a burning fever." He pressed on for three days, during which he delivered eight sermons. At Lurgan he collapsed. Wesley was never without prosperous supporters, and a "gentleman of means" provided the bed in which he was expected to die. Long periods of catatonic sleep were interrupted by violent convulsions. Then, according to his own account, he was offered medicine and, in a moment of rare lucidity, decided, out of courtesy to the man who was watching over him, "I will, if I can swallow . . . for it will do me neither harm nor good."[30] He was wrong. The convulsions increased. He was violently sick. His pulse, which had almost disappeared, resumed its regular strong beat. The wife of his host, who was kneeling by his bedside, rose and cried,

"The prayer is granted." Six days later he set out for Dublin to resume the itinerancy.

There are two possible interpretations of Wesley's frequent illnesses and his almost invariable recovery at a speed which astonished both his friends and his medical advisers. One possibility is that most of his complaints, the hydrocele being an obvious exception, were psychosomatic and that they came and went with changes in his state of mind. The other explanation is that because of his physical strength and mental stamina, nothing afflicted him for very long. Whatever the cause of the swift restoration of health, he always attributed it to divine intervention and was, in consequence, strengthened in both his faith and his conviction that he was called by God to preach His gospel. The fever of 1775 ended with a "miracle" which was spectacular even by Wesley's normal standards. The condition was contracted in Dublin, but somehow the news of his sickness reached England, and a newspaper, sure that Wesley was mortally ill, announced that he was dead. Alexander Mather, a Jacobite who had survived the Battle of Culloden and then fled south and become a Methodist preacher in Kent, read the news and turned in consolation to his Bible. He opened it at Ezekiel 38:5, "Behold I will add unto thy days fifteen years." He began at once to pray that the prophecy would be fulfilled. That was in June 1775. John Wesley lived on until March 1791. It was easy for early Methodists to believe that Wesley had in fact died and that he had risen from the dead when Mather (who believed his own escape from Butcher Cumberland had been an act of Providence) had pleaded with a merciful God to spare his humble but essential servant. Unfortunately Wesley's powers of recovery, whether the result of divine intervention or a robust constitution, were not shared by all his supporters.

Like all early Methodists, John Wesley lived in the constant shadow of death. So he gave much thought to the leadership of his connexion after he had gone to glory. For many years he had assumed that his brother Charles would be his successor. But Charles had begun to fear that a break with the Church of England could not be avoided. His theological doubts had been reinforced by a reluctance to spend his life as a traveling preacher once he had settled down with an amiable wife and fathered two sons, whose prodigious musical talents convinced him that God was not opposed to the occasional enjoyment of a symphony or sonata. John Wesley considered other names but rarely, if ever, discussed them with anyone except Vincent Perronet. At one point William Grimshaw of Haworth seemed the natural choice. But he was too inclined to speak his mind. By 1772, seventy years old and conscious of his mortality, Wesley had decided that John Fletcher (already his literary executor and assumed by many conference members to be the obvious candidate) should follow him. At the beginning of the following year the heir presumptive was formally notified that he had become heir apparent.

In many ways it was a strange choice. Jean Guillaume de la Flechère was born in Nyon in the Pays de Vaud and believed himself to be the descendant of Savoy aristocrats. He was educated for the Calvinist ministry at Geneva but rejected the doctrine of predestination and lost his vocation, without, he later claimed, abandoning his faith in Cartesian logic. He decided to become a soldier and was commissioned, for reasons which were never explained, into the Portuguese Army. After service in Brazil and the Low Countries he found peace 'disappointing" and moved to England, where he became tutor to a prosperous Shropshire family. Impressed by his intellect and piety, they persuaded him to take holy orders. He was ordained in the Chapel Royal and became vicar of Madeley. In 1768, his enthusiastic association with Methodism convinced John Wesley that Fletcher was the one man he knew who might one day achieve Christian perfection. That made him, in Wesley's eyes, the natural successor.

The momentous letter which offered him the leadership of the connexion began with a detailed description of the qualities which were required in a Methodist leader. It then continued: "But has God provided one so qualified? Who is he? *Thou art the man.* God has given you a measure of loving faith and a single eye to His glory. He has given you some knowledge of men and things, particularly of the whole plan of Methodism. You are blessed with health, activity and diligence together with some degree of learning."[31]

It was a highly qualified commendation and has been interpreted by some of Wesley's critics as proof that the offer, far from being sincere, was an attempt to demonstrate that the founding father was implacable. Fletcher's response was even more equivocal. "Should Providence call you first, I shall do my best, by the Lord's assistance to help your brother gather the wreck." He had agreed, with some reluctance, to become president of Trevecka College. But "being shut out there it appears to me that I am called again to my first work. . . . I would not leave this place without further persuasion that the time has quite come." Wesley, not unreasonably, took the letter to be the first self-effacing step along a road which would lead to Fletcher's accepting the succession. His heir wanted, perhaps even needed, to be persuaded that he was the right man, as long ago Benjamin Ingham had needed to be convinced that God wanted him to convert the Native Americans of Georgia. Fletcher was left to ponder his position for some months and then John Wesley visited him at Madeley. Fletcher remained reluctant. On his return to London, Wesley wrote a highly uncharacteristic letter which neither reproached nor bullied but got very near to pleading for a change of mind. Fletcher's fears that he might be unacceptable to the society membership were brushed aside with an assurance which revealed John Wesley's relationship (at least as he imagined it) with his followers. He accepted that there were "grievous wolves" and "many . . . to speak perverse things" who would rebel at the appointment of a successor. "But the one and the other stand in awe of me and do not care to encounter me. So I am able, whether they will or no, to deliver the flock into your hands."[32] Fletcher would not change his mind. So he received from John Wesley not the expected rebuke but a rare compliment. "I can never believe it was the will of God that a burning light should be hid under a bushel. No, instead of being confined to a country village it ought to have shone in every corner of the land."[33] It seemed that, at last, Wesley had found a friend.

The friendship was not destined to last. In 1776 Fletcher developed "a violent cough, accompanied by spitting blood," the symptoms of tuberculosis. Wesley, notoriously unsympathetic about other people's illnesses, immediately suggested his famous cure, "taking a journey of some months with me through various parts of England."[34] Fletcher was understandably suspicious. He offered his services as a "travelling assistant." But "your recommending me to the Societies as the one who should succeed you (should the Lord call you hence before me) is a step to which I could by no means consent." Wesley assured him that the invitation had been offered with no other hope than that it would improve his health. And the tone of his letter, quite different from that which he normally employed to remind associates of their mutual duty to him and to God, confirms that he had a real affection for the man he hoped would follow him.

Unfortunately, Wesley's prediction of restored health was not fulfilled, and within a month or two Fletcher was forced to return home. He lived for another nine years. But most of them were spent struggling against tuberculosis, in semiretirement in England and then in the bracing air of Switzerland. Wesley was late in looking for real friendship. No sooner had he realized that there was a gap in his life than he lost the man who might well have been the companion of his old age as well as his successor.

Fletcher's contribution to the clarification of basic Methodist theology was incalculable. And Wesley gladly acknowledged it. As the Calvinist controversy raged on into the late 1770s he wrote to Alexander Knox, "You should read Mr. Fletcher's *Essay on Truth*" and went on to explain, in his usual highly patronizing language, how the notion of sudden and immediate justification had been modified without abandoning the doctrine of salvation by faith alone—with good works as the result, not the cause, of redemption. Fletcher describes the situation with absolute certainty: "Put it beyond all doubt that [there is] a medium between a child of God and a child of the Devil—namely a servant of God. This is your state. You are not yet a son, but you are a servant and you are waiting for the Spirit of adoption which will cry in your heart, 'Abba, Father.' You have 'received the Spirit of Grace' and *in a measure* work righteousness."[35]

When Wesley set off for Ireland with Fletcher, he was seventy-three. The Calvinist controversy, which had raged for most of the last decade, raged on. Each year the arguments grew more bitter and the language in which they were conducted more abusive. Shortly after John Wesley's return to England, Richard Hill published his *Imposture Defeated*. Again, Wesley chose to react with lofty disdain rather than meet the arguments head-on. He claimed that he "stood amazed" by Hill's truly "wonderful performance. . . . Compared to him Mr. Toplady himself is a very civil, fair-spoke gentleman." But there must have been moments when he longed to retire, if only temporarily, from the fray and spend a few hours of his declining years in congenial company. Fletcher, who described Wesley as a man with whom he "would gladly live and die," could have provided it. Mary Wesley certainly could not.

Although Mary Wesley left her husband (vowing never to return) in 1771, they were reunited from time to time in a state of matrimony which could reasonably be described as armed neutrality. Occasionally real war broke out. One day Mrs. Wesley, after following her usual practice of stealing and examining her husband's private papers, had first doctored them to suggest that he was more attracted to "redemption by good works" than he publicly admitted and then showed them to his critics on the *Morning Post*. The article which followed, written under the bylines of Scorpion and Snapdragon, was perhaps the most painful assault on his integrity he had to endure. Whether or not Mary Wesley was directly responsible for the calumny, she was certainly not available to provide comfort and support at the end of a long and difficult day.

In early middle age Wesley had announced, "[L]eisure and I have taken leave of one another. I propose to be busy as long as I live if my health is so long indulged me." Before the end of his life John Wesley gave his own explanation of why he had found it so easy to keep that promise. God, who works in mysterious ways, had arranged "the prolonged sorrow for his own good." Henry Moore, the recipient of that sad confidence, shared his view. "If Mrs. Wesley had been a better wife, and had continued to act in the way which she knew well how to act, he might have been unfaithful to his great work and might have sought too much to please her according to his own desire."[36] That explanation of Wesley's unremitting energy would have been more plausible had he not, on his wedding night, when we must assume he was full of hope for his marriage, announced that the acquisition of a wife must not reduce his evangelism by a single minute. Mary Wesley was clearly an intolerable wife. But John Wesley was equally obviously an impossible husband.

It may be that servants of the Lord were not destined to find earthly happiness. They certainly did not search for it in the usual way. George Whitefield, forced to consider marriage because he needed someone to help him manage his American Orphan House, had been explicit on the subject of how a clergyman should propose. "The passionate expressions which carnal courtiers use I think should be avoided by those who would marry in the Lord." So he wrote to the father of a lady who seemed to possess the essential qualifications with the explanation that like Abraham, he needed a "helpmeet" and asked for a frank opinion on her suitability to play the part of Rebekah. "I am free from the foolish passion which the world calls love. I write only because I believe it is the will of God that I should alter my state, but your denial will finally convince me that your daughter is not the person appointed for me." The parents—whether out of love of God or respect for their daughter we do not know—replied that they could not give Whitefield the assurances he needed. The young woman was seeking the Lord, but they could not swear that she had yet found Him. So the offer of marriage was withdrawn.

On his return to England, Whitefield had been told of a suitable widow in Abergavenny, a woman aged between thirty and forty who had become a "a despised follower of the Lamb." The marriage was successful in so much as it produced a son—who died at the age of four months. His wife's death, shortly afterward, was said by a friend "to set his mind at rest." He was free to set out his view on marriage. "It remains that those who have wives be as though they had none." A married friend was instructed, "Let nothing intercept or interrupt your communion with the Bridegroom of the Church." Despite his many dalliances, John Wesley held almost identical views about the priest's first obligation. It is not surprising that his marriage was not a success and that although surrounded by adherents, he led a lonely life.

Between January 1771 and October 1781, Mr. and Mrs. Wesley lived in virtually permanent separation. During those ten years they occasionally wrote bad-tempered letters to each other and sometimes met in order to express their mutual dislike. Had there been the prospect of a final reconciliation, Providence would have prevented it. For John Wesley, who set out for Bristol on 7 October 1781 and preached his slow way back to London through the Cotswolds, arrived home to hear the news of Mary's death. His *Journal* entry for 12 October reflects not the slightest regret. "I was informed my wife died on Monday. This evening she was buried though I was not informed of it till a day or two after." Then, without mentioning his bereavement to any of his followers, he set off again to Oxford and beyond.

Mary Wesley left five thousand pounds, the remains of the fortune which her husband had forgone, to her son. In a rare show of sentiment she bequeathed John Wesley a ring. The memorial which marks her grave in the churchyard at Camberwell pays tribute to "a woman of exemplary piety, a tender parent and a sincere friend." No mention was made of her qualities as a wife.

It is hard to believe that in his declining years, John Wesley would not have welcomed both comfort and companionship. Increasingly estranged from his brother, aloof from his preachers, whom he could never regard as equals, he faced the trials of doctrinal dispute alone. Fortunately his temperament, as well as his physique, allowed him to work on, and he assumed that however His love was manifested, the rage for work was a gift from God. "How is this that I find just the same strength as I did thirty years ago, that my sight is considerably better now and my nerves firmer than they were then, that I have none of the infirmities of old age and have lost several I had in my youth? The grand cause is the good pleasure of God who doeth whatever pleases him."[37] He helped God to perform that particular miracle, rising early, giving up drinking tea, traveling on horseback for at least forty-five hundred miles every year. But it was God who kept him fit and well so that His work could be continued. As he passed his seventieth birthday, his energies were increasingly devoted to establishing an independent identity for the connexion which he would leave behind. His *Journal* for Monday 11 August 1777 records, in highly inappropriate casual language, two more steps by which he moved the Methodist cause further along the route to permanent independence. The entry covers several days: "I returned to London. Thursday the 14th I drew up the proposals for the Arminian Magazine. Friday the 15th the committee for the building met, which hitherto God has helped us."[38]

The magazine was created in direct response to what, at the 1777 conference, had briefly appeared to be the disintegration of Methodism. John Hutton, the Bristol assistant, had desperately weakened what should have been one of the strongest circuits in England by openly describing his attraction toward the Society of Friends. Some of the ministers feared that if a breach with the Church of England did not come in the lifetimes of the Wesley brothers, it would quickly follow their deaths. And many of the most reliable Methodists, Fletcher among them, were losing health and influence. The *Arminian Magazine* was a way of holding the societies together. Combined with a new chapel on London's City Road, the magazine marked a proclamation of Methodist permanence. The reassurance of paper and property made Wesley more aggressive in his opposition to what he clearly believed was the path to damnation. "O, beware of Calvinism and everything that has a tendency thereto. Let a burnt child dread the fire."[39]

The City Road chapel was, like so many new Methodist ventures, the product of necessity. The Foundry, always a ruin, was to be pulled down. So, in late 1776, John Wesley appealed to the whole membership of every society for funds to build a new headquarters. By November enough money had been guaranteed to justify the approval of plans. The work was formally inaugurated on 21 April 1777. Wesley recorded that "the rain befriended us much by keeping away the many thousands who proposed to be there. But there were still such multitudes that it was with great difficulty that I got through them to lay the first stone."[40] The crowd stood in absolute silence to hear his sermon. It celebrated the "rise and progress" of an "extraordinary work of God," which was not a new religion but the faith of the Bible and the Primitive Church. To confirm his loyalty, he announced that preaching in the new chapel would be restricted to ordained Methodists. As a result, the pulpit was more or less monopolized by Charles Wesley, with the result of—because Charles had the reputation for preparing sermons which were "dry as dust"—swelling the congregation in the West Street meeting-house, near Seven Dials, which had been opened as a local chapel more than thirty years earlier.

Combined with publication of the *Arminian Magazine*, the City Road chapel seemed like a declaration of independence. But once again what looked like an independent initiative was a reluctant reaction to forces outside John Wesley's control. The *Spiritual Magazine* and the *Gospel Magazine* were beginning to influence opinion, partly by their theological articles but mostly by their cheerful abuse of Methodism. The *Arminian Magazine* aimed at a higher moral tone than that which its rivals adopted. Arguments in support of universal redemption were augmented by accounts of the lives of holy men, experiences of pious persons who could bear witness to God's love and devotional poems. From time to time, in a display of confidence, it published the sermons and pamphlets of Methodism's critics, but only when their views coincided with Methodist beliefs. In the long term it was a potent aid to the evangelical cause. In the short, it demonstrated that the connexion was a permanent part of British religious life.

Permanence did not guarantee peace. And because it was a new and expanding movement in which theology, as well as organization, was continually developing, Methodism was constantly beset by arguments in which a clash of personalities was confused with more fundamental disputes about doctrine and liturgy. Often they revolved around the relationship between ordained clergy and itinerants, itself an aspect of the old disagreements over who was entitled to administer the sacrament and whether or not Methodists should remain loyal to the Church of England.

In 1775 Joseph Benson, who had failed in his attempts to achieve ordination by the usual route, had proposed that Wesley should examine all the preachers and ordain those he regarded as fit to become ministers without concern for the canons of the church. John

Fletcher, ever ingenious if not always practical, then produced a counterproposal which he convinced Wesley would satisfy the impatient itinerants without precipitating a formal breach with the Church of England. Methodists, he proposed, should become "a general society and daughter Church of our holy mother." The connexion was to be called the Methodist Church of England, and its liturgy and articles should be revised to conform, wherever practical, to the beliefs of the Established Church. The matters of disagreement should be represented to the archbishop of Canterbury as "the liberty of Englishmen and Protestants to serve God according to the dictates of their own conscience." On the assumption that the primate of all England accepted, he should then be asked to ordain suitable preachers.

Wesley, as always, allowed the argument to run on in the hope that it would run itself out and that when it was all over, there would remain that the balance between loyalty and independence which allowed Methodism's work to continue. But dissatisfaction with his position, from critics on both sides of the argument, was increased by the knowledge that he always disobeyed the Church of England when it was personally convenient for him to do so. He constantly administered communion in unconsecrated premises, and both the London Foundry and the Bristol New Room had been regularly used for formal services. When other societies wanted to follow suit, Wesley refused them permission. But they were minor issues of dispute compared with the real cause of crisis, which was not unconsecrated premises but ordination. There were still not enough Methodist clergy to meet the demand, and the preachers were beginning to feel that the refusal to regard them as priests was a calculated denial of their calling.

The itinerants grew increasingly irritated by the way in which the ordained clergy dominated Sunday services. Criticism was concentrated on the City Road chapel, where according to his detractors, Charles Wesley was compounding his failures as a preacher by organizing services not to glorify God and redeem sinners but to display the talents of his two musical sons. The preachers' demands for greater respect were first heard in London, but they quickly spread to the provinces. The dispute reached crisis point in Bath when Edward Smyth, an ordained minister who had moved to Bath for his wife's health, was told by Wesley to preach there every Sunday. Smyth had in the previous year argued for immediate separation. So Wesley's decision might have been an attempt to reconcile him to the status quo, though the official explanation was that the initiative was part of an attempt to reduce the continuing loss of members which had first been reported to the 1774 conference and was still affecting twenty circuits including London. The attempt to impose Smyth on a reluctant society provoked an open revolt and public defiance of John Wesley's authority. Alexander McNab, the Bath assistant, refused to recognize the usurper, claiming that only the conference was entitled to allocate "preaching stations." Wesley thought he could resolve the situation by visiting Bath himself and reading the society a paper which he had prepared, twenty years earlier, for the Norwich Society. "The rules of our preachers were fixed by me before any Conference existed. . . . Above all you are to preach when and where I appoint."[41] McNab was suspended from preaching "till he was of another mind." Wesley recorded that "every body was satisfied by the outcome," but Charles, as well as claiming that McNab was praying for Wesley's death, saw the incident as another example of the preachers' determination to seize control of the whole society. The verses which he composed to expose the malcontents could not be described as one of his poetic triumphs.

> Like hireling priests, they serve for hire
> And through ambition blind aspire
> Without the cross to reign.[42]

Charles Wesley was always inclined to see conspiracies where none existed. But the status of the preachers, represented by the demands for either ordination or powers which Church of England ordination provided, had become a cause of real rebellion. A rebellion of a different sort, four thousand miles away, was to make the demand for independent ordination irresistible.

16

SHEEP WITHOUT A SHEPHERD

According to Samuel Johnson, England's American colonies possessed the rights and status enjoyed by "the vestry of a large parish which may lay a tax on its inhabitants" but was subject to the senior power of Parliament like any other "Corporation" in England. That was not a view that the colonists shared. But it was a judgment which the Church of England reflected in its attitude toward the American churches and their clergy. They were part of the Established Church. They owed allegiance to its supreme governor, King George III, and were part, administratively, if not geographically, of the London diocese.

The Great Revival had come early to North America, though it was a revival which differed fundamentally from the one which followed in the mother country. In New England, before the beginning of the eighteenth century, sudden explosions of faith, sometimes Pietist in character and often Lutheran in doctrine, temporarily transformed local communities. Occasionally the news of God's work spread through a whole colony. More often the sudden enthusiasm for faith and piety, usually inspired by some "miraculous" happening and often concentrated on reforming the "ungodly" who were already part of the church community, was a cause of awe and wonder only in the locality where it occurred. In England the revival was inspired by God but initiated by men who went out into the world to save the souls of sinners who would never be part of a spontaneous return to religion.[1] The connexion crossed the Atlantic to America because as well as being part of John Wesley's worldwide parish, Methodism was a constituent part of the Church of England.

There was no general plan. Societies were formed abroad as the result of sudden individual enthusiasm. Francis Gilbert, who returned home from Antigua in disgrace and debt, was persuaded by Vincent Perronet that missionary Methodism offered him the prospect of social as well as spiritual redemption. Nathaniel, Gilbert's brother, who remained prosperous and respectable in the Leeward Islands, read John Wesley's *Appeal to Men of Reason and Religion* and followed his wayward brother into the society. When he visited England in 1758, he brought with him his black servant. John Wesley was inspired by the event to write, "The first African Christian I have known. . . . But shall not our Lord, in due time, have these heathens also for His inheritance?"[2]

By the time of the Nathaniel Gilbert's death in 1774 the society in the Leeward Islands had two hundred members. But it was chance, not the encouragement of early success, which prompted the spread of Methodism in the New World. British soldiers took Methodism to Canada. Loyalists, who fled New England in anticipation of the American Revolution, established societies in Nova Scotia. Lawrence Coughlan, a Methodist itinerant who had been ordained and sent to Newfoundland by the Society for the Propagation of the Gospel, announced on his arrival that his admission to holy orders had in no way changed his beliefs. "I am and do confess myself a Methodist."

The SPG's ardor for sending missionaries to mainland America had been immensely increased by a denunciation of the character and conduct of settlers in the southern states which Thomas Secker, the bishop of Oxford, had delivered shortly before he died in 1758. Colonists, he complained, "carried but little sense of Christianity abroad with them—and their children grew to have yet less than they—No teacher was known, no religious assembly was held. The sacrament of Baptism was not administered for near twenty years together."[3] The colonies languished in sin and ignorance, at least in part for want of clergy to instruct them, and the Church of England dignitaries at home did little to satisfy their need. When the ecclesiastical commissioner for Virginia petitioned the queen for a contribution toward building "a college to educate and qualify young men to be ministers of the gospel," the attorney general of the day urged the rejection of his request on the grounds that Britain was fighting an expensive war against France and Spain. Urged to consider the souls of the colonists, he replied, "Souls! Damn your souls! Make tobacco!" The shortage of clergy in North America was to take Methodism another step toward becoming an independent church. To the end John Wesley was reluctant to precipitate the final break. But when a choice had to be made, he preferred it to the end of his worldwide itinerancy.[4]

John and Charles Wesley had been early pioneers of a process which hoped to keep the colonists close to God through the ministrations of clergy from the Established Church. They, and George Whitefield, were spreading God's word in Georgia long before Methodism was thought of as an organized connexion. Their evangelical impulse was encouraged in America by members of English religious societies who had emigrated to the New World and taken the most pious of their old habits with them. In 1760 Barbara Heck and her cousin Philip Embury, refugees from the Palatinate, arrived in New York via Ireland, where Embury had been a local preacher. Initially they settled into membership of the Church of England and then the Lutheran Church. But Barbara, horrified by the discovery that the playing of cards was a common pastime among the colonists, told her cousin that unless he began to preach, the whole community would go to hell. His subsequent sermons allowed him to lay claim to being the founding father of American Methodism.

At about the same time, Robert Strawbridge, an Irish Methodist, arrived in Maryland. He extended his work of preaching and founding societies into Pennsylvania. Membership grew at such a pace that in 1768 the leaders of the Pennsylvania societies wrote to England with a request for preachers to be sent out to assist in their own version of the revival. It is not clear whether Strawbridge resented the idea of other ministers encroaching on his territory or he was frustrated by Wesley's refusal to respond to the societies' pleas. Whatever the reason, he began to administer the sacraments. Having precipitated a head-on collision with the Church of England, he continued to preside at communion services throughout the long and crucial controversy which raged within Methodism as well as between Methodists and their critics in the Established Church.

In New York, Philip Embury's work was supplemented and enlivened by Captain Webb, a one-eyed veteran of General Wolfe's campaign in Quebec. Webb had been converted (during a period of postservice depression) while listening to Wesley preach in Bath in 1760. Shortly afterward, while attending a Methodist meeting in the same city, he had been moved (he claimed by spiritual instruction) to preach in the place of the unaccountably absent itinerant, a manner in which God often revealed himself to early Methodists. Webb, just like other good men who had heard the same call, had no doubt that the whole incident had been engineered by the Lord. So when he returned to the state of New York as barracks master in Albany, he began freelance preaching—often in uniform.

In America societies were formed and grew in the haphazard pattern of the earlier New World revival. For better or for worse, John Wesley was drawn into a new series of "connexions" which were not of his design or making. Initially, recalling that his first expedition had ended in near disgrace, he was disinclined to involve himself in North America for a second time. Whitefield was always far more enthusiastic about the work in New England. In 1764 he had asked Wesley to help by sending some of his itinerant priests to the eastern seaboard. The request was politely declined on the grounds that all the itinerants were needed in England, but to soften the blow of refusal, he suggested that local preachers ("equal in both grace and gifts") might be available to take their place.[5] But it was not until 1768 that Wesley's interest was stirred, and then it was the management of American Methodism rather than its prospects of saving souls that caught and captured his attention. Thomas Taylor wrote from New York to ask advice about the proper legal ownership of the meetinghouse, the management of the society's money and the stationing of itinerant preachers. Despite his undoubted spirituality,

John Wesley was always fascinated by the mundane business of organizing the connexion. At the 1768 conference he reported that Robert Strawbridge had requested help for the Methodists who were evangelizing from Maryland to the south. It was decided that there was no real chance of help for at least a year. But America had forced its way on to John Wesley's agenda.

Pressure to save America began to grow. In the October of the same year, Dr. Wrangel, a Swedish Pietist minister, traveled to Bristol expressly to implore Wesley to take pity on the "sheep without a shepherd" in Pennsylvania.[6] Captain Webb renewed his appeal, and Thomas Bell of Charlestown employed, in more dramatic language, the metaphor with which Wrangel had hoped to persuade John Wesley to change his mind. "Mr. Wesley says that the first message of the preachers is to the lost sheep of England. Are there none in America? They have strayed from England into the wild woods here and they are running wild after this world. They are drinking their wine in bowls and are jumping and dancing and serving the Devil in the groves and under the green trees. Are these not lost sheep?"[7] He went on to ask rhetorically about the whereabouts of specific preachers—Brownfield, Pawson and Manners. They all were men he believed were failing in their duties.

The conference of 1769 discussed what members called, and accepted as, a "pressing call" to save America. Two preachers, Richard Boardman and Joseph Pilmoor, volunteered to go and were sent west with the societies' blessing and a generous contribution toward the cost of a new chapel in New York. Boardman, the more senior, remained in New York while Pilmoor, the more able, moved on to Philadelphia, where he immediately introduced John Wesley's *General Rules* for the governance of societies and forbade discussion of even the possibility of separation from the Church of England. He also lent his voice to the common complaint that the connexion was in desperate need of ordained ministers to administer the sacraments.

Boardman also reported the difficulties he found in controlling the conduct of local preachers. The settlers were being taught that "There is no Church that is Established more than another. All sects have equal authority with the Church of England."[8] As a result,

Webb felt entitled to appoint himself an itinerant, and Strawbridge believed that he could create an independent "Connexion" in the southern states. Wesley's reaction was to persuade the 1771 conference to send two more volunteers. One of them was Francis Asbury.

Asbury was twenty-six when he set sail for America. But he was already a veteran evangelist with four years' experience as a circuit preacher. He had begun to preach as a boy of seventeen in Staffordshire, and his commitment was so great that he agreed to work his passage from Bristol to New York with the explicit intention of spreading the gospel in the New World. On his arrival he immediately complained about the habit of concentrating evangelical efforts in the towns and was rewarded for his impertinence by being given responsibility for New York.[9] Asbury had to wait for five years before he could preach the gospel in the way he chose. Then he rode forty or fifty miles a day over the rough terrain of New England, preaching somewhere every day and three times on Sundays. The success with which he followed Wesley's example established his reputation as an American Methodist rather than as an English preacher sent to redeem the lawless colonists.

Asbury, unlike other English volunteers, determined to make America his permanent home and Methodism in the New World his life's work. Together with Thomas Rankin, who arrived to support him in 1773, he called the first American Methodist conference and began to impose the discipline which Wesley required of his English members. Sawbridge, too powerful in the South to be brought within the conference's control, continued, against the rules of the societies, to administer communion. But Methodism in America was becoming a coherent movement. In 1775 there were over three thousand registered society members. The colonists, particularly in the south, had embraced Methodism as the proper creed for a people who, having detached themselves from the crown, felt no instinctive loyalty to the Established Church. The American Connexion would have made uninterrupted progress into the nineteenth century had the North American states remained loyal to King George. But in the early months of 1775 the prospect of armed insurrection had become so pressing that Lord North, the prime minister, thought it necessary to prepare for open rebellion. On 9 February the two houses of Parliament presented a loyal address to the king requesting powers to "take the most effectual measures to enforce obedience to the laws and authority of the supreme legislature." With the king's agreement the naval and military estimates were revised.

John Wesley usually allowed great political events to pass him by. He did, however, react to the upheaval which led up to the Declaration of Independence. His chief concern was not the merit of the revolution but its effect on his members. According to his *Journal*, Methodist congregations were made particularly anxious by the publication of the Bill of Rights, in their view "a threatening posture of public affairs," since it enshrined liberties which Methodists thought dangerous. In response, Wesley "strongly enforced our Lord's words 'Why are ye fearful O ye of little faith?' "[10] Three weeks later he preached on the text (Daniel 4:27) "Let my counsel be acceptable to thee and break off thy sins by righteousness and thine iniquities by showing mercy to the poor." He deviated from his chosen theme with what the *Westminster Journal* called "an awful sermon on the horrid effects of a civil war." He concluded "that, of all scourges from God, war was the most to be deprecated because it often swept away all traces of religion and even of humanity."[11]

That was a perfectly acceptable opinion for a clergyman to advance. But Wesley chose to go further. Dr. Johnson, who had described the American colonists as "a race of convicts [who] ought to be thankful for anything we allow them short of hanging," published his *Taxation No Tyranny: An Answer to the Resolutions and Addresses of the American Congress.* It compared the northern states with a parish council. Shortly afterward John Wesley published *A Calm Address to Our American Colonies.* It was written not for the "quality" but for the people, and it sold for one penny.

Wesley's work reflected, in barely less brutal form, Johnson's low opinion of the American colonists. They had "sunk down" from the state of nature which they originally enjoyed and become dependent on a superior authority. The third-generation Americans were "descendants of men who either had no votes or resigned them by emigrating. You had therefore exactly what your ancestors left you;

not a vote in making laws nor in choosing legislators; but the happiness of being protected by laws and obeying them."[12] In a letter to Lord North—certainly written in the hope of gaining favor but, nevertheless, confirming the sincerity with which his prejudices were held—Wesley described the genesis of his opposition to the colonists. "I do not intend to enter upon the question of whether the Americans are in the right or in the wrong. Here all my prejudices are against the Americans; for I am a High Churchman, the son of a High Churchman, bred up from my childhood in the highest notions of passive obedience and non-resistance."[13] Wesley's views coincided with Dr. Johnson's in every detail. Indeed there is every reason to assume that as with so many theological works, he methodically copied out *Taxation No Tyranny* in his own style and published the result in his name.

There is no reason to believe that Johnson objected to the plagiarism. The two men knew each other well enough for Johnson to write about Wesley in the cheerfully dismissive tone which he often employed when describing friends. "John Wesley's conversation is good. But he is never at leisure. He is always obliged to go at a certain hour. This is very disagreeable to a man who loves to fold his legs and have out his talk as I do."[14] There was, however, nothing disagreeable to Johnson about the adoption of *Taxation No Tyranny*. He wrote to Wesley with "thanks for the addition of your important suffrage to my argument against the America question. To have gathered such a mind as yours may justly confirm me in my own opinion."[15] It was, however, disagreeable to some of Wesley's long-term critics.

Johnson's note—not, it seems, ironic, for irony was not his style—confirms that Wesley was becoming influential at least among the clerical classes in which he moved. There was, from some figures of literary London, mild criticism of his failure to acknowledge how heavily he had relied on Dr. Johnson's *Taxation No Tyranny*. But the real damage was done by men who, anxious to take any opportunity to undermine Wesley's reputation, reminded the reading public that five years earlier he had written *Free Thoughts on Public Affairs*, a defense of the colonists' rights to govern and tax themselves. Once again Wesley had changed his mind, and once again he was determined to prove how constant he had been.

The campaign against Wesley was led by the Reverend Caleb Evans, a Bristol Baptist minister and an open supporter of the rebellious colonists. In his *Letter to the Rev. John Wesley Occasioned by his Calm Address* he recalled that, during a visit to the West Country, Wesley himself had possessed and commended a book titled *An Argument in Defence of the Exclusive Right Claimed by the Colonists to Tax Themselves*. Wesley conceded that his pamphlet contained little original thought and could easily have gone on to say that reading Johnson had changed his mind. But although William Pine, his printer, and the printer's friend James Rouquet both conceded that they too read the defense of the colonists on Wesley's recommendation, he refused to admit that he had either read the book or sympathized with the colonists.

Another pamphlet war broke out. "TS" in *A Cool Reply to A Calm Address* claimed that Wesley's "religious principles are a species of popery." "WD" published *A Wolf in Sheep's Clothing*. Patrick Bull described Wesley as "a chaplain in ordinary to the Furies or minister extraordinary to Bellona, goddess of war." Toplady, recognizing the opportunity to relaunch the offensive against his old adversary, contributed *An Old Fox Tarr'd and Feather'd*. Wesley was not without allies. But they had only one defense of his apparent dishonesty. When he had claimed that he had never sympathized with the colonists, he had genuinely believed it to be the case. The Reverend Thomas Olivers' *Full Defence of the Reverend John Wesley* explained that "Mr. Wesley is now an old man and yet has such a variety and multiplicity of business as few men could manage even in the prime of life. . . . When all these things are considered, no one will think it strange that his memory should often fail."[16]

A plea in mitigation based on the claim that Wesley was senile was not a defense which was likely to be welcomed by a man who still rightly regarded himself as the leader of a continuing Christian Revival. Nor was it any more justified than the allegation that the "popular" version of Dr. Johnson's polemic had been swiftly produced in denial of Wesley's true beliefs because the author of the diatribe knew that a cheap pamphlet which denounced the colonists would both endear him to the government and earn a small fortune. However, *A Calm Address* produced both those results. Forty thousand copies were sold in the three weeks after its publication. And the government spent public money to guarantee that it was distributed outside all the metropolitan churches on four consecutive Sundays. For the first time Wesley was offered official patronage, fifty pounds from the privy purse for any charity of his nomination. Wesley accepted but later regretted that he had given his critics such an excuse to libel his integrity. The accusations that Wesley had sold his principles for the profit on a penny pamphlet grew so loud and became so compelling that he thought it necessary to meet the allegations head-on with a letter to *Lloyd's Evening Post.*

> I have been seriously asked, From what motives did you publish your Calm Address to the American Colonies? I seriously answer, Not to get money. Had that been my motive I should have swelled it into a shilling pamphlet and have entered it at Stationers' Hall. . . . I contributed my mite toward putting out the flame which rages all over the land. . . . There is no possible way to put out this flame or to stop it rising higher and higher but to show that Americans are not used either cruelly or unjustly.[17]

The reference to the fortune which he might have made, a strangely demeaning argument to be used by a man who usually stood on his dignity, revealed how disturbed he was by the allegation. John Wesley was always particularly sensitive to the accusation that he was motivated by the hope of either honors or riches. On the rare occasions when he expressed a political opinion, he did so "not to get money, not to get preferment for myself or my brother's children, not to please any man living or dead. . . . I know that they that love you for your political services love you less than their dinners; and they that hate you hate you worse than the Devil."[18] And he was even more zealous in the preservation of his reputation for plain living. When, in 1776, the Commission for Revenue suggested that he possessed plate for which he had "hitherto neglected to make an en-

try" in the required tax inventory, his reply was more than an assertion of his fiscal probity. It was a slightly injured declaration of faith.
"I have a silver teaspoon at London and two at Bristol. This is all the
plate I have at present and I shall not buy any more while so many
round me lack bread."[19] Wesley's contempt for riches was genuine.
So he was easily able to refute the charge that he had turned on the
American colonists for money. The complaint that he had changed
his mind was irrefutable because it was true.

The sincerity with which Wesley held his new views was supported, if not quite confirmed, by the cancellation of his contract
with his publisher, William Pine. The final breach was certainly
brought about by Pine's open espousal of the colonists' cause, but by
then relations had already been strained by the publisher's chronic
inefficiency. However, what at least appeared to be constant demonstrations of loyalty to crown and country endeared him to the king
and court. It was affection which he deserved. For whatever his
change of heart and mind about America, he was unequivocally and
consistently the king's man.

What he gained in London, he lost in Philadelphia. The American
Methodists who supported independence were outraged. And even
those who wished for continued union with England resented his
"High Tory and High Church" attitude. His autocracy encouraged
support for the creation of a separate American Methodist Connexion. Francis Asbury could not deny the strength of the antagonism, even though he tried to moderate its effect. "There is not a
man in the world so obnoxious to the American politicians as our
dear old Daddy; but no matter, we must treat him with all the respect we can and that is due to him."[20]

Wesley opposed the American revolutionaries with a sincere passion that was entirely consistent with his political prejudices. His
mistake, which he was incapable of admitting, at least publicly, was
his earlier defense of their calls for liberty or death, an aberration
which, in so loyal a king's man, can be explained only in terms of
what, by then, had become his ruling passion. His other considerations were secondary when compared with the greater good of the
connexion. His initial support for insurrection was undoubtedly in-

fluenced by the knowledge that some active Methodists numbered among the insurgents. Once he had read Dr. Johnson, he knew that he must speak up for the king. His birth and upbringing allowed nothing else. *A Calm Address* expressed his true opinion of "the mob" which he believed to be united by a common enthusiasm for destruction in both Britain and America, though his claim to objectivity was, as his letter of loyalty to Lord North had made clear, at best, disingenuous.

> I have no prejudice to any man in America. I love you as my brethren and countrymen. My opinion is this. We have a few men in England who are determined enemies to Monarchy, whether they hate his present majesty on any other ground than because he is King, I know not, but they cordially hate his office and have for some years been undermining it with all diligence. . . . These good men hope it will end in the total defection of England for America.[21]

The war, which Wesley had predicted, began with the shot at the Lexington bridge that echoed around John Wesley's worldwide parish. The Battle of Bunker Hill followed. More than a thousand English soldiers were killed and wounded. Monarchism turned into patriotism, and on 12 November 1775 Wesley was "desired to preach in Bethnal Green church a charity sermon for the widows and children of the soldiers who were killed in America." The sermon dealt less with the war than with the revolutionary message which Wesley believed was spreading throughout England and would soon destroy the whole country, thousands "standing in the streets with pale looks, hollow eyes and meagre limbs . . . families who, a few years ago, lived in an easy, genteel manner . . . [living by] picking up turnips which the cattle had left." The malaise was, he judged, the result of previously "calm, mild and friendly mannered men . . . screaming for liberty till they were utterly distracted and their intellects quite confounded."[22]

Unfortunately, John Wesley's conclusions on the state of the nation were not so much based on careful observation and steady judgment as on political prejudice. Less than a year after he had described the terrible prospect of England incapacitated by revolution, he made an equally partial judgment about the economic consequences of attempting to quell the American revolt. Dr. Price, a Unitarian minister who had published *Observations on the Nature of Civil Liberty, the Principles of Government and the Justice and Policy of War with America*, attributed the nation's stagnation and decline to the time and money spent on fighting a colonial war with which he did not agree. Wesley denied that rural England faced decline and depopulation. He claimed to know the contrary, having seen ten times more of England every year than most men in the nation. "All our manufacturing towns, as Birmingham, Sheffield, Manchester, Liverpool increase daily. So do many villages all over the kingdom, even in the mountains of Derbyshire."[23] Revolution would damn England. Fighting revolution saved both its soul and its industry.

It seems that at least for a time he was oblivious of the effects his capricious opinions were having in the societies of North America. Then he realized that his opposition to the American Revolution was damaging New England Methodism. The advice which he eventually sent to American preachers was hard to reconcile with the strident views which he had expressed in England. "It is your part to be peacemakers; to be loving and tender to all, but to addict yourself to no party." Charles wrote, shortly afterward, to reinforce his brother's instruction. His judgment—"private Christians are excused and exempted; privileged to take no part in civil troubles"[24]—at least carried the conviction of consistency. But it was no easier to follow. Attempts were made by some Methodists to keep Wesley's true opinions from the colonists. One rich society member bought up all the copies of *A Calm Address* that reached America and destroyed them before they could be distributed outside the churches. But Wesley's intractable opposition to independence was reported to the colonists in letters and by immigrants' word of mouth. The more extreme revolutionaries began to attack the preachers. There were reports, probably apocryphal, of tarring and feathering.

The problems of the preachers were complicated by disagreements between Thomas Rankin and Francis Asbury. Asbury was for the Revolution. Rankin was not. A letter from Antigua, inviting Asbury to replace Gilbert on that island as pastor of the three hundred Methodists, seemed to offer a suitable way of ending the conflict. But Asbury doubted that a man who was not ordained could meet the Antiguans' needs, and Wesley was reluctant for any declared friend of the separatists to stay in the New World. Correspondence on the subject began in March 1775 and went on until October. As a mark of his disapproval, Wesley usually wrote to Rankin rather than Asbury, even when Asbury's future was the main topic of discussion. As the year passed, more and more Church of England priests chose to return home claiming that most Methodists were loyal and that their loyalty put their lives in danger.

The minutes of the 1776 conference noted that there were 3,148 Methodists in America[25] and claimed that most of them remained loyal to King George. During January 1777 John Wesley received "two letters from America [confirming] that all the Methodists there are for the Government and on that account persecuted by the rebels only not to death. . . . The preachers are still threatened but not stopped . . . The work of God increases much in Maryland." Both the loyalty of the members and the extent of the threat were overstated.

Thomas Rankin and George Shadford, the most outspoken of the preachers, were briefly persuaded to stay in America by Asbury's argument that the more wicked the new nation, the more they were needed. But by the end of the year both had returned to England. Asbury remained. Yet despite his sympathy for the new union of states, he refused, because of his obligation as a preacher, either to bear arms or to promise to do so at a time of emergency. He accepted what amounted to voluntary exile in Delaware, leaving the Methodist flock of North America without an English shepherd.

Denied the day-to-day guidance of even the sympathetic Asbury and despite the wild talk of persecution, American Methodism still prospered. Thirty-four itinerant preachers, appointed from the local societies, helped to spread the word among the fifteen circuits. According to Asbury, membership was twice as large, almost seven thousand, as the total reported to the previous year's conference. Most of them trusted Asbury but felt nothing but antagonism for the

Church of England. Whether or not they were on the side of the colonial authority, they were hostile to the Established Church, which had deserted them. And the "London Methodists" remained inseparable from York and Canterbury. In consequence the American Methodists decided to imitate the Continental Congress, which had created a new nation, and form an organization of their own. They were motivated by more than resentment at what they saw as betrayal. They had been taught that regular communion was essential to their continued status as "real Christians." After the Church of England clergy returned to England, that was no longer possible. Without Methodist preachers to guide them, the American societies had to decide for themselves how to meet the new danger to their members' souls. Their dilemma was a reflection of the problem faced by English Methodists. The Americans responded in proper Methodist fashion by organizing a conference.

Because of the size of the territory, as much as the result of differences in attitude, two conferences were convened, one in the North, the other in the South, where numbers were far greater. The conferences met formally in 1779. In the North a resolution was passed requesting that Asbury became "superintendent," a status which left open the question of his right, without formal ordination, to administer the sacrament. The southern Methodists, meeting at Fulvanna, Virginia, voted by nineteen to ten to form a presbytery of their four senior members, who would first ordain one another and then do the same to other preachers who were judged worthy to officiate at communion. Asbury, still in exile in Delaware, described the decision as "effecting a lame separation from the Episcopal Church which will last about one year."[26]

Despite his initially dismissive reaction, Asbury clearly took the prospect of separation seriously. In 1780 he attended the northern Methodists' conference and persuaded it to accept an entirely emollient resolution, "to sit in Conference on the original plan as Methodists," in effect postponing any decision indefinitely. Armed with the news that the southern Methodists faced separation from their brothers and sisters in the North as well as their English brethren, Asbury visited the southern conference and warned the delegates that they faced isolation. He also read them a selection of John Wesley's thoughts on separation from the Church of England as well as more recent opinions expressed in letters from London, all of them carefully addressed to the "General Assistant" rather than the "General Superintendent." The southern conference was convinced that schism should be avoided but, fearing that the societies might not be so easily persuaded, asked Asbury to help secure the postponement of independent ordination. Wesley's doctrinal authority was, in consequence, reestablished, and Asbury became, in fact, if not in name, the leader of American Methodists in both the North and South.

Asbury, although a profound opponent of both separation and the provocative acts which might, unintentionally, bring it about, had no doubt that the absence of ordained priests left the American Methodists in peril of their souls. He therefore, assuming an authority which, despite its magnitude, did not defy the ordinances of the Established Church, announced that "want of opportunity suspends the force of duty to receive the Lord's Supper."[27] Although he was in no doubt that observing the laws of ordination was more important than providing opportunities for constant communion, he believed it was his duty to warn John Wesley that the dilemma must be speedily resolved. He could not guarantee that American Methodists would tolerate for long a situation which denied them the essential sacrament.

It was not only the independent Americans who were growing restless about the continued refusal to countenance Methodist ordination. Some English societies were in open revolt. Anticipating dissent at the 1780 conference, John Wesley changed the rules of attendance. Only preachers of whom he approved were invited. But as a gesture to the democratic spirit of the societies he extended the number of days allowed for debate. He also allowed, for the first time, a preacher to preside over the deliberations[28] and, in order to guarantee that he had allies in any of the debates which proved contentious, appointed an inner cabinet of six delegates to advise and support him. It included the ever-reliable John Fletcher and the Reverend Thomas Coke, an Irishman with a passion for foreign missions.

John Wesley's loyalty to the Church of England was made all the more remarkable (commendable, some people would say) by the fact that he had serious and plausible doubts about the doctrine of ordination as practiced by the Anglican episcopate. He had long been convinced that the historic office of presbyter covered both priest and bishop. And on 8 June 1780 he wrote to his brother reiterating both his belief that he possessed the right to ordain and his determination, out of respect for the Established Church, not to exercise it for as long as forbearance could be continued without destroying the Methodist Connexion. "Read Bishop Stillingfleet's *Irenicon*, or any important history of the ancient Church and I believe that you will think as I do. I verily believe that I have as good a right to ordain as to administer the Lord's supper. But I see an abundance of reasons why I should not use that right unless I was turned out of the Church. At present we are just in our place."[29]

The 1780 conference complained about autocracy. But nothing very serious with which Wesley disagreed was read into the record of the proceedings. The most provocative conclusion, reached as part of the process of revising the "Longer Minutes," was agreement that Methodists need no longer concentrate their efforts in parishes where their ordained preachers were welcome. That meant that in most of Britain, the connexion was free to challenge the Established Church. But the undercurrent of secession was running too strongly to be wholly ignored. At the close of the conference Wesley wrote to Mary Bosanquet (soon to become Mrs. Fletcher) to congratulate her on beginning prayer meetings in Hunslet. He added, with evident relief, "The case of the church we shall fully consider by and by."[30] Charles found the mood of antagonism to the church intolerable and left the final day's meeting vowing never to attend a conference again. He celebrated his decision with a poem:

> Why should I longer, Lord, contend
> My most important moments spend
> In buffeting the air?
> In warning those who will not see
> But rest in blind security
> And rush into the snare?[31]

Ordination was not the only snare into which the aging John Wesley rushed during the year. At its beginning and its end he made excursions into politics, certainly the politics of faith but politics nevertheless. His uncharacteristic behavior added to the fear that he was beginning to suffer the disabilities of old age. His antagonism to Rome was long-standing and had been set out as early as 1749, in his "Letter to a Roman Catholic." And in 1779 he published *Popery Calmly Considered*, a tract that opposed the Catholic Relief Act of the previous year, even though the latter's prospects for the removal of some civil penalties fell far short of full emancipation. Wesley based his objection to the limited extension of civil rights on a crude version of John Locke's philosophy of government. Catholics owed an allegiance to the pope, a foreign power. So they should not enjoy the full benefits of citizenship. A letter reiterating his view that "no [Protestant] government ought to tolerate men of Roman Catholic persuasion"[32] was published in the *Public Advertiser* in January 1780. The belief that there was "no faith to be kept with heretics" was acceptable to contemporary opinion. But Wesley went a step farther. He gave his public support to the militantly anti-Catholic Protestant Association, an organization which was regarded as unattractively extreme even by the standards of the eighteenth century.

In June 1780 the association, led by Lord George Gordon, marched on Parliament to demand the repeal of the Catholic Relief Act and then, under the influence of drink and bigotry, attacked Catholics and Catholic property throughout London. The four days of violence came to be called the Gordon Riots. At their conclusion, Lord George Gordon was arrested and placed in prison, where, to the consternation of moderate opinion, John Wesley visited him. Wesley, realizing the damage which he had done to his own reputation, tried to retrieve some of the old esteem by announcing that prison had "proved a lasting benefit" to the man who had led the Protestant mob.[33] It was another sign that John Wesley was growing old.

Wesley's grip on the Methodist Connexion was beginning to weaken. He was still in charge. But it was necessary for him to respond to criticism in a way which twenty years before he might have dismissed out of hand. The connexion itself was flourishing. In the decade since 1770 the number of circuits had risen from fifty to sixty-four and membership had increased from 29,406 to 43,830. The annual Kingswood Collection, by which the societies were financed and preachers' expenses met, had almost doubled from £218. 4s. 1d. to £402. 1s. 9d. But members, both new and old, continued to complain about the related problems of infrequent communion and the shortage of ordained priests. John Wesley was finding it increasingly difficult to insist on solutions which both held the connexion together and maintained its loyalty to the Church of England. In what amounted to a last desperate effort to meet both obligations, he proposed a solution wholly within the ordinances of the Church of England. Suitable Methodists should be offered to the church as candidates for holy orders. He therefore approached the one authority which could resolve the genuine crisis of conflicting consciences. If Church of England bishops were prepared to ordain Methodists who wished to preach the gospel in America, the societies' needs could be met without affront to established doctrine.

The first possible candidate was Brian Bury Collins, a Cambridge graduate who, in his admiration for both Wesley and Whitefield, had announced, "I could freely die to see the Tabernacles and the Foundry reconciled."[34] His application for ordination was rejected by the bishop of Chester on the provocative grounds that "you have never expressed to me . . . the least degree of concern for your wandering mode of life and preaching."[35] Itinerancy was not the Church of England's way. It was built on incumbency. Wesley made no great issue of the rejection or its reason, not wanting to appear committed to the cause of a man who hovered between Calvinism and belief in universal redemption.[36] And he correctly assumed that Collins would eventually be admitted into holy orders. The case of John Hoskins caused far more offense, for he was intended for America. And the stated reasons for his rejection, set out with uninhibited clarity by Robert Louth, the bishop of London, were a particular offense to Wesley's principles of evangelism. Hoskins was rejected because he had no formal education. Wesley wrote a magisterial rebuke to the bishop, which included what must have been an implied threat. "Perhaps it is the last time I shall trouble your Lordship." Dr. Louth was left to decide for himself whether the correspondence would end with Wesley's death or disaffection. The letter congratulated the bishop on his diligence in personally examining candidates for ordination but asked:

> Examining them! In what respects? Why, whether they understand a little Latin and Greek and can answer a few trite questions in the science of divinity! Alas how little does this avail! Does your lordship examine whether they serve Christ or Belial. . . . Your lordship did not see good to ordain [John Hoskins] but your lordship did see good to ordain and send to America other people who knew something of Latin and Greek but knew no more about saving souls than of catching a whale.[37]

The letter was not to be the last communication between Wesley and Dr. Louth. Having failed in his attempt to secure Hoskins's ordination, Wesley wrote to the bishop, who included North America in his diocese, with a formal request that additional ordained clergy, of the church's own nomination, be sent to meet the spiritual demands of the revolutionary colonists. The bishop's reply—that there were already three Church of England clergymen in Canada—contained the clear implication that if America left the empire, it also left the London diocese.

In September 1783 the Treaty of Paris established and recognized the new country of America, and Edward Drumgoode, a locally recruited itinerant, immediately wrote to London with a request for help. Wesley replied that they must first discover "how Providence opens itself." But he added, "Brother Asbury is raised up to preserve order among you and do just what I should do myself if it pleased God to bring me to America."[38]

The endorsement of the American hierarchy should have marked a graceful acceptance in Wesley that he could no longer dominate New World Methodism. But he was not yet ready to relinquish paternal rights over the connexion which he had come to believe was the child of his inspiration. In the northern states of the new Union, there was a brief enthusiasm for creating the Methodist Church of England in America, but the idea was quickly abandoned. Wesley thought of seizing the chance provided by the colonists' indecision by making a personal visit to the new country and, by force of character, securing the North American societies for the Methodist Connexion. For once his nerve or energy failed him, and he decided to send a representative rather than make the perilous crossing himself. The announcement that Thomas Coke would take his place was regarded by Methodists who worried about the succession as proof that he had already decided who should take John Fletcher's place as the heir apparent.

Thomas Coke, a gentleman commoner of Jesus College, Oxford, ordained episcopal minister and curate of South Petherton, had paid court to John Wesley at Taunton in 1776 and impressed the old man with his zeal and devotion. Wesley recorded the meeting in the most complimentary terms. "A union then began which I trust will never end."[39] From then on, everything that Coke did appeared to support the hope and fear that he expected that Wesley's cloak would one day fall upon him. Cynics suggested that for years his conduct had been designed to secure the succession.

It seems unlikely that Coke contrived to be dismissed from his curacy. The reasons given for his expulsion—persistent preaching in cottages, barns and the open air, combined with the assertion that he was a Methodist—might have been calculated to appeal to John Wesley. Without parish or income he offered his full-time services to the Methodist Connexion and was appointed director of the Tract Society, a scheme to distribute Wesley's pamphlets according to the principle which was set out in bold letters on their cover, "Not to Be Sold but to Be Given Away." Wesley vetoed Coke's plans to create a Society for the Establishment of Missions Amongst Heathens on the principle that there was "no call neither yet no invitation, no Providential opening of any kind."[40] Wesley was in theoretical sympathy with the ideas, as he made plain in his sermon "The General Spread of the Gospel,"[41] but he had other pressing business to which he must attend. John Wesley always took questions of property seriously.

The trustees of the Birdsall meeting room had signed a deal which gave them the power to appoint and dismiss preachers, an autonomy which John Wesley regarded as verging on mutiny. Attempts to persuade them to adopt the model trust deed set out in the *Large Minutes* were met with the claim that even if they wanted to meet Wesley's demands, the title deed could not be legally altered or ignored. Then the trustees of the New Room in Bristol—to Methodists the equivalent of Jerusalem's holy places—found that they too owned the premises on terms which were not in line with the model trust deed. They expressed their regret but insisted that the document could not be revised. It was then that Coke reminded Wesley that he held a law degree. There were about four hundred meetinghouses in England and applications to establish two dozen more each year. John Wesley suggested that Coke should ride through England, discouraging what the 1783 conference called "the needless multiplication of preaching houses," and require those that were already established to accept the model deed laid down by the conference.

Acquiring the power to regularize the way in which meetinghouses were owned, used and run made Coke a profoundly influential figure within the connexion. For property—the rights of trustees and their freedom to ignore the conference rules of management—always agitated Wesley. But by either personal design or the good fortune of the old man's concern for his mortality, Coke acquired a much more important role in the connexion. John Wesley was legally the only authority which the whole movement possessed. Decisions resided with him alone. His was the only power to appoint preachers, distribute funds and confirm regulations. As things stood in 1783, Wesley's death would be followed by a legal vacuum and anarchy.

Coke suggested that the whole situation be regularized, and Wesley, true to the Methodist tradition which he had established, agreed that one essential element in the "good death," to which all Christians should aspire, was the bequest of a well-ordered inheritance. William Chilow, a solicitor who was already a society member, and John Maddocks, a barrister of Lincoln's Inn, were recruited to help Coke draw up a deed of declaration, which was presented to the 1784 conference. Its effect was to formalize a new form of conference, a gathering made up of a "legal hundred" members who should have the powers of the connexion's executive. Of course the new constitution did nothing to "extend, to extinguish, lessen or abridge the life estate of John Wesley and Charles Wesley" in any chapels where they "have or may have an estate or interest, power or authority." But it did a great deal to extinguish the interests, powers and authority of those conference members who were not included in the legal hundred.

Coke had been against the limitation of numbers and, in what was thought to be a bid for popularity, told the assistant to the Sarum Society, "I had no hand in nominating or omitting any of my brethren." Inevitably the excluded members attempted to change the deed in a way which guaranteed their reinstatement. John Hampson, who was later to write the most authoritative contemporary account of John Wesley's character, resigned from the connexion. But not least thanks to the loyal eloquence of the dying John Fletcher, the deed was endorsed by a conference that (since it had no constitution and was essentially Wesley's creation) had no power either to reject or to accept it. It was enrolled in the High Court of Chancery on 28 February 1784 and made the Methodist Connexion a legal entity. Because of its importance, it guaranteed that after the death of John Fletcher in August 1785, Thomas Coke, the deed's originator, became the de facto second-in-command to John Wesley.

It might be argued, in Coke's defense, that his prospects of inheriting the Methodist leadership would have been best served by a long period in England, advising and influencing the increasingly feeble John Wesley. But on either his own initiative or that of his patron, it was decided that Coke should follow his missionary inclinations by taking his place, alongside Francis Asbury, in America. It was conceded that the New World needed a new approach. It had begun in 1784, when a new liturgy, *The Sunday Services of the Methodists in North America with Other Occasional Services*, was published. The Methodists were to have their own prayer book.

The preface to *Sunday Services* made it clear that John Wesley's reverence for the Book of Common Prayer was beyond doubt or question. "I believe there is no liturgy in the world, either in ancient or modern language, which breathes more of a solid, scriptural, rational piety than the prayer book of the Church of England. And though the main of it was compiled more than two hundred years ago, yet the language is not only pure but strong and elegant in the highest degree." Despite what was to become one of Methodism's defining characteristics, Wesley declared, as late as 1778, "I myself find more life in the church prayers than in the formal extemporary prayers of Dissenters." Yet although he thought the King James Version a literary masterpiece inspired by God, he had from time to time expressed his reservations about some of its contents. At the 1755 conference he set some of them out. They included "the Athanasian Creed (though we firmly believe the doctrine contained therein) . . . the thanksgiving in the burial service" and, most significantly, "those parts for Ordaining Bishops, Priests and Deacons which assert or suppose an essential difference between bishop and presbyter."

So despite his affection for the Prayer Book, making amendments to accommodate the needs of American Methodism was not as traumatic as a totally new enterprise might have been. Some of the changes, probably suggested by Coke, were purely stylistic. "Our Father which art in heaven" became "who art," and "Thy will be done in earth" was changed to "on earth." The existence of the new Republic was accepted and accommodated by prayers for the sovereign and royal family being replaced by prayers for "supreme rulers." But there were also more material changes and omissions. Some of them reflected the changes of 1755. The preface explained, "The service of the Lord's Day . . . has been considerably shortened. . . . Some sentences in the offices of Baptism and for the Burial of the Dead are omitted. . . . Many psalms [are] left out." The result was a volume just a little more than half the size of the Book of Common Prayer.

Clearly Wesley's principal aim was to construct a prayer book which both satisfied the Methodists chiefly in America and kept them as close as possible, both constitutionally and doctrinally, to the Church of England. But he clearly seized the opportunity to rectify some of what he saw as faults in the prayer book he claimed to revere. And the new prayer book was to become the holy writ of a new priesthood.

The American Connexion was to be governed by "joint superintendents" watching over the north and south and two "elders" who were to be given the right to administer the Eucharist. Methodism was on the bank of the Rubicon. And Wesley knew it. The agreements with which he justified his actions sounded unusually defensive. "The case is widely different between England and America. Here, therefore, my scruples are at an end."[42] In March 1785 a letter to Barnabas Thomas, "a very sensible man, possessed of a fertile mind and retentive memory," was written with the bogus certainty of a man who wants to convince himself as well as others. "I am now as firmly attached to the Church of England as I ever was since you knew me. I know myself to be as real a Christian as the Archbishop of Canterbury."[43]

The undoubted heresy of extending the right to administer Holy Communion was the cause of the greatest outrage. But John Wesley's agreement to a continual revision of the liturgy produced almost equal offense. In his *Little Sketch for American Sunday Services* the Thirty-nine Articles were reduced to twenty-four. The Book of Common Prayer, in use since it was composed by Cranmer, was further abridged with the advice that its contents could be supplemented by the extempore words of the preachers. One-sixth of the psalms were discarded. America was beginning to exert its influence on the future of the mother church in England. The only way in which the old man could maintain his authority was, he had decided, to demonstrate that he understood the colonists' needs. That required him to meet some of the their demands. The adjustments were bound to affect the governance of English Methodism, even though, in his broadsheet circular *Our Brethren in America*, Wesley tried to establish a distinction between his Old and New World "parishes."

Lord King's account of the Primitive Church convinced me many years ago that bishops and presbyters are the same order and consequently have the same right to ordain. For many years I have been importuned from time to time to exercise this right by ordaining part of our travelling preachers. But I have still refused, not only for peace' sake, but because I was determined as little as possible to violate the established order of the national Church to which I belonged.

But the case is widely different between England and North America. Here there are bishops who have a legal jurisdiction. In America there are none, neither any parish ministers, so that for some hundred miles together there is none either to baptize or to administer the Lord's Supper. Here, therefore, my scruples are at an end, and I conceive myself at full liberty, as I violate no order and invade no man's right by appointing and sending labourers into the harvest. I have accordingly appointed Dr. Coke and Mr. Francis Asbury to be joint superintendents over our brethren in North America; as also Richard Whatcoat and Thomas Vasey to act as elders among them, by baptizing and administering the Lord's Supper. And I have prepared a liturgy little differing from that of the Church of England.[44]

Coke claimed to be astonished by the suggestion that he should become "superintendent." But there is no doubt that the idea of becoming some sort of American consul came from him. "If some one in whom you could place the fullest confidence . . . were to go over and return," he wrote, "you would then have a source of sufficient information to determine on any points or propositions." So his enemies were probably right to insist that he had insinuated the idea into the half-formed plans of a near-senile old man. Whatever its origins, Wesley put his plans for reorganizing the American societies before the 1784 conference. The scheme was outlined step by step, beginning with the call for volunteer missionaries. He then told his "inner cabinet" of his plan for ordination. John Pawson, a member of the group, told his brother that "the preachers were astonished when this was mentioned, and, to a man, opposed it. But I plainly saw it would be done, as Mr. Wesley's mind seemed to be quite made up." Fletcher thought that one last attempt should be made to persuade the bishops to do their duty. The suggestion was ignored on the reasonable assumption that the bishops would again refuse to meet the Methodists' needs. Wesley continued to consult friends. None supported his proposal. Sometimes Wesley chose to argue, and sometimes he abandoned the conversation before the case against his scheme had been fully set out.

Coke then tried to bring the question to a conclusion by writing to Wesley to say that he accepted the offer of the superintendentship, which he had kept "under consideration." Since the offer had been made several months earlier, his critics said that he was afraid that Wesley would change his mind. His friends agreed that he was doing no more than urging the implementation of a decision that had been taken quite independently of his intervention. Whatever the truth of the rival claims, Coke clearly decided that in his own interests or those of the American Connexion, it was necessary for him to become a Methodist "bishop." And he wrote to Wesley saying so. "The more maturely I consider the subject, the more expedient it appears to me that the powers of ordaining should be received by me from you." Authorities on common law drew attention to one sentence in Coke's letter. "It is well to provide against all events and an authority *formally* received from you will be fully admitted by the people and my exercising the office of ordination without that formal authority may be disputed if there be any opposition on any other account." They judged that, whatever his motives, he was right to warn Wesley that in the traditions of church government, a formal act was necessary to give him the authority Wesley proposed. More cynical men might have thought that he wanted to make clear—in case of catastrophe—that he was acting under explicit orders.

According to his *Journal*, John Wesley "appointed Mr. Whatcoat and Vasey to go and serve the desolate sheep of America" and "added to them three more." The reasons that their names were withheld is not to Wesley's credit. The "three more" whose existence was not admitted included Whatcoat and Vasey, who (having been ordained deacons) were then ordained a second time as "elders." The third "appointment" was Coke, who was ordained "superintendent." Coke's promotion to what amounted to a bishop extended Wesley's offense against church law. It also contradicted the principle on which he claimed to act. He justified his actions with the argument that in the Primitive Church, all priests were presbyters of the same rank and that they were all qualified to ordain. Yet he gave Dr. Coke an elevated status with the express intention of making it possible for him to ordain others. The letter of authorization which Coke demanded of Wesley justified the irregular conduct in more practical and more plausible terms. "Whereas many of the people in the southern provinces of North America . . . are greatly distressed for a lack of ministers to administer the Sacraments . . . and whereas there does not seem to be any other way of supplying them with ministers, know all men that I, John Wesley, think myself to be providentially called to set apart some persons for the work of the ministry in America." Setting Coke so far apart caused nothing but trouble.

If John Wesley believed that concessions to American demands would guarantee him continued control over the American Connexion, his hopes were soon shattered. Once America was independent of England, American Methodists took it for granted that they would not be ruled by an English priest. But Wesley tried to cling on to his empire. In 1787 he instructed that a conference should be held in Baltimore and that it should appoint Richard Whatcoat as an "additional general superintendent." The American Methodists, having first repealed the "binding minute" which committed them to follow Wesley's lead, ignored the injunction. Asbury, too popular with the Americans for them to agree to his power being diluted, explained. "For our old Daddy to appoint Conference when and where he pleased, to appoint a joint superintendent with me, were strokes of power we did not understand."[45] He explained that no one who was not "omnipotent, omniscient and omnipresent" could govern America from England. He also explained the underlying causes of what he clearly regarded as a power struggle. "Mr. Wesley and I are like Caesar and Pompey. He will bear no equal and I will bear no superior."

Relations further deteriorated when Coke assumed the full title and dignity of "bishop" and then wisely used his episcopal powers to confer the same style and status on Asbury, who would certainly have been the societies' choice of leader of the American Connexion. In the name of that church the two men then sent a letter to General Washington congratulating him on his appointment as president and swearing loyalty to the new nation.

Charles Wesley's reaction to the events, as well as coming as close to humor as anything he ever wrote, illustrated his talent for representing complicated ideas in simple verse.

> How easy now are bishops made
> At man or woman's whim.
> Wesley his hand on Coke hath laid,
> But who laid hands on him?

It was, in a way, an epitaph for the Wesleys' years of work together. John could not or would not recognize the awful consequences of what he had done. His brother could not ignore it. So he wrote, "Our partnership is finished, though not our friendship."

Wesley's friends regarded the elevation of Coke as further evidence of "pure weakness of mind" exploited by the "well-meaning but very inconsiderate"[46] superintendent of American Methodism. And they argued with one another about the regret that Wesley felt, but hid, at the discovery that Coke had assumed episcopal airs as well as powers and, in the name of American Methodism, had paid homage and sworn fealty to the man who had raised so successful a rebellion against King George. Whatever his immediate reaction to these events, John Wesley certainly resented an entry in the American conference's minutes which equated him with the two "bishops" he had created. It asked, in the customary style, "Who are the persons that exercise the Episcopal office in the Methodist Church of Europe and America?" The answer, which drew no distinction among the three men, was "Wesley, Coke and Asbury."[47] John Wesley never felt the slightest inhibition in reminding his followers that divine inspiration distinguished him from other men. So he wrote to Asbury, without embarrassment, to explain the minutes' error. "You are the elder brother of American Methodism. I am, under God, the father of the whole family." The man (subject to the sins of pride and envy) then took over from the saint. "I study to be little; you study to be great. I creep, you strut along. . . . How can you dare to suffer yourselves to be called Bishops? I shudder, I start at the very thought. Men may call me a knave or a fool, a rascal, a scoundrel and I am content; but they shall never, by my consent, call me bishop."[48] The monster he had created was about to swallow him up.

Coke and Asbury had fallen into the error which Wesley so assiduously avoided, failure to maintain a proper balance between respect for the Church of England and response to the needs of the Methodist Connexion. But the final personal blow was still to be struck. Asbury agreed that all mention of Wesley's name should be struck out of the American minutes. All reference to "Old Daddy" was removed from what, in effect, was the statement of American Methodism's doctrine, governance and history. When he heard of the decision, Wesley reacted with mortified dignity. "This completed the matter and showed that he had no connection with me."[49]

The pain of rejection must have been immense. But by turning its back on Wesley, the American Connexion was demonstrating more than a personal distaste for Wesley's autocracy. Methodism was growing up. The Americans were determined to find their own way of ensuring regular communion for their members. The Americans were a microcosm of the wider movement. Methodist members were no longer prepared to have their right to worship as they chose circumscribed by John Wesley's sentimental attachment to the Church of England. The wholesale creation of Methodist presbyters could have only one conclusion. According to Charles Wesley, Lord Mansfield, the lord chief Justice, had summed it up in three words: "Ordination is separation."

17

PRAISE WHILE I HAVE BREATH

According to John Creighton, clerical assistant to John Wesley, the first ordinations were performed in haste and regretted throughout the remaining years of the old man's life. The "letters" which purported to give Whatcoat and Vasey the rights and responsibilities of a priest contained a hint of uncertainty. "I John Wesley think myself to be providentially called at this time to set apart some persons for the work of the Ministry in America." And his "Letter to Methodists," published in the autumn of 1784, justified his decision in a way which, ten years earlier, he would have thought beneath his dignity. "By a very uncommon chain of providence many of the Provinces of North America are totally disjoined from the Mother Country. . . . The English Government has no authority over them either civil or ecclesiastical." He then switched the argument from the constitutional position of the new country to the doctrines of the old church. Lord King was again called in aid. "Bishops and presbyters [are] of the same order and consequently have the same rights to ordain." He went on to explain that attempts had been made to persuade the bishop of London to lay hands on new clergy. The implication that he would have preferred the orthodox course profoundly undermined his earlier contentions that episcopal authority was not necessary. Both the logic and the language suggest that the ordinations were made out of necessity rather than conviction. His final explanation was the most revealing, and the least elevating, of all his various justifications for a step which he must have known would lead to separation. It also contradicted the previous implication that the bishops forced his hand. If the Church of England bishops had complied with his request and ordained more priests for Methodist America, "they would likewise expect to govern them. And how grievously thus entangle us." He had begun to think of the connexion as a church in its own right.

The American ordinations, and the explanations which followed them, raised questions about John Wesley's motives, and therefore his integrity, which dominated his declining years. Robert Southey judged that the old man was "led towards separation step by step," but, despite accepting that Wesley was not the driving force behind schism, believed that "it was not to his honor that he affected to depreciate it to the last while he was evidently bringing it about by measures which he pursued."[1] Southey asked Alexander Knox, a friend and disciple of Wesley's in his old age, to help with the difficult problem of deciding how genuine the protestation of love for the Established Church had been. Unfortunately, Knox responded after Southey's biography had been published. So his judgment, instead of influencing the whole work, appeared at its conclusion as an annex. Knox, relying on firsthand evidence, had no doubt that for many years "two dissonant principles wrought in Mr. Wesley's mind. He was unfeignedly attached to the Church of England, but he was more sensitively and practically attached to his own Society."[2] For much of his life Wesley had successfully struggled to reconcile those two conflicting affections, sometimes making concessions to the demands of his more intemperate followers, sometimes insisting that the canons of the church must be obeyed. In old age he was no longer able to hold the balance or to withstand the pressures of society members who had less concern for the established order. But his apparent equivocations were the misjudgment and mistakes of an octogenarian. His early biographers expected him to possess the strengths of a saint. They were therefore disappointed when he exhibited the weakness of a man.

Methodists were not the only North American Protestants to be confounded by the War of Independence. The Episcopalians had always relied on their nominees for holy orders being ordained in England and the ranks of their local clergy being augmented by immigrant English priests. The American Revolution cut off both sources of supply. In 1782 a Dr. William Smith convened a meeting of what he called the Protestant Episcopalian Church and had himself declared its bishop. There was talk of cooperation with the other dispossessed denominations and sects, including the Methodists. The notion of amalgamation fell through when it was learned that (with or without the knowledge of "Old Daddy") cooperation depended on "Mr. Wesley [becoming] the first link in the chain on which that Church is suspended."

Even the suggestion of federation alarmed traditional church opinion. In 1783 fear of latitudinarianism prompted a body, calling itself the Connecticut High Churchmen, to nominate Samuel Seabury to seek consecration. Seabury was a loyalist who had led the White Plains Protest against "unlawful congresses and committees" at the time of the first colonial risings. He had, in consequence, been attacked by both Alexander Hamilton, soon to become secretary of the Treasury, and the New York mob. His loyalty to the crown was confirmed by his agreement to become chaplain to one of King George's American regiments. But once the new nation was created, he believed that he owed his allegiance to America. He could not, in consequence, take an oath of fealty to the English monarch. That meant that the Established Church would not make him a bishop.

Seabury was consecrated bishop by Scottish Nonjurors in 1784. Six years later he was made bishop of Long Island, and in 1796 his elevation and appointment were acknowledged by the General Convocation of the Church of England. Typically, the whole Protestant movement had been slow to recognize the needs of the New World. Wesley at least realized that America offered the church special challenges and unique opportunities. The evangelical movements of the United States—in their different ways, his heirs and successors—have proved him right.

Wesley also believed, less plausibly, that by setting out the special circumstances of North America he avoided his first independent ordinations' becoming a precedent. But other "special circumstances" set the precedent on its head and made the American initiative an example of fearless evangelism which had to be followed wherever a shortage of priests threatened the future of the connexion. It was only a matter of time before a new crisis arose. Scotland's "special circumstances" were diagnosed in the spring of 1785.

Scottish Methodists, although small in number, were no less in need of communion than their English brethren. Yet the weakness of the connexion north of the border (largely the result of the strength of the indigenous churches) meant that there were no ordained ministers who were prepared to provide the sacrament in a way or in places that met the societies' needs. Scotland, as did America, could provide a constitutional justification to reinforce the argument for action. The English church, in which Wesley had sworn to live and die, had no authority there. The reluctance with which Wesley took the next leap toward separation is made clear by the entry in his *Journal* for 5 August 1785. "Having with a few select friends weighed the matter thoroughly, I yielded to their judgement and set apart three of our well-tried preachers, John Pawson, Thomas Hanby and Joseph Taylor to minister in Scotland."

The news was badly received by Charles Wesley, who wrote to his brother urging him to read again the pamphlet *Reasons Against Separation*, which John had published in 1758. The letter ended with a reproof which John Wesley must have known contained the indisputable truth that he was already traveling the road to separation. "When you began ordaining in America, I knew and you knew that your [English] preachers would never rest until you ordained them."[3] John Wesley, realizing that it was impossible to dispute that foresight, relied, in his reply, on an assurance that the Scottish ordinations were not as bad as they seemed, an assertion of his own integrity and an appeal for Charles's fraternal affection. "I walk still by the same rule I have done for forty and fifty years. I do nothing rashly. It is not likely that I should. The high day of my blood is over. If you will go hand in hand with me do. But do not hinder me if you will not help. Perhaps if you had kept close to me I would have done better. However, with or without your help, I creep on."[4] Charles was neither convinced nor impressed and expressed his disapproval with a trenchant disregard for John's pleas for brotherly understanding. The result was John Wesley's acceptance that the evangelical partnership was ended forever. "I see no use of you and me disputing together. You say I separate from the Church. I say I do not. There let it stand."[5]

The assurance that the Scottish ordinations would carry no rights in England was an important indication of John Wesley's wish to limit the danger of schism as far as his first concern for the connexion (and the pressures of its members) made possible. The desire, indeed the determination, to go no further than he was pushed was even more dramatically illustrated by his attitude toward baptism. In his view, the urgent need to find ministers who could administer the Eucharist was not matched by an equal necessity to christen infants, whose justification and sanctification would, in any event, come later through a quite different process. When in 1783 Joseph Benson admitted that he had, "with some reluctance, consented to baptize a young man who appeared to be very penitent and to experience a measure of faith," Wesley's reply was unambiguous. "I do not and never did consent that any of our preachers should baptize as long as we profess ourselves to be members of the Church of England."[6] A year later he announced his intention to "drop all the preachers who will not drop" baptism.[7] He then wrote to John Hampson with the specific instruction "Whoever among us undertakes to baptize a child is *ipso facto* excluded from our Connexion."[8] The Scottish ordinands were given advice which they must have found profoundly disturbing—and no doubt attributed to the old man's failing powers. "As we have not yet made a precedent of any one who is not ordained administering baptism, it is better to go slow but sure."[9] The implication of that instruction was that the Scottish "priests" were not quite the real thing. Perhaps that was John Wesley's secret opinion. What is not in doubt is his continuing desire to offend against the canons of the Church of England no more than was necessary to protect and preserve his precious connexion.

However, true to Charles Wesley's prediction, the Methodist conference of 1786 extended the apostasy. Joshua Keighley and Charles Atmore were ordained for Scotland, William Warrener for Antigua and William Hammatt for Newfoundlands. But a year later yet another attempt was made to mitigate offense against the church by prohibiting practices which set the Methodist Connexion apart. Preachers were again reminded that meetings were not to be held while church services were taking place. But in order to assuage the pressure of more rebellious members, an important caveat was added. If the pulpits were occupied by "wicked preachers," competition was not so much justified as demanded. The moral obligation to make invidious distinctions between different classes of clergy was illustrated with an anecdote. "The last time I went to Scarborough I earnestly exhorted the people to go to church and I went myself. But the wretched minister preached such a sermon that I could not, in conscience, advise them to hear him any more."[10] The ad hominem attack was reinforced with a general observation. "One may leave a church (which I would advise in some circumstances) without leaving the Church."[11]

However, in his sermon "On Attending the Church Service," John Wesley made a strange concession. It might have been the product of intellectual integrity, the result of a desire further to placate the Church of England or no more than an old man's wandering. Whatever its motives, it implied a view of the priesthood which certainly undermined the Methodist demand for more ordinations. Although it was reasonable and right to reject a priest whose sermons offended true believers, that was no reason to refuse communion from the same source. "The unworthy minister," Wesley wrote, "does not hinder the efficacy of God's ordinance. The reason is plain. The efficacy is derived not from him that administers but from him that ordains." The distinction can be rationally justified. But the likelihood is that logic was far less important in the formulation of proper Methodist attitudes toward the Established Church than the desire to please both society members and the episcopate at the same time. His judgment was prejudiced by pressures which increased from day to day. Weeks before his death Wesley told Creighton, "the preachers are now too powerful for me." This was more than an admission that Charles Wesley had been right to predict that they would force the pace of separation. It confirms that during the last years of his life John Wesley was fighting a rearguard action. He knew that separation could not be avoided forever. But it could be postponed until his death. Then he would be spared expulsion from the church into which he had been born and which he still loved. When he said, "I have no desire or design to separate till my soul separates from my body," he meant it. He remained determined to live and die an ordained minister of the Established Church. But he was approaching the point at which a choice had to be made.

The pressures on John Wesley increased with the years. The patience of Methodists who longed for regular communion was exhausted. The principle that ordination was acceptable if it was intended to guarantee the sacrament in "a desolate place" or performed outside the Church of England's jurisdiction was all the justification they needed for demanding that presbyters be created in England. At first they argued that North Yorkshire was as inaccessible and inhospitable as North America. That contention was resisted at the 1788 conference, but it was clear, even then, that the line could not be held for long. In 1788 John Wesley ordained Alexander Mather, a senior preacher, for unspecified duties. Mather was later to insist that he had also been made elder and deacon and that Wesley intended that he should succeed to the leadership of the connexion. Two years later Henry Moore and Thomas Rankin were ordained without Wesley's specifying whether their duties were to be discharged in "desolate places" in or outside England. The break had come in all but name. The Methodists were, in fact, if not in law, a separate church. Ordination was separation.

Once again John Wesley attempted to restore his waning influence by issuing new regulations. In 1786, immediately after Keighley and Atmore had been ordained for Scotland and Charles's reproof had been received, Wesley had revised the rules which governed Methodist conduct. The new "instructions to preachers" were technical. "Never scream. . . . It is disgustful to the hearers." A year later his revision of duties and obligations was more related to the continuation of a cohesive connexion. "Anyone who wishes to preach (apart from regular preachers)" must possess "a note from Mr. Wesley or the assistant of the circuit." And while he attempted to tighten, or at least maintain, his hold on the connexion, he continued his theological battle against its external critics. The need to define more clearly the nature of true faith still troubled his restless mind. Christian perfection had to be defended, final perseverance (in the extensive Calvinist form) rejected and assurance of God's love and salvation re-enforced as a central tenet of Christian belief. John Wesley still believed that he remained capable of guiding—in matters both spiritual and temporal—a connexion which was increasing daily in sophistication as well as size. His response, and therefore his reputation, were immensely impaired by his refusal to accept the limitations of age.

Time did bring one blessing. As John Wesley redefined his beliefs, he embraced a new moderation: the formal and explicit tolerance of "part Christians" who, in the distant past, had not been accepted as Christians at all. The final revision of a belief about which he had agonized for years was set out in the sermon "On Faith," given and published in 1788. It returned to the distinction between the faith of a servant and the faith of a son—or child, as he chose to redesignate the superior condition in a concession to female virtue. "He that believeth as a child of God 'hath the witness in himself.' This the servant hath not." But although the servant might lack full assurance, they who "feareth God and worketh righteousness" remain real Christians.[12] Faith remained the key to redemption. But righteous works—the result, not the cause, of holiness—became, in Wesley's old age an increasingly important element in his definition of a true Christian life. And the way in which the emphasis on *sola fide* (a doctrine which was right in itself) had prejudiced him against "half Christians" became the cause of publicly expressed regret. "Nearly fifty years ago when the preachers commonly called Methodists began to preach the grand scriptural doctrine salvation by faith, they were not sufficiently appraised of the difference between a servant and a child of God. They did not clearly understand that every one who feareth God and worketh righteousness is accepted of him."[13]

As a result the eighties—of both Wesley's life and the eighteenth century—marked an increasing Methodist emphasis on good works. It began with a sermon against wealth. "The Dangers of Riches," given in 1780, had warned that prosperity "led to some other . . . hurtful desires." Eight years later he made the same point with greater insistence. The poor, he claimed, possessed "an advantage over the rich." They "receive with meekness the engrafted word which is able to save souls."[14] The notion that money corrupts could not have been more plainly stated. "It would not be strange if rich men were, in general, void of all good disposition and easy prey to evil ones since so few of them pay any regard to that solemn declaration of our Lord without observing which we cannot be his disciples. . . . 'If any man will come after me, let him deny himself and take up his cross daily and follow me.'"[15]

Following Him required, in John Wesley's revised theology, more than simply forswearing wealth. It was "better . . . to go to the poor than to the rich and to the house in mourning than the house of feasting."[16] The 1780s were, for Methodism, a didactic decade. So John Wesley laid down the way in which the ministry of service should be performed. The sick must be succored. But each charitable act should lead toward the greater good of salvation.

> It may not be amiss usually to begin with inquiring into their outward condition. You may ask whether they have the necessities of life. Whether they have sufficient food and raiment. If the weather be cold, whether they have fuel. . . . Those little labours of love will pave your way to things of great importance. Having shown that you have regard for their bodies you may proceed to enquire concerning their souls . . . while you are eyes to the blind and feet to the lame, a husband to the widow and a father to the fatherless see that you keep a still higher aim in view.[17]

The higher aim was still the purpose of evangelism, the purpose of Methodism and the destiny of John Wesley. All that mattered was salvation. But age—age and the deaths of the handful of men and women to whom he felt close had mellowed him. John Fletcher had died in 1785, leaving Wesley very near to friendless. His brother, never the most fervent of evangelists, had lost enthusiasm and found caution. The joys of a happy married life, combined with fears that the Methodists were in headlong flight toward separation, had served to encourage Charles's increasing detachment from the connexion, but he still sent his brother (generally unwelcome) advice. "I leave America and Scotland to your latest thoughts and recognition, only observing . . . keep your authority while you live and after your death *detur digniori* or rather *dignioribus*. You cannot see the succession. You cannot define how God will settle it."[18]

That last letter from Charles Wesley to his brother was written in the pain of what turned out to be a terminal illness. John was as didactic about the treatment of illness as Charles was about the management of Methodism. But he at least responded to the news of his brother's fast-deteriorating health with advice which was inspiring, if not very practical. "He has a little more work for you to do, you must now take up your cross."[19] It was also generous in spirit. "Never mind expenses. Do not die to save charges. I can make that up. You certainly need not want for anything as long as I live."[20] There was no shortage of medical advice. Much of it was bizarre. "I hope you keep to your rule of going out each day . . . keep to this but one month and I am persuaded you will be as well as you were this time twelvemonth."[21] Letters to his sister-in-law contained alternative remedies. "I wish he would see Dr. Whitehead. I am persuaded there is not another such physician in England, although to confound human wisdom he does not know how to cure his own wife."[22] Two weeks later John Wesley had another helpful idea which he passed on to his niece Sarah. "Mr. Whitefield had, for some time, thrown up all the food he took. I advised him to slit a large onion across the grain and bind it across the pit of his stomach. He vomited no more. Pray apply this to my brother's stomach the next time he eats."[23] The suggestions for recovery were interspersed with the persistent reminder that his brother was "suffering the will of God." Perhaps Charles found comfort in that.

Whether or not Sally Wesley took her brother-in-law's advice, Charles Wesley died on 29 March 1788. It was, by Methodist standards, a good death, confirmed by a poem which Charles, enfeebled and almost unable to speak the words, dictated to his wife.

> In age and feebleness extreme
> Who shall a helpless worm redeem?
> Jesus my only hope Thou art,
> Strength of my failing flesh and heart.
> O could I catch a smile from Thee
> And drop into eternity!

It was the last verse to be written by a poet whose words are still sung in every church in England.★

John Wesley was preaching in the north when the end came and did not hear of his brother's passing until 4 April. His condolence letter to his sister-in-law is a model of remorse combined with a desire for vindication. "Half an hour ago I received a letter from Mr. Bradburn informing me of my brother's death. For eleven or twelve days before I had not one line concerning him. The last was from Charles, which I delayed to answer, expecting every day to receive some further explanation."[24]

Charles's will stipulated that he be buried in consecrated ground. So he was laid to rest in Marylebone churchyard, rather than the Dissenters' cemetery at Bunhill Fields or in the grounds of the City Road chapel. John did not hide his regret at his brother's final rejection of Methodism's pretensions to be treated as a church in its own right. The City Road burial ground was, he said, as "holy as any in England and contains a large quantity of bony dust." The pain was also personal. "'Tis pity but the remains of my brother had been deposited with me," he wrote. For some days preachers marveled that John showed so little feeling. Then two weeks after Charles's death he was about to preach in the Bolton meetinghouse. When the

★ Charles Wesley's hymns include "Jesu Lover of my Soul," "Soldiers of Christ Arise," "Love Divine All Loves Excelling" and "O for a Thousand Tongues to Sing." He also wrote a Christmas carol, "Hark How All the Welkins Ring." When George Whitefield published it, he changed the first line to "Hark the Herald Angels Sing."

congregation reached the line of a hymn which offered their lives to God with the explanation "My company before is gone, and I am left alone with thee," John broke down. It was some time before he was able to begin his sermon.

The exhibition of human emotion was not John Wesley's usual style. A few months after Charles's death he heard that Grace Murray, widowed in 1759 and reconciled with the Methodists, traveled from her home in Derbyshire to visit her son, who had become a minister at Pavements in Moorfields. She asked to meet John Wesley again. Friends expected a heartrending reunion. On all the evidence, then and now, Grace was the love of his life. Had they married, she might have helped him to find the personal happiness which, without her, he was denied. Henry Moore, young acolyte and eventual biographer, recorded, with clear apprehension, that "Mr. Wesley, with evident feeling, resolved to visit her." But he need not have worried. "The next morning he took me with him to Colebrook Row where her son then resided. The meeting was affecting, but Mr. Wesley preserved more than his usual self-possession."[25]

John Wesley was growing frail. In 1782 he had been able to boast, "I entered into my eightieth year, but blessed by God my time is not laboured in sorrow. . . . I find no more pain and infirmities than I did at five and twenty."[26] He attributed his good health to the power of God, the regularity of his preaching and settled habits, which ranged from "rising at a set hour" to "still travelling four or five thousand miles a year." Eight years later neither faith nor regular exercise could hold back the ravages of time. On New Year's Day 1791 he wrote, "I am now an old man, decayed from hand to foot. My eyes are dim, my right hand shakes much, my mouth is hot and dry every morning. I have a lingering fever almost every day. My motion is weak and slow. However, blessed be God, I do not slack my labors. I can preach and write still."[27] It was the constant preaching and the writing, combined with the still-incessant traveling, which had laid him low during the last decade. John Wesley was incapable of accepting the limitations of his mortality even when he recognized its symptoms. Only actual infirmity could ever slow him down.

At the age of eighty-four, John Wesley made his second visit to Holland in two years. On his return he was struck down by what his *Journal* called "a most impetuous flux." Modesty prevented an identification of its source. Doctors prescribed a grain and a half of opium to be taken in three rapid doses. The pain was eased, but the drug had hideous side effects. "It took away my speech, hearing and power of motion and locked me up from head to foot, so that I lay a mere log."[28] He never really recovered and was from then on unable to continue his work—at least in the way which he thought right. In the autumn of 1789, aged eighty-six, he had to admit, "I cannot easily preach above twice a day."[29] But he still preached to some purpose. John Wesley had found a new cause.

In 1787 Granville Sharp, a future member of the British and Foreign Bible Society and a New Testament scholar, had succeeded in founding his colony for freed slaves in Sierra Leone. In October of that year John Wesley wrote to tell him, "Ever since I heard of it . . . I felt a perfect detestation of the horrid slave trade, but more particularly since I had the pleasure of reading what you have published on the subject."[30] A month later he wrote to Thomas Funnell to offer "whatever assistance I can give those generous men who join to oppose that execrable trade I shall certainly give. I have printed a large edition of *Thoughts on Slavery*." For the rest of his life he campaigned unremittingly for emancipation.

John Wesley had written his tract against the slave trade back in 1774, but it was not quite true to say that he had been opposed to slavery ever since he had heard of its existence. One of his duties in Georgia—according to John Burton, speaking on behalf of the Society for the Propagation of the Gospel—was "the conversion of Negro slaves." He had tried to do his Christian duty. But in both Frederica and Charleston he had been disheartened by his lack of success. He had made a couple of converts, but his plan to identify and convert susceptible slaves had foundered. Wesley certainly felt compassion for those among them who were mistreated. David Jones, a white slave of his acquaintance, committed suicide after being abused by Captain Williams, his owner. But there is no evidence that the Georgia missionary ever thought about emancipation. That came later, when Sharp and Funnell stirred the conscience of the nation.

The new enthusiasm added to the demands upon his energy. And he still, after almost half a century leading the Methodist Connexion, had to face and, if he could, to resolve the controversies which had raged in the societies since they were founded. And that task was proving increasingly difficult to accomplish. In 1788 John Wesley was still valiantly attempting to preserve his own authority while the preachers, represented at the conferences and the "cabinet" which he had created, were increasingly determined to impose their will upon him.

In 1788 he was persuaded by his solicitor that all the preachers and meetinghouses should, for their own protection, be licensed under the Conventicle Act. His eventual, and deeply reluctant, agreement was, in its way, the biggest change of heart and mind of all. Not only did it represent the reversal of a view which, fifty years earlier, had been held with unconcealed passion, but it was a concession that legally Methodism existed outside the Church of England. Some of Wesley's followers refused to accept that interpretation of their status. So some applications were refused because of local protestations that Methodists were, and would remain, part of the Established Church. More often the distinction which Methodists tried to make between "Dissenters" or "preachers of the gospel" was either ignored or not understood so the attempt to remain half in and half out of the Church failed. Whether or not the licenses were granted, the notion that Methodism was an autonomous church had become irresistible. It was increasingly assumed—by both members and critics—that it was only a matter of time before the connexion announced that it intended to break away.

Against all the evidence, John Wesley continued to assert his loyalty to the Established Church. But his influence was rapidly diminishing. Every aspect of the connexion—its governance, its dogma and its organization—was examined by the senior members of the conference in its relationship to the succession. It was assumed that Wesley would soon either die or go. Few of the possible contenders wanted to take his place. None of them looked forward to being superseded by a colleague. Only Dr. Thomas Coke displayed open ambition.

The societies began openly to question John Wesley's judgment and frustrate his will. Dublin Methodists, denied the right to attend connexion meetings on Sunday mornings because of the prohibition on competing with the Church of England, began to attend the Dissenters' chapel. Henry Moore, assistant on the Dublin circuit and a personal friend of John Wesley's, was saddened but could think of no legitimate way in which it could be prevented. Coke was more ingenious. Acting as Wesley's representative (though without Wesley's authority), he ordered that the Dublin Methodists hold services, at church times, on three mornings a month and attend St. Patrick's Cathedral on the fourth. Moore complained, more about the usurping of his authority than the offense to the Established Church. Wesley's initial response was unequivocal in its general support for continued loyalty. "I am a Church of England man; and as I said fifty years ago, so I say still. In the Church of England I will live and die, unless I am thrust out."[31] The final proviso was an addition to the original assertion. It almost certainly represents apprehension rather than disenchantment. But four days after he seemed to disown Coke's suggestion by announcing, "The doctor is too warm," another letter to Moore (followed by instructions to Coke) endorsed the plan wholly in principle and largely in practice. "I allow two points. (1) that while Doctor Coke is in Dublin, he may have services at eleven o'clock as before. (2) That on condition that our brethren will attend St. Patrick's one Sunday in four, you may read prayers on the other three in the room."[32]

It seems unlikely that Moore was consoled by a solution which made plain that Coke could conduct services while he must confine himself to prayers, but he was the old man's friend and must have realized that Wesley's judgment, like his powers, was failing. About only one thing was Wesley certain: the importance of doing all in his power to postpone immediate formal separation. The confidence in continued unity, which he continued to express, has little justification. But in his tract *Further Thoughts on Separation from the Church*, he even offered reassurance about the connexion's constancy after his death. The schism, he promised, would not come about. "I do not believe the Methodists in general design it when I am no more seen."[33] The assurances about what would follow his death were undermined by the constant demonstration that even in life, he was not the power that once he had been.

The pattern of movement toward separation which Charles Wesley had predicted was repeated year after year. First a specific decision, justified as an exception, was taken in defiance of church laws. Then within months it became the general rule. The Coke formula, promulgated for the special circumstances of Dublin, was made lawful in all Methodist circuits by the minutes of the 1788 conference. "The assistants shall have the discretionary power to read the Prayer Book in the preaching houses on Sunday mornings where they think it expedient." Wesley was no longer master in his own connexion.

There were revolts against Wesley's authority in the chapels. At Dewsbury, there was a long and complicated legal dispute about the right to appoint and dismiss ministers. It ended with the book steward's assuming power and declaring independence from the connexion. Then the chapel at North Shields announced its intention to make its own appointments. John Wesley wrote in the sternest terms to the three itinerant preachers who served the Newcastle circuit. They were "required" to instruct the trustees "of the house at Milburn Place" to follow "the Methodist plan." If the trustees failed to comply, then the itinerants were instructed to "renounce all connection with the dissidents." In a postscript Wesley added, offering a true sign of his uncertainty, "I am at a point. I will be trifled with no longer."[34] The requirement was not met. Wesley's letter to Edward Coates, the leader of the rebellious trustees, began with a complaint which was clearly a concession of defeat. "You have used me basely and ungratefully after I have served you between forty and fifty years."[35] Newcastle, one of Methodism's earliest outposts, no longer accepted that Wesley's word was law. The rebellions spread. Thomas Hanby, whose ordination in Scotland had been justified by the insistence that his ministry ended at the English border, moved to Nottingham and began to administer the sacrament there. John Wesley forbade him to continue. Hanby announced that if he had to choose between following Wesley and following his conscience, only one decision was possible.

Assailed on all sides, John Wesley, old and weary, lost all stomach for the fight. In 1790, when he was "nearly worn out and his faculties were very much impaired, especially his memory,"[36] his proposals for the stationing of preachers were amended by "mutual consent." Gone were the days when he announced that the stations were decided by him and him alone. At the ceremony "for admission into full connexion" of young preachers it was Dr. Coke, home from America, who played the key role. The copy of the *Large Minutes* with which they were each presented contained Wesley's welcome to "fellow labourers." But it was Thomas Coke's hand which was laid on their heads.

The time had come for last things. The determination even to govern his own life with rules of iron had begun to fade. In June 1790 he made the first voluntary concession to old age. "For upwards of eighty years I have kept accounts exactly. I will not attempt it any longer being satisfied with constant conviction that I save all I can and give all I can. That is all I have."[37] Mortality began to force itself upon him. At Winchelsea on 20 November he preached his last open-air sermon. The heady days of field preaching—competing with wind and weather for the attention of thousand-strong crowds, which had begun so long ago in Bristol—were over forever. The last *Journal* entry, meant like the rest for publication and posterity, was dated 24 November and ended too suddenly to have any meaning. Diary notes continued until six days before his death, but the zeal to tell his story to the world had passed. His health improved toward the end of the year, and by Christmas he seemed to have recovered some of his old vigor. But in the New Year there was a relapse. His friends and confidants urged him to rest. There was never a chance that he would accept their advice even though he knew that the end was near. "I am half blind and half lame, but by the help of God I creep on still."[38] On 17 February 1791 he was preaching again.

On Saturday, the nineteenth, he felt too unwell to do anything except read and write and next day he was unable to perform all of

his usual Sunday observances. But he rallied and was sufficiently recovered to dine with friends in Twickenham and Islington within
the space of three days. On Monday, the twenty-second he preached
for the last time at the City Road chapel—his home as well as his
headquarters—and rose early on the following morning to travel to
Leatherhead, where he had "agreed to preach for a gentleman there
who had lately buried his wife and who, till then, was an entire
stranger."[39] He chose as his text Isaiah, chapter 55, verse 6, "Seek ye
the Lord while he may be found."

Much of the day before the journey to Leatherhead was spent
reading *The Interesting Narrative of the Life of Gustavus Vasa*. The book
was probably finished during the journey. Vasa had been born in
Africa in 1745, kidnapped while still a child and sold into slavery.
After a series of adventures at sea he arrived, a free man, at Bristol,
was converted to Christianity and baptized at St. Margaret's, Westminster. Wesley was immensely moved by the story, particularly the
revelation that a black man's word was never accepted in court
against the testimony of a white man. On 24 November he wrote to
William Wilberforce that he regarded slavery as "an execrable vil-
lainy which is the scandal of England and of human nature." He was
particularly shocked by the thought that "when a man has a black
skin if he [is] wronged or attacked by a white man [he] has no re-
dress." The valediction was essentially evangelical in content and
tone. "Go on in the name of God and in the power of His might,
till even American slavery (the vilest that ever saw the sun) shall banish before it."[40] The last letter of the greatest evangelist in modern
history urged Wilberforce, as Wesley had urged the world, "Be not
weary in doing well."

The Leatherhead sermon was not a great success. "The plain
country people who had come plodding through the mire seemed
rather out of their depth."[41] However, Wesley returned to London
"cheerful and nearly as well as usual"[42] and settled down comfortable and at home in his apartment alongside the City Road chapel.
Unfortunately, neither happy condition lasted long. His housekeeper, Miss Elizabeth Ritchie, a thirty-nine-year-old spinster "high
in the confidence of the whole Connexion," sent for Dr. Whitehead,

Wesley's physician. The prognosis was so bad that Whitehead suggested that Miss Ritchie record the dying man's last days. Her account of the week that followed ran to more than five thousand words. A précis would be produced and read at the funeral which Dr. Whitehead knew would swiftly follow.

John Wesley's robust constitution, fortified by careful diet, regular exercise and constant prayer, meant that he did not go quickly to meet his Maker. But he went joyfully and with the proper respect for the laws of discipline and order which had characterized his life. To Methodists, a good death was essential proof of an assurance which did not falter to the very end. Good deaths were used in evidence to convince doubters and backsliders of the peace which passeth all understanding. Evidence of joyful passing was essential. So the old man was spared nothing. It was necessary that he should know that he was about to die in order that he might face the end with the necessary righteous fortitude.

Joseph Bradford, a preacher and Wesley's traveling companion during the last year, anticipating "the awful event . . . asked if he wished things to continue as determined when debated at the last conference, or if he desired—in the case of his removal—that any or all of them should be convened?" For once he lacked the energy to argue for change and improvement.

When John Wesley fell into a coma, Miss Ritchie prayed that he would be aroused before death in order that "we might at least receive his dying charges and enjoy comfort (amid the awful scene) of hearing him repeat, with his own last breath, the blessed truths which we had so long been accustomed to receive from God through him." When he did briefly recover consciousness, he quoted a hymn which he had first sung long ago in Bristol and had asked his friends to sing for him during an earlier illness. "I the chief of sinners am. But Jesus died for me." The remorseless Miss Ritchie asked him, "Is this the present language of your heart and do you feel now as you did then?," and he replied that it was. It is hard to believe that the cross-examination did much to help the dying man through his last moments. But for a time the old passion for evangelism returned. He struggled on for another four days. Then, after hours of coma interspersed with sudden revivals and hymn singing, he asked for his sermon "The Love of God" to be reprinted and circulated to the societies. There was to be one last message to the world. Pen and ink were brought to his bedside. Writing was beyond him. So he asked Miss Ritchie to transcribe a letter. The request was followed by a long silence. Then she asked what he wanted the note to say. He replied, "Nothing but the best of all, God is with us." There was another brief recovery, during which he repeated the words of Isaac Watts's hymn "I'll Praise My Maker While I've Breath." But it was clear that the end was near. After a long silence, he said, "Farewell," and on 2 March 1791, surrounded by twenty of his most devoted followers, including Mrs. Charles Wesley and her daughter, Sarah, John Wesley died.

True to his meticulous character, Wesley's affairs were in complete order, and he had laid down precise rules about his burial. There were substantial changes to the will which he had made, anticipating early death, in 1768. Then the principal beneficiaries had been Kingswood School and the poor of London. In 1789, as if to acknowledge Methodism's new status, most of the money went to the connexion's general fund. Wesley's sister Martha received forty pounds. In the will he had written twenty years earlier she had been bequeathed nothing, for then her errant husband, Westley Hall, was still alive, and her brother had not been prepared to risk his laying his hands on the hard-earned money. Directions about the form of the funeral were precise. The body was to be wrapped in wool, and six poor men were to be given twenty shillings for carrying his coffin. Despite those indulgences, he was to be given what he called a modest funeral. The sorts of excesses he was anxious to avoid are illustrated by the accoutrements of mourning which his old adversary Augustus Toplady had forbidden to be produced to mark his own death, mourning rings, commemorative scarves and memorial hatbands. Wesley was similarly explicit in his prohibition. "I particularly wish that there shall be no hearse, no coach, no escutcheon, no pomp except the tears of those who love me and are following me to Abraham's bosom."

The Methodists did their best both to respect his modest wishes and, at the same time, to arrange a funeral which they thought appropriate to his greatness. Originally they planned for his body to lie in state at the City Road chapel, and for many years Methodists hung engravings on their walls which depicted the somber scene. But Henry Moore, an eyewitness to the obsequies, insisted that the idea was abandoned as inconsistent with John Wesley's instructions. The chapel was, however, draped in black. After the service the material was used to provide "decent dresses for sixty poor women."

To avoid unmanageable crowds and the consequent dangers to the funeral congregation, the service was held at five o'clock in the morning. The words of the funeral service were amended to reflect the feelings of the mourning Methodists. "For as much as it has pleased Almighty God to take unto Himself the soul of our dear brother" seemed inappropriate for the committal of a man who towered above his contemporaries. So "father" was used in place of "brother." When they heard the word, most of the Methodists who had filled the chapel and crowded the open ground outside, recognizing the change, broke down in tears.

True to the belief that concern for burial in consecrated ground was a "Popish conceit," John Wesley was interred in the graveyard at City Road. Theological principle triumphed over the undoubted personal preference to lie next to his brother. In death they were divided unnecessarily. Fifty years after Charles had been laid to rest it was discovered that the Marylebone churchyard, in which he had insisted he was to be buried, had never been consecrated.

Almost forty years before his passing, John Wesley had composed his own epitaph in anticipation of imminent death and ordered that if any inscription were placed on his tombstone, it must be his own simple work. His wishes could not be respected. The passage of time had, his followers decided, made the original epitaph out of date and inappropriate. So his friends wrote a threnody describing him as the true disciple of "the pure apostolical doctrine and practice of the Primitive Church" and expressing their "inexpressible joy" at the way in which his labors had, for half a century, "born witness in the hearts and lives of many thousands." The encomium was well deserved. But perhaps even in old age, and conscious as he undoubtedly was of his greatness, he would still have preferred "not leaving, after his debts were paid, Ten Pounds behind him" to be included. And to the end, after all the struggles with conscience, the battles with the Established Church and the intellectual uncertainties that he strove so long to overcome, he remained, in his own view, saved from damnation only by the love of God and the sacrifice of Christ, His Son. He died, still "a brand plucked from the burning."

18

TINCTURED WITH IMPERTINENCE

Leaders of dissident minorities often argue that they represent the one true faith and that it is the ruling majority who are the apostates and heretics. It was convenient for John Wesley to believe—and the belief might have been sincere—that it was the episcopal hierarchy that had betrayed the faith of the ancient fathers. The obvious conclusion, to which he regularly came, was that primitive purity would be recaptured only by the religious revival which he led. Yet he still insisted, though with diminishing conviction, that his only intention was a reinvigoration of the Church of England which his family had served for four generations, albeit the first two had been dissenters. The final task to which he set his hand was not simply to proclaim a new truth to a neglected people but to convince an entrenched Established Church that it should embrace the old truth which it had abandoned. However, by the time of his death the once-disparate societies had become a connexion, with their tight rules of order and behavior, their own edited version of the Prayer Book, their précis of the Thirty-nine Articles, their exclusive revision of Archbishop Cranmer's *Homilies* and strict instructions to accept John Wesley's writing as the only acceptable commentary on the Scriptures. So he must have known that he had founded a new church.

It is impossible exactly to determine how much John Wesley was motivated by personal ambition and how much by devotion to the cause. It never is with visionaries. Southey, whose biography relied heavily on Wesley's contemporaries, was certain that "[h]owever he might have deceived himself, the love of power was the ruling passion of his mind." Hampson, who left the connexion because of Wesley's autocracy, wrote of his "absolute and despotic power." Whitehead, who knew and admired him, excused his obsession with the explanation that he "considered his power as inseparably connected with the unity and prosperity of the Societies over which he presided." One thing, however, is certain: He had no doubt that his future and that of his connexion could not be separated.

The idea of the connexion, related societies with common beliefs and aims, came to him gradually. Early Methodism in general and Wesleyan Methodism in particular had many of the characteristics of a "holiness sect," groups of introspective and exclusive Christians which proliferated during the eighteenth century. Georgia planted the missionary seed. From then on, the idea of an itinerancy grew, and John Wesley began to experience the joy of multiple conversions at mass meetings. But the notion that Wesley set out to redeem the whole nation remains a romantic myth created by his early biographers. Until the connexion became effectively independent, his objective was to reach out—on behalf of a reformed and reinvigorated Established Church—to those sections of the population that had been denied the blessing of hearing God's holy word. They were by and large the new industrial proletariat.

The notion of class, as it has come to be understood, had no meaning for Wesley and his generation. He exhibited real concern for the poor, though Hampson wrote that "his charities rather seem to have been the result of a sense of duty than of any tenderness of nature." But whether or not he was motivated by compassion or the belief that God expected good works, his relationship with the laboring class was the product of pragmatism. Methodism chose to evangelize among them for the sole (and totally unideological) reason that they were neglected by the traditional priesthood. Wesley had no ideological view about the nature of eighteenth-century society. He certainly believed that modest living was a virtue, and from time to time he denounced the "quality" for their profligacy as well as their godless decadence. But he was happy to receive assistance from evangelically inclined aristocrats, and there was nothing in either his theology or his character that made him the enemy or friend of one social group. Wesley took what converts he could find: the coal miners of Kingswood, the fishermen of Norfolk, the tin miners of Cornwall and the weavers of the West Riding. That changing economy, which the Church of England refused to accept or even acknowledge, combined with Wesley's search for ready recruits, made Methodism crucially influential among the workers who were about to become the backbone of Victorian Britain.

Élie Halévy, in his classic *History of the English People in the Nineteenth Century*, judged that it was Methodism which held back the forces of violent resentment. "Why was it that of all the countries of Europe, England has been the most free from revolutions, violent crises and sudden changes? We have sought in vain to find the explanation by an analysis of her political institutions and economic organisation."[1] He went on to conclude that "the elite of the working class, the hard-working and capable bourgeoisie, had been imbued by the evangelical movement with a spirit from which the established order had nothing to fear."

Eric Hobsbawm, examining the nineteenth century from a different philosophic perspective, first quotes Lenin's explanation that a revolution needs, as well as a "deterioration in the conditions of life," a "crisis in the affairs of the ruling order and a body of revolutionaries capable of leading the movement." Those essential requirements, he argues, were not met in Britain for reasons wholly unrelated to Methodism and Methodists—not least (pace the Great Reform Act of 1832) the willingness of the "ruling order" to bend in the wind of popular dissatisfaction rather than allow it to break them. Hobsbawm then reinforces his argument with examinations of Methodist behavior in the areas where they were strongest. Some of them, in variance with what Halévy implied, were the leaders of popular agitations. "When Lord Londonderry evicted strikers after the 1844 coal strike, two-thirds of the Durham Primitive Methodist circuit became homeless."[2] However, the Wesleyan Methodists, from whom the "primitives" had separated, were at the same time "congratulating themselves because their members did not take part in strikes except under duress."

According to Charles Wesley, it was because of their Methodism that the colliers of Kingswood, although forced by class loyalty to take part in the Bristol grain riots of 1740 and 1753, conducted themselves with commendable restraint.[3] But that does no more than confirm Hobsbawm's conclusion that some Methodists were militant and others were not, that after the movement had begun to divide, it was impossible to attribute any political attitude to Wesley's posthumous influence and that the numbers of Methodists—Wesleyan, New Connexion, Primitive and Bible Christians—were never enough to have a significant effect on national attitudes. Prudently, Halévy insisted that "the influence of Wesleyan ideas was not confined to the 200,000 members of official Wesleyanism."[4] That judgment reveals a scholar's proper inclination toward understatement. To have influenced society against revolution in Wesley's own lifetime, Methodism would have had to have been far more firmly embedded in the working classes. It was the nineteenth century which Wesley and Wesleyanism helped to form.

After John Wesley's death, Methodism, which even in his day had been divided between believers in preordination and universal redemption, split into a series of factions for reasons which ranged from the autocracy of Wesley's successors to the heretical decision of the trustees of Leeds's Brunswick chapel to install an organ. However, John Wesley's influence on all the factions was immense. It had the effect of making Wesleyans of every stripe, reactionary and radical, preoccupied with propriety. Methodism made men and women respectable. And respectability was an essential element in the character of the aspiring working-class Victorians who built an empire abroad and prosperity at home.*

The connexion which Wesley had created had, in consequence,

---

* E. P. Thompson in *The Making of the English Working Class* described their attitude more critically. Nineteenth-century Methodists, he wrote, saw it as "their peculiar mission to act as apologists for child labour."

an influence in Great Britain which he neither intended nor anticipated. Because he preached that the whole Christian—the man or
woman sanctified by faith—aspired to be an "imitation" of Christ,
he influenced the character and conduct of his converts. Joseph
Priestley, scientist, Unitarian and fierce critic of Wesley's theology,
had no doubt about the influence Methodism had on both its members and the wider public who were impressed and influenced by the
way the Methodists behaved. "By you chiefly is the gospel preached
to the poor of this country and to you is the civilization, the industry and sobriety of great numbers of the laborious part of the community owing, though you are a body unknown to government and
look not to your rewards from men." That made John Wesley a
social as well as a religious revolutionary. But instead of Liberty,
Equality, Fraternity, he proclaimed Piety, Probity and Respectability.

The paradox of John Wesley's position was that although he encouraged the characteristics which led to prosperity, he was, at most,
ambivalent about those who achieved the fruits of hard work and sobriety. Good Methodists worked hard with the explicit intention of
enjoying material success. Yet once achieved, material success was,
he believed, usually inconsistent with sanctity. In old age he sadly reflected, "The Methodists in every place grow diligent and frugal.
Consequently they increase in goods. Hence they proportionally
increase in pride and anger, in the desires of the flesh, the desires of
the eyes and the pride of life. So, although the form of religion remains, the spirit is swiftly vanishing away."[5] And the richer a man became, the more Wesley disapproved of him. His sermon "The Use
of Money" denounced luxury and warned against "the dangers of
wealth." The paradox is most dramatically illustrated by the decision
of Robert Peel (father of the Tory prime minister) to employ only
Methodists as foremen in his cotton mill and calico printing factory.
The news that spread through Lancashire concerned the supervisors'
characters, not their convictions. Methodist virtues—respectability,
sobriety, responsibility—were seen as the prerequisites of success.
Wesley was so encouraged by Peel's decision that he made a special
visit to Lancashire. But as he left the mill, rejoicing in the high esteem in which his Methodists were held, he told the preachers who

had accompanied him that the owner's wealth made it extremely unlikely that he would ever enter the kingdom of heaven.

Although Methodism encouraged its working-class members to aspire to the status and habits of their "betters," Wesley was unremitting in his criticism of the "quality," a class of people whom he believed to be at best indolent and at worst corrupt. John Pawson, a Methodist preacher who wrote to defend Wesley's posthumous reputation, described him as having "far more charity in general in judging a person's reputation (except the rich and the great) than his brother had."[6] Wesley, in his lifetime, confirmed the parenthesis. "To speak the rough truth, I do not desire intercourse with any person of quality in England."[7]

Most persons of quality felt much the same about him. Indeed they detested Methodism in general. The duchess of Buckingham wrote to the countess of Huntingdon thanking her for supplying information about the revival. Her letter ended with her opinion of the new Christians. "Their doctrines are most repulsive and strongly tinctured with impertinence and disrespect towards their superiors. It is monstrous to be told that you have a heart as sinful as the common wretches which crawl the earth."[8]

Wesley was the enemy of the privileged classes but not because he was against privilege itself. He observed in them a tendency willfully to disregard the laws of God. The same morally fateful flaw was tragically obvious in the working classes, though they were slightly less culpable than their betters. However, they were guilty of a secular fault from which, by definition, the upper classes were immune. Workingmen demanded a voice in government. That, to John Wesley, was an insupportable pretension. The message which he spread among the lower orders was that they should aspire to achieve the economic status that was the reward of an upright existence but should not attempt to play a part in the political life of the nation. At first his followers accepted it. As a result, his disciples were exactly the men the country needed: diligent in their determination to improve, but constant in their modest conviction that they should aspire to copy their betters without challenging the hegemony of the ruling classes.

Doubts about middle-class morality did not prevent Wesley from advocating, and in some cases adopting, middle-class mores. Order and personal discipline were the mark of the virtuous Methodist. "Dying well," an essential element in the good life, required, as well as the joyful acceptance of God's will, up-to-date accounts. "From these words 'Set thy house in order,' I strongly exhort all who have not done so already to settle their temporal affairs without delay. It is a strange madness which still possesses many, that are in other respects men of understanding, who put off from day to day, till death comes in an hour when they looked not for it."[9]

The obsession with propriety grew as the fear of being associated with the Puritans of the Commonwealth diminished. Attending playhouses, dancing and playing cards—all regular activities of Wesley's youth—were forbidden. So was reading fiction, although exceptions were occasionally made for novels with a clear moral purpose. Methodists were thus denied the pleasure of reading *Sir Charles Grandison*, Samuel Richardson's portrayal of a "good man," which he wrote to complement his novels of good women. In volume 5, the eponymous hero writes: "Mrs. O'Hara is turned Methodist. Thank God she is anything that is serious. These people really have great merit with me in her conversion. I am sure that our own clergy are not as zealously in earnest as they. They have really given a face of religion to subterranean colliers, tinkers and the most profligate of men."

Methodists followed their leader. And Wesley had no more time for democracy than he had for frivolous literature. In 1768, *Free Thoughts on the Present State of Public Affairs*, his first political pamphlet, denounced John Wilkes, his claim to sit in Parliament and the riots which followed his exclusion from the House of Commons. But it also condemned "cobblers, tinkers, porters and hackney coachmen" who claimed the right "to instruct both the King and his council." He associated the demands for representation with the hope of patronage, the principle on which the eighteenth-century Parliament as well as the church did business, and the willingness to reap the rewards of corruption. So he ended the pamphlet with the boast that he "wanted no man's favour, having no hopes and no fears from any man." That, he thought, made him an honest and reliable judge of Wilkes's views on liberty.

> Encumbered with no religion and disappointed in his application for place and power, Wilkes had set up for patriot, vehemently inveighed against evil councillors and grievances and was paid in French *louis d'or* for his agitative services. Supposing things to take their natural course, they must go from bad to worse. The land will become a field of blood and many poor Englishmen will sheath their swords in each other's bowels for the diversion of their good neighbors.

The detestation of democracy was reflected in Wesley's changing judgment on the American War of Independence. When he began to fear that the demands for parliamentary representation might spread to Britain, he abandoned all sympathy with the colonists—Methodists or not—and accused them of "screaming of liberty till they were utterly distracted and their intellects quite confounded."[10] His *A Calm Address to Our American Colonies* extended the principle in a reflection of his father's views on the interregnum: "No governments under heaven are so despotic as the republican—no subjects are governed in so arbitrary a manner as those of a commonwealth."[11] He extended the thought in *Some Obstructions to Government.* "The greater the share the people have in Government, the less liberty, either civil or religious, does the nation generally enjoy."[12]

By the time that the Bastille was stormed in 1789, John Wesley was too old and too tired to react to what he would have undoubtedly believed, with Edmund Burke, to be "an irrational, unprincipled, proscribing, confiscating, plundering, ferocious, bloody, tyrannical democracy." He had made his views on France's imperial pretensions clear in 1744, when he had abandoned plans to travel north, so as to avoid being associated with "papists" who had been ordered to leave London in case they gave succor and support to an anticipated invasion.

To make sure that there were no doubts about his loyalty, Wesley had petitioned King George with a humble address. "Silver and gold, most of us must own, have we none. But such as we have, we humbly beg your majesty to accept together with our hearts and prayers." Sending the message in the name of the whole connexion amounts to an admission that Methodism had become a distinct organization separate from the Church of England. The message was carefully worded to minimize the risk that it would be used as proof that a church had been created within the church. However, the risk could not be completely eliminated. Nevertheless, despite his determination never to admit even the inclination to separation, the message was sent. In his head, as well as his heart, Wesley was a king's man even as he became increasingly detached from the king's church. He expected his followers to be the same. The king was ordained by God. The aristocracy could claim no such distinction. Even so, he did not want to disturb their place in the established order of things. He aspired to no more than to make them godly, and his only objection to their riches was his suspicion that their wealth encouraged behavior which jeopardized their chances of redemption.

Support for the crown made Wesley a patriot. When French invasion was again threatened, or at least feared, in the early months of 1759, 16 February was appointed a day of national prayer and fasting in the hope that an act of worship would encourage God to support England. Wesley responded to the call by preaching at five o'clock in the morning at Wandsworth, nine and three in Spitalfields and half past eight at the Foundry. The countess of Huntingdon attended the evening service and, when it was over, invited Wesley to preside at a prayer meeting which she had arranged in her house as a contribution to the patriotic effort. Charles Wesley and George Whitefield also took part, and the congregation was as distinguished as the preachers. It included the earl and countess of Dartmouth, the earl and countess of Chesterfield, Sir Charles and Lady Hotham and a variety of Cavendishes and Carterets. Patriotism and the belief that influential associates helped the connexion to prosper made Wesley participate in the event. Yet, true to his belief in the aristocracy's moral vulnerability, he chose as the text of his sermon an amalgamation of Isaiah 40:15 and 2 Kings 18:19, "O what are the greatest men to the great God? A small dust in the balance."

John Wesley was not a thoroughgoing or consistent iconoclast. There were times in his life when he was profoundly impressed by both wealth and distinction. But his ambivalence mirrored the attitude of his followers, men and women who simultaneously despised the rich men whose entry into heaven was unlikely and yet aspired, by hard work and plain dealing, to become like them. John Wesley wanted to encourage men and women to be more godly. When he spoke of "new men" being the necessary preparation for a "new world," the changes to which he referred were entirely spiritual.

His belief in strong government—men of destiny deciding the fate of followers who accepted the station to which God had called them—was reflected in the ruthless organization of his connexion. Methodism was connectional rather than congregational because it was emphatically not a collection of independent churches with independent rights to appoint their own ministers. Democracy was, to John Wesley, the work of the devil. Methodism, until old age sapped both Wesley's will and capacity to govern, was essentially an autocracy. And autocracy was his ideal of government. He appointed the preachers and nominated their stations. The meetinghouses were built and managed on principles which he laid down. The dogma of Methodism was set out in his lectures, sermons and pamphlets. The proper conduct of members of the societies was described by him, often in risible detail, before it was incorporated into the minutes of the annual conferences. Methodism was created in John Wesley's image, not as a reflection of its members' hopes and aspirations. Because it mirrored its leader's energy and determination, his connexion became the most dynamic and cohesive body of opinion in eighteenth-century England.

The scope as well as the nature of that achievement is easily misunderstood. John Wesley did not create a national mood of spiritual renewal. He did not even reinvigorate the Church of England, although in early middle age that was certainly his hope and intention. In his lifetime, the size and character of the Methodist membership (comparatively small numbers of the politically dispossessed, materially disadvantaged and spiritually disappointed) made it impossible for that ambition to be realized. Nor did he totally succeed in creating a "people's church." Toward the end of the nineteenth century, when William Booth raised the banner of another great evangelical campaign, he echoed John Wesley's complaint that the Church of England (living off its tithes and pew rents) would not go out into the streets and find souls to save. The founder of the Salvation Army believed that Methodists of every sort (studying for their doctorates) had fallen into the same error. But by then Methodism, in all its forms, was a religious force to be reckoned with.

Certainty—of both God's love and his own special role in promoting its understanding—made him hated by the Calvinists, parts of the Established Church and some of his colleagues in the Great Revival. It might even have contributed to the hatred his wife felt for him toward the end of her life. It also made him both loved and revered by the thousands of followers who heard him preach and joined him in prayer. Without their affection he could not have founded his new church and become the leader of the Second Reformation. They both admired him and aspired to become the "whole Christians" who, by Wesley's reckoning, were at least on the route to heaven even if their arrival could not be guaranteed. Because they imitated as well as followed him, they became a vital influence on the character of nineteenth-century society. Methodism encouraged the working poor to be ambitious, industrious and respectable, the qualities which made them the indispensable backbone of industrial and imperial England.

Had John Wesley done no more than found the Methodist Church, he would have deserved a place in the pantheon of great Englishmen. What he created and led was strong enough to survive his death. The membership rolls of the connexion in Great Britain and Northern Ireland exploded from 79,000 in 1791 (the year Wesley died) to 230,000 in 1815. And there were another 210,000 Methodists in North America. For the rest of the century membership steadily increased on both sides of the Atlantic, and Methodism, the manifestation of the Second Reformation, embedded itself in the life of Victorian England. Although founded in the eighteenth century, it became an essentially nineteenth-century institution which not so much illustrated the values of the age as helped to shape them. Not in his own lifetime, but certainly by proxy during the hundred years which followed his death, Wesley was one of the architects of modern England. John Wesley's Second Reformation created a new church and helped to build a new nation.

AUTHOR'S NOTE

John Wesley's *Journals and Diaries*, edited by Nehemiah Curnock, were published in eight volumes in 1909. An eight-volume edition of John Wesley's *Letters*, edited by John Telford, was published in 1931. The Curnock and Telford editions remain the most accessible editions of both the *Journal* and *Letters* and wherever possible, they are the sources quoted in the text.

However, in recent years Frank Baker, Richard Heitzenrater, Albert Oulter and Reginald Ward have published material which does not appear in the Curnock and Telford editions. Additional entries in the coded diaries have been deciphered. The notes clearly distinguish between the different, but equally authoritative, sources.

One small, but frequently repeated, alteration to Wesley's original work must be reported. He was devoted to the colon and semicolon. I am not. In consequence, his complete sentences have been ended with the full stops which he neglected.

NOTES AND REFERENCES

ABBREVIATIONS

Green   V. H. H. Green, *The Young Mr. Wesley* (London: Arnold, 1961)

Heitz   R. P. Heitzenrater, *Wesley and the People Called Methodists* (Nashville: Abingdon Press, 1995)

Journal Nehemiah Curnock, ed., *The Journal of Rev. John Wesley* (London: Epworth Press, 1995)

Letters John Telford, ed., *The Letters of John Wesley* (London: Epworth Press, 1931)

Rack   Henry Rack, *Reasonable Enthusiast: John Wesley and the Rise of Methodism* (Abingdon Press, 1992)

Southey *The Life of Wesley and the Rise and Progress of Methodism*, Devonshire edition with notes by J. A. Atkinson and biographical essay by Alexander Knox (London: Frederick Warne & Co., 1889)

Telford J. Telford, *The Life of John Wesley* (London: Wesleyan Methodist Book Room, 1899)

Tyerman Luke Tyerman, *The Life and Times of the Reverend John Wesley* (London: Hodder & Stoughton, 1870, 3 vols.)

Wallace Charles Wallace, Jr. ed., *Susanna Wesley: The Complete Writings* (New York: Oxford University Press, 1997)

References to the bicentennial edition of John Wesley's *Collected Works* (Nashville and Abingdon) appear as "B-works," preceded by the name of the editor of the volume.

CHAPTER 2   AMONG OUR FOREFATHERS

1. Southey, p. 3 (note).
2. Matthew, *Calumny Revisited* (London: 1832), p. 457.
3. Ibid.
4. Samuel Wesley, Sr., "A Defence of a Letter Concerning the Education of Dissenters at Their Private Academies," in R. Heitzenrater, *Mirror and Memory: Reflections of Early Methodism* (Nashville: Kingswood Books, 1989).
5. Samuel Wesley, Sr., "Letter from a Country Divine," ibid.
6. Southey, p. 5.
7. Ibid.
8. Tyerman, vol. 1, p. 30.
9. Edmund MacClure and William Osborn Bird Allen, (eds.), *Two Hundred Years: The Hisory of the Society for Promoting Christian Knowledge,* London, 1898.
10. John Wickham Legg, *The English Church from the Restoration to the Tractarian Movement* (Longmans & Co., London, 1914), p. 292.
11. J. H. Plumb, *England in the Nineteenth Century* (Penguin, 1950).
12. Heitzenrater, *Mirror and Memory,* p. 44.
13. Samuel Wesley, Sr., "Letters Concerning Religious Societies," in Heitzenrater, *Mirror and Memory,* loc. cit.
14. Wallace, p. 35.
15. Ibid., p. 36.
16. Ibid., p. 37.
17. Ibid., p. 38.

CHAPTER 3   THE SOUL OF THIS CHILD

1. Wallace, p. 38.
2. Ibid., p. 40.
3. Norman Sykes, *William Wake: Archbishop of Canterbury* 1657–1737, Cambridge, 1957. p. 48.
4. Rack, p. 46.
5. Green, p. 48.
6. Southey, p. 11.
7. Ibid., p. 98.
8. Wallace, p. 52.
9. Clarke, *Memoirs of the Wesley Family* (London: 1823).
10. Wallace, p. 67.

11. Ibid.
12. Ibid.
13. Grace Elizabeth Harrison, *Son to Susanna: The Private Life of John Wesley* (London: Nicholson & Watson, 1937), p. 57.
14. Wallace, p. 67.
15. *Arminian* magazine, No. 1 (1778).
16. Harrison, *Son to Susanna*, p. 57.
17. Southey, p. 11.
18. Rack, p. 67.
19. Susanna Wesley's Papers, Wesley College, Bristol.
20. Wallace, p. 67.
21. Ibid.
22. Telford, p. 18.
23. Ibid.
24. Wallace, p. 370.
25. Ibid., p. 369.
26. Ibid.
27. Telford, p. 21.
28. Wallace, p. 370.
29. Ibid., p. 382.
30. Tyerman, vol. 1, p. 317.
31. Clarke, *Wesley Family*
32. Tyerman, vol. 1, p. 412.
33. Green, p. 57.
34. Southey, Note VI.
35. *Arminian* magazine, no. 1 1778, pp. 448–50, 606–08, 654–56.
36. Telford, p. 27.
37. Ibid.
38. Tyerman, vol 1., p. 21.
39. Henry Moore, *Life of the Reverend John Wesley* (London: 1824), vol. 1, p. 117.
40. Telford, p. 30.

CHAPTER 4   BEAUTY AND VIRTUE

1. W. Ward and R. Heitzenrater, Bicentennial-works (1988), vol. 7, p. 310.
2. Letters, vol. 1, p. 8.
3. Ibid., p. 30.
4. Wallace, p. 103.

5. Letters, vol. 1, p. 9.
6. Ibid., p. 31.
7. Wallace, p. 105.
8. Tyerman, vol. 1, p. 44.
9. Wallace, p. 105.
10. Telford, p. 35.
11. Tyerman, vol. 1, p. 11.
12. Cheyne, *Book of Health and Long Life* (Newcastle-upon-Tyne: Oriel Press, 1976), p. 95.
13. Ibid.
14. *Westminster Magazine* 1774, p. 180.
15. Tyerman, vol. 1, p. 13.
16. Ibid., p. 14.
17. Ibid., p. 10.
18. John Reynolds, *Anecdotes of the Reverend John Wesley*, p. 5 (London, 1828).
19. Tyerman, vol. 1, p. 8.
20. Ibid., vol 2, p. 12.
21. Ibid., vol. 3, p. 141.
22. Henry Moore, *Life of Rev. Charles Wesley*, vol. 2, p. 366.
23. Journal, vol. 1, p. 467.
24. Ibid., p. 469.
25. Frank Baker, *The Works of John Wesley* (Oxford, 1980) vol. 25.
26. Ibid., p. 160.
27. Ibid., p. 154.
28. Ibid., p. 160.
29. Green, p. 65.
30. Ibid.
31. John Whitehead, *Life of John Wesley* (London: 1793), vol. 1, p. 384.
32. Ward and Heitzenrater, B-works, (1976), vol. 18, p. 244.
33. Letters, vol. 1, p. 40.
34. John Pollock, *John Wesley* (Australia: 1992), p. 40.
35. Ibid.
36. Green, p. 208.
37. *Wesleyan Magazine* (1845).
38. Rack, p. 79.
39. Letters, vol. 1, p. 56.
40. Ibid., p. 72.
41. Ibid., p. 92.
42. Ibid., p. 16.

43. Green., p. 80.
44. Journal, vol. 1, p. 466.
45. Green, p. 112.
46. Letters, vol. 1, p. 23.
47. Tyerman, vol. 1, p. 44.
48. Whitehead, *John Wesley*, vol. 1, p. 355.
49. A. Oulter, Bicentennial-works, 2003, vol. 1, p. 4.
50. Green, p. 80.
51. Tyerman, vol. 1, p. 46.
52. Ibid.
53. Green, p. 83.
54. Letters, vol. 1, p. 30.
55. Sir Arthur Thomas, Quiller Couch, *Hetty Wesley* (London, 1903), p. 154.
56. Ibid.
57. Green, p. 110.
58. Ibid.
59. Whitehead, *John Wesley*, vol. 1, p. 40.
60. Green, p. 118.
61. Ibid., p. 119.
62. Ibid., p. 121.
63. Ibid., p. 122.
64. Ibid.

CHAPTER 5   EVERY WIND OF DOCTRINE

1. Journal, vol. 1, p. 89.
2. Green, p. 145.
3. Telford, p. 58.
4. John Whitehead, *John Wesley*, vol. 1, p. 420.
5. J. H. Overton, *John Wesley*, Methuen, London, 1891, p. 28.
6. Benjamin Ingham, *The Diary of an Oxford Methodist* (Durham, N.C.: Duke University Press, 1985), p. 12.
7. Letters, vol. 1, p. 152.
8. Journal, vol. 1, p. 55.
9. Heitz, p. 52.
10. Telford, p. 61.
11. Thomas Jackson, *Works of Reverend John Wesley*, vol. 7, p. 21.
12. Ibid., vol. 1, p. 99.
13. Letters, vol. 1, p. 48.

14. Journal, vol. 4, p. 409.
15. Jackson, *Works*, vol. 2, p. 367.
16. F. Baker, *John Wesley as Revealed by His Letters* (Epworth Press, London, 1948), vol. 1, p. 168.
17. Ibid.
18. Ibid., p. 377.
19. Ibid., p. 378.
20. Journal, vol. 8, p. 281.
21. Letters, vol. 1, p. 120.
22. Ibid., p. 122.
23. Ibid., p. 121.
24. Ibid., p. 143.
25. Ibid., p. 147.
26. Ibid., p. 154.
27. Ibid., p. 149.
28. Ibid., p. 134.
29. Ibid.
30. Rack, p. 94.
31. Letters, vol. 1, p. 182 (note).
32. *Wesleyan Times* (28 October 1861).
33. A. L. Maddox ed., *Aldersgate Reconsidered* (Nashville: Kingswood Books, 1990), p. 61.

CHAPTER 6   THE FAITH OF A SERVANT

1. *House of Commons Journal*, 1729.
2. Luke Tyerman, *The Oxford Methodists* (London, 1873), p. 64.
3. Moore, *Life of John Wesley*, vol. 1, p. 204.
4. Heitz, p. 57.
5. Letters, vol. 1, p. 190.
6. Heitz, p. 58.
7. Journal, vol. 8, pp. 285–88.
8. Ibid., vol. 1, p. 138.
9. Ibid., p. 140.
10. Ibid.
11. Ibid., p. 142.
12. Ibid.
13. Telford, p. 77.
14. Journal, vol. 1, p. 124.
15. Southey, p. 57.

16. Ibid., p. 58.
17. *Diaries of Lord Egmont* (London: 1923) vol. 4, p. 313.
18. Heitz, p. 62.
19. Fitchett, *Wesley and His Century* (Smith Elder and Company, 1906), p. 102.
20. Journal, vol. 1, p. 234.
21. Green, *John Wesley*, p. 45.
22. Journal, vol. 1, p. 307.
23. Heitz, p. 63.
24. Telford, p. 81.
25. Journal, vol. 1.
26. Ward and Heitzenrater, Bicentennial-works, vol. 18, p. 204. The entry in Curnock edition differs.
27. Journal, vol. 1, p. 352.
28. Ibid.
29. Ibid., p. 424.
30. Baker, *Letters*, vol. 1, p. 454.
31. Rack, p. 157.
32. Southey, p. 52.
33. Ward and Heitzenrater, B-works, vol. 9, p. 209.
34. Kenneth J., Collins, *A Real Christian* (Nashville: Abingdon Press, 1999), p. 45.
35. Ibid.
36. Journal, vol. 1, p. 315.
37. Ibid., p. 323.
38. Journal, vol. 1, p. 315.
39. Rack, p. 125.
40. Collins, *A Real Christian*, p. 48.
41. Journal, vol. 1, p. 333.
42. Ibid., p. 334.
43. Ibid., p. 367.
44. Ibid., p. 379.
45. Ibid., p. 391.
46. Ibid., p. 397.
47. Ibid., p. 399.
48. Ibid., p. 393.
49. Ibid., p. 207.
50. Rack, p. 132.
51. Ibid, p. 133.
52. Ibid.

CHAPTER 7   RITES AND CEREMONIES

1. T. Jackson, ed., *Journal of Charles Wesley* (Kansas City: Beacon Hill Press, 1980), vol. 1, p. 115.
2. Baker, B–Works, vol. 25, p. 526.
3. Murray, ed., George Whitefield's Journals, (Edinburgh: Banner of Truth Trust, 1960), p. 157.
4. Rack, p. 137.
5. *Wesleyan Magazine* (1854), p. 96.
6. Heitz, p. 77.
7. Journal, vol. 1, p. 455.
8. Southey, p. 86.
9. V. H. H. Green, *John Wesley* (London: Nelson, 1964), p. 72.
10. Letters, vol. 1, p. 289.
11. Ibid., p. 240.
12. Collins, *A Real Christian*, p. 60.
13. *Jackson Journal of Charles Wesley*, p. 88.
14. Ibid.
15. Ibid., p. 146.
16. Ibid.
17. Journal, vol. 1, p. 475.
18. John Wesley, *Oulter*, p. 51.
19. Journal, vol. 1, p. 480.
20. Ibid., vol. 2, p. 125.
21. Letters, vol. 1, p. 250.
22. Ibid., p. 251.
23. Journal, vol. 2, p. 13.
24. Telford, p. 110.
25. Letters, vol. 1, p. 255.
26. Ibid., p. 262.
27. Collins, *A Real Christian* (London: Adams & Co., 1856), p. 68.
28. Daniel Benham, *Memoirs of James Hutton*, p. 40.
29. Letters, vol. 1, p. 286.
30. Telford, p. 117.
31. Journal, vol. 2, p. 167.
32. Ibid., p. 172.
33. Murray, *George Whitefield's Journals*, p. 240
34. Telford, p. 130.
35. Journal, vol. 2, p. 221.
36. Baker, B–works, vol. 25, p. 542.

37. Ibid., p. 694.
38. Ibid., p. 660.
39. Ibid.
40. Letters, vol. 1, p. 354 (note).
41. Wallace, p. 16.
42. Rack, p. 210.

CHAPTER 8   THE ALMOST CHRISTIAN

1. Journal, vol., 2, p. 211.
2. Telford, p. 126.
3. Letters, vol. 1, p. 258.
4. Tyerman, vol. 1, p. 279.
5. Ibid., p. 297.
6. Ibid.
7. Journal, vol. 2, p. 327.
8. Ibid., p. 312.
9. A. Oulter, ed., *Sermons* (Nashville: Abingdon Press, 1984), vol. 2, p. 137–39.
10. Collins, *A Real Christian*, p. 74.
11. Ibid.
12. Journal, vol. 2, p. 328.
13. Ibid.
14. Tyerman, vol. 1, p. 298.
15. Ibid., p. 299.
16. Journal, vol. 2, p. 401.
17. Tyerman, vol. 1, p. 303.
18. Journal, vol. 2, p. 366.
19. Ibid.
20. Heitz, p. 112.
21. Journal, vol. 2, p. 35.
22. Letters, vol. 1, p. 302.
23. Rack, p. 199.
24. Ibid., p. 198.
25. Tyerman, vol. 1, p. 311.
26. Journal, vol. 2, p. 353.
27. Ibid., p. 185.
28. Tyerman, vol. 1, p. 318.
29. Ibid., p. 319.
30. Telford, p. 130.

31. Tyerman, vol. 1, p. 316.
32. Ibid.
33. Ibid., p. 320.
34. Ibid., p. 342.
35. Heitz, p. 121.
36. Telford, p. 142.
37. Journal, vol. 2, p. 423.
38. Ibid.
39. Tyerman, vol. 1, p. 325.

CHAPTER 9   ALL THINGS HIMSELF

1. Journal, vol. 2, p. 274.
2. Ward and Heitzenrater, B-works, vol. 19, p. 96.
3. Telford, p. 175.
4. Ibid.
5. Ibid., p. 176.
6. Moore, *Life of John Wesley*, vol. 2, p. 3.
7. A. Oulter, *John Wesley's Sermons* (Library of Protestant Thought, 1970), vol. 6, p. 393.
8. Journal, vol. 3, p. 98.
9. Ibid.
10. Ibid., p. 100.
11. Ibid., p. 101.
12. Ibid.
13. Journal, vol. 2, p. 257 (note).
14. Thomas Jackson, *Lives of Early Methodist Preachers* (London: Wesleyan Conference Office, 1849), vol. 1, p. 14.
15. Journal, vol. 3, p. 14.
16. Tyerman, vol. 1, p. 393.
17. Journal, vol. 3, p. 19.
18. John Hampson, *Memoirs of the Late John Wesley* (Sunderland, 1791), vol. 2, p. 91.
19. John Harrold Whiteley, *Wesley's England* (London: Epsworth Press, 1938), p. 64.
20. Ibid.
21. Hampson, *Memoirs of the Late John Wesley*, vol. 2, p. 190.
22. Tyerman, vol. 2, p. 212.
23. Journal, vol. 6, p. 119.
24. Ibid.

25. Jackson, Sermon 60, *Collected Works*, vol. 6, p. 248.
26. Journal, vol. 5, p. 360.
27. Ibid., vol. 3, p. 388.

CHAPTER 10   ASHAMED OF NOTHING

1. Telford, p. 145.
2. Ibid.
3. Journal, vol. 3, p. 67.
4. Tyerman, vol. 1, p. 391.
5. Journal, vol. 3, p. 31.
6. Heitz, p. 119.
7. Jackson, *Lives of Early Methodist Preachers*, p. 258.
8. Jackson, *Journal of Charles Wesley*, vol. 1, p. 267.
9. John Wesley, *Methodist Societies: History, Nature and Design*, (Nashville: Abingdon Press, 1989).
10. Journal, vol. 2, p. 84.
11. Ibid., p. 86.
12. Ibid.
13. Jackson, *Journal of Charles Wesley*, vol. 1, p. 333.
14. Journal, vol. 3, p. 143 (note).
15. Tyerman, vol. 1, p. 444.
16. Journal, vol. 3, p. 144.
17. Ibid. (note).
18. Journal, vol. 3, p. 144.
19. Jackson, *Works*, vol. 8, p. 276.
20. Ibid. p. 293.
21. Letters, vol. 2, p. 64.
22. Moore, *Life of John Wesley*, vol. 2, p. 297.
23. Tyerman, vol. 1, p. 508.
24. Jackson, *Works*, vol. 8, p. 293.
25. Letters, vol. 2, p. 90.
26. Tyerman, vol. 1, p. 509.
27. Jackson, *Journal of Charles Wesley*, vol. 1, p. 303.
28. Letters, vol. 2, p. 18.
29. Jackson, *Journal of Charles Wesley*, vol. I, p. 249.

CHAPTER 11   ALONG THE FLOWERY WAY

1. Journal, vol. 3, p. 323.
2. Ibid., p. 395.
3. Ibid., p. 273.
4. Ibid., p. 336.
5. G. Smith, ed., *History of Methodist Church in Great Britain* (London: Longman, 1862), vol. 4, p. 649.
6. Minutes of Methodist Conference, 1748.
7. Tyerman, vol. 2, p. 9.
8. Ibid., vol. 1, p. 562.
9. Ibid.
10. Southey, p. 430.
11. Ibid.
12. Rack, p. 228.
13. Élie Halévy, *History of English People in Nineteenth Century* (Ernst Benn, 1924), vol. I, p. 462.
14. John Brand, *History and Antiquities of the Town and County of the Town of Newcastle*, (London: White & Son, 1789).
15. Letters, vol. 2, p. 41.
16. Ibid.
17. Ibid., p. 51.
18. Tyerman, vol. 1, p. 505.
19. Jackson, *Journal of Charles Wesley*, vol. 2, p. 36.
20. Ibid.
21. Journal, vol. 3, p. 112.
22. Tyerman, vol. 2, p. 45.
23. Ibid., p. 46.
24. Jackson, *Journal of Charles Wesley*, vol. 1, p. 224.
25. Telford, p. 246.
26. Ibid.
27. Ibid.
28. Rack, p. 260.
29. Telford, p. 241.
30. Journal, vol. 3, p. 435 (note).
31. Ibid.
32. Ibid.
33. Ibid., p. 439.
34. Telford, p. 249.
35. Journal, vol. 3, p. 512.

36. Ibid., p. 514.
37. Ibid., p. 512.
38. *Gentleman's Magazine* (February 1751).
39. John Pollock, *John Wesley* (Oxford: Lion Publishing, 1989), p. 204.
40. Journal, vol. 3, p. 514 (note).
41. Telford, p. 252.
42. Hampson, *Life of John Wesley*, vol. 2, p. 262.
43. Journal, vol. 3, p. 512.
44. Ibid.
45. Ibid.
46. Ibid.
47. Baker, *Letters*, vol. 26, p. 451.
48. Ward and Heitzenrater, B-works, vol. 20, p. 200 (note).
49. Letters, vol. 3, p. 65.
50. Baker, *Letters*, vol. 26, p. 456.
51. Ibid., p. 457.
52. Journal, vol. 3, p. 517.
53. Letters, vol. 3, p. 65.

CHAPTER 12   EXTRAORDINARY PROPHETS

1. Letters, vol. 2, p. 148.
2. Heitz, p. 183.
3. Ibid., p. 185.
4. Ibid., p. 184.
5. Ibid., p. 185.
6. Moore, *John Wesley*, vol. 3, p. 226.
7. Heitz, p. 184.
8. Tyerman, vol. 2, p. 129.
9. Ibid., p. 137.
10. Thomas Jackson, *Life of Charles Wesley* (London, 1841), vol. 2, p. 576.
11. Journal, vol. 4, p. 11 (note).
12. Ibid., p. 52.
13. Tyerman, vol. 2, p. 162.
14. Ibid.
15. Ibid., p. 176.
16. Journal, vol. 4, p. 90.
17. Letters, vol. 4, p. 150.
18. Ibid., p. 148.
19. Collins, *A Real Christian*, p. 98.

20. Ibid.
21. Letters, vol. 3, p. 289.
22. Ibid., p. 35.
23. Baker, *Letters*, vol. 24, p. 491.
24. Letters, vol. 3, p. 131.
25. Thomas Jackson, *Lives of Early Methodist Preachers* (London, 1837–8), vol. 2, p. 7.
26. Leslie Frederick Church, *The Early Methodist People* (London: Epworth Press, 1948), p. 132.
27. F., Baker, *William Grimshaw* (London: Epworth Press, 1963), p. 183.
28. Church, *Early Methodist People*, p. 5.
29. Baker, *William Grimshaw*, p. 249.
30. Tyerman, vol. 2, p. 207.
31. Jackson, *Journal of Charles Wesley*, vol. 2, p. 116.
32. Letters, vol. 3, p. 144.
33. Tyerman, vol. 2, p. 208.
34. Ibid.
35. Letters, vol. 3, p. 143 (note).
36. R. Davies, ed., *The Methodist Societies*. Bicentennial Edition of Works. (Nashville: Abingdon, 1989), vol. 9, pp. 569–73.
37. Rack, p. 299.
38. Letters, vol. 3, p. 186.
39. Jackson, *Journal of Charles Wesley*, vol. 2, p. 131.
40. Letters, vol. 3, p. 195.
41. Heitz, p. 194.
42. Tyerman, vol. 2, p. 245.
43. Ibid., p. 247.

CHAPTER 13   THINGS I DISLIKE

1. Telford, p. 254.
2. Jackson, *Journal of Charles Wesley*, vol. 2, p. 247.
3. Letters, vol. 3, p. 65.
4. *Letters* (Baker), vol. 26, p. 455.
5. Ibid.
6. Letters, vol. 3, p. 68.
7. Tyerman, vol. 2, p. 285.
8. Stanley Ayling, *John Wesley* (Nashville: Abingdon Press, 1979), p. 224.
9. Letters, vol. 4, p. 4.
10. Baker, *Letters*, vol. 26, p. 494.

11. Tyerman, vol. 2, p. 109.
12. Ibid., p. 110.
13. Telford, p. 256.
14. Heitz, p. 181.
15. Journal, vol. 4, p. 303.
16. Charles Wesley (Letters), p. 99.
17. Frank Baker, *John Wesley and the Church of England* (London: Epworth Press, 1963), p. 134.
18. Frank Baker, *William Grimshaw*, p. 250.
19. Reverend Tom Benyon, *Howell Harris: Reformer and Soldier* (Caernarvon: The Calvinistic Methodist Bookroom, 1958).
20. Heitz, p. 209.
21. Letters, vol. 4, p. 99.
22. Rack, p. 335.
23. Tyerman, vol. 2, p. 417.
24. Oulter, *Sermons* vol. 1, p. 328.
25. Journals, vol. 4, p. 535.
26. Tyerman, vol. 2, p. 432.
27. *Arminian Magazine* (1790) p. 42.
28. Southey, p. 418 (note).
29. Tyerman, vol. 2, p. 433.
30. Journal, vol. 4, p. 539.
31. Ibid., p. 535.
32. Ibid., p. 537.
33. Ibid., vol. 5, p. 5.
34. Tyerman, vol 2, p. 462.
35. Ibid.
36. Tyerman, p. 402
37. *Methodist Magazine* (1797), p. 35.
38. Southey, p. 418.
39. Journal, vol. 5, p. 10.
40. Ibid., p. 12.

CHAPTER 14   CHURCH OF ENGLAND MAN

1. Journal, vol. 5, p. 47.
2. Ibid., p. 39.
3. Letters, vol. 4, p. 305.
4. Baker, *John Wesley and the Church of England*, p. 783.
5. Letters, vol. 3, p. 224.

6. Letters, vol. 4, p. 243.
7. Baker, *John Wesley and the Church of England*, p. 180.
8. Letters, vol. 4, p. 147.
9. *Arminian Magazine* (1781), p. 219.
10. Heitz, p. 216.
11. 7 December 1764.
12. Baker, *John Wesley and the Church of England*, p. 208.
13. Minutes of Methodist Conference, pp. 51–52.
14. Tyerman, vol. 2, p. 578.
15. Letters, vol. 5, p. 16.
16. Journal, vol. 5, p. 244.
17. Sermon 128.
18. Oulter, *Sermons*, vol. 2, p. 161.
19. Letters, vol. 3, p. 163.
20. Ibid.
21. Jackson, *Works*, vol. 4, p. 409.
22. Journal, vol. 4, p. 203.
23. Rack, p. 445.
24. Heitz, p. 217.
25. Ibid.
26. Clive Field, "The Social Structure of English Methodism: Eighteenth-Twentieth Centuries," *British Journal of Sociology*, vol. 28 (June 1977), pp. 199–225.
27. Collins, *A Real Christian*, p. 122.
28. Tyerman, vol. 4, p. 15.
29. Ibid., p. 49.

CHAPTER 15   THROW AWAY THE SCABBARD

1. Letters, vol. 5, p. 47.
2. Ibid., p. 9.
3. Ibid., p. 49.
4. Ibid., p. 108.
5. Ibid., p. 86.
6. Ibid., p. 65.
7. Ibid., p. 105.
8. Journal, vol. 5, p. 282.
9. Tyerman, vol. 1, p. 526.
10. Journal, vol. 5, p. 111 (note).
11. Ibid., p. 159.

12. Collins, *A Real Christian*, p. 127.
13. Tyerman, vol. 3, p. 83.
14. Journal, vol. 5, p. 243.
15. Tyerman, vol. 3, p. 73.
16. Letters, vol. 5, p. 252.
17. Ibid.
18. Tyerman, vol. 3, p. 77.
19. Ibid.
20. Ibid., p. 24.
21. Ibid., p. 96.
22. Ibid., p. 99.
23. Journal, vol. 5, p. 425.
24. Whitehead, *John Wesley*, vol. 2, p. 394.
25. Tyerman, vol. 3, p. 103.
26. Letters, vol. 6, p. 51.
27. Collins, *A Real Christian*, p. 138.
28. Tyerman, vol. 3, p. 160.
29. *Lloyd's Evening Post* 2 April 1773.
30. Tyerman, vol. 3, p. 213.
31. Letters, vol. 6, p. 10.
32. Ibid., p. 35.
33. Ibid.
34. Tyerman, vol. 3, p. 212.
35. Letters, vol. 6, p. 272.
36. Telford, p. 261.
37. Southey, p. 537.
38. Journal, vol. 6, p. 169.
39. Letters, p. 250.
40. Journal, p. 144.
41. Ibid., p. 263.
42. Smith, *History of Methodist Christian Britain*, vol. 4, p. 190.

CHAPTER 16   SHEEP WITHOUT A SHEPHERD

1. J., Kent, *Holding the Fort* (London: Epworth Press, 1978).
2. Journal, vol. 4, p. 227.
3. Southey, p. 461.
4. Benjamin Franklin, *Correspondence*, vol. 1, p. 158.
5. Letters, vol. 5, p. 45.
6. Journal, vol. 5, p. 290.

7. Southey, p. 461.
8. Smith, *History of the Methodist Church in Britain*, vol. 10, p. 57.
9. Rack, p. 487.
10. Journal, vol. 6, p. 55.
11. Tyerman, vol. 3, p. 185.
12. Jackson, *Works*, vol. 11, p. 83.
13. Letters, vol. 6, p. 161.
14. James Boswell, *Life of Johnson* (London: Charles Dilly, 1791).
15. *Gentleman's Magazine* (1797), p. 455.
16. Olivers, *A Full Defense of Reverend John Wesley* (London, 1823).
17. Tyerman, vol. 3, p. 92.
18. Southey, pp. 467–68.
19. Tyerman, vol. 3, p. 235.
20. A. C. Oulter, *Asbury's Journals* (Nashville: Abingdon Press, 1971), vol. 3 p. 62.
21. Southey, p. 463.
22. Tyerman, vol. 3, p. 193.
23. Southey, p. 465.
24. Ibid., p. 468.
25. Tyerman, vol. 3, p. 248.
26. A. C. Oulter, *Asbury's Journals*, vol. 1, p. 304.
27. Ibid., p. 25.
28. Journal, vol. 6, p. 330.
29. Tyerman, vol. 3, p. 332.
30. Letters, vol. 7, p. 29.
31. Tyerman, vol. 3, p. 330.
32. Letters, vol. 6, p. 371.
33. Journal, vol. 6, p. 301.
34. Tyerman, vol. 3, p. 335.
35. Baker, *John Wesley and the Church of England*, p. 261.
36. Tyerman, vol. 3, p. 335.
37. Ibid., p. 333.
38. Rack, p. 508.
39. Tyerman, vol. 3, p. 214.
40. Journal, vol. 6, p. 476.
41. Oulter, *Sermons*, vol. 2, p. 493.
42. Letters, vol. 7, p. 238.
43. A. C. Oulter, *Asbury's Journals*, vol. 3, p. 63.
44. Southey, p. 476.

45. J., Vickers, *Thomas Coke: Apostle of Methodism* (Nashville: Abingdon, 1969), p. 116.
46. Letters, vol. 8, p. 91.
47. Ibid., p. 183.
48. Ibid., p. 91.
49. Ibid., p. 183.

CHAPTER 17   PRAISE WHILE I HAVE BREATH

1. Southey, p. 580.
2. Ibid., annex 1.
3. Jackson, *Charles Wesley*, vol. 2, p. 394.
4. Letters, vol. 7, p. 285.
5. Ibid., p. 288.
6. Ibid., p. 179.
7. Ibid., p. 203.
8. Baker, *John Wesley and the Church of England*, p. 259.
9. Letters, vol. 8, p. 23.
10. Ibid., p. 326.
11. Ibid., p. 327.
12. Oulter, *Sermons*, vol. 3, p. 130.
13. Ibid., p. 497.
14. Journal, vol. 7, p. 436.
15. Oulter, *Sermons*, vol. 3, p. 527.
16. Ward and Heitzenrater, B-works, vol. 23, p. 235.
17. Ibid.
18. Tyerman, vol. 3, p. 523.
19. Letters, vol. 8, p. 42.
20. Ibid., p. 41.
21. Ibid., p. 42.
22. Tyerman, vol. 3, p. 526.
23. Letters, vol. 8, p. 49.
24. Ibid., p. 51.
25. Moore, *JohnWesley*, vol. 2, p. 171.
26. Telford, p. 342.
27. Ibid.
28. Ward and Heitzenrater, Bicentennial-works, vol. 23, p. 179.
29. Journal, vol. 8, p. 17.
30. Letters, vol. 8, p. 17.
31. Ibid., p. 58.

32. Ibid., p. 59.
33. Methodist Societies, *History, Nature and Design*, p. 540.
34. Letters, vol. 8, p. 131.
35. Ibid., p. 133.
36. Jackson, *Lives of Early Methodist Preachers*, p. 418.
37. Letters, vol. 3, p. 510.
38. Letters, vol. 8, p. 257.
39. Journal, vol. 8, p. 134.
40. Letters, vol. 8, p. 265.
41. Journal, vol. 8, p. 134.
42. Ibid.

CHAPTER 18   TINCTURED WITH IMPERTINENCE

1. Elie Halévy, *History of the English People in the Nineteenth Century* (Ernst Benn, S.1. 1924).
2. Eric Hobsbawm, *Labouring Men* (London, Weidenfeld & Nicolson 1986), p. 24.
3. Halévy, *History of the English People*, vol. 1.
4. Ibid.
5. John Harrold Plumb, *England in the Eighteenth Century* (Hammondsworth: Penguin Books, 1950), p. 97.
6. Rack, p. 541.
7. John Harrold Plumb, *England in the Eighteenth Century* (Hammondsworth: Penguin Books, 1950), p. 92.
8. Gibbs, *Complete Peerage*, vol. 2, p. 40.
9. Tyerman, vol. 3, p. 15.
10. Ibid., p. 187.
11. Thomas Jackson ed. *The Journal of the Reverend John Wesley* (London: Wesleyan Conference Office, 1903).
12. Ibid., p. 105.

INDEX

435

Locke, John—*continued*
  Toleration, 10; *On the
  Reasonableness of Christianity*, 84;
  Thoughts on Education, 29
Lodder, 189
Lollards, 148
London Magazine, 244
London, 96, 145–6, 150, 161, 165,
  166, 203, 214, 228, 291, 336;
  Aldersgate Street, 136–7, 139,
  143; Bedlam, 150; Bethnal Green,
  359; Blackheath, 150;
  Bloomsbury, 140; Bunhill Fields,
  199, 388; Camberwell, 343;
  Chelsea, 256; Christ Church,
  Spitalfields, 275; City Road, 344,
  345, 346, 388, 395, 398;
  Colebrook Row, 389; Dean's
  Yard, 40; Deptford, 153, 165;
  Fetter Lane, 133, 146, 157, 163;
  Fleet Prison, 99; Foundry, 163,
  169–70, 174, 179, 198, 206, 218,
  219, 232, 244, 266, 273, 300,
  321, 344, 346, 408; Holborn,
  140; Islington, 146, 395;
  Kennington, 150, 186; Leadenhall
  Street, 9; London Bridge, 243;
  Marshalsea Prison, 99, 171, 258;
  Marylebone churchyard, 388,
  398; Moorfields, 150, 186, 275,
  328, 389; New Chapel, 73; St.
  Botolph, Aldersgate, 10; St.
  Clement Danes, 194; St. Giles,
  Cripplegate, 10; St. James's,
  Piccadilly, 203; St. Katherine's,
  146; St. Margaret's, Westminster,
  32, 395; St. Paul's, Shadwell, 189;
  Seven Dials, 244, 345; Snowfields,
  203, 292; Southwark, 184;
  Spitalfields, 284, 408;
  Threadneedle Street, 241, 244;
  Tottenham Court chapel, 328;
  Tottenham Court Road, 287;

West Street, 203, 345;
  Wandsworth, 408; Wapping, 140,
  151; Woolwich, 169
London Methodists, 362
Londonderry, Lord, 402
Lopez, Gregory, 85
lots, drawing of, 120, 128, 154, 168,
  170
Louth, Robert (bishop of London),
  366–7
love feasts, 133, 163, 298, 309
Lowestoft, 189
Ludlow, 241
Lurgan, 336
Luther, Martin, 82, 100, 134, 136,
  304
Lutherans, 86, 161, 348, 350

McNab, Alexander, 347
Maddocks, John, 369
Madeley (Shropshire), 289, 324, 338,
  339
Man, Isle of, 316
Manchester, 131, 195, 255, 360
Mansfield, Lord, 377
Mar, earl of, 38
Marienborn, 141
Marlborough, duke of, 14, 98, 227
marriage contracts, 233–8
Married Women's Property Act,
  245
Maryland, 350, 352, 361
Mather, Alexander, 337, 384
Maxfield, Thomas, 153, 154–5, 283,
  285–6, 287, 288, 289–93
Maxwell, Lady, 296, 320
medicine, 219, 317
meetinghouses, 150, 152, 351, 369,
  409; Birdsall, 369; Bolton, 389;
  Bristol New Room, 150, 191,
  200, 202, 346, 369; Brunswick
  chapel (Leeds), 403; City Road,
  344, 345, 346, 388, 395, 398;

443